Terry Savage's
New Money Strategies
for the '90s

ALSO BY TERRY SAVAGE

Terry Savage Talks Money:
The Common-Sense Guide to Money Matters

Terry Savage's New Money Strategies for the '90s

Simple Steps to Creating Wealth and Building Financial Security

Terry Savage

HarperBusiness
A Division of HarperCollinsPublishers

A hardcover edition of this book was originally published in 1993 by HarperBusiness, a division of HarperCollins Publishers, Inc.

HarperCollins books may be purchased for educational, business, or sales promotional use. For information please write: Special Markets Department, HarperCollins Publishers, Inc., 10 East 53rd Street, New York, NY 10022.

First paperback edition published 1994.

The Library of Congress has catalogued the hardcover edition as follows:

Savage, Terry.
    Terry Savage's new money strategies for the 90s : simple steps to creating wealth and building financial security / Terry Savage.—
1st ed.
        p.   cm.
    Includes index.
    ISBN 0-88730-602-0
    1. Finance, Personal.   2. Investments.   3. Estate planning.
4. Tax planning.   5. Insurance.   I. Title.   II. Title: New money
strategies for the 90s.
HG179.S243   1993
332.024—dc20   92-53340

ISBN 0-88730-668-3 (pbk.)

95 96 97 98 PS/RRD 10 9 8 7 6 5 4

Contents

Acknowledgments   xi
Preface to the Paperback Edition   xv

PART I—Mind Over Money

1 Motivating Your Mind   7
2 The Purpose of Planning   12
3 Money Stages   16
4 The Wheel of Fortune—A Brief History of Economic Fashion 23
5 Breaking Bad Money Habits   32

PART II—Making Money Work

6 Starting to Plan   39
7 Setting Goals—and How to Get There   44
8 Getting Help with Financial Planning   46
9 Risk and Reward   53
10 Choosing Your Risks: Asset Allocation   62
11 The Impact of Taxes on Your Financial Plan   69
12 Power, Politics, and Money   74

PART III—Investment Strategies

13 Investment Concepts   83
14 Safe Money Strategies   94
15 Mutual Fund Investing—The Basic Concepts   104

16   How to Buy Mutual Funds   110
17   Simple Mutual Fund Investment Strategies   114
18   Strategies for Choosing a Mutual Fund   120
19   The Stock Market   126
20   How to Choose Stocks   134
21   Investing Using Leverage   143
22   Understanding Interest Rate Investments   148
23   Strategies to Increase Yields   154
24   Tax-free Investment Strategies   167
25   International Investing   176
26   Strategies for International Investing   183
27   Investing for Financial Self-Defense   193
28   Tax-deferred Annuities as an Investment Strategy   203
29   Variable-rate Annuities   210
30   Guaranteed-rate Annuities   216

PART IV—Everyday Living Strategies

31   Strategies for Everyday Money Handling   225
32   Using Credit Wisely   232
33   Credit Card Strategies   240
34   Quick Cash and Bigger Borrowing Strategies   248
35   Marriage and Money   256
36   Dollars and Divorce   262
37   Money Strategies for College   267
38   Financial Aid for College   283
39   Children and Money   290
40   Strategies for Getting, Keeping, and Leaving a Job   294
41   Strategies for Creating Your Own Business   303
42   Mortgage Strategies   311
43   Strategies to Save Big Bucks When Buying   322
44   Retirement Planning Strategies   331
45   Everyday Tax Strategies   349

PART V—Insurance Strategies

46   Homeowners Insurance   361
47   Automobile Insurance   370
48   Health Insurance   381

49	Disability Insurance	391
50	Life Insurance	398
51	Understanding Term Insurance	403
52	Cash Value Life Insurance	411
53	Life Insurance Strategies	423
54	Strategies for Saving Money on Insurance	434

PART VI—Strategies for Seniors . . . and Those Who One Day Will Be!

55	Planning Your Estate/Passing It On	447
56	Estate Planning Strategies	453
57	Estate Tax-Saving Strategies	461
58	Charitable Trusts and Estate Planning	469
59	Estate Planning Strategies: Giving Away Power	474
60	Social Security	477
61	Medicare and Medicare Supplement Insurance	489
62	Catastrophic Illness and Nursing Home Care	499
63	Strategies to Save Your Estate from Nursing Home Costs	509
64	Lifecare Communities	516
65	Pension and IRA Distributions	519
66	Senior Income Strategies	526
	Conclusion	534
	Appendix A: No-load Mutual Fund Companies	535
	Appendix B: Federal Reserve Banks	540
	Index	547

Acknowledgments

Many people were kind enough to provide information and spend their time reading and commenting on these chapters. Indeed, it would have been impossible to research and write this book without their help.

I am truly indebted to Rick Nelson, who really knows the ins and outs of the life insurance business. Watching his testimony before a Senate committee sparked my desire to shed light on the sales techniques of the insurance industry. Similarly, insurance experts Ted Bernstein and David Phillips read and reread manuscripts and were generous with their time and thoughts—as well as their staffs, who quickly came through with the numbers I needed. Also, sincere thanks to Peter Katt and James Hunt for their insights into the insurance industry.

For historical perspective on the financial markets, the work of Larry Siegel at Ibbotson & Associates was invaluable. Jerry Perritt of Investment Information Services and Don Sallee of Invesco MIM, Inc., relate past market trends to future performance in a most understandable way. My thanks to all the analysts at Morningstar Mutual Funds and publisher Don Phillips. Steve Norwitz of T. Rowe Price Associates is certainly the most creative communicator in the mutual fund industry. Don Hoppe has been my guide through the history of economics for several decades now, and has taught me the importance of perspective. Economist Gary Shilling has a unique insight into trends and allowed the use of his charts that demonstrate those concepts.

When it comes to numbers, no one is better than my favorite actuary,

Art Tepfer; ditto with taxes and Matt Kessler and Mark Mann. Mortgage expert Bob Rowen of Bell Federal Savings once again came to my rescue when I needed numbers, as did John Pfister of Chicago Title and Trust. Municipal bond trader Fred Uhde continued lending his insights into the tax-free market, as he did 20 years ago when I was a stockbroker. Doug Youngren of the Savings Bond Division is another old friend who keeps my knowledge current. I welcome mail from the IRS when it comes from Steve Mongelluzzo of the public affairs department! Mike McGrail of the IRS knows every tax regulation and quickly responded to all my questions.

Annuity experts Greg Yost and Tina Baughman of Independent Advantage Financial Services let me sit in on their sales presentations to appreciate the practical as well as theoretical aspects of these investments. Steve Persky once again made sure no one would lack for disability insurance. Allstate Insurance was generous in providing illustrations and statistics; special thanks to Al Orendorff, Bob Lapinski, and Brooke Ohrman for working on that part of the project.

The subject of "senior strategies" became personally dear to my heart in recent years. Many thanks to Harley Gordon (*How to Protect Your Life Savings*) and to Adriane G. Berg (*Warning: Dying May Be Hazardous to Your Wealth*), whose writings set the standard on these topics. John Gras of AARP-Prudential, estate planning attorney Michael Hartz, annuity authority Jerome Alexander, and Robert Davis of David Phillips & Co. all made invaluable contributions to this section. Also my appreciation to Larry Keillor of the Social Security Administration and Ron Benjamin of the Health Care Financing Administration.

Hewitt Associates, through Christine Seltz, was gracious enough to lend their workplace studies. Labor attorney Richard Menson of Gardner, Carton, & Douglas, executive search expert Scott Shelton of Spencer Stuart, and Don Wilson of Jannotta, Bray, & Associates, Inc. provided consultation on the jobs section, a relatively new topic for financial planning in the nineties.

The financial planning industry is better off for the talents of Marv Tuttle of the Institute of Certified Financial Planners. Peter Roberts, chairman of the College Savings Bank, generously provided the most current charts and statistics. Jack Hinz of the College Scholarship Service advised on the latest rules for financial aid. And my thanks to countless others at various organizations—especially at the many no-load mutual fund companies—who cheerfully responded to my questions.

Technical support from Bill Straka made my new computer program less intimidating. A special nod to Fedex delivery man Dennis Beier, who cheerfully brought packages of research and carted off copy to my editors. Kim Guiliano, Tina Mosley, Brenda Houston, and Joe Ostopak provided office support without bending under pressure. And Andrea Clark and Cheryl Villari diligently kept me in shape for this project.

Thanks to copy editor Pat Stahl who, once again, devoted her sharp pencils and even sharper mind to editing my copy. And my very special thanks to editor Stephanie Gunning, who calmly and consistently showed her faith that this book would be a great success!

My good friend Clyde Harrison not only provided support and encouragement, but a living example of the benefits that come from a combination of market knowledge and self-discipline, along with an undeniable optimism. He and Warren Shore have always encouraged me to take the next step into my future. And sincere appreciation to Edward Harshfield for his invaluable financial advice and support.

My most special thanks are given in the dedication of this book—to the generations dearest to me, each of whom has taught me valuable lessons in financial planning.

Preface to the 1995 Paperback Edition

1995 has brought Americans new financial challenges. The volatile stock market reached new highs, while the U. S. dollar plunged in value. A new Congress attempted to balance the federal budget and revise the tax code. Interest rates gyrated as the Federal Reserve tried to engineer an unprecedented "soft landing" for the economy.

In the midst of all these changes, the investment strategies and attitudes in this book are proving even more appropriate and helpful in guiding your financial planning today as they were when I first set them to paper two years ago. And the warnings that I insisted be set in bold type in the first edition have, I hope, saved many readers from expensive mistakes.

For instance, in Chapter 22 I pointed out the risk in locking up your "chicken money" for longer periods of time just to get a slightly higher rate of interest. And I explained that you could lose money even in "safe" government bonds when interest rates rise.

The higher the interest rate you receive, the greater the risk you are taking.

Bond prices move in the opposite direction of interest rates.

Following that advice kept conservative investors from losing as much as 25 percent of their principal as the bond market had its worst bear market in 1994. For conservative investors in 1995 this advice is still true:

> *I'm not so concerned about the return ON my money, as I am about the return OF my money!*

Also, in the past few years many investors rushed into international mutual funds—without understanding the concept of currency risk which was highlighted in Chapter 25. The resulting Mexican peso collapse cost investors profits in many global markets.

> *The key to international investing: Only switch out of your own currency when you think it is falling in value—or when you are optimistic that the profits to be made overseas will more than compensate for any currency risk.*

A major bull market in stocks contains lessons of its own. An entire generation of investors has not lived through the wrenching decline of a bear market. Yet there have been eleven bear markets since, but not including, 1929. The average decline in the Standard & Poors 500 stock index during those bear markets was 35 percent. It took, on average, 7.5 years to *break even* if you held on to stock positions as opposed to switching into money market funds at the top.

Of course, no one ever gets out right at the top. And for *long-term* investors (as you can see in Chapters 9 and 19) stocks have always outperformed safer investments. Still, it's emotionally difficult to stick with a long-term plan when prices are plunging. In a bear market, wealth simply disappears. That's why it's wise to honestly evaluate in advance your ability to take—and live with—risk in the markets. Then allocate your investments accordingly.

Looking ahead in 1995 and beyond, it has never been more important to create a financial security plan. Amidst financial crisis and economic change there is tremendous opportunity. Knowledge gives you the ability to profit from the financial opportunities that lie ahead.

Every day gives us a new chance to make a decision about how we will spend, save, or invest our money and our time. Each of us can choose to turn away from the mistakes of the past. The future offers no guarantees. But with knowledge, self-discipline, commitment, and optimism, I firmly believe we can create a more secure financial future for our country, our families and ourselves.

PART 1

Mind Over Money

GETTING CONTROL over your financial life is one of the most rewarding personal commitments you can make. The goal is simple: to make your money work for you as hard as you work for it. The rules are basic—easy to understand and learn. The strategies do not have to be complicated to be successful. It's the need for self-discipline that stops many people from putting their money to work.

The money decisions you make today will be magnified many times into the future. Correct decisions can lay the groundwork for financial security and fortune. Mistakes can cost both valuable time and money. The worst strategy of all is to do nothing.

To make the correct decisions, you need to understand how the future will require different choices from those that may have been profitable in the past.

For example, suppose you decide to make a $2,000 purchase this month and charge it to your Visa or MasterCard. That makes you one of the millions of Americans who today have more than $165 billion charged on their bankcards!

If you can't pay the entire $2,000 bill this month, the card issuer will be quite accommodating. You can keep your credit in good standing by making the required minimum monthly payment. You may be surprised to know that if you have a card that charges 19.8 percent interest and a $40 annual fee, and if you make only the required minimum monthly payment every month,

It will take you *31 years and 2 months* to pay off that $2,000!

And, along the way, you'll have paid an additional $8,202 in nondeductible finance charges.

This is a classic example of how being in debt can bury you. And it's a safe assumption that whether that $2,000 charge represented clothing, furniture, or a vacation, the pleasure of your purchase will be long gone in 31 years when you make the last payment.

On the other hand, what if you took $2,000 and invested it in the stock market today? Suppose that instead of buying just one or two stocks, you could buy a broad cross-section of the whole stock market—such as the Standard & Poor's index of 500 stocks. (You can easily open an account to buy that stock index for as little as $100, and we'll show you how to do it later in this book.) What would your $2,000 be worth in 31 years if you invested in equity instead of debt?

That requires making some assumptions about market performance. Not every year is the same for the stock market. For instance, in 1991, the S&P 500 Index gained nearly 30 percent. In 1992, it gained 7.62 percent.

For the past 31 years—from 1960 through 1991—this broad-based index of the stock market has had an average growth rate of 10.6 percent, including reinvestment of dividends paid on those stocks.

If the stock market continues to gain at the same average rate over the next 31 years, and if you invested the same $2,000 in the stock market instead of borrowing on your bankcard and being buried in debt,

In 31 years your $2,000 would have grown to $45,540!

If you made that investment in your tax-sheltered Individual Retirement Account, you wouldn't have had to worry about paying income taxes on the gains along the way.

The big picture is a $53,742 difference—$45,540 in investment gain, plus $8,202 in interest that you didn't send down the drain.

And investing regularly is a good habit. If you put aside $2,000 in your IRA every year for 31 years, growing at 10.6 percent, you'd have $453,252 in your retirement account.

The difference between these two paths is the most graphic example I can give you of the dangers of playing the money game using outdated strategies. It's not only what you *lose* in playing by the old rules; it's what you *fail to gain* by not redirecting your mind-set toward the new money environment.

Using debt to build wealth was one of the major success strategies of the 1980s: borrow, leverage, use other people's money. And for those who got in—and out—early, it was an investment and lifestyle strategy that worked. On the other hand, for those who didn't recognize the changing rules of the money game, debt proved disastrous.

It's all a matter of timing. In the early 1980s, when inflation and tax laws made it easier to use debt to your advantage, fortunes were made by buying assets—everything from houses to entire companies—with borrowed money, and then selling at a profit when inflation pushed prices higher.

By the end of the 1980s, the rules had changed. Inflation was under control. Tax laws for investment real estate had changed. Interest on consumer debt was no longer deductible. New regulations for banks and savings and loans meant that easy credit dried up. And those who kept playing by the old rules found their fortunes in ruins. From Donald Trump to Robert Maxwell, from Macy's to Olympia & York, the financial collapse of these empires has made front-page headlines. On a more personal scale, excessive debt pushed a record 1 million Americans into personal bankruptcy in 1992.

If you thought that piling up debt was the "easy" way out of your financial problems, you were not alone. The federal government used the same strategy. It hasn't had a balanced budget since 1969. And the total of all those annual budget deficits—the National Debt—is now more than $4.6 trillion dollars!

Of course, the federal government has virtually unlimited borrowing (and printing) power to maintain its debt burden. Individuals eventually come face-to-face with credit limits and the burden of spiraling interest costs on that debt.

Leaving behind the consumption and debt mentality of the past decade will take some discipline. Old habits are difficult to break. But the new lessons are easy to learn and very rewarding. Whether your goal is to build a huge fortune or just to create financial security for yourself and your family, you'll need to understand the new strategies for making your money work for you in the 1990s and beyond.

Chapter 1

Motivating Your Mind

When it comes to managing your money, the two greatest motivating forces are **fear** and **greed**! They're the financial equivalent of the carrot and the stick. Depending on your individual personality, one or the other will be a stronger incentive. Both fear and greed can motivate you wrongly, as well. It's up to you to control and direct your mind, as well as your money.

For example, fear of being poor in old age may be a strong incentive to set money aside while you're young. On the other hand, fear of being "unable to keep up with the neighbors" can motivate unwise spending for appearance's sake.

"Greed" became a word symbolic of the excesses of the 1980s. Yet, however you label the desire for money, it can be a potent motivating force. But if you're motivated by greed you must also guard against the downside, which is irrational thinking. Greed can blind you to risk and push you into making unwise decisions guaranteed to cost you money.

Knowledge and self-discipline are the two keys to making these forces work *for* you instead of against you. To get started, though, you must be motivated.

SOME MOTIVATING FACTS

In 1948, the median income American family paid 2 percent of its income in taxes to the federal government. In 1994, that same family paid 24 percent of its income in taxes to the federal government—and an additional 6 to 9 percent in state and local taxes!

As you can see from chart I-1, even *before* taxes, the median American family income stalled out in the 1970s. No wonder you're not feeling better off than your parents were at the same age.

If you were born after 1945, the Social Security trust funds will almost certainly be depleted by the time you're ready to retire. (Or else those still working—your children—will have to pay 40 percent of their paychecks in payroll taxes to support their elders.)

If you have a three-year-old child, the first year at Harvard will cost about $54,000. For today's nine-year-old, one year of expenses at a public college will cost more than $37,000, if college costs keep rising at the current pace.

If you don't make a will or living trust estate plan, the cost of dying can be as expensive as the cost of living. Your estate—the money you worked hard for and meant to leave to your family—could be taxed at rates as high as 55 percent!

CHART I-1
Real Median Household Income
(pretax)

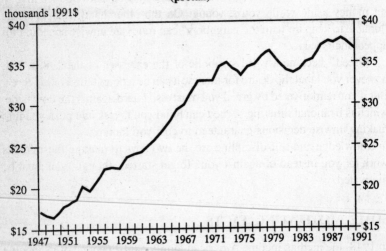

DATA: Department of Commerce.
SOURCE: A. Gary Shilling & Co., Inc.

Plan to live longer than you think—and think about the cost of living that much longer. The average American will live to be age 74, and many will live into their eighties or beyond. It has been forecast that more than 40 percent of all Americans turning 65 in 1992 will spend time in a nursing home. The odds are even greater that this nursing home experience will wipe out all of the family's savings.

As shown in chart I-2, it's worth saving and investing for your future, and even better to save in a way that shelters your investment from income taxes.

If you save $2,000 a year at 6 percent for 30 years, and if you pay income taxes of 30 percent on the interest earnings every year, the total savings account will be worth $120,862.

If, instead, you shelter that $2,000-a-year savings by placing it in an Individual Retirement Account (IRA) or other tax-deferred safe investment earning 6 percent, the total savings will be worth $167,603 in 30 years.

It's important that your income keep up with inflation, and even more important that your after-tax return on investments actually *beat* inflation. Chart I-3 shows what inflation can do to your buying power.

Even relatively low rates of inflation can do a lot of damage over time. Assuming a 5 percent inflation rate, the cost of living for someone retiring in 1993 will nearly triple in 20 years. That is, it will take more than $130,000 a year in 2013 to buy the lifestyle that costs $50,000 a year today.

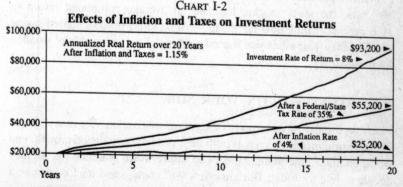

CHART I-2
Effects of Inflation and Taxes on Investment Returns

Annualized Real Return over 20 Years
After Inflation and Taxes = 1.15%

Investment Rate of Return = 8% ► $93,200 ►

After a Federal/State $55,200 ►
Tax Rate of 35% ▲

After Inflation Rate $25,200 ▲
of 4% ◄

SOURCE: Courtesy of H. L. Hopewell, The Monitor Group, Inc., Falls Church, Virginia.

CHART I-3

**How $20,000 Declined in Purchasing Power Over Past 20 Years
1971–1991**

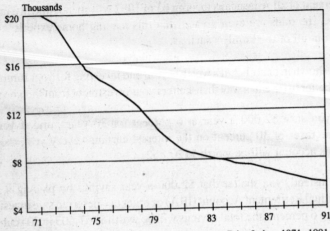

SOURCE: T. Rowe Price Associates, Inc. Based on Consumer Price Index, 1971–1991.

It doesn't take a lot of money to make a lot of money! If you save $2,000 a year, every year, and invest it to earn 10 percent compounded annually and sheltered from income taxes, in 30 years your nest egg would be worth $361,886. Even with annual inflation running at 3 percent, that's still $194,508 in today's dollar.

Is it still possible to earn 10 percent annually? Remember, over the past 30 years, the stock market has had an average compound return of 10.6 percent. Think how far ahead you'd be today if you'd started saving that $2,000 a year when you started working! Fear and greed are wonderful motivators!

OPPORTUNITY IS ON YOUR SIDE

Planning for the future requires long-term motivation. Yet many people look at world problems such as pollution, poverty, population growth, and world conflicts, and assume there's no future worth planning for. So they decide to live for today. But tomorrow *will* come—and it's likely to be a better world, not a worse one.

If you look around, there are sound reasons to be optimistic. First, we have technology on our side. Just when it appeared the world would grind to a halt because it was running out of oil and energy prices were soaring, along came technology to develop fuel-saving devices and to develop alternative energy sources. The result: Instead of $50 a barrel, crude oil trades at inflation-adjusted prices not far above those in the early 1970s, and the United States is no longer held hostage to oil-producing countries.

There are many other examples of technology at work. In the late 1970s, people started to hoard pennies for their copper content. Rising raw copper prices, plus political uncertainty in copper-producing countries, combined to send the price of copper to $1.67 a pound in 1980—a price where the copper in a penny would be worth more than 1 cent. But technology created fiber optics, which lessened the need for copper in all those telephone transmission lines, and copper prices plummeted.

Today we are introducing light bulbs that can burn for 20 years using a fraction of the electricity required for regular light bulbs. Technology creates answers to seemingly insurmountable problems—from population growth to waste disposal—and in the process creates opportunities for new investment.

A second reason to be optimistic involves demographics. Yes, we're living longer and that creates its own costs. But the largest generation ever born—the baby boomers—is now reaching the years when instead of spending and consuming it will start to save and invest. We'll talk more about the impact of the boomers in a later chapter, but in the coming years the boomers could form an explosive force for savings and capital investment and growth in our economy. These demographics are on our side.

And certainly, we must be optimistic as we see the forces of democracy and free enterprise triumphing around the world after a 50-year cold war. While not without problems, our economic system has attracted the attention and desire of people around the world. And the world will provide an incredible marketplace for American ideas, technology, products, and marketing experience. The free market trend is on our side.

It's worth planning for your future, because so many long-term trends are on our side. The best way to predict the future is to create it!

Chapter 2

The Purpose of Planning

The art of financial planning is actually very simple. The first step is to examine where you are now, financially—and where you want and need to be in the next five, ten, thirty years.

The next step is to assess the amount of money you need to set aside regularly to meet your goals, based on the potential returns you can earn, the risks it is prudent to take in your situation, and the amount of time you have to make your money grow.

Then you must sort out and balance different investments to keep from putting all your eggs in one basket. Today, that process goes by the fancy name of "asset allocation." As you'll see, there are many techniques to evaluate potential investments. Diversification is, in itself, a strategy to help build your wealth.

Finally, you must organize your financial life to protect the investments you are making. That means setting up a system to monitor your investments and files to keep track of your documents. It can be as simple as a cardboard file box and folders, or as technical as a personal finance computer program.

Financial planning is not only about setting money aside to grow for the future. It means making smart decisions about how and when to purchase and finance things you need today—from a home or car to consumer products. It means using credit wisely and knowing when to borrow.

Financial planning means understanding how money issues affect relationships: in marriage or divorce, in raising children and planning for their education, in growing older and protecting assets when an elderly parent or spouse needs custodial care. All of these issues are handled better when financial plans are made in advance.

And financial planning also means reassessing your insurance needs— using cost-effective strategies to protect your current assets, such as your property, to protect your working income through disability insurance, and to protect the value of your life by purchasing the correct amount and type of life insurance.

Last, but certainly not least, you need to create and update an estate plan to protect your family and your assets from the high costs of dying, or of a long-term illness.

Who needs financial planning? Everyone, no matter what age, can benefit from taking a "snapshot" of his or her current money situation and making some plans for the future.

It's the first thing we teach a small child planning to open a corner lemonade stand. What do the ingredients cost? How many are you likely to sell? What price will give you a profit? Both the logic and the arithmetic are simple.

The teenager allocating his allowance between hamburgers and music videos, the homemaker juggling expenses such as groceries and childcare, the corporate executive making decisions about new products and expansion—all practice a form of financial planning. Yet how many people translate these everyday skills into making investments for their own future?

Ask yourself some questions.

Am I hiding from my financial future?
We make all sorts of excuses: no time, not enough extra cash, too young to start worrying about retirement. The bottom line is that there is only one major reason to avoid planning: *fear*. It's the incredible worry that if we take a real look at our finances, we'll have to acknowledge that the problems appear insurmountable. We fear we'll wind up old and impoverished—and why worry about that now.

It may sound confident to say, "We'll take care of one day's financial problems at a time," but that's really the coward's way out. With very little time spent on a plan and with a small initial investment, you can ensure that your future will be much more secure.

What are my goals?

There is one overriding goal: **to make your money work for you as hard as you worked for it!** One day your accumulated savings and investments will generate enough income and profits to allow you the financial freedom to work less and enjoy life more.

You may have intermediate goals such as buying a home, educating your children, or taking regular vacations. The ultimate goal is a comfortable retirement. As you'll soon see, it's a pipe dream to count on Social Security or even your company pension to finance your retirement.

How much time do I need to set aside to work on my financial goals?

In terms of current time to create and implement a financial plan, you're talking about several hours of homework and a regular schedule of watching your money-making decisions perform. That may mean setting aside time weekly when you read the Sunday newspapers to check the value of your mutual funds. Or it may simply mean being aware of front-page news such as changes in interest rates or tax bills being debated in Congress. On an ongoing basis, you may come to check your financial picture about as often as you check the weather forecast to decide whether to carry an umbrella tomorrow.

How long will it take to achieve my goals?

If you're asking how much time it will take to make your financial plan work, the answer is, the more time the better. That is, the earlier you start, the longer you have to make your money grow and compound. Even if you only start setting aside a small sum of money on a regular basis, having a long time horizon is like having the wind constantly at your back when you're sailing.

Can I do it myself?

There's no reason you can't manage your own finances, just as there's no reason you can't become a gourmet cook, or repair your own car, or play tennis. Like succeeding in any other field, it's simply a matter of making financial planning a priority. Like any other skill, it's easy if you know it!

Some people do pay for professional help in financial planning for several reasons: to get expert advice on a full-time basis, to get outside help in imposing discipline on the financial plan, or to have a personal teacher of financial techniques.

If you do get professional advice, remember that it's *your* money—and ultimately your responsibility to review the plan and take action. It's worth paying for good financial advice; but how will you know the advice is good unless you understand what the planner is recommending?

If you decide to seek advice from a professional, you'll want to know how to make that decision and how the planner is compensated. You'll find more on that subject in chapter 8. And you'll need to know the questions you should be asking a planner—plus the questions a planner should be asking of you.

Why can't I seem to get started?

Just by picking up this book, you've shown the desire to gain control over your financial life. You want to believe you can do it, and that's the first step. I firmly believe that you can accomplish *anything* you put your mind to. Success in life depends on setting your goals, working on your dreams, and taking control over your destiny.

Limited goals create limited lives. Passion and dreams win every time—*if* they are harnessed to a plan. Remember, a goal without a plan is simply a dream. If you want to make those dreams come true, the time to start planning is now. It's all a matter of mind over money!

Chapter 3

Money Stages

We all move through different financial stages, and each stage has one thing in common: Unless you win the lottery and wipe out all worries about your financial future, at each stage your current financial needs and required expenditures make it difficult to save and invest for the future. It's a problem shared by all generations.

If you're just starting out, the overwhelming financial need is to find the first job, and some sort of financial independence. The young family worries about mortgage payments, furnishing a home, and saving for college for children. There are always cash emergencies—car repairs, home repairs, a child's marriage.

Eventually, those tasks are accomplished and retirement is around the corner, requiring a different set of financial sacrifices. Even those already comfortably retired are not immune to financial worries. Inflation could destroy the value of retirement income, and medical expenses or nursing costs could wipe out a lifetime of savings.

The generations are no longer isolated from each other financially. More and more empty-nesters are finding their children coming home to roost as postcollege job plans do not work out. Many families with teen-age children face not only the burden of college but the unexpected need to pay for nursing home care for their parents. And retired parents are often called upon to dig into their savings to rescue middle-age children who have lost jobs and careers.

16

No one can rule out expensive financial surprises; but there are ways to minimize the impact of unexpected events, as well as those costs you know will be coming up in the future. It's important to insure against the unexpected and to build investment reserves for future needs.

It seems that each generation rebels against the strictures of its parents when it comes to managing money. In fact, it has been noted that some long-term economic cycles are generational: just when the grandparents' generation is gone, the younger generation needs to relearn financial lessons of a previous era. Unfortunately, the lessons that teach the most often cost the most to learn.

You should understand the general financial characteristics of your age and generation, but don't skip the profiles of those older—and younger—than you. You may have something to learn, and something to teach!

THE BABY BOOM GENERATION

The baby boom generation is moving into its peak power years—both financially and politically. For the first time, the President and Vice-President of the United States are baby boomers. You're a member of the baby boom generation if you are one of the 76 million Americans born between 1946 and 1964. It's a generation that seemed to have stumbled into incredible financial opportunity. Most were born too late for the Vietnam War and were young enough to adjust to the 1970s era of inflation. This was also the generation that enjoyed many of the fruits of the 1980s economic boom.

There were some financial dilemmas during this era. Notably, housing prices soared, making the American dream of owning your own home less affordable. But these Yuppies (young urban professionals) conquered that problem by transforming themselves into Dinks (double income, no kids). With two incomes it seemed once again possible to live the American dream—until the babies arrived and childcare took a big bite out of the combined paychecks!

The typical baby boomer's original investment scenario in the 1980s: Buy the biggest house with the largest mortgage. Home prices were sure to appreciate. Furnish the home using credit. Personal possessions became symbols and stereotypes: the BMW became the status car although it was far outsold by Japanese imports.

Like every generation, the boomers had their own music. Perhaps the theme song of this generation should have been the 1988 hit "Don't Worry, Be Happy." But this was a generation that decided to have its own musical hardware as well as software. Its entire inventory of popular music on cassette tapes became obsolete when boomers decided to start over with compact discs, creating an entirely new multi-million-dollar market for both disc players and the recordings.

Jobs on Wall Street seemed to coin money. One young broker, Michael Lewis, wrote a best-selling book, *Liar's Poker*, about the fortunes to be made by even the least informed. The path upward seemed to be smooth—following the trail of the stock market, which soared upward from a low of 776 on the Dow Jones Industrial Average in 1982 to reach 3400 a decade later. Why plan? Why worry?

The baby boom generation was buoyed by the stock market increase, but they were not big shareholders. By 1989, equity holdings as a percentage of family wealth had dropped to less than 20 percent from a high of more than 40 percent a generation earlier. In part, the decline was due to the incredible increase in the value of home equity as a percentage of family wealth.

But the boomers have not been investors, as a whole. They have been spenders and consumers. As this generation came of age, retail sales in the United States soared dramatically. And along with the expansion of retail sales came an unprecedented expansion of consumer debt.

It's obviously unfair to characterize an entire generation in a few sentences. Individuals have taken different paths in this generation. Some made breakthroughs in medical technology that turned into profitable business ventures. Many were entrepreneurs, while others pushed corporate America into new technologies and international expansion. And others were among the first to fall victim to a welfare system that seemed determined to create generations of dependency.

Of the baby boomers on the success path, however, it seems fair to say that relatively few were overly worried about retirement or making a will or estate plan as they entered the 1990s. The economy of the 1980s was also booming. The recessions of 1973–74 and 1980–83 were forgotten. Ever-rising salaries, bonuses, and home values would provide for children's college education when the time came. Retirement was a distant shadow; after all, their parents were living reasonably well.

Then along came the recession of 1990–92. Unlike previous recessions, this one hit hardest at white-collar workers whose jobs were eliminated in corporate downsizing and restructuring. Jobs in financial services, advertising, and media which had seen the largest increases in compensation in the 1980s were among the ones most often eliminated. While middle managers represent only 6 or 7 percent of the nation's workforce, nearly 17 percent of corporate layoffs came from their ranks in the early 1990s.

The boomers' prized assets—their homes—not only failed to increase, but started to decline in value. In 1991, the national median price of a new single-family home was $122,900. A year later it had dropped to $120,000. Those losses were moderate in comparison to substantially larger declines in many of the urban areas in which boomers are concentrated.

Clearly a home is no substitute for a savings or investment account. In fact, owning a home without a job (or two jobs in many two-income families) and having to make mortgage payments has become a recipe for financial disaster. A whole new term for this generation was coined: Dumpies (downwardly mobile professionals).

The baby boom generation has largely been ignored in the marketplace for financial planning. After all, the motto of the boomer generation had been "I see it; I spend it" when dealing with cash on hand.

All of that is about to change. According to *The Great Income Reshuffle*, a report issued in 1992 by the Conference Board, a private research group, the nineties will be "a decade of extensive demographic change. Households under age 35 will become much less significant, while those age 35–55 will become more important."

The report notes that baby boomers have tended to marry late, but in the nineties as the last of the baby boomers marry, husband-wife families will account for 60 percent of the increase in households, compared to only about a quarter of household growth in the 1980s, when there was explosive growth in single-income households.

Baby boomers are moving into their peak earning years. The oldest boomers will turn 50 in five years. The Beatles' Paul McCartney turned 50 in 1992! In 1991, those older than 50 held more than half of all discretionary income and 80 percent of the money on deposit in banks and S&Ls, according to the Conference Board.

As the huge boomer generation acquires both the earnings and the awareness that they are the next generation to retire, they may build an incredible pool of savings and investment capital that could propel the economy—and eventually the stock market—into its next stage of dynamic growth. This generation's attention to investing for a better future could become a self-fulfilling prophecy.

Individuals currently hold a lower proportion of their financial assets in stocks, including mutual funds, than at any time in the last four decades. In 1968, individuals had 45 percent of their financial assets in stocks; by 1990 that figure had hit a low of 18 percent, and it had rebounded to 20.5 percent in 1992. A study by the Babson Group of mutual funds points out that just a one percentage point increase in individuals' equity share ratio would add $120 billion in buying power. That's three times the amount of money that moved into stock market mutual funds in 1991—a year when the market gained 29 percent!

If you're a member of the huge baby boom generation, and if you recognize the changing times, you have before you the greatest profit opportunities of a lifetime. As in every generation, the first to recognize the changes are those who profit most. Forget looking backward and acquire the habits of future prosperity.

MATURE MONEY

Those currently in the age group between 55 to 64 form a bridge generation between the baby boomers and the already retired. Compared to the general population, this group is both healthy and wealthy. The number of Americans aged 55 and older is projected to increase 11 percent between 1990 and 2000, compared with a 7 percent increase for the overall population of the country.

In some respects, the generation closest to retirement has the most flexibility to act quickly to create a financial plan. This preretirement generation has a median household income of $32,000—7 percent more than the average for all households. Most are empty-nesters; only 7 percent have children under age 18 living in their homes. Of course, many still have children in college, but within a few years they will get their largest pay raise ever—when college bills stop! That makes this group a major target market for financial planning.

According to the U.S. Census Bureau, about 78 percent of these households have at least one person in the workforce, and about 40 percent of these households contain at least two current wage earners. The majority of their income comes from wages, with only 30 percent of these households collecting Social Security, and 24 percent receiving a pension.

Interest income does not reach a significant proportion of total household earnings.

The average age of retirement for this group is just past 60 years, although many who retire later decide to return to the workforce for a short period of time. Men at age 55 have a life expectancy of an additional 22 years, and women can expect to live 27 more years.

So, if you fall into this bracket, there is good news and bad news. You'll live longer, but you will need more money at retirement than your parents' generation did. You'll also be faced with more expensive medical care (unless there is a major overhaul of national healthcare policies) and a greater chance of having to spend time in a nursing home. The best news is that you are aware of these facts while you still have at least ten years at your highest income levels to set aside and invest funds for retirement.

OLDER AND WISER AND WEALTHIER

Senior citizens—officially those over age 65—now make up 12 percent of America's population. They are better off than any previous group of seniors, and perhaps better off than any subsequent group will ever be. This generation of seniors has used its political clout dramatically.

According to *Fortune* magazine, federal, state, and local governments spent slightly more than $11,000 on every American over 53 in 1990. That compares to $4,200 spent on every child under age 18. With 12 percent of the population, seniors receive 54 percent of federal social spending through Medicare and Social Security. Seniors vote in greater numbers than other segments of the population.

Older people constitute only 20 percent of America's households but own 40 percent of the nation's wealth, says former Social Security Commissioner Dorcas Hardy in her best-seller, *Social Insecurity*. Families headed by a person age 65 or older have a median income of $20,000 per year—40 percent of which comes from Social Security. In the last 30 years, poverty among the elderly has dropped from 35 percent to about 12.5 percent.

Still, incomes do fall dramatically after retirement. The median income for households aged 54 to 74 is just over $20,000, according to the Census Bureau. That is 37 percent less than the median for households aged 55 to 64. Social Security contributes a substantial amount to households in this age bracket: 91 percent of this group receive Social Security, and more than half receive more than $8,200 a year from Social Security.

That is not to say that all seniors are well off; millions of them do live at the poverty line, and this generation is closer than any previous one to finding itself pushed under the line by one disastrous medical experience. That's all the more incentive to create strategies to protect the benefits seniors already have earned.

In many respects, the parents of the baby boom generation should provide an object lesson for their children. All those years of savings and working at one company until retirement have not guaranteed today's seniors a secure retirement. The oldest in this group were devastated by the inflation of the late 1970s that cut into the living standards of those already on fixed incomes. When they learned to play the interest rate game and adjusted their lifestyles accordingly, they were whipsawed when interest rates plunged in the early 1990s.

Today, the realities of medical costs cause seniors to debate between giving assets to their children, thus turning over control of their financial lives, or watching their life savings be eaten up by nursing home costs, possibly leaving a surviving spouse or children with little or no estate. We'll examine the investment and planning options available to senior citizens in the face of these uncertainties in Part VI.

THE GENERATION GAP

The baby boom generation must recognize how unlikely it is that they will receive the same benefits as their parents. In fact, it has been suggested that for those who retire in the year 2020 to receive the current level of Social Security benefits, future workers may have to pay as much as 40 percent of their paychecks in Social Security taxes!

A generation war is in the making. The generation now aged 18 to 29, sometimes called the "X generation" or "baby bust" generation, will be far less likely to support their parents in today's style. It is far more likely, according to Dorcas Hardy, that the main Social Security trust fund will run out of money somewhere around the year 2010—or even earlier if something is not done to curb Medicare costs.

Some solutions include raising the retirement age, lowering cost-of-living increases, or making Social Security benefits available based on need, instead of to all who have contributed over the years. The real solution is for the younger generation to start early to create their own retirement funds. It's just one more lesson for these parents to teach their children.

Chapter 4

The Wheel of Fortune—A Brief History of Economic Fashion

To make the most of your money now, you'll need to break the habits of the past and take a fresh look at what's likely to succeed in the future. Money styles move in and out of fashion—just like clothing. What looks right to one generation may seem old-fashioned to the next. Styles that work to make fortunes in one era may be totally inappropriate in other times.

There is good reason to believe that values are changing again in the 1990s and becoming more traditional. A recent study by Yankelovich Partners, Inc., a consumer research organization, expresses that value shift in graphic form (see chart I-4). If these neo-traditional values take root in the coming years, they should be reflected in changing financial habits.

Once-popular sayings like "A penny saved is a penny earned" seem quaint. But if this generation heeds the lessons of its grandparents, we may have a return to some old-fashioned customs. "Mortgage-burning" ceremonies may become the social event of the late 1990s, as a new generation considers financial solvency to be the height of style. (Then again, if it doesn't catch on, we may see another dramatic increase in the bankruptcy rate!)

CHART I-4

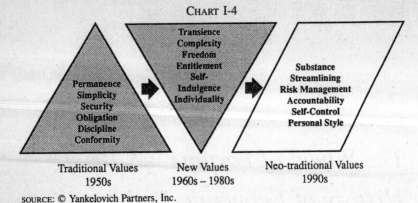

Permanence
Simplicity
Security
Obligation
Discipline
Conformity

Transience
Complexity
Freedom
Entitlement
Self-
Indulgence
Individuality

Substance
Streamlining
Risk Management
Accountability
Self-Control
Personal Style

Traditional Values
1950s

New Values
1960s – 1980s

Neo-traditional Values
1990s

SOURCE: © Yankelovich Partners, Inc.

WHAT GOES AROUND COMES AROUND

A look back at the past 60 years confirms the changing fashion of handling money—and how each generation was affected by the style. The Roaring Twenties stands out as a decade of wild speculation, capped by the stock market crash of 1929. But social values also were relatively wild: speakeasies, flappers, and gangsters.

Stocks were purchased on credit (low margin), and almost everyone expected the boom to continue—or that they would get out of the market first, before stocks sold off. Ultimately, of course, most got trapped in the crash. But that's one of the oldest rules of the stock market: It always fools the greatest number of people.

LESSONS OF THE LAST DEPRESSION

The Great Depression of the 1930s left an indelible mark on the style of the generation that lived through it. Those growing up in the depression remembered poverty and need, and even desperation. For ever after, this generation has felt compelled to set money aside in safe places—even under the mattress—just in case the depression were to come again. To succeeding generations their style seemed old-fashioned.

It took World War II to bring America out of the depression, and even after the war ended, many were worried that the depression would resume. In 1948, they were afraid to invest in the stock market for fear it would crash again. Ironically, the market once again fooled the greatest number of people, because those few who were brave enough to buy stocks at bargain prices sowed the seeds of fortune.

FEAR . . . AND A GREAT OPPORTUNITY

The 1950s and early 1960s have been termed by many the "golden years" of this century. Prosperity and growth were the themes, along with a move to suburbia where every American family would own its own affordable house. Even though this generation fought a war in Korea and feared the cold war, the iron curtain, and the military-industrial complex, there was a sense of domestic growth and prosperity. Savings interest rates were 3 percent and mortgage rates were 4 percent. Inflation was almost nonexistent. This generation has remembered the lessons of its parents, setting some money aside in savings.

STARTING IN THE SIXTIES

The decade of the 1960s ended in unrest. The war in Vietnam heated up, and the younger generation rebelled against the values of their parents. The stock market in the late sixties was dominated by a new fashion trend: conglomerates. The credo of those who purchased diverse companies and combined them to "create value" was: "One plus one equals three." Those who had built companies in the postwar boom sold them for stock in the new conglomerates, believing the stock value of diverse companies combined under one management would be even greater. If that sounded vaguely like the investment pools of the 1920s, few from that generation were around to remember.

SCARES OF THE SEVENTIES

The stock market fell sharply in 1973–74 from over 1000 to 570 on the Dow Industrials, but that wasn't the greatest worry. America had its first taste of global interdependency. The OPEC oil cartel pushed oil prices higher, and America was brought to a crawl. A government that was determined to pay for both the war in Vietnam and significant social programs made a conscious decision to pay for them by creating new money.

To have the flexibility to create that money, in August 1971 President Richard Nixon took the United States off the gold standard—in effect, saying that the United States could create as much money as necessary without worrying about whether there was gold in Fort Knox to back the currency. From that point on, the U.S. government would try to spend its way to prosperity. All it really did was unleash a massive inflation upon the country—creating a financial whirlwind that would leave its mark on the generations to follow.

In the mid-1970s America did seem to prosper, even though it was fighting a devastating war in Vietnam. Salaries were rising, and working people could afford more luxuries. Among the "hot" stock groups were the shares of mobile home and recreational vehicle manufacturers. The expectation was that every worker would have time and money to enjoy life more.

THE IMPACT OF INFLATION

By the late 1970s, the full force of inflation caused by that newly created money and credit had impacted American society. Home prices were rising, but those fortunate to have purchased houses in the 1960s and early 1970s with low fixed-rate mortgages were delighted. They profited at the expense of the bankers who were stuck with those old, low-interest mortgages on their books.

Meanwhile, free market interest rates were starting to rise to protect lenders against inflation. But savings and loans were restricted by law to paying relatively low interest rates. The smart money moved out of the low-rate banking accounts and into money market funds, which could invest in Treasury bills and commercial paper—and pass the high yields along to individuals.

Everyone, even grandmothers, had an up-close lesson on how to chase high interest rates in an inflationary market. But those living on fixed incomes such as pensions could not keep up with inflation. Prices went up, but their buying power could not keep up. In fact, it became apparent that the real trick to making a fortune in inflationary times was to purchase assets that increased in value faster than inflation.

Real estate, oil, and natural resources were the winners in this trend. Another OPEC oil shock in 1979 pushed energy prices even higher. By 1980, the public had caught on to the fashion of investing to beat inflation. The price of gold soared to over $850 an ounce. The idea was to hold anything except paper money, which was losing value so quickly. And that's not surprising, considering the United States was creating money at an unprecedented rate.

Meanwhile, the savings and loan industry was deregulated, so it could offer depositors higher, competitive interest rates instead of watching deposits fly out the door. In order to earn the higher rates they were paying depositors, the S&Ls also were allowed to make riskier loans instead of the simple home mortgages that had been their original business. So the industry started making commercial real estate loans on everything from shopping centers to ski resorts. Its lack of experience in this arena did not stop the industry from making money available. The yields on these loans were higher, and the fees earned were greater. And, after all, the deposits used to make the loans were guaranteed by the federal government.

Inflation not only spurred a trend to "buy now, before prices rise," but it also created a new awareness of the burden of income taxes. Incomes rose, but higher incomes pushed people into higher tax brackets. A new phenomenon was created: "tax bracket creep." And a new mania was created: tax shelter, tax avoidance.

THE INFLATION/RECESSION REACTION

By the time the process came to a head in the spring of 1980, even the president of the United States was calling for restraint, urging consumers to cut up their credit cards and stop charging purchases. The Federal Reserve, the nation's central bank, stepped in to raise interest rates even higher in order to slow down the economy. The prime rate—the rate banks charge their best customers—rose to an unprecedented 20½ percent late in 1980, and the economy did slow down. In fact, it fell into a deep recession that lasted most of the next two years. President Jimmy Carter was not reelected in November 1980.

Eventually, as the result of the recession, interest rates came down and oil prices fell. Tax rates were cut and brackets were fixed, ending tax bracket creep. Inflation turned downward. But a generation that was hooked on the fear of inflation (just as its grandparents had been hooked on fear of depression) was unable to change its habits quickly. Consumption became the mode of the 1980s, which would later be dubbed the "generation of greed." Real estate and oil tax shelters based on predictions of inflation and deductibility of debt continued to be sold throughout the decade—eventually resulting in huge losses.

THE EIGHTIES: "GREED IS GOOD"

In the 1980s it was the common wisdom that fortunes were made by taking on debt. Corporate raiders emerged to purchase companies whose stock prices were viewed as "too low" in relation to the value of company assets. The takeover mania was financed by debt. Often the debt was of questionable value, so it was called "junk bonds." The raiders promised high rates of interest to attract bond buyers because it was questionable whether the company could actually make the interest payments and ultimately repay the cash it had borrowed.

The takeover procedure became a formula for creating wealth. Sell junk bonds to borrow money to take over a company. When the company was purchased, expenses could be cut and divisions sold to raise cash to repay the debt. The new owners then had control of the valuable remaining pieces of the company for little or no cash investment. It all worked fine— if the assumptions were correct about the amount of expenses that could be cut and the prices that could be realized on the sale of parts of the company, and if the company could generate enough earnings to pay the high-priced interest on the remaining debt.

DEBT AND DELUSION

Fortunes were built on debt. In some respects, the takeover craze was reminiscent of the conglomerate empires of the late 1960s. Only instead of selling their companies for stock, this time the vehicle was debt. Once again, when styles changed, many latecomers would be left holding the bag.

With debt in fashion, consumers quickly caught on to the game. Consumer debt soared during the 1980s. Where previous generations took on mortgage debt, the baby boomers took on unprecedented consumer debt. Credit card charges outstanding soared to more than $165 billion; auto loans were stretched to five years, and new products were introduced to allow consumers to tap the equity that was growing in their homes.

By 1991, consumer mortgage debt reached an unprecedented 84 percent of personal disposable (after-tax) income (see chart I-5). And there were few places left for consumers to borrow, as home equity was nearly tapped out (see chart I-6).

It wasn't just business and consumers that wallowed in debt. Government also took on debt at an unprecedented rate. Some blamed it on the tax cuts, but the numbers showed that tax revenues actually increased dramatically in the 1980s, in spite of the tax cuts. Congress, catching the mood of the decade, was spending more than ever—and paying for it by borrowing money.

Federal spending in 1981 totaled $697 billion, and the budget deficit for the year was $59 billion. By 1988, the government was spending $1.1

CHART I-5

Consumer and Mortgage Debt Outstanding as a % of Personal Disposable Income   last point 93:II

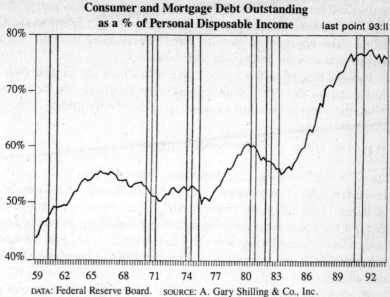

DATA: Federal Reserve Board.   SOURCE: A. Gary Shilling & Co., Inc.

CHART I-6

Total Equity of Owner-Occupied Real Estate as a Percentage of Total Value

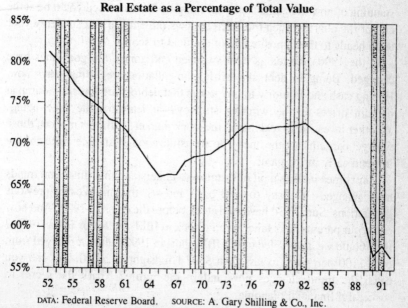

DATA: Federal Reserve Board.   SOURCE: A. Gary Shilling & Co., Inc.

trillion a year, and the budget deficit was $137 billion. The trend actually accelerated from 1988 through 1992, in spite of sharp tax increases. For 1992, the government spent $1.38 trillion and the budget deficit was $290 billion. The government spending trend is even more dramatic when viewed over a longer period (see chart I-7).

The sum total of all those annual budget deficits is our *National Debt*. At the start of the 1980s, it totaled just under $1 trillion. By the end of 1994, the National Debt had soared to more than $4.6 trillion!

WHAT'S NEW IN THE NINETIES

As we've seen, in each generation those who were able to discern the trends first made the most money. Those who caught on at the end were left as losers. In the 1920s, the smart money got into the stock market game early; it was the general investing public that pushed the market to new heights in 1929 and bought at the top. In the 1980s, once again the least informed lost the most—getting in on the inflation and debt game when it was already over.

Think of it in terms of watching a football game. Even if you have only a vague understanding of the rules, you at least know you're rooting for your team to get into the end zone and score. But with only a surface understanding of how the game is played, imagine how confused you'll be at the end of the quarter when the referee blows the whistle and suddenly your team heads to the opposite end of the field to score!

In the 1990s the teams have switched end zones; the goal lines have changed. Being in debt and betting on inflation are losing plays now. Having cash and liquidity to buy assets that debtors are forced to dump at bargain prices is the winning strategy—at least for the time being. Whether investing in real estate, the stock market, or the art market, those who get bargains are the ones who are astute enough to discern the change in trend early in the game.

Sometimes it takes a bit of distance to understand that times and trends have changed. It's easy to look back and see the mistakes of previous generations. Sure, we'd have sold stock before the crash in 1929. And how could our parents have failed to buy stock in IBM and Xerox in the 1950s? How could we have failed to sell IBM short in 1992 before it plunged from over $100 per share to less than $50? Hindsight is 20/20. But can you catch the trend changes now and in the future? That's the secret to successful financial planning.

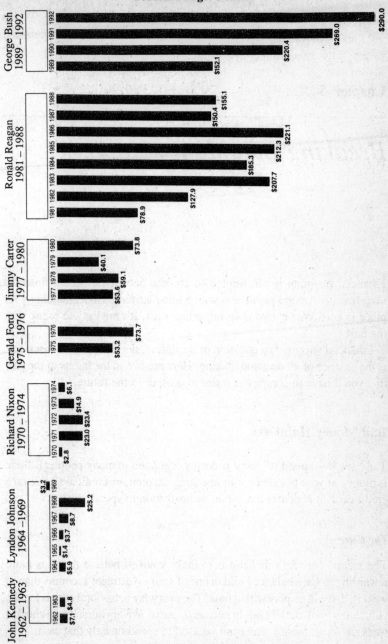

CHART I-7
Federal Budget Deficits

George Bush 1989 – 1992
1992 $290.0
1991 $269.0
1990 $220.4
1989 $152.1

Ronald Reagan 1981 – 1988
1988 $155.1
1987 $150.4
1986 $221.1
1985 $212.3
1984 $185.3
1983 $207.7
1982 $127.9
1981 $78.9

Jimmy Carter 1977 – 1980
1980 $73.8
1979 $40.1
1978 $59.1
1977 $53.6 $53.2

Gerald Ford 1975 – 1976
1976 $73.7
1975 $53.2

Richard Nixon 1970 – 1974
1974 $6.1
1973 $14.9
1972 $23.4
1971 $23.0
1970 $2.8

Lyndon Johnson 1964 –1969
1969 $3.2
1968 $25.2
1967 $8.7
1966 $3.7
1965 $1.4
1964 $5.9

John Kennedy 1962 – 1963
1963 $4.8
1962 $7.1

SOURCE: National Taxpayers Union, Washington, D.C.

Chapter 5

Breaking Bad Money Habits

Financial planning is not limited to choices between different financial investments. A good plan starts with a good attitude. Understanding your place in economic cycles is an important start. It's not easy to break with the past.

Financial success is a question of discipline, not denial. Self-discipline is the essence of all decision making. Here are two of the habits of the past that you'll have to conquer in order to prosper in the future.

Bad Money Habit #1

The **"see it—spend it"** habit is deeply ingrained in many people. If there is money in your pocket or your checking account, or credit available on a credit card, it becomes almost an authorization to spend.

The Cure

The mental cure for this habit is to make yourself believe that it is more rewarding to see a balance build in one of your investment accounts than to wear it, drive it, or play with it now! The everyday behavioral cure is to take your checkbook out of your briefcase or purse. Write yourself one check a week, as an allowance, and limit yourself to spending only that cash.

Take your credit cards out of your wallet and only carry the one or two that are necessary for business use or emergencies. Don't sign a credit card charge slip without looking at the exact amount on the bottom line. Then keep a small notebook in your bag—one that's about the size of the checkbook you used to carry. Every time you charge, write down the amount of the charge instead of just tucking the charge slip away.

You'd be amazed at how spending money can disappear from your wallet on small and often unnecessary purchases. Use that notebook to record everyday cash expenditures—newspapers, morning coffee, cigarettes. Just knowing where your money is going is an important element in gaining control.

To help you break the "see it—spend it" habit, we'll show you some strategies designed to take the money right out of your account and put it into worthwhile investments *before* it disappears into a cash register.

Bad Money Habit #2

Another expensive habit that can destroy your financial future is the **"bigger is better"** or **"status is significant"** attitude. Have you noticed that you'll walk through a store and seek out the most expensive product in the line, or that you'll buy an appliance that offers far more uses and gadgets than you'll ever be willing to learn? "Top of the line" has become a way of life.

The "bigger is better" habit applies to very large purchases as well as small. Top-of-the-line cars have become a very profitable niche for car makers. When European imports priced themselves too high, Japanese car makers created their own version of luxury and status—less expensive than the European imports, but expensive enough to confer a special status upon the owner.

Consumers pay for the marketing of status symbols. Would you be better off buying the less expensive car and taking the $20,000 savings and investing it for your future? That concept made for an interesting series of Cadillac commercials in 1991 and 1992.

The combination of credit and status has created some very expensive bad habits. Twenty years ago the use of credit cards in a restaurant or store was a mark of status, indicating that the holder "qualified" to make a credit purchase. As credit cards proliferated, gold and even platinum cards were offered (at higher annual fees) to confer even more "status" on the holder. In the nineties, the true mark of status will be the person who pays the restaurant bill in cash!

The ultimate "status habit" manifests itself in designer labels on clothes. While it is undeniable that some more expensive clothes are more stylish and better sewn, you must be aware that the same offshore factories often turn out identical products with different labels. Those with designer labels may sell for twice the price.

The Cure

Ask yourself: Are jeans really any different because they carry a different label? We object to commercials for alcohol and cigarettes when they are targeted toward impressionable young people. Don't status ads also carry a certain risk of ingraining dangerous financial habits?

Designer labels are often worn on the outside of the garment; checking account balances or mutual fund statements arrive in sealed envelopes. It takes self-confidence to find status hidden inside an envelope instead of on a label.

Everyday choices contribute to the success of your investment plan. It's not a question of sacrificing for your future; it's a question of evaluating your current purchases and balancing the current benefits against the opportunity cost. It's deciding whether that $2,000 would be better off invested in the stock market than spent on a vacation, or better off saved in a money market account for a down payment on a home than spent on new clothes today.

Sometimes you can make a good case for current consumption. If the new clothes help you land a better-paying job, then you can consider them an investment in your future. If a larger car bolsters your appearance as a successful salesperson, it might be helpful in making more commissions. But you have to draw a very careful line between appearance and reality. It's always easy to rationalize the difference between "needing" and "having."

Even the realization of opportunity lost won't change social pressures. But, as in any trend, following the crowd doesn't bring you out ahead. Making a reasonable financial plan based on disciplines that you willingly accept is the key to success.

PART II

Making Money Work

The Goal: to make your money work for you as hard as you work for it.

Investing money regularly and making smart money decisions in your daily life are not the only ways to get rich. In fact, really big money has been made in America by two groups of people: those who start, build, and then sell their own companies; and those who master the art of selling products or services to others. The combination of selling a product and owning the company that serves or manufactures it has been an American wealth strategy upon which great fortunes have been built—from Andrew Carnegie to H. Ross Perot.

At times in our country's history, it has also been possible to get rich through speculation in financial assets. The fortunes created on Wall Street in the 1980s come to mind, but similar fortunes were made (and lost) in the 1920s and even as far back as the Civil War. There is, of course, a great difference between speculation and investment.

There are plenty of motivational and inspirational books for those who want to build companies, sell products, or trade assets. But even those successful people need strategies to put their fortunes to work. Whether you work for a paycheck every week, count your earnings in hourly wages, or are an entrepreneur building your own business, you need to understand the financial techniques that can leverage your own hard work.

Don't believe the myth that you have to *have* a fortune to *make* a fortune. That's a defeatist attitude that keeps many people from getting started. You don't need a lot of money to get going; there are strategies that work with as little as $30 a month, or a few dollars a week taken out of your paycheck.

Money Strategy #1: Pay Yourself First

It has been said that "you can't get rich on a salary." The truth is, you can't get rich if you *spend* your entire salary. There is no question that you can and will grow your own fortune if you *pay yourself first*.

You must set money aside regularly in planned investments that are slightly out of your everyday reach. As you'll see in chapter 14, choosing a money market mutual fund is better than letting your extra cash sit in your checking account. In chapter 17, you'll learn how to have money transferred out of your regular checking or savings account and into a stock market mutual fund.

Money Strategy #2: Make an Investment Plan

Now that you're setting money aside regularly, you're ready to consider some savings and investment strategies. But all those strategies must fit into a plan. Every plan must have realistic goals. The earlier you start your plan, and the more disciplined you are about sticking to it, the better your chances of success. If you listen to the latest hot stock tip or revise your investments with the latest issue of every investment newsletter, you limit the chances of success.

Let's start planning!

Chapter 6

Starting to Plan

The first step in making a financial plan for your future is figuring out where you stand right now. Whether you decide to seek help from a financial planner or other advisor, or whether you decide to use the strategies in this book to direct your finances, you must get a clear picture of two issues: your *balance sheet*: what you owe and what you own; and your *cash flow*: how much you earn and how much you spend.

Planning Strategy #1: Your Balance Sheet

A balance sheet is simply a list of what you own in assets and what you owe in debt. It does not necessarily have to balance out! You can follow the listing we've included here, or just take a blank sheet of paper and draw a line down the middle.

You can divide your assets into categories. Here's how a standard list should look, although you may not have assets in every category:

Assets
Cash
  Checking account
  Money market bank account
  Money market mutual fund
  Certificates of deposit (CDs)

Securities
   Stocks
   Bonds
   Mutual funds
   Unit investment trusts
   Partnerships or other investment plans

Real estate
   Residence
   Vacation home
   Investment property

Life insurance (death benefits and cash value)
   Variable life
   Whole life, universal life
   Term life (death benefit only)

Retirement accounts
   401(k) or 403(b) plans
   IRA
   Keogh
   Profit-sharing, defined benefit plans
   Annuities
   Current estimate of Social Security benefits

Equity in business owned

Trust funds

Personal property
   Jewelry, furs
   Artworks
   Collections
   Other

You'll notice that your list of assets generally consists of things that could be used to raise cash if you need it. But not all assets are equally saleable. For instance, you'd take a 10 percent federal tax penalty if you had to break into your IRA, Keogh, or annuity plan to raise cash. And your baseball card collection or signed lithograph might not bring the price you think it's worth if you're forced to sell it through a newspaper ad or at an auction. Your term life insurance is an asset to your family if you die suddenly, but it has no current cash value for borrowing purposes.

Now it's time to look at what you owe. On the other side of the paper make a list of your debts. Also note the interest rate you are paying on each debt.

Liabilities
Mortgage loans
    Primary residence mortgage
    Second mortgage or home equity loan
    Home equity line of credit
    Vacation home mortgage
    Mortgage loans on investment property

Installment loans
    Car loan
    Education loan
    Unsecured bank loans

Credit card debt
    (list individual credit cards, amount outstanding, and interest rate)

Other debt
    Loans from family members
    Stock market margin loan
    Insurance policy loans
    Loans from 401(k) plan

It's a natural instinct to total both lists and compare the balances. But in financial planning the elements of the list are more important than the totals. While your debt may total up to a huge amount, it's important to distinguish "good" debt from "bad." That is, your mortgage debt may be large, but the interest you pay on it is deductible, and the monthly payments contribute to building up your net worth as the underlying asset—your home—increases in value.

Credit card debt and other forms of consumer debt are no longer deductible, so they can be a big drag on other hard-working parts of your money strategies. If you pay more than $1,000 in nondeductible annual interest on your $5,000 credit card balance, you might as well sell your 100 shares of a $10 stock and pay off your consumer debt. The stock would have to gain more than 10 percent a year just to break even with the money you're throwing down the drain on credit card interest—and that's not counting taxes you'd owe if you sold the stock for a gain!

If you're honest with yourself, this balance sheet should point out both the accomplishments and the glaring mistakes of your past financial strategies.

If you're burdened with nonproductive debt, your first priority should be paying it off.

Planning Strategy #2: Cash Flow Statement

Where does all the money go? It's time to track it down. For most people, a simple budget will provide the best description of your income and spending habits. You can get started by looking over your checkbook for the past few months and categorizing your major monthly expenditures. But making a budget is not that simple unless you're willing to keep track of *every* expenditure over a period of several months.

Start by buying a budget notebook, available at any stationery store. If you really want to make a project out of your budget, I highly recommend *The Budget Kit* ($15.95, Dearborn Financial Publishing, in bookstores or to order by mail, 800-322-8621). This handy book guides you through the process of creating budget categories and matching your cash flow to your spending plan, while setting aside money for savings and investment. Another alternative is to use one of the computer programs described in chapter 31, "Strategies for Everyday Money Handling." Whatever your style, the idea is simply to keep track of your spending habits—and get them under control!

Your cash flow statement simply tracks the monthly inflow of cash—paychecks, interest, dividends, etc.—and balances it with your known spending habits. The two sides of this statement should definitely balance out for the year, or preferably wind up with a surplus that is going into investments. If you're spending more than your income, it will come as no surprise that you're either going into debt or digging into your capital reserves to maintain your lifestyle.

Analyzing your cash flow statement will help you figure out how you're going to get ahead in financial terms. The additional money that you will be setting aside for regular investments has to come from somewhere. You will either have to spend less or you will have to earn more!

Planning Strategy #3: Create a Need for Money

That brings us to one of the most interesting financial aspects of human nature. *We can all spend as much as we earn!* Did you ever dream you'd be making as much money as you are today? Did you think that if you made this much money, you'd certainly be willing to set some aside for investment? You started out by living reasonably well on less money. But every time you earned a raise or a promotion, the additional money was easily spent as part of an expanding lifestyle.

There's no question that part of the motivation for working hard is to afford a better lifestyle. But within that lifestyle definition it's important to include a category called "investing for the future."

Human nature says needs are satisfied first; then you turn to wants. Make a secure financial future one of your needs. Once you create a need for investing, and start earning the money to fill that need, you're on your way to making the most of the strategies in this book.

Chapter 7

Setting Goals—and How to Get There

Want to have one million dollars? All you have to do is set aside $1,000 a year for 40 years at 12.5 percent and you'll have $991,791—almost a million dollars!

This illustration has been used by financial salespeople with great success. The possibility of having a million dollars does stimulate your imagination, and the example is correct in the arithmetic, as far as it goes. But in financial planning it's probably less useful than suggesting you buy a ticket to your state lottery.

What will $1 million be worth in 40 years? Well, if inflation runs at 3 percent annually, then your $1 million will be worth $306,557 in today's spending power. If inflation averages 4 percent, your buying power in 40 years will drop to $208,289 in today's dollars. Is that enough for you to live on for all your retirement years?

The second problem with the illustration above is the assumption that you could invest $1,000 every year at a rate of 12.5 percent—and keep reinvesting the interest earned at the same rate. We did have long-term interest rates on government bonds at 13.5 percent for one year in this century: 1980–81. At the same time, inflation was running at an official rate of 13.5 percent, so you were not beating inflation even with such high interest rates.

Finally, this illustration does not include the effects of taxation on your interest every year. Of course, we can fix that simply by investing the money in an IRA or 401(k) plan, but sheltering your savings from taxes is an important component of any long-term investment plan. In the illustration above, if you had to pay taxes on the interest every year at a 30 percent tax rate, you'd be left with only $343,688 in actual dollars. And you'd have a lot less in buying power—only $113,744 in today's dollars if inflation averages 4 percent over the 40-year period.

There are three financial issues to deal with when you're trying to build your fortune through a program of regular savings and investing.

1. How much money will I need?

That question involves making assumptions about inflation and the costs of the purchase you're saving for: the income you'll want in retirement, the college education your children will need, or the down payment on the home you'll want to purchase.

2. How much money do I have to set aside, at what rates of return, over how long a period of time, to reach my dollar goal?

This question involves analyzing different assumptions about rates of return on investments, and the risks you'll have to take to earn those rates of return. In combination with question 1, these assumptions are best illustrated with a spreadsheet showing how the numbers change with different assumptions. In chapter 44 you'll see how you can do this yourself with an inexpensive home computer program, or free charts offered by several mutual fund companies.

3. Which investments can shelter my income from taxes, while still allowing flexibility to use my assets productively?

It makes good sense to use simple tax-deferral strategies to build your wealth. The 1980s mania for tax shelters has given tax-saving strategies a bad name because so many involved investments in illiquid and over-priced assets. But there are many places to invest your savings in plans that give you control over your investments along with tax deferral. Some of these plans may be offered by the company for which you work; others you must choose for yourself. There may be penalties, however, for early withdrawal of funds from most of these plans, so it's important to understand the restrictions before you invest your money.

Chapter 8

Getting Help with Financial Planning

Can you answer the questions raised in chapter 7 by yourself, or do you need help? The process can be intimidating, and that's why so many people turn to financial planners for assistance. But there's no way you can entirely turn over the responsibility for your financial future to someone else. Even if you decide to get professional help, in the end it's your responsibility to approve the investments and cooperate with the plan. That's why it's important to understand every investment or purchase that is recommended to you.

In fact, you may decide that once the strategy is created, you can do the actual investing, saving fees and commissions. Or you may choose to turn your financial affairs over to a planning firm that will handle everything from investments to tax and estate advice. Still, you'll need to meet with your planner regularly to update your situation and approve changes in investment strategy.

Choosing a financial planner is much like choosing a doctor or attorney. The first place to start is with personal references. You can ask your accountant or attorney for names of planners, or ask friends who have worked successfully with a planner. Also, listed in this chapter are the telephone numbers of financial planning registries that will introduce you to planners in your city.

Some planning firms provide many services; others advise only on your investments. Any planner or firm you choose should be willing to work with your current tax accountant and attorney to build your total plan. You may want to contact several planners by phone to get started, but before making a decision you should definitely have a face-to-face meeting lasting at least an hour, for which there should be no charge.

Financial planning is a huge business, and it promises to grow every year as the baby boom generation turns its attention to planning for the future. Unfortunately, the title "financial planner" does not require licenses or credentials such as those given to doctors or lawyers. The name "financial planner" has also been assumed by many stockbrokers, accountants, and insurance salespeople. Not all planners have the same education, qualifications, or method of compensation.

The *International Board of Standards and Practices for Certified Financial Planners, Inc.* (303-830-7543), is the one organization that officially certifies financial planners who have completed a degree course offered at more than 40 colleges and universities around the country or through home study courses. To earn the designation *Certified Financial Planner (CFP)*, candidates must complete the required courses in six broad categories ranging from investment advice to tax and estate planning. A CFP must also pass a ten-hour examination given by the board, demonstrate proof of financial planning-related experience, and agree to abide by the group's code of ethics.

More than 23,000 individuals have earned the right to place the initials CFP after their name. So far, it is the one designation that really signifies a broad-based background and training in the entire field of financial planning.

The International Board of Standards and Practices for CFPs will not recommend individual financial planners, but they will help you by checking the credentials of anyone claiming to be a CFP. If you're interested in pursuing a certification in financial planning, this board will direct you to the colleges that offer the required courses.

The *Institute of Certified Financial Planners* (800-282-7526) in Denver, Colorado, is a professional association for more than 7,300 Certified Financial Planners. This group does maintain a database, and at no charge will send you information, including a biography and statement of practice, about three financial planners in your area.

The *American College* in Bryn Mawr, Pennsylvania (215-526-1000), has an accredited degree program leading to the designation of *Chartered*

Financial Consultant. This institution primarily trains insurance professionals in the techniques of financial planning, and you might ask any insurance agent who does financial planning if he or she is qualified as a Chartered Financial Consultant or as a CFP.

The largest trade association of financial planners is the *International Association for Financial Planning* (800-945-IAFP). This is not a licensing group for its 11,500 members, but the group does publish a registry of financial planners and will send a list of qualified financial planners in your area. Not every member of the trade association qualifies for the registry; only about 850 are listed. All planners in the registry must have practiced for at least three years, submit references from six clients for whom they have done comprehensive financial planning for at least two years, and successfully complete the IAFP practice/knowledge examination. All pledge to comply with a stringent code of ethics.

Some people prefer to deal with advisors who charge a fee only and do not charge commissions on the products they sell. The *National Association of Personal Financial Advisors* (708-537-7722) is an association of fee-only financial planners. They will send you a list of their members in your area.

WHAT YOU SHOULD PAY FOR PLANNING SERVICES

Financial planners may be compensated in several ways. The most common are straight fees for creating a plan, or commissions on products like insurance and mutual funds they sell you, or a combination of both. It all depends on the advice you seek, but you should know in advance how you are being charged. A total financial plan may range in cost from $1,500 to many thousands of dollars, depending on the complexity of your financial situation and the range of services that the planner offers. There may also be annual charges for meetings to update your plan and investments. And, of course, this cost may be in addition to the commissions you pay on the products you purchase.

Your accountant may give you financial advice and simply bill you for a few extra minutes of his or her time. Or you may choose to pay to have your accountant present at a session with a financial planner, to contribute a tax perspective to the discussions.

Your stockbroker will charge you a commission every time you buy or sell a product. The amount of those commissions can almost always be negotiated, depending on the size of your account and the frequency of your trades. (Even if you don't see a commission charge listed separately on your trade confirmation, you can be sure the broker is being paid for that transaction.) There is a new trend for brokerage firms to charge fees for *wrap accounts*—that is, to direct you to individual money managers who will charge a fixed fee of about 3 percent of your assets. (In chapter 19, we'll show you some less costly alternatives.)

It is always difficult to understand how insurance agents are compensated. Generally speaking, with policies that build cash value such as whole life, universal life, and variable life policies, your agent will keep 55 to 80 percent of the first year's premiums and at least 5 percent of the premiums you pay in the next nine years. (In chapter 54 we'll show you how to buy "low-load" life insurance and build your cash value more quickly by paying smaller commissions.) First-year commissions on term insurance may run between 45 and 75 percent of the premium paid.

An estate planning attorney may quote you a fixed fee for the entire set of documents you'll need, or you may pay for this service by the hour. (More on setting up an estate plan in chapters 55–59.)

QUESTIONS TO ASK YOUR FINANCIAL ADVISOR

This is *your* money and you are always entitled to ask how much commission the salesperson or advisor is making on the transaction. It is a question that should be answered honestly and without resentment—or you have the wrong advisor. One way to get a feel for the amount that is being taken out of your account to pay commissions is to ask how much of your original investment you'd get back if you decided to sell in three or six months. Of course, changing markets can cost you money in many investments, but you should be aware of those risks, apart from the simple cost of doing business.

It is certainly important to understand your advisor's motivation for recommending an investment. If substantial fees are involved, you can always ask if there are other similar investments and compare costs. It helps to know how much you'd be paying in fees and charges if you were acting without an advisor. That will give you a basis for comparison.

At a full-service brokerage firm you may pay as much as 3 percent of your investment dollars as a commission on stocks. That cost can be negotiated, or you can use a discount firm that can cut your commissions by half if you do enough trading (see chapter 19).

You can purchase a "no-load" (no-commission) mutual fund and expect to pay less than 1.5 percent per year in management fees and charges, but no additional charge to buy or sell your shares in the fund (see chapters 15–18). That compares very favorably with some funds sold by brokers and planners that charge as much as 8.5 percent of your initial investment in commissions.

Obviously, you can save money if you decide to "do-it-yourself," but then you don't have the benefit of the investment advice and "hand-holding" that many advisors provide. That can be a valuable service to help keep you on the right path. And it may be well worth paying an extra $50 or $100 commission on a stock purchase if your broker recommends a stock that doubles in price.

The bottom line: Only you can decide your comfort level with the advice you're receiving and how much you're willing to pay for it. The important thing is that you understand going in just how and how much you'll be paying for the advice you accept.

OTHER QUESTIONS YOU SHOULD ASK

Cost is not the only determinant in choosing a financial advisor. You should not only check the qualifications of the person who will be handling your money, but also ask for references. The references may be current clients, or business references such as banks or brokerage firms. When checking a business reference, ask not only if the firm has been doing business there, but if there is an individual contact who has an idea of the advisor's track record with clients.

Planners who give investment advice should be registered with the Securities and Exchange Commission (*SEC*) in Washington, D.C.; and with state securities commissioners. It's worth checking on these registrations, although these agencies will not pass any judgment on the advisor's qualifications, nor will they inform you of any pending enforcement actions against individuals or firms.

A planner may give you names of "rich and famous" clients, but in itself that is not necessarily a recommendation. He or she may be too busy with those important clients to pay much attention to your smaller account. Ask how many clients the firm has, and how frequently you will meet personally with the planner for a review of your investments and goals. Will you be dealing with an assistant or clerk after your first meeting?

It's also important to understand how your cash will be handled. Generally speaking, you should not hand over stock certificates or write checks to the planner. Instead, you will have an insured account in your own name at a brokerage firm or mutual fund to handle transactions. Money or certificates should be sent directly to that account. If the planner is earning commissions on your trade, the fund company will take the commission out of your purchase price and send it directly to the planner. If you are paying a quarterly fee based on the dollar value of your assets under management, the planner may bill you for the service or you may arrange to have the fee paid directly out of your account.

What else should you ask your planner? One interesting question: Ask for a description of his or her best—and worst—investments of the past ten years. Find out why those recommendations were made in the first place and what went wrong as well as right. Ask for the planner's current economic outlook and how he or she reached that conclusion.

You're not looking for an investment genius who always beats the market. You're looking for a professional who will help give you the edge on making your money work for you. Your personal comfort level is an important factor in that decision. Trust your instincts—once you have the facts.

QUESTIONS THE PLANNER SHOULD ASK YOU

You'll want to judge a prospective financial advisor not only by the answers to your questions—but by the questions you are asked. Beware of planners who immediately jump to conclusions about which investments you "need." They may simply be trying to peddle products that pay the largest commissions.

The planner should start by asking for a list of your assets and liabilities, and asking about your current cash flow. If you have prepared the lists we described in chapter 6, you'll give the planner a head start on understanding your needs. Then the planner should ask you about your goals for the future, because he or she will need to know something about your family, your dreams, and your fears.

While you may be talking to the planner strictly about investment advice, the full-service planner will need to know more about your personal finances in order to balance the recommendations with your needs. So, you should know what retirement and other benefits your company offers, and bring the documents with you to your meeting. The planner will ask about your estate plan—whether you have a will or living trust (more about that in chapters 55–59) and how much of your estate you want to leave to your children.

The planner should question your insurance coverage—including health, disability, and property insurance, as well as life insurance. All of these issues have an important bearing on your future financial plans. If you haven't covered some of your insurance needs, then your investment gains could be wiped out by a catastrophe. And, of course, you'll need to set aside money to pay for the needed insurance premiums. (More on that in Part V.)

After your meeting with the planner, give some thought to the entire process. You may want to talk with some of the planner's clients, or discuss the situation with your attorney or accountant. This is not a relationship to be entered into without some real consideration. Above all, do not mislead yourself into believing that you are now turning over all your financial worries to someone else. It's still your money, your future—and your responsibility to work with the planner.

Chapter 9

Risk and Reward

Every financial strategy is based on trade-offs—the balance of risk and reward. Measuring risk is the most difficult part of choosing a strategy. Many people have an intuitive perception of risk—a sense, for example, that investing in the stock market is riskier than leaving your money in the bank. But when it comes to financial strategies, relying on intuition may be the greatest risk you'll ever take. It's far better to be guided by the facts of any investment decision.

THE RISK IN AVOIDING RISK

In fact, it may actually be far riskier to your fortune to leave your money in fixed-rate investments than to choose a good stock market mutual fund. In part, the risk in this decision is related to your time horizons. If you know you will need your entire principal returned to you in a short period of time, you'll want to follow the Safe Money Strategies in chapter 14. Those strategies are also designed for older people who are living on their savings interest and have no other income to make up for losses that might occur in more risky investments.

But over a longer time horizon, safe money strategies may actually be less wise.

Consider the following chart, II-1, showing the real rate of return on certificates of deposit over the past 20 years. Even in periods where CD

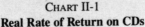

CHART II-1
Real Rate of Return on CDs

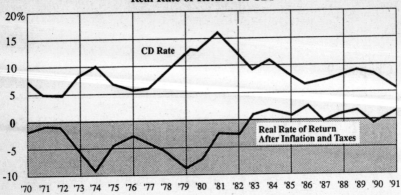

rates were highest, the after-inflation return was actually negative. You could earn 15 percent on CDs and actually be losing ground to inflation at a rate of 2.5 percent. So, investing in "safe" CDs was actually a losing strategy and far from riskless. The guaranteed safety of CDs only eliminated the risk of losing money through fraud or institutional failure because of the government guarantee against those losses.

RISK AND THE LONG RUN

On the other hand, a good case can be made for the fact that *over the long run* the stock market is actually *not* very risky. A study by Ibbotson & Associates, stock market historians and analysts, shows that there has been no 20-year period in which you would have *lost* money in the stock market—as defined by the Standard & Poor's 500 Stock Index—going back to 1926.

Chart II-2 shows the compound returns you would have received over the past 65 years on investments such as common stocks, long-term government bonds, and Treasury bills. You can measure their performance against inflation. Clearly, common stocks have outperformed the traditionally safer bonds and Treasury bills over the long run. What about the risks? Of course, over shorter periods of time, such as the few months in the fall of 1987, it is possible to face huge losses in stock market investments. However, over the long run, the risk in owning common stock actually diminishes. Chart II-3 illustrates the declining risk associated with owning common stocks over a longer period of time.

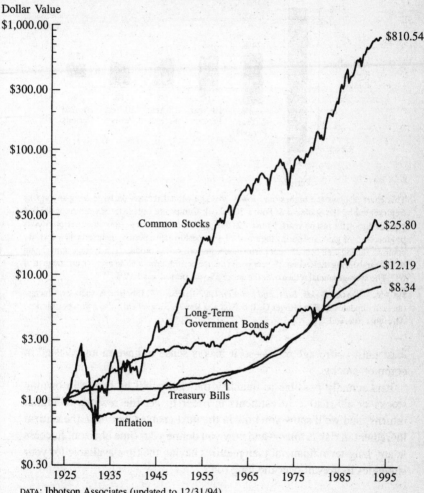

CHART II-2

**Investments in the U.S. Capital Markets
1926 to Present
(assumes Initial Investment of $1.00 at year-end 1925
with income reinvested)**

DATA: Ibbotson Associates (updated to 12/31/94).
SOURCE: INVESCO

Many younger people make the mistake of choosing only the most conservative investments such as fixed-rate guaranteed contracts (GICS) when they are called on to allocate their assets in a company pension or 401(k) plan. But the assets in these plans are set aside for the long run—at

CHART II-3
How the Risk on Common Stock Investments Is Reduced by Lengthening Your Investment Period

Common Stock Returns 1926–1990

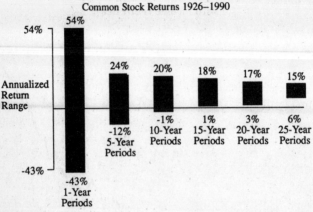

This chart displays the highest and lowest average annual returns on large company stocks (represented by the Standard & Poor's 500 Stock Composite Index) for six different holding periods during the last 65 years. Notice that during their best 1-year performance period, stocks produced a 54% gain, and during their worst 1-year performance period, incurred a 43% loss. By contrast, during their best 25-year performance period, stocks produced an average annual gain of 15% and during their worst 25-year performance period, produced an average annual gain of 6%. The average annual return over the entire 65-year period was 10.1%.

SOURCE: © *Stocks, Bonds, Bills, and Inflation 1992 Yearbook*™, Ibbotson Associates, Chicago (annually updates work by Roger G. Ibbotson and Rex A. Singuefield). Used with permission. All rights reserved.

least until you're age 59½—so it makes sense to have more invested in common stocks.

It is actually possible to quantify the risk you'll be taking in owning stocks or alternative investments in order to get the rewards of higher returns, and we'll show you how in the next chapter. For now, the critical ingredient in risk is *time*—and how you define your time horizon. Success in any long-term financial plan requires having the time available for your strategies to prevail over the long run.

RISK AND YOUR ASSUMPTIONS

It's also very important to base your assumptions on realistic time periods. Most people base their expectations for performance on their own recent experience. That can be a mistake. For example, during the ten years between 1982 and 1991, the S&P 500 Stock Index had a total return of 17.6 percent compounded annually. That return far exceeds the 40-year return of 11.7 percent in the years from 1942 to 1982. The only other ten-year period in which the stock market matched the performance of the 1980s was the period from the end of World War II to the early 1950s.

In fact, the 1980s were a decade in which most financial assets performed relatively well. Long-term Treasury bonds had a compound return of 15.6 percent during this period, three times their historical average since 1950. Even Treasury bills earned 7.7 percent annually—or 3.8 percent more than the rate of inflation, on average, during the past decade. But over the past 50 years, the rate of return on Treasury bills only equaled the annual rate of increase in consumer prices.

The eighties were a special period, when financial markets reacted to dramatic reversals in interest rates and inflation. While tangible assets such as real estate, gold, and art were big winners in the inflationary 1970s, the eighties were a decade to own financial assets. In the 1990s, percentage returns on financial assets are hardly likely to match those of the eighties. We have never had two decades of back-to-back, double-digit average annual growth in the stock market.

It's important to use a realistic set of assumptions if you're planning to grow your money for a college fund or retirement. Otherwise you're not assessing risk accurately and are unlikely to reach your goals.

HISTORICAL RISK AND REWARD

Chart II-4 measures the maximum and minimum returns for 20-year holding periods for various assets. Common stocks once again top the list

CHART II-4
Maximum and Minimum Returns for 20-Year Holding Periods
(Compound annual rates in percent)

	Maximum	Minimum
Common Stocks	16.9%	3.1%
Long-Term Government Bonds	9.0	0.7
Intermediate-Term Government Bonds	9.4	1.6
Treasury Bills	7.7	0.4
Inflation	6.4	0.1

SOURCE: Investment Information Services.

of long-term gainers among these investment choices. In every 20-year period in this century, the minimum gain (compound rate of return) you would have received from an investment in the Standard & Poor's average of 500 stocks was 3.1 percent, while the largest compound rate of return in any 20-year period was 16.9 percent.

As you can also see from that table, the rate of return on long-term government bonds, intermediate government bonds, and Treasury bills has a far narrower spread over 20-year periods in this century. That means there has been less *volatility* in the performance of these investments. For instance, with Treasury bills, the maximum 20-year return was 7.7 percent compounded annually, and the minimum was 0.4 percent.

Narrower swings in market performance lead to the intuitive concept of lower risk. But you still need to factor in performance relative to inflation, to figure out if you're making a good investment. As you can see from the same chart, the maximum and minimum inflation rates over any 20-year period are 6.4 percent and 0.1 percent.

TRADITIONAL RETURNS

Treasury bills historically reflect the rate of inflation plus ½ of 1 percent. That's because the weekly Treasury bill auction market is a huge free market that quickly adjusts rates to changing economic conditions. So, if you expect the rate of inflation to average about 4 percent, you could assume you'll get an average rate of return of about 4.5 percent when you invest in Treasury bills over the long run.

A portfolio of money market funds might increase your return by another 0.5 to 1 percent over the inflation rate, on average. And a portfolio of long-term bonds can generally be expected to return between 0.5 and 2 percent more than Treasury bills.

At other times this relationship between long- and short-term interest rates (called the *yield curve*) may change. In September 1992, the difference or *spread* between short- and long-term rates widened to 4.6 percentage points—the widest differential in the twentieth century. Rates on short-term Treasury bills were 2.75 percent, while rates on 30-year government bonds reached 7.38 percent. The yield curve was said to be very *steep*.

In December 1980, the reverse situation occurred. Short-term Treasury bill rates rose to 16.55 percent, while long-term government bonds yielded only 11.89 percent. The resulting negative 3.77 percentage point difference was the largest yield curve *inversion* in history. As you can see, traditional relationships may sometimes be pushed to extremes.

Over the long run, it is possible to make some judgments about the relative risk of a portfolio of common stocks. This so-called "risk premium" has averaged about 8.5 percent over the rate of return on Treasury bills. So, if you predict that Treasury bills will yield about 4 percent over the next 20 years, based on past history, a portfolio of common stocks should return about 12.5 percent on average (4 plus 8.5).

MEASURING STOCK MARKET RISK

Many individual stocks or portfolios of stocks may be inherently riskier than the entire S&P 500 Stock Index. That's why the concept of *beta*, or relative risk, was created to quantify risk using a computer. Individual stocks and even entire mutual fund portfolios have a beta, or risk premium, to the market as a whole, which has a beta of one. You can find this beta number right at the top of any *Value Line* stock report, which is easily available through your broker or at most public libraries. To find the beta of any mutual fund portfolio, check analyses such as those printed in the *Morningstar* reports (see chapter 18).

The higher the beta or volatility of any stock or fund, the greater the perceived risk—but also, the greater the potential return. Some market analysts debate the ability of beta to truly measure market risk, but it's a much better way to judge risk than by using your intuitive feelings about whether you'll make or lose money. And if you're going to design an investment strategy, it's important to take risk into account.

HIDDEN INVESTMENT RISKS

There are other risks that are not so easy to quantify, but can have a significant impact on your investment performance. These risks should be carefully investigated *before* you commit any money to an investment. These are the risks involved in getting *out*!

Many investments have significant penalties, or *back-end* charges, if you decide to exit early. Some mutual funds charge a fee if you sell your shares in the first few years. Insurance annuities may charge as much as 8 percent surrender charges in the first year, and a declining percentage in subsequent years, if you change your mind. In addition, there is usually a

10 percent federal tax penalty for taking money out of a qualified retirement plan before age 59½.

Other costs of taking money out of your investment are not so obvious. If a broker or salesperson takes a commission on your investment, that money will not be recouped if you sell quickly. For example, if you purchase a mutual fund that charges an 8 percent sales commission, or load, that amount will be deducted from your investment. Only $9,200 of your $10,000 investment will go to work for you.

The way to check on the cost of getting out is to ask how much of your money would be returned if you changed your mind within one month or one year of making that investment. Of course, market movements can also cause losses; but penalties, surrender charges, and commissions are sure losers.

One other risk in getting out of an investment is not so easy to measure in advance. It is called "liquidity risk." You can sell 100 shares of stock on the New York Stock Exchange any working day. It is not so easy to sell an investment for which there is no ready marketplace. Limited partnerships are an example of investments that may be valued at one price, yet difficult to sell at any price (see chapter 27). Illiquidity adds substantial risk to your investment.

OTHER RISK DECISIONS

It's fairly easy to measure risk in financial assets such as stocks and bonds. But there are plenty of other risks you decide to take, or hedge against, with your assets. Few wealthy people would leave their homes or cars uninsured—both for protection against damage or loss, and protection against the liabilities that come with ownership of these assets. Yet many otherwise insured people fail to take out a low-cost "umbrella" insurance policy to protect against liabilities from huge judgments in lawsuits, which are now commonplace.

Most people understand the importance of life insurance, yet surprisingly few people remember to insure their ability to earn a living with disability insurance. On the other hand, many people will pay extra cash up front to take out an insurance policy on a newly purchased appliance without understanding that major retailers will stand behind the products they sell even if the manufacturer won't. Or they pay far too much to insure risk when they purchase an accidental death policy in an airport before getting on an airplane or rent a car for two days.

THE RISK OF EMOTION

There is one other concept of risk that cannot be quantified or predicted. That's the risk of being ruled by emotion. As you will note, all of these historical rates of return are based on *long-term* investments and averages. Yet, if you take an honest look at yourself, you'll recognize that it might be difficult for you to keep a long-term commitment to an investment strategy—especially when everything seems to be collapsing around you.

That's why the majority of investors tend to sell at market bottoms and buy at the top. It's a question of crowd psychology that has been documented all the way back to the "tulipmania" in Holland in the mid-seventeenth century, when people were willing to trade their farms and livestock for one rare tulip bulb. It's not so dissimilar from the mania that pushed the price of gold to $850 an ounce in 1980.

In the late 1980s, the real estate and stock market valuations in Japan definitely qualified as one of these crowd manias. In the end, all of these markets come crashing back to earth—sometimes resulting in values far *below* the asset's real worth. Eventually, over the long run, these extremes will average out. But extremes are not only averaged in price, they are averaged in time—and it may take years for these markets to regain a semblance of relative value.

It requires self-discipline to stick to a financial strategy when the market moves against you. It's difficult to stick to a monthly investment plan in a stock market mutual fund, for instance, when the market has just taken a nosedive. The instinct is just the opposite: to sell out before all is lost.

The lesson in creating any financial strategy: understand the real risks based on historical information, and understand your own ability to accept those risks and stick with the strategy.

COVERING ALL RISKS

Obviously, not all financial risk can be quantified in any formula. There is always the risk of war, domestic violence, or natural disasters that could disrupt the very workings of the market system. That's why government and businesses have so-called "disaster plans" and backup systems. But you'll never be able to protect yourself against all unexpected risks. That's life. Fear of inherently unpredictable risk should not blind you to the opportunities to be gained if you're willing to take and manage recognized risk.

Chapter 10

Choosing Your Risks: Asset Allocation

After you've given some thought to the real risks you're willing to assume for the sake of making your assets grow, you can make some decisions about categories of potential investments. That's a simple description of one of the big buzzwords in financial planning: *asset allocation*. It's just a process of deciding how your investment dollars should be divided among different types of investments.

ASSET CHOICES AND RISK

Professional money managers use the concept of asset allocation to divide portfolios into categories such as stocks, government bonds, corporate bonds, money market investments, and perhaps international stocks, or international bonds, or even gold, real estate, and venture capital investments. Then the manager makes decisions about the appropriate mix of these investments to achieve targeted returns, taking into account considerations such as risk and historical performance records.

It is definitely possible to determine the inherent risk in different kinds of assets, and the returns you would have received for taking those risks over the years. Looking at charts II-5 and II-6, you'll see the results of investing in different kinds of assets over the past 46 and ten years.

CHART II-5
**Major Asset Classes
Risk/Return
1945–1993**

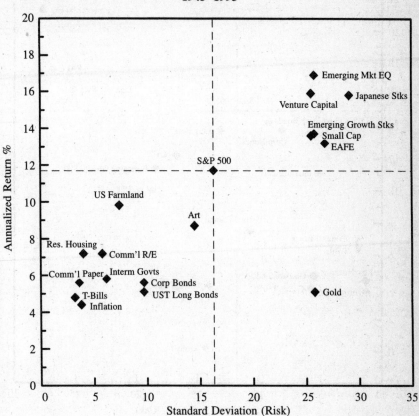

DATA: Morgan Stanley.
SOURCE: INVESCO

CHART II-6
Major Asset Classes
Risk/Return
Past 10 Years (Ending 1993)

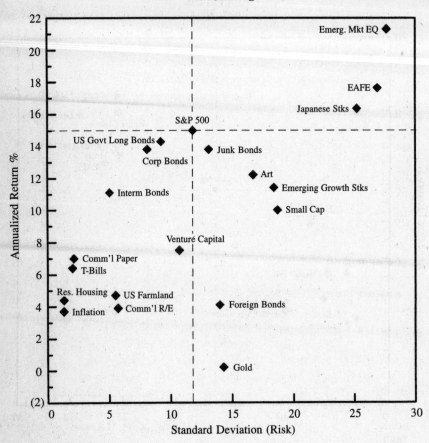

DATA: Morgan Stanley.
SOURCE: INVESCO

The idea is to move up the return scale (on the vertical axis) while minimizing the risk taken (which increases along the horizontal scale).

Make special note of the square representing inflation on these charts. That's the real number you're trying to beat, and some of the results on these charts may be surprising. Take a look at gold, the renowned inflation hedge, on both charts. Over the past ten years, if you had owned gold you would have lost ground to inflation, and gold barely beat inflation over the past 46 years. Yet, owning gold has been pretty far out along the risk scale in both charts.

Of course, you could have made a fortune in gold by purchasing it in the early 1970s at about $45 an ounce. (On December 31, 1974, when gold bullion was once again legalized for American citizens to own, gold was trading at around $180 an ounce.) To make that fortune required selling when prices peaked at more than $800 an ounce in 1980. Trading success requires adding another, more difficult talent to your investment decisions—market timing. More about that later.

When it comes to your investment decisions, it makes sense to choose an asset category that performs well over the long run, at relatively minimal risk, and allocate a substantial portion of your assets to that group. Diversification helps minimize risk, but when making those decisions it helps to have historical perspective.

Take one more look at the two charts and find the circle that represents common stocks, the Standard & Poor's 500 Stock Index. Over the long run, common stocks have outperformed inflation by a large margin while having a relatively low profile on the risk scale. Yet there's a widespread misperception that common stocks are very risky. In fact, stocks are always viewed by the general public as *most* risky just when the risks are lowest.

It helps to have hindsight. In August of 1982, when the country was in a recession and the Dow Jones Industrial Average was at a low around 778, the stock market was viewed as extremely risky. Yet in the following decade, the DJIA moved higher than 3400. After the frightening October 1987 stock market crash to 1738, the market rebounded 1,500 points in less than five years. The day Operation Desert Storm started in January 1991, the Dow touched 2460; six months later, it was trading at over 3000. Fear is an emotion; risk is a mathematical calculation.

YOUR OWN ASSET ALLOCATION

Do you have a picture of your own current assets? Take the time to sit down alone, or with your financial advisor, and sort out your present distribution of wealth. Refer to the balance sheet you made (in chapter 6) and be sure to include all your assets. The idea is to get the "big picture" of your current financial allocations, not only your investment portfolio.

For example, under real estate, you'll list the current market value of your home, vacation home, and any other real estate you own either individually or in an investment partnership, along with the current market value of those assets.

Next, make a list of the ways in which your assets are invested in the stock (equity) market. You may own stocks in your Individual Retirement Account, or perhaps you've allocated a portion of your company profit sharing or 401(k) savings plan to the stock market. Are your stock market assets diversified, or are they concentrated in one stock—perhaps shares in the company for which you work? Don't forget to include stock options granted by your company as part of your stock market equity exposure.

You may also have a portion of your assets invested in bonds, either through your own direct purchases or as part of an allocation in your company pension or savings plan. Some of your assets may be considered short-term "liquid assets"—even if they are included in a qualified and restricted company profit-sharing plan. Still, you have the option to move those liquid assets into stocks, bonds, or other investments offered within the plan, so you'll include them in the category of short-term, liquid assets for investment decision purposes.

Don't forget to list other assets: cash value insurance policies, equity value of ownership of your own company, or any valuable collections you own and could potentially sell to diversify your assets.

CHANGING YOUR ASSET MIX

When you look at this list of assets, you realize you have basically three choices. You can add to your assets; you can deplete your assets; or you can change their mix to make them grow faster within the limits of the risks you're willing to take. If you like to play with computers—or crayons— you can make a pie chart to illustrate the percentages of your assets in each category. Are you comfortable with the way they balance out, or do you need to make some adjustments?

The "correct" mix of assets will be different for every individual or family, depending upon factors such as age, health, total portfolio size, and willingness to assume risk. Often you'll find that within your family two adults will differ about the correct mix because each has a different tolerance for risk.

You might decide to change the mix of your assets for one of two reasons. You could decide that your assets are too heavily concentrated in one category—having too much tied up in your company stock for your advancing age, or too little exposure to stock market growth considering how young you are. If your home is your greatest asset, you'll need to start a program of savings and investing in other areas. If a good portion of your annual earnings comes in the form of stock options granted by your company, then maybe you ought to diversify the investments in your company 401(k) savings plan.

MARKET TIMING AND YOUR ASSET MIX

Or you could decide that your mix of assets is wrong for an entirely different reason: market timing. You may decide to eliminate some stocks or mutual funds from your investment portfolio because you think the market is going to drop. Or you may decide that declining real estate prices have made some bargains available. If you are going to change the mix of your asset allocations because of your market timing predictions, you must be willing to forecast future price changes.

Most people make their asset allocation decisions based on market timing considerations. And that may be one of the biggest mistakes an investor can make, according to some recent reports. A study by Brinson Associates followed the performance of 91 huge U.S. pension funds over ten years. The study concluded that nearly 94 percent of the difference in performance between those funds was determined by how the investments were allocated between various assets. Only about 6 percent of the differences in track record was a result of the portfolio manager "choosing the right stocks" or "getting in and out at the right time."

Mark Hulbert, author of *The Hulbert Financial Digest* (see chapter 20), which tracks the performance of investment newsletters, did a study that reported essentially the same results. Hulbert found that "asset allocation decisions alone can account for fully 71 percent of the average newsletter's performance. . . . Market timing and security selection appear to add relatively little above and beyond asset allocation."

So, unless you want to make investing a full-time hobby, you'll be better off deciding on the right mix of assets rather than spending your time picking individual stocks or deciding when the market is most likely to rise or drop.

In chapters 19 and 20 on stock market investments, we'll introduce some simple strategies you can use that are based on both asset allocation and market timing techniques. In the meantime, before you start to allocate *within* your investment portfolio, you need to make sure your overall asset picture is well balanced to suit your long-term growth needs and risk profile.

Chapter 11

The Impact of Taxes on Your Financial Plan

The debate over the Tax Act of 1993 brought the question of income tax rates into sharp focus for many Americans. What is the level of "wealth" at which Americans feel "rich?" Will raising tax rates bring in more revenues, or will higher rates simply result in more (legal) tax avoidance maneuvering? Are higher tax rates on the wealthy a question of "fairness"—or do they destroy investment incentives for those who create jobs? Will higher taxes bring down the federal budget deficit, or merely slow down the economy and thereby increase deficits?

Whatever your personal response to these issues, you must deal with the question of taxes in your personal financial planning. If you think back to your high school physics classes, you probably remember that most of the experiments were done "in a vacuum." The teacher told you the experiments would work perfectly if there were no real-world "friction" to slow things down and alter the results. When you're making financial plans, consider income taxes as the "friction" that slows your money plans. And don't make any assumptions in a vacuum without considering the effects of taxes.

HOW TAXES AFFECT YOUR INCOME

Most people understand the impact of taxes on income. After all, the deductions are listed right on your paycheck stub, or you have to write a check for estimated taxes every quarter. You know that if you're in the 31 percent tax bracket, that's the amount you'll pay the government out of your next dollar of earnings. If you live in a state that taxes income, that's one more cut out of your paycheck. And the trend is toward tax increases.

In 1995, highly paid workers will have as much as $4,681 taken out of their paychecks over the year for FICA—the Federal Insurance Contributions Act, more commonly known as Social Security or the payroll tax. The tax is levied at a rate of 7.65 percent on the earnings up to $61,200. On all earnings above that level, workers pay an additional 1.45 percent in payroll taxes to fund Medicare. The employer contributes an equal amount. If you're self-employed, you'll be paying a 15.3 percent tax, up to a maximum of $9,363 in taxes, but you are allowed to deduct one half of the self-employment tax you pay.

The Tax Act of 1993 raised marginal tax rates to the highest levels in more than a decade. Those who file single returns with taxable income of more than $115,000 or joint returns with taxable income over $140,000 moved into the 36 percent tax bracket. Those with taxable income over $250,000 (whether joint or single return) are in the 39.6 percent bracket. But effectively those tax brackets may really be as high as 42 or 43 percent because of the phaseout of certain deductions and personal exemptions at those income levels. Check with your accounting professional.

HOW TAXES AFFECT YOUR BUYING POWER

The tax burden on the American family is most dramatic when you consider the impact of taxes on the cost of things the family must buy. After all, most people work to earn money to buy the basic necessities in life before they start thinking about having extra cash to invest. A recent report by the Cato Institute gives dramatic evidence of the burden of taxes.

Suppose that a middle-income worker earning $34,000 a year wants to buy a new $10,000 car. If that worker lives in an average-tax state, he or she must earn an additional $17,038 to pay for the car. That total includes the $10,000 purchase price, plus $7,038 to pay the sales tax on the car and the income and payroll taxes on the earnings used to pay for the car!

Viewed from another perspective, the worker must work three and a half months of the year to pay for the car, and then two and a half more months to pay the taxes on the income used to purchase the car!

For a self-employed, middle-income worker, the true cost of that car is even higher—$18,320—because the self-employed person pays a 15.3 percent self-employment tax to cover both employee and employer shares of FICA.

The Cato study gives the true cost of some other major purchases of the American family. In each case, the worker lives in an average-tax state and earns $34,000 per year. The taxes considered include federal and state income taxes, employee's FICA contribution, and state sales tax. For example:

One year college tuition. Cost: $8,000. Amount of earnings needed to pay the bill: $13,307.

Personal computer. Cost: $1,500. Earnings needed to pay the bill: $2,748.

One year's gasoline for typical driver. Cost: $479, exclusive of all taxes. Income needed to buy the gas: $1,145.

In other words, if you live in a high-tax state, you should figure that you need to earn roughly twice as much as the purchase price of the item you are buying. Or consider that half the time you spend working is to pay taxes to various governments! That's the real burden of taxes.

HOW TAXES AFFECT YOUR INVESTING POWER

Income and gains taxes have an equally powerful effect on your ability to build wealth by investing your money. That's why sheltering income from current taxes became such a mania in the early 1980s, when tax rates were high, and inflation-led wage increases kept pushing people into higher tax brackets.

In the early eighties, income tax cuts and indexing of tax brackets to keep up with inflation took some of the sting out of the tax bite. But in 1990 the federal government enacted a five-year, $200 billion tax increase. The

1993 Tax Act is estimated to add $300 billion to the tax burden over five years. And rising state taxes are estimated to add another $40 billion in new taxes to the burden.

There are ways to escape or postpone paying taxes. Tax law has become an industry of its own, and the federal tax code has more than 7,000 pages plus four volumes of official regulations. But sheltering your income from taxes does not require getting involved with uneconomical investments or schemes with debatable legal consequences.

TAX-FREE INVESTMENTS

It's important to understand the difference between tax-*free* and tax-*deferred*. States, cities, and certain other municipal taxing bodies are allowed to sell tax-free municipal bonds, where the income you earn is totally free from federal taxes and, in some cases, free from state taxes as well. But the interest rate you receive on those bonds is correspondingly lower than the rates paid on other investments. (See chapter 24.)

CHART II-7
IRA Beats Taxable Accounts
assumes 9% annual rate of return and $2,000 annual contribution

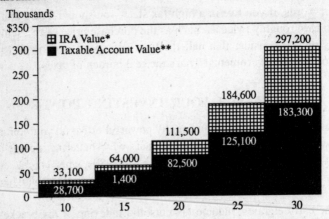

* Tax-deferred account value. Upon withdrawal, taxes will have to be paid on earnings.
** Account value after federal taxes (28%).

SOURCE: T. Rowe Price Associates, Inc.

TAX-DEFERRED INVESTMENTS

Tax-deferred investments are simply regular taxable investments such as stocks, bonds, and mutual funds that are purchased *within* an officially approved, qualified investment plan. Examples of this type of plan are annuities, company 401(k) savings plans, pension plans, and Individual Retirement Accounts. (See chapters 28–30 and 44.)

Deferring the impact of income taxes is worthwhile because of the dramatic increases in investment returns you can achieve. Simple strategies for deferring taxes are available to everyone, although many people fail to take advantage of them. Perhaps they don't understand the financial bonanza that occurs when taxes are deferred on interest income and profits.

Chart II-7 shows the dramatic difference between investment returns in a taxable account (28 percent tax bracket) and a tax-deferred account. The graph assumes an annual $2,000 contribution to an IRA that earns a 9 percent annual rate of return.

In the early years, there appears to be very little impact because of income taxes. But at the end of 30 years the difference is dramatic. You'd have $297,200 in your IRA account, and only $183,300 if you'd saved the money outside this tax-sheltered investment.

Of course, when you take the money out of your IRA, you'll still have to pay income taxes. But few people take the money out all at once, so the account can continue to grow even as you use a portion of it for retirement expenses.

When you have the combination of a long amount of time and tax deferral working in your investment plan, you have an unbeatable formula for accumulating wealth. Unbeatable, that is, unless the government changes the rules again. That's why you need to understand the power of the government and the Federal Reserve System as described in the next chapter—and why you need to keep alert to changing tax laws and monetary policies.

Chapter 12

Power, Politics, and Money

Winning financial strategies depend on making assessments about the direction of the general economy. In order to be a winner, you must understand where the power lies to change financial trends. Understanding those trends is the key to being there first to make a fortune, instead of getting in last and losing.

The most important power to move the economy and the value of money is divided between the government and the Federal Reserve, the nation's central bank. Congress can pass laws that change the tax code and create or destroy investment opportunities. The Fed determines the amount of money in the banking system and the interest rates that are charged to borrow that money. Both of these powerful entities have been known to take surprising actions.

THE POWER OF CONGRESS

The 1993 Tax Act raised top marginal rates to 39.5 percent on ordinary income. However, capital gains tax rates (taxes on gains on the sale of assets held for one year or more) were left unchanged at 28 percent. As you can imagine, this disparity in rates creates a powerful incentive for those in upper brackets to seek capital gains instead of ordinary income.

For example, under this tax differential it may make more sense to invest in a stock that pays low dividends but has the potential for big price appreciation than to search out high-dividend paying stocks. Dividends are taxed as ordinary income while gains on the sale of the stock, if held for at least a year, are taxed at the lower rate.

Lower tax rates on long-term gains may affect your investment decisions. Do I sell now before the market drops and pay ordinary income taxes on short term gains, or do I wait a full year and accept market risk of losing some (or all) of my profits?

The 1993 Tax Act also put into place a special capital gains provision for gains on the sale of certain small business stocks that have been held for at least five years. Individual shareholders who hold qualified stock (stock originally issued by the company after the date of the tax law change) and sell it after five years can exclude 50 percent of the gains on the stock from any taxes. This provision does not include gains on the sale of Subchapter S corporations.

The complexity and changes in the tax law may require you to seek professional advice in your investment planning. But taxes should not be a deterrent to financial planning; they're really a form of motivation to make you think about your financial future!

Congress and Tax Law

For example, the Tax Reform Act of 1986 effectively destroyed the market for investment real estate. Under the guise of reform, the new tax laws made it more difficult to finance real estate and benefit from tax deductions in the purchase of real estate. The result: a massive collapse in commercial real estate prices and major bankruptcies that threatened the entire banking system. But then, it was Congress that created those tax incentives in the first place, causing an excess of money to be directed to an overheated real estate market in the mid-1980s. In 1993, Congress once again changed the tax laws, including the entire direction of personal income tax rates, one of the greatest incentives—or disincentives—of all.

Congress and Regulations

Another classic example of the power of government to affect the economy is the savings and loan bailout bill, officially titled the Financial Institutions Reform, Recovery, and Enforcement Act (FIRREA) of 1989. Having deregulated the savings and loans in the early 1980s to allow them to pay higher interest rates to depositors, Congress failed to establish any oversight regarding the loans the S&Ls were making to earn those high rates which were then passed on to depositors. Ordinarily, that oversight wouldn't be important, except that Congress officially guaranteed the savers' deposits that were being used to make those loans.

As borrowers defaulted on those loans, taxpayers were left holding the bag. And the 1989 attempt to bail out the industry may have made the problems worse, forcing S&Ls to dump assets into a declining market. Certainly there was chicanery in the S&L business, with many operators pocketing illegal kickbacks and owning properties on which their institutions made loans. But it was bad laws that made the situation possible, and worse laws that cost billions of dollars in an attempt to patch up the situation.

At year-end 1992, another important law went into effect: the Federal Deposit Insurance Corporation Improvement Act (FDICIA). It put into effect a whole slew of new banking regulations that impact on banks' willingness to make loans. Regulatory excess had the effect of slowing the entire economy while banks have poured money into investments in safe government securities instead of lending money to companies that could create new jobs. In the first eight months of 1992, banks purchased more than $37 billion of government securities, while bank loans declined by $7 billion.

The moral of this story is that laws can and do change—in the process creating new incentives and rules in the economy and in investments. And those changes are not always for the better. That is the reason investors need to keep an eye on what's happening in Washington, D.C., as well as on Wall Street and Main Street.

THE POWER OF THE FEDERAL RESERVE

The other great power in the economy is the Federal Reserve System, with its ability to create new money and affect the level of interest rates. Every few years the Fed is given the task of helping the economy out of a recession. One of the oldest rules of investing is: **Don't fight the Fed!** If the Federal Reserve decides to unleash all its economic weapons, it will have a definite impact on financial markets.

Creating Credit

One way the Fed can try to get the economy going is to create new money or credit. The process is very simple and doesn't involve printing money, as most people imagine. Instead, the Fed can go into the huge trading market for government securities and buy Treasury bills, notes, and bonds, paying for them with newly created credit. Nobody questions whether the check is good when the Fed pays for those securities! And so the money represented by the Fed's check goes right into the banking system. But if the Fed creates too much new credit in the system, the result is inflation.

Cutting Rates

The Fed's biggest weapon in a recession is to cut interest rates, encouraging business investment and economic growth. When the Fed cuts interest rates, stock market investments also become more attractive. Interest rates on bank deposits drop, encouraging people to take the risk of putting money into the market. The money moving into the stock market pushes prices higher.

When the Fed decides to lower interest rates by cutting the rates it charges on loans to member banks, then short-term rates throughout the economy will come down. It's a bit harder for the Fed to affect long-term rates, which are based not only on the current supply of money, but on fears for its value in the future: inflation.

The Results

Often the Fed is in a delicate situation. Creating excess money may make the price—interest rates—drop in the short run. But if the Fed creates too much money, inflation fears will cause long-term interest rates to rise.

In 1992, the Fed found itself in an unusual situation. It was creating plenty of money and cutting its interest rates regularly, but the economy was not reviving in spite of lower interest rates. Inflation did not seem to be a worry. So why was the economy failing to respond?

The answer soon became obvious. Think of the economy as a giant bucket. As the Fed poured money into the economic system, the bucket was not running over. Instead, the credit was draining out of a hole in the bottom of the bucket because of declining asset values and write-offs in huge bankruptcies.

As real estate values were written down by banks, insurance companies, and other financial institutions, the new money pouring in barely made up for the loss of the old values leaking out of the system. The bankruptcy of real estate giant Olympia & York caused write-offs estimated to reach $15 billion, and credit card charge-offs because of bankruptcy and fraud cost an additional $8 billion.

So, like Congress, the Fed is not infallible. Sometimes all its powers may be unable to reverse economic trends on schedule. And sometimes the Fed itself miscalculates the money power needed to change the trend. In fact, by 1993 the Fed had announced that it would no longer use one of its best known measures of money growth—M-2. It had simply become unpredictable.

By 1995, the Federal Reserve was confident it could engineer a "soft landing" for the economy, creating a low level of economic growth without inflation. But at the same time, Fed Chairman Alan Greenspan was criticizing the Consumer Price Index as an accurate measure of inflation.

THE POWER OF THE PRESIDENCY

The ability of the nation's chief executive to change economic policy is greatly enhanced when Congress is controlled by the same party. The American people voted to end the gridlock of the early 1990s by electing both a Democratic President and Congress.

There are two dominant economic issues for the Clinton presidency. First is dealing with the deficit through a combination of tax increases and spending cuts. The balance between cutting spending and raising taxes could tip the scales between growth and stagnation. Equally important are decisions about how much direct involvement government will have in the business of the country. Programs to change tax incentives, target business investment, deal with trade imbalances, and shift the cost burden of programs such as healthcare will all affect the economic and investment outlook.

The congressional elections held in fall, 1994 changed the balance of power and the economic agenda. The "Contract With America" focused, in part, on attempts to balance the budget by cutting welfare and social programs, and changing the tax code. While the long-term effects of a balanced budget would be beneficial, the process of getting there would cause economic disruptions along the way.

Into this world of uncertainties comes the individual investor, struggling to put together a financial plan that will guarantee future security. That's why it's important to keep a watchful eye on Congress, the President, and the Federal Reserve. Fear of change should not paralyze you. On the contrary, it's important to create strategies that require discipline but are flexible enough to change with the trends. That's why financial planning is not a one-time event, but an ongoing process.

PART III

Investment Strategies

IN ORDER to meet your goals of financial independence you need to know how to invest the money you earn and save. All of the other strategies of everyday money management are only tools to create money for investment, so that your money can work for you.

This section of the book will introduce you to simple investment strategies that you can initiate without professional help. Or you may use these concepts to help you understand the plan suggested by your financial advisor.

The most important thing to remember when it comes to investments is *never* to purchase any investment you don't completely understand. Always read about the investment and ask questions *before* you invest. The person selling the investment to you may not be completely objective, so you have to do your own homework.

Never be pressured into an investment by someone who tells you it's a once-in-a-lifetime opportunity. Markets are like trains: If you miss one, there's always another coming along. Always deal with reputable people when it comes to any investment, and don't hesitate to ask for—and check into—references.

Remember, it's *your* money, and ultimately *your* responsibility to make decisions about the people, strategies, and individual investments before you get involved.

Chapter 13

Investment Concepts

Everything you've already learned about risk and asset allocation (chapters 9 and 10) will take on new meaning when you actually start investing your money. Whether you're investing in the stock market or buying a home, here are some more basic financial concepts that you'll need to understand.

Basic Investment Strategy #1: Develop Dollar Discipline

Dollar discipline means setting limits when buying or selling—and sticking to those limits.

Whether you're making investments, negotiating a major purchase, asking for a raise, or bidding at an auction, the secret of success is *dollar discipline*. The discipline required at an auction, or when bidding on a house, is obvious. Auction fever or emotions have often resulted in people paying not only more than an object may be worth, but more than the buyer can afford.

When it comes to making investments in the stock and bond markets, you need some perspective on what those limits should be. If the market is moving quickly, it makes sense to enter a buy or sell order with a limit on the price you'll pay to purchase the stock or accept to sell the stock.

But it makes very little sense when entering a purchase order to place your limit a quarter of a point *below* the current trading price if you really want to own the stock. Ultimately, one quarter of a point difference in the purchase price should make very little difference if the reason you're buying the stock is a hope that the price will double. The same holds true when placing a sell order. If you really want to get out, you should do it at the market price—unless you suspect the marketplace itself is inefficient.

Only very short-term speculators concern themselves with eighths and quarters. And those who chart stock prices might want to buy a stock only if it moves above a preset price level.

Terry's Tips:

$$$ One way to set limits on stock losses is to place a stop-loss order when you purchase a stock. Set a specific price level below the current trading price at which you want to limit your losses and get out. That price might be 10 or 15 percent below your purchase price. If the stock rises in price, ask your broker to raise your stop-loss order price a commensurate amount. Then you won't face the nerve-wracking task of deciding when to sell in a falling market. When the stock dips to your preset price, your order will automatically become a market order to sell.

$$$ Don't place your stop-loss order at a round number. Frequently a stock will trade down (or up) to a round number and then rebound. So, if your stock is trading in the mid-thirties and you definitely want to get out if it drops to $30 a share, but also want to avoid getting whipsawed, you'd place your stop-loss order at $29^7/_8$.

Basic Investment Strategy #2: Use Dollar Cost Averaging

Dollar cost averaging is simply the process of making a regular investment in a stock or mutual fund of a fixed amount of money at a preset time.

Did you ever talk to a person who advises you to buy when he sells, or sell when he buys because he's always wrong? He or she is not alone. That's what makes market tops: people rushing in too late and pushing prices to levels where there are no more buyers. Of course, for every buyer there must be a seller of those shares, but not necessarily the same number of people on the winning and losing side.

A wise old trader once told me that the stock market makes fools of the greatest number of people. One sophisticated seller—perhaps a fund manager or large shareholder—may sell to dozens of individual buyers at the top. Those are the people that lament their "luck" in the stock market. You don't have to be one of those losers. In fact, there is a surefire way to avoid buying at the top: *dollar cost averaging*.

For instance, you could decide to invest $100 a month in a mutual fund on the fifth day of every month. Most mutual funds will gladly arrange to deduct that amount from your paycheck, checking account, or money market fund, and have it credited to your mutual fund account. (More on that in chapter 17.)

Here's what you accomplish: An equal amount of dollars buys an investor more shares when the market is low than when prices are high.

When the market is high, your $100 will buy fewer shares of the mutual fund. If stock prices drop, your $100 monthly investment will automatically purchase more shares. (Mutual fund shares are sold in thousandths of a share, so you don't have to worry about purchasing a full share when you invest; every dollar goes to work for you.) It's a little more expensive to use dollar cost averaging to buy individual stocks, since you may pay higher commissions to buy an odd number of shares.

Dollar cost averaging does not guarantee against loss. If the overall trend of the market is down, then you will wind up with a loss for that period of time. That's why you should plan a dollar cost averaging program to last at least several years. Success requires sticking to the plan in spite of market fluctuations.

One thing is for sure with dollar cost averaging: You'll never buy all your position at the top. Maybe some of it will be purchased at the highest prices, but not all of it. You will have been buying all the way up.

Example: You decide to invest $1,000 in a mutual fund every six months.

Purchase #1: You buy 100 shares at $10 each. Investment: $1,000. The market then rises sharply in the following six months, and the fund share price rises to $20.

Purchase #2: Your regular $1,000 investment now buys 50 shares at $20 each.

The market drops a bit and the fund share prices falls to $15.

You might think you're now even. But actually, you have a good profit. Your total $2,000 investment purchased 150 shares. At $15 a share, your total investment is now worth $2,250—a 12 percent gain over your original $2,000 cost.

Example: Here's a real-life example of how dollar cost averaging worked in a T. Rowe Price stock fund over the last decade (see chart III-1). The chart represents a $100 investment at the end of each month from 1980 through 1990, and the reinvestment of all dividend and capital gains distributions. Over the 11-year period, there was a total of $13,200 in monthly contributions; and at the end of the 11-year period, the account had a market value of nearly $32,000— including the value of the shares purchased when dividends and gains were reinvested.

From the chart you can see the average cost per share each year in relation to the fund's real price range for the year. The overall average cost per share for the entire period was $16.67—lower than the highest price in every year but one.

Terry's Tips:

$$$ It's *never too late* to start a program of dollar cost averaging, even though the stock market may appear to be high. One historical study shows that a program of dollar cost averaging in the Dow Jones Industrial Average, starting at the market highs in 1929, and purchasing at the *high* price every year through 1966, would have been very successful.

In this study, although the stock market did not retain its 1929 peak until 1954, the dollar cost averaging program had already doubled in value. By 1969, the Dow was 160 percent above its 1929 high, while the hypothetical investment program using dollar cost averaging showed a gain of 336 percent. If you have the discipline to take a very long-term perspective, it's never too late to start a program of dollar cost averaging in the stock market.

$$$ This is a strategy that works very well for college savings programs. You'll see how to choose mutual funds to use this strategy in chapters 17 and 18.

CHART III-1
A Dollar Cost Averaging Program
Investments in a T. Rowe Price Stock Fund

Year Ended 12/31	Total of $100 Monthly Investments	Shares Purchased*	Average Cost Per Share	Fund's Price Range Lowest	Fund's Price Range Highest	Cumulative Market Value of All Shares Owned*
1980	$ 1,200	110.492	$10.91	$ 9.66	$12.79	$ 1,288.34
1981	1,200	98.971	13.05	11.15	17.45	3,655.13
1982	1,200	72.829	18.93	14.58	27.23	7,133.52
1983	1,200	85.095	21.37	15.88	25.53	7,105.26
1984	1,200	191.156	13.89	11.38	19.35	8,674.17
1985	1,200	102.474	16.57	14.97	18.60	12,189.15
1986	1,200	146.894	16.79	15.14	18.94	13,839.52
1987	1,200	179.203	16.18	15.76	18.87	18,429.42
1988	1,200	287.480	18.23	17.45	20.84	22,636.79
1989	1,200	263.968	18.67	17.10	25.17	27,817.20
1990	1,200	161.086	18.78	17.37	20.60	31,936.39
	$13,200	1,699.648	$16.67	$ 9.66	$27.23	$31,936.39

SOURCE: T. Rowe Price Associates, Inc.

* Reflects reinvestment of all dividend and capital gain distributions made during the period.

This table is a hypothetical illustration intended to demonstrate the effects of dollar cost averaging; it is not intended to indicate future results for a specific security or fund.

Basic Investment Strategy #3: Know the Dangers of Averaging Down

Averaging down is the process of purchasing more of your investment as prices decline.

Dollar cost averaging should not be confused with the concept of *averaging down*. Generally speaking, averaging down is used as an excuse to purchase more of a losing investment and rationalize that the overall average cost of the total investment will then be lower. It's completely different from dollar cost averaging in that it's a strategy that moves you in only one direction. You can average yourself into a deep hole by averaging down.

For example, if you purchased 300 shares of a $10 stock, you spent $3,000. The stock then drops to $5 a share. You purchase another 200 shares of stock, spending an additional $1,000. But now your average cost on the 500 shares is $8 a share. The stock is still below your average purchase price, and will have to rise to $8 in order for you to break even.

Remember, you started out thinking the shares would rise in price. If you had known the price would drop, wouldn't you have waited? If averaging down is a rationalization for an earlier error, you're making a mistake and compounding the error. Always reassess your original reason for purchasing the stock before buying more at a lower price.

Terry's Tip:

$$$ You'll be much better off if you average *up* in a rising market— purchasing additional stock as the market rises, not as it falls. It's always better to trade *with* the trend than against it.

Basic Investment Strategy #4: Use the Rule of 72

The Rule of 72 is a formula for calculating the time it will take for your money to double when invested at any compound rate of interest.

The Rule of 72 not only explains how long it will take your money to double through compounding, but also how long it will take for the spending power of your money to be cut in half by inflation.

Simply take any number and divide it into 72. The resulting answer is the number of years it will take your money to double. For instance, if you can earn a 6 percent interest rate, divide 72 by 6, and the resulting answer—12—is the number of years it will take your money to double if you are earning 6 percent. If you're earning 8 percent, it will take only 9 years to double your money.

On the other hand, if inflation is running at 5 percent, and you divide 72 by 5, the resulting answer—14.5—is the number of years it will take for inflation to cut your buying power in half!

Basic Investment Strategy #5: Understand the Time Value of Money

Every dollar has a present value—what you can purchase with it today— and a time value—the amount by which it could grow if invested over time.

Whenever you make an investment decision, you have to consider the alternative uses of your money. Money you leave in a bank account earns interest that compounds over the years, and that has to be taken into account when considering alternative investments.

If you choose one investment over another, there is an *opportunity cost.* That is, if you had made a different choice, you might have had a better result. Unfortunately, it is easiest to see the true opportunity cost in hindsight! But you should attempt to balance the alternative uses for your money—not just the potential profit in any one investment choice.

For instance, you might decide to purchase a vacation condo instead of renting for a few months, because the monthly mortgage payments are lower than the rent. But don't forget to account for the down payment you must make on the condo. You'll be losing the interest that money could have earned in the bank.

Or perhaps you could have invested that down payment in the stock market and earned even more than the bank interest rates. Other factors may come into play, including the potential appreciation of the condo, or the convenience of owning your own vacation spot.

The basic time value of money is usually computed using short-term interest rates. But, as you can see, it is impossible to compute in advance the real time value of money because you can never know for sure what increases (or losses) you would have had in alternative investments.

Just don't forget the reality of the opportunity cost when making your decision.

Basic Investment Strategy #6:   Know When to Use Leverage

Leverage is a technique for using a small amount of money to control a large amount of assets.

The concept of *leverage* is a simple one. All it means is getting more work out of the same input. When you purchase a house with a 20 percent down payment, you are using leverage. The money you put down supports a much larger purchase price. When you buy stocks on margin, you are using leverage. Instead of paying cash for the full purchase price, you are only required to put up 50 percent in your margin account; the brokerage firm lends you the balance. Instead of paying $4,000 for 100 shares of a 40 stock, you would be allowed to put up only $2,000.

The most important thing to know about leverage is that it can work *for* you or *against* you.

Example: If your home or stock increases in value, your gain is magnified. If the stock you bought at 40 rises to $60 a share, you have a gain of $2,000. Since you only invested $2,000 to buy the stock in your margin account, you have doubled your money. Notice that the stock did not have to double in price; it rose only 50 percent. It was the leverage of your margin account that allowed you to earn a 100 percent return.

But what if the stock were to fall in price? If the stock dropped 50 percent, to $20 a share, your entire investment would be wiped out. (Of course, the brokerage firm would call you to put up more cash in your margin account long before that happened.) The concept of leverage is often called a "two-edged sword" because it works both for and against you, magnifying your gains and losses.

The term leverage is often associated with sophisticated and potentially costly financial strategies, such as trading commodities where as little as a 5 percent good-faith down payment may be made on the full value of a futures contract. But in the most recent recession many people started to appreciate the leverage in their everyday financial lives.

Those who purchased a home with a 10 or 20 percent down payment suddenly realized they had no equity left when home prices dropped by a similar amount. If they then wanted to refinance a high-interest-rate mortgage, they found the bank would require them to put up additional cash equity in order to qualify for a new mortgage at lower rates. That's a classic example of leverage working *against* you.

Terry's Tip:

$$$ The use of leverage is tempting. Many people have been suckered into risky commodity speculation with the promise that a small "investment" can yield huge returns. The commodities markets can move so dramatically that not only will the initial investment be wiped out, but the brokerage firm can sue for additional dollars beyond what was first put at risk. Leverage is often touted as a way to "get rich quick"; it can also be a way to get poor quickly.

Basic Investment Strategy #7: Understand the Risks of Selling Short

Selling short is simply the strategy of making a bet that prices will fall.

Selling short means selling something you don't own, in hopes of buying it back later at a lower price. Selling short is a very real strategy that has strict rules when used in the stock market.

Suppose XYZ stock is trading at $50 a share, and you believe that it will fall to the twenties. If you already own the stock, you'll sell it and deliver the stock certificate to the broker, who will then send you a check for the money from the sale.

But if you don't own the stock, you can sell it anyway—and profit by buying it back when it reaches the lower price level. That's called selling short. If you sell the stock short at $50 and then buy it back ("cover") at $22 a share, you'll have a profit of $28 a share.

Now the rules: You must notify the broker before you sell a stock short. That's because you will be obligated to deliver the stock certificate within five business days on a normal sale and, of course, since you don't own the stock, you won't have a certificate to deliver. The broker will literally borrow 100 shares of stock to put in your margin account.

The broker will collect the proceeds of the short sale and hold on to that money in your account as an assurance that there will be cash available to buy back that stock (covering your short position). If the stock rises in price instead of moving lower, the broker could ask you to put up even more money as security against your short sale.

There's another important rule about short sales: You can't sell short while the stock is collapsing in price. That rule is designed to keep short-sellers from pushing a stock down even farther. In order to sell short, the stock must have traded higher—even if just by $1/8$ of a point—in its last differently priced transaction. So if that stock trades at 50, then $49^1/2$, then $49^1/4$, you can't sell it short. But if it suddenly trades slightly higher, say $49^3/8$, then you can sell the stock short.

Terry's Tips:

$$$ There's a huge risk in selling a stock short. After all, your profit potential is limited. The stock can only fall to zero. But if you're wrong and the stock climbs, your potential losses are unlimited.

$$$ It may be risky and even unprofitable to sell a stock short, but it is not unpatriotic or un-American! Markets tend to fall faster than they rise, so huge profits can be made on the downside. Short-selling is for those who watch the markets closely and have strong stomachs. If you still don't understand it, don't let anyone talk you into doing it!

Basic Investment Strategy #8: Learn to Rate Investment Performance

Rating investment performance is the process of using objective measurements to evaluate your investment success.

Some people decide that they are not successful investors unless they beat the market averages. Others are pleased if their investments just match certain averages. If you're buying a home, you might want to find out the average sale price of similar homes in the neighborhood so you don't pay too high a price. If you're applying for a job, you might want to know the average pay for that line of work so that you can point out to a potential employer why you should be paid more.

As an investor, you need to understand the averages by which performance or price is judged. When it comes to the stock market, the averages are a performance index of certain stock groups such as the Dow Jones Industrial Average (30 large blue-chip stocks); the Standard & Poor's 500 Stock Index; the Value Line Composite Index of 1,700 stocks, which includes many smaller companies; and the Wilshire Small Cap Index and Russell 2000 Index, which track the stock performance of smaller companies. Some of these popular measures are "weighted" indexes based on market capitalization, such as the S&P 500. Even the Dow Jones Industrial Average is not, strictly speaking, an average of the 30 stocks in the index. But each is a standard measure of performance.

Sometimes performance standards are called *benchmarks*—standards reached by other investors such as professional money managers. So an investment advisor will rate the skills of one money manager against a benchmark—the recent performance of other managers using similar strategies, or against a market average or index.

Terry's Tips:

$$$ One thing to keep in mind about averages: They are just that, an arithmetic leveling of diverse performance. There's an old saying about the man standing with one foot in a bucket of ice water and the other in a bucket of boiling water. His comment: "On average, I feel fine!"

$$$ When choosing an investment manager, ask for performance comparisons against several benchmarks as well as the performance of other managers with similar goals. Compare ratings year by year, in up as well as down markets, to evaluate a manager's past performance.

Chapter 14

Safe Money Strategies

There are certainly people and situations that require minimal risk. In my first book, *Terry Savage Talks Money*, I introduced the concept of the "bulls, bears, and *chickens*"—a labeling system that really caught on, especially with senior citizens. Some people are simply not in a position to take *any* risks with their money—and that's nothing to be ashamed of. In fact, it's very important to answer the question of just how much, if any, risk you can afford to take *before* you start considering individual investments or strategies.

> *"Chicken money" is money you cannot afford to lose.*

There are two basic categories of "chicken money." The first is money that cannot be replaced if lost. For those who are retired and no longer earn income but instead depend on Social Security, fixed pensions, and interest income to make ends meet, it is unwise to take risks with capital that has been saved over the years. That does not mean your investment strategies are restricted to insured deposits. As we'll explain in chapter 66, there are several ways for seniors to increase monthly income and still not run out of money in their lifetime.

The second category of "chicken money" belongs to those who have a very short time horizon. For example, you may have used stock market mutual funds over a period of 15 years to accumulate money for a child's college education. But when the child is actually a year or two from entering college it may be time to switch a large portion of those funds to a money market fund. That way, a sudden market decline won't wipe out sophomore-year tuition.

While some people need to stick strictly to these safe investments because of their risk profile, or because of their time horizon, everyone needs to have an understanding of how to use these virtually risk-free investments for the times when you temporarily have excess cash.

The news headlines about savings and loan and bank failures in the past few years, plus the need for a multi-billion-dollar bailout of the industry, have caused many people to fear for the safety of even their insured deposits in financial institutions. You might be surprised at how many people reveal to me that they actually have a substantial amount of cash hidden in a mattress or coffee can. Usually these are older people who remember standing in line trying to get money out of banks during the depression.

It may be useful to keep a small amount of currency on hand for unexpected emergencies. But leaving substantial sums of money around the house is not only dangerous, it is a guaranteed losing strategy. Even if inflation is only 3 or 4 percent a year, your money is losing value and you are losing interest you could have earned. And the government has amply demonstrated its determination to stand behind the promise of federal backing for insured deposits.

The following short-term investment strategies are designed to give you *liquidity*—a very important concept in financial planning. Even if you are willing to accept more risks, these investments are a place to park your money for a short period of time while you are deciding on how to allocate your investment assets. For example, if you sell a house or receive an insurance settlement, you'll need an interest-bearing account in which to deposit your money temporarily before investing it or purchasing a new home.

"Chicken money" investments guarantee that your money will be there in the short run when you need it. Remember, these investments do not guarantee the value or spending power of your money over the long run. You can keep your money perfectly safe in a bank, yet watch your buying power erode because of inflation and taxes.

Safe money, or chicken money, investments are *one-decision* invest-ments. That is, you only need to make the decision to buy. You'll never be forced by market circumstances to decide *when* to sell. You will take money out only because you want to or need to, or because the investment comes to maturity, but not because something in the market has added risks to this investment.

All "chicken money" strategies keep your money safe from loss, available when needed, and pay low, but market-competitive, interest rates.

Safe Money Strategy #1: Money in the Bank

Short-term, insured *certificates of deposit* (CDs) in a bank or S&L are safe, one-decision investments. When your CDs mature, you may be faced with another decision, such as whether to take out a shorter- or longer-term CD at the then-prevailing rates. But market forces won't force you to decide to sell your insured CD out of fear of losing money.

The rare exception to this rule occurred in the early 1980s, when interest rates were rising so quickly that many people decided to break their CDs, accept the penalty, and reinvest in higher-yielding CDs. That's why I emphasize that only *short-term* CDs are meant for chicken money.

Banks and S&Ls also offer *money market deposit accounts*, which may pay lower rates of interest that can change as frequently as every week. These accounts do offer complete liquidity, because you can write as many as three checks a month, allowing you to withdraw some or all of your cash at any time, or to continue earning interest while using the checking privilege to pay several bills a month. Money market deposit accounts also allow additional unlimited transfer privileges so you can move money into your regular checking account.

Terry's Tips:

$$$ Make sure you are buying a *federally insured* CD, and not some other investment product that is sold through your bank or S&L.

$$$ When putting money into bank accounts, it's important to watch the Federal Deposit Insurance Corporation (FDIC) limits of $100,000 per separately titled accounts. You can leave more than $100,000 in a financial institution and remain fully insured by creating joint and trust accounts—

but you should check to make sure each account is separately insured. For instance, just changing the order of the names on the title of the account is not enough to generate insurance on separate accounts.

$$$ Local competition usually guarantees that interest rates on CDs are fairly competitive. If you want to get the highest rates being offered in the nation and are willing to make the effort to open an account at an out-of-state institution, contact *100 Highest Yields* (407-627-7330; cost $98/year). This weekly publication surveys the highest interest rates offered on a variety of CDs and money market accounts, giving safety ratings on the institutions and toll-free telephone numbers to open an account.

If you shop for the highest rates yourself, keep in mind that an extra eighth of a percentage point in interest may not be worth the time and paperwork of shipping your money to an out-of-state bank unless you have a very large CD.

$$$ Avoid certificates of deposit offered through stock brokerage firms, even though they promise that your CD is individually insured. The brokerage firm takes a small bite out of your yield as a service fee, so you are not getting as high a yield as you deserve on your CD.

$$$ The nation's banking system currently has $2.53 trillion in deposits. About 23 percent of that amount is currently in "jumbo" deposits—above the $100,000 insured limit. Depositors who purchase jumbo CDs receive higher rates because they are insured only up to the $100,000 limit. Presumably, those depositors are sophisticated enough to judge the risk involved. But in 1992, only 50 percent of deposits over $100,000 were protected when banks failed, according to *100 Highest Yields*.

If you're considering placing money above the insured limit in any banking institution, contact Veribanc (800-44-BANKS) and ask for their bank safety rating on that institution. The cost is $10, and it can be charged to your credit card.

Safe Money Strategy #2: Money Market Mutual Funds

Money market mutual funds are another good place to invest money with convenient access while avoiding risks. Money market mutual funds are offered by most major mutual fund companies and by some brokerage firms. It's hard to believe, but 15 years ago money market funds were unknown to the general public. Today, there is as much as $500 billion invested in money market funds.

Money market mutual are not federally insured, but they invest in only the highest-quality, short-term, interest-bearing instruments, such as government Treasury bills, government agency IOUs, commercial paper (IOUs) of highly rated companies, and bank CDs. So, although they do not carry a promise of federal insurance, money market mutual funds are among the safest short-term investments.

The interest paid on the funds reflects the general level of short-term interest rates, and the yield on a money market fund changes daily. A very small management fee (usually less than $\frac{1}{2}$ of 1 percent) is deducted from the fund and reflected in the yield.

Money market mutual funds are perfectly liquid in that you can write a check for all or part of your money at any time. Most money market funds will place a limit on the minimum check amount you can write. You can also arrange to have your money wire-transferred directly to your bank account. The money market fund will mail you a monthly statement of the value of your account.

Money market mutual fund accounts are usually opened via toll-free telephone and through the mail, although some major fund companies do have service centers around the country. When choosing a money market mutual fund, call the toll-free telephone number and ask them to send you a prospectus and application. Ask about the minimum required to open an account and the minimum dollar amount for writing checks on your account.

For a list of major mutual fund companies that offer money market funds, see Appendix A.

Terry's Tips:

$$$ If you're concerned about maximum safety, choose a money market fund that invests only in short-term U.S. Treasury securities and avoids bank certificates of deposit and commercial paper. As an added bonus, money market funds that purchase only Treasury bills are not subject to state income taxes, thereby increasing the true return on your money if you live in a state that taxes investment income.

Some Treasury securities money market funds:
Capital Preservation Fund
(800-4-SAFETY)
Dreyfus 100% U.S. Treasury Fund
(800-DREYFUS)
T. Rowe Price U.S. Treasury Money Market Fund
(800-638-5660)
United Services Treasury Securities Cash Fund
(800-USFUNDS)

$$$ There are also tax-free money market funds, which invest in very short-term municipal IOUs from cities, states, and local taxing authorities. These funds pass along the tax-free interest, which is correspondingly lower than rates on taxable money market funds. (See chapter 24 for an explanation of how tax-free funds work, and how to calculate whether they offer you a better after-tax yield than taxable money market funds.)

Safe Money Strategy #3: U.S. Treasury Bills

One of the safest ways to invest your money is to lend it directly to the United States government. Treasury bills are direct, interest-bearing IOUs from the government. They are sold at weekly government auctions in maturities of 13 weeks, 26 weeks, or one year. Auctions take place every Monday, except when there is a bank holiday.

The interest rate on Treasury bills changes each week and is set by huge institutional bidders on the government's debt. The yield they are willing to accept at auction is based on the institutional bidders' perceptions of the outlook for the economy, inflation, the money supply, and other such considerations. When individuals purchase Treasury bills, they agree to accept the average rate set at auction by these institutional investors. That average rate is announced late in the day, after the auction is complete.

Individuals may purchase Treasury bills either in person at any of the Federal Reserve banks in major cities around the country, or by mail. Minimum purchase for individual investors is $10,000, with additional increments of $5,000. Treasury bills can also be purchased through your local bank, but those institutions often add on a service charge that lowers your return.

There are some important things to note about Treasury bill interest. Individuals purchase Treasury bills through the Treasury Direct system, which means your interest is deposited directly into your bank account or money market account as you specify. When you purchase Treasury bills, you'll need to supply your bank or money market account number and the bank routing number of the institution that will be receiving the interest for your account. You can get the routing number from your bank or mutual fund company.

Your bank account will be credited for the entire amount of the interest on the Treasury bill within a few days of the auction. Since that interest is paid to you immediately, your true yield or return on Treasury bills will be higher than the stated auction "discount" rate because you actually have less than the full $10,000 tied up in your investment. Your true yield (or *bond equivalent yield*) is also announced at the time of the auction. In fact, your ultimate yield could be even higher since the interest you earn can sit in your bank or money market fund and earn additional interest.

Several weeks before your Treasury bills mature, you'll receive a letter from the Federal Reserve asking you whether you'd like the proceeds deposited to your local bank account, or whether you want to "roll over" the Treasury bill when it matures and accept the average rate at the next week's auction. Or at the time you purchase the T-bills you can request automatic rollover at maturity. If you do not elect to roll over your Treasury bills, at maturity the full proceeds (i.e., your original investment) will be automatically credited to your bank account. Remember, you already received your interest check immediately after you purchased the Treasury bill.

Terry's Tips:

$$$ When purchasing Treasury bills through Treasury auctions, you should plan to hold them to maturity because they are expensive and difficult to sell before they mature.

$$$ One big advantage of Treasury bills is that interest earned on them is not subject to state income tax. If you live in a high-tax state, it means your comparable return on Treasury bills is even greater because you don't pay taxes on the interest. (The same applies to money market funds that invest exclusively in Treasury bills.)

$$$ Although you receive the interest on your Treasury bills within a few days of the auction, for income tax purposes that interest is considered taxable in the year in which the Treasury bill *matures*. That is, if you purchase a six-month Treasury bill in September of this year, and it matures in February of next year, the interest is not taxable in the current year. That fact may be useful for tax planning purposes.

$$$ The Treasury also holds regular monthly and quarterly auctions of longer-term notes and bonds ranging from two to 30 years. Rates are set at auction and interest is paid every six months. For more information on purchasing Treasury bills, notes, and bonds, contact your nearest Federal Reserve Bank or branch. See Appendix B for the addresses and telephone numbers.

Safe Money Strategy #4: Series EE U.S. Savings Bonds

Series EE U.S. savings bonds qualify as "chicken money" investments because of their high level of safety—even though they require you to lock your money away for at least five years to earn the promised returns.

U.S. savings bonds offer market rates of interest, tax deferral, and ease of purchase in small dollar amounts. They can also be used to get a special tax break on money saved for college. In fact, while savings bonds were once marketed as a strictly "patriotic" investment, they have some dramatic advantages over other safe money strategies.

The interest rate paid on all outstanding savings bonds changes every six months (May and November), and is guaranteed to be 85 percent of the rates paid on five-year Treasury notes. For bonds purchased after May 1, 1995 and held less than five years, interest earned will also be pegged to market rates. The short-term rate on savings bonds is 85 percent of the average of six-month Treasury bill yields. There is no longer a guaranteed *minimum* rate of 4 percent, as there is on previously-issued savings bonds. However, if Savings Bonds are held at least 17 years, there will be a one-time adjustment that guarantees a minimum rate of return that is slightly higher than 4 percent.

U.S. savings bonds can be purchased through banks and other financial institutions, or through regular payroll deductions at most major companies. Savings bonds are purchased at a discount from face value. For example, a $50 face value bond has a purchase price of $25. Over the years, the interest buildup will increase the value of the bond.

There is no set time period for the bond to reach full face value; that depends on the interest rates being paid for each six-month period. After you have held your bonds for the required minimum five years, the total interest you earned is computed by averaging the semiannual rates during the time you've held the bond.

As long as you hold your U.S. savings bonds, they will continue to accrue interest at the floating rate—up to 30 years. In fact, even older bonds purchased before rates started "floating" in 1982, now earn the market rates of interest.

The highest six-month rate paid since savings bonds started floating was 11.09 percent in 1982–83. The average rate paid since 1982 is 7.66 percent.

Savings bonds have some additional features that make them even more attractive. You never pay any state income tax on savings bond interest. And you don't pay any federal income tax on the interest you earn until you cash the bonds in at some time in the future.

Starting in 1990, savings bonds purchased in the *parents' names* and cashed in to pay for college tuition may be completely tax-free in certain income brackets. (See chapter 37 for the strategy of using U.S. Savings Bonds to save for college education.)

There are limits to how much you can invest in savings bonds each year. An individual may purchase only $30,000 face value ($15,000 purchase price) of savings bonds in a calendar year. However, you can expand those limits by purchasing bonds in joint names with different people.

If you don't want to pay taxes on the interest buildup in your Series EE savings bonds, you can convert their current market value into Series HH bonds, which since March 1, 1993 pay a fixed 4 percent annual interest rate. Then, you'll only pay taxes on the interest income you receive every six months. Series HH bonds come in minimum denominations of $500, and if you are converting a smaller amount of EE bonds you can add cash to reach the next $500 level.

NOTE: When cashing in HH bonds, make sure you do so in the month in which interest is payable. The interest is not prorated, so if you cash them in during the first four months after interest is paid, you'll lose out. If you cash in HH bonds in the fifth month, the Treasury will hold them one month and then pay you the full six months' interest.

Terry's Tips:

$$$ Savings bonds make great gifts for children on birthdays, graduation, etc. The system for purchasing savings bonds was changed in 1992. You fill out an application for a bond purchase at a bank or savings and loan, and the bond will be mailed to you within two weeks, instead of being given to you immediately. If you've waited until the last minute to make your purchase, ask the financial institution for an official gift announcement form.

$$$ Don't think of savings bonds only for small investments. You can buy up to $15,000 purchase price ($30,000 face value) in savings bonds each year, unless you stretch the limit by adding different co-owners with different Social Security numbers. When bank CD rates are low, the 4 percent minimum yield and tax-deferral features make savings bonds an extra good investment.

$$$ Savings bonds may be the perfect investment for people who are a few years away from retirement and would like to defer taxes until after retirement when they are in a lower tax bracket. Remember, there is no income tax paid on the interest until the bonds are cashed in.

$$$ If you want to know what your old savings bonds are worth today, or find out whether they've stopped paying interest (bonds more than 40 years old), call 800-4US-BOND, or contact your local bank.

Safe Money Strategy #5: Higher Yields with Safety

Interest rates paid on Treasury bills, money market funds, and bank certificates of deposit represent the free market evaluation of the proper yield for the lowest-risk investments. If an investment offers a slightly higher yield, you can be sure that there is a slightly higher degree of risk. Sometimes it's worth taking a bit more risk to increase your return—*if* you understand and are willing to accept that additional risk.

For higher-yielding money strategies turn to chapter 23, which has strategies for increasing your investment income.

Chapter 15

Mutual Fund Investing—The Basic Concepts

Mutual funds became one of the most popular ways to invest in the stock market during the 1980s. In 1979, there were just 444 equity, bond, and income mutual funds holding $8 billion in assets in 7.5 million shareholder accounts. By 1994, there were 4,408 different mutual funds (excluding money market funds and short-term municipal bond funds). Those funds held $1,553 billion in assets in 76.8 million shareholder accounts.

Here's the attraction: Mutual funds offer diversification of your investment dollars and professional money management at a very low cost. Plus, they're easy to buy and sell.

Mutual funds can be used to simplify your investment strategies, but you need to understand how they work, their costs, and how to choose a fund that meets your needs.

Open-end mutual funds accept money from new investors and issue additional shares in the fund to represent the dollars invested. The price of the shares is determined every day, based on the current market value of the stocks, bonds, or other investments owned by the fund. For no-load funds, that price per share is called the *net asset value* and is calculated at the close of business every day.

THE COST OF MUTUAL FUND INVESTING—LOAD VS. NO-LOAD

Some funds charge a commission—or *load*—on top of the net asset value per share when you purchase the fund. The commission is paid to the brokerage firm, broker, or financial planner who took the time to explain and sell you the fund. The commission, which may range as high as 8.5 percent, is taken out of your initial investment.

If you are being sold a mutual fund investment by a broker or financial planner, ask how much commission you are paying. Larger purchases may result in reduced commission charges. A 1992 survey by Market Facts, an independent research company, shows that 46 percent of investors who own load funds didn't know how much sales charge they paid to purchase their funds.

Paying a sales commission or load is worthwhile if you feel you need help in choosing a fund, diversifying among funds, or encouragement to stick with your mutual fund investment plan. But you don't necessarily need a professional advisor to help you choose a mutual fund.

The strategies in this chapter are designed to allow you to make fund investments on your own. In that case, you will want to choose a *no-load fund*. No-load means no commission, so no broker will call to sell these funds to you. Many financial planners will advise clients on purchases of no-load funds, charging their clients a small fee for asset management instead of receiving a commission on the sale of the fund itself.

No-load mutual funds are marketed primarily through advertising, and are usually explained to you by fund company representatives whom you contact by calling the fund's toll-free telephone number. Of all 1994 stock, bond, and income fund sales, $474.3 billion (about 50 percent of fund sales) were made through salespeople such as brokers or financial planners. No-load stock, bond, and income funds had sales of $192.3 billion, or 40 percent of the total. The remaining 8.4 percent resulted from reinvested dividends and variable annuity investments.

There have been many studies on the subject of performance of load versus no-load mutual funds. Every study has concluded that there is no measurable difference between the two types of funds when it comes to investment performance. There *is* one advantage to buying a no-load fund, in that more of your money goes to work directly for you in fund investments.

Whether the fund is load or no-load, each fund management company charges a fee to pay the fund manager, and to cover mailing and clerical expenses. These annual management fees should total about 1 percent of fund assets for equity (stock) funds and less for bond and money market funds.

In addition, many no-load funds charge what is called a 12b-1 fee, which is a separate fee named after a government rule that lets funds charge each shareholder up to 1 percent of assets (effective July 1993) every year for advertising, mailing, and other marketing expenses. Most funds charge less than 0.25 percent for 12b-1 fees; those that charge more should be avoided.

Every mutual fund will give you a *prospectus*—a little booklet that describes the fund's investment objectives, costs, current investments, and management. To receive a prospectus, call the fund's toll-free telephone number or, in the case of a load fund, ask the sales representative. No mutual fund sales may be made without the buyer having seen a prospectus. See Mutual Fund Buying Strategy #1 in the following chapter for more information on buying no-load mutual funds.

Terry's Tips:

$$$ Some funds do not charge an up-front commission, but instead charge a fee when shares are sold. That's called a *back-end load*. Some deferred sales charges are only imposed if the fund is sold during the first few years. Avoid funds with back-end loads. These charges may be expressed as a percentage of your account value and can be substantial if your assets grow in the first few years.

$$$ Also avoid mutual funds that charge a commission or load when you reinvest your fund dividends.

HOW MUTUAL FUNDS ARE ORGANIZED

When you start considering mutual funds, you'll notice that they come in "families," or groups of funds offered by the same management company. You may be familiar with some of the larger fund families, such as Fidelity, Dreyfus, Vanguard, and T. Rowe Price. There are more than 100 fund management companies. (See Appendix A for a listing of the toll-free phone numbers of some of the major no-load mutual fund management companies.)

Within each fund family there may be a dozen or more individual mutual funds, each with a separate investment objective and its own portfolio manager. Most no-load fund management companies allow you to switch between the funds in their group at no charge. Some fund management companies such as Fidelity Funds manage both no-load and load funds.

The major fund categories are stock, bond, or money market funds. But within those categories there are also many choices.

FUND OBJECTIVES

Growth (invest in large growth companies and blue-chip stocks)

Aggressive growth (often newer, smaller capitalization stocks)

Growth and income (dividend paying stocks, preferred stocks, some bonds)

Balanced portfolio (strives for some growth, some income)

Precious metals (shares of gold, silver companies, natural resources)

International stocks (global diversificaton, or shares of just one country or region)

Money market funds (invest in short-term Treasury securities, bank CDs, and corporate notes)

Tax-free money market funds (very short-term municipal obligations)

U.S. government bond funds (long-term Treasury bonds and debt backed by government agencies)

Ginnie Mae funds (invests in insured mortgage securities)

ARM funds (adjustable rate, insured mortgages)

Corporate bond funds (higher-grade corporate debt)

High-yield bond funds (riskier corporate debt, "junk bonds")

Long-term municipal bonds (tax-free state, city, and local taxing authority bonds; may be limited to issues of just one state)

International bonds (debt obligations of one country or region)

Unfortunately, there are no strict rules about how funds are labeled. Rather, the categories tend to be more of a marketing tool for the fund companies. This list is included to give you an idea of the choices you'll have.

Don't be intimidated by the large number of mutual funds listed in directories, newspapers, or financial magazines. The idea is not to pick the one "perfect" fund, but to get started on your investment program. The strategies listed later in this chapter will make those choices easier.

Terry's Tip:

$$$ If you're just starting on your own to invest in mutual funds, choose a fund management company that has a variety of funds and offers the opportunity to switch between them at no cost. That will give you more flexibility in your investment program.

Sticking with one large fund family also offers advantages in simplicity of recordkeeping. Most fund management companies now issue one simplified monthly statement for all of your individual fund accounts.

CLOSED-END MUTUAL FUNDS

There is another, completely separate type of investment company called a *closed-end fund*. Unlike open-end funds, which take in additional money from investors at any time, closed-end funds are formed by selling a fixed number of shares. The proceeds raised from the sale of the shares may be invested in stocks, bonds, or a combination of the two, depending on the stated goals and objectives of the fund.

The closed-end fund has a professional manager making decisions about investments within the fund, but he or she must allocate assets within the fund, as no new money can be invested once the fund has made its initial offering. The only way the fund manager can have more money to work with is to sell investments within the fund at a profit.

Every day the value of the fund investments can be divided by the fixed number of shares outstanding to find the *net asset value* per share. But that is not necessarily the selling price of the fund. Usually the shares of the fund are listed on a major stock exchange where, as with all stocks, the price is determined by supply and demand.

Sometimes the shares may trade at a value higher than the net asset value per share. The shares are then said to trade at a *premium*. If the share price is lower than the net asset value per share, then the shares are said to trade at a *discount*. The amount of the premium or discount may change as investor sentiment changes.

It's important to understand this basic difference between open-end and closed-end mutual funds. Open-end funds take in new money from shareholders at a price that is equal to the net asset value per share—plus, in the case of load funds, a sales commission. The price of a closed-end fund is based on net asset value per share, but it may be substantially higher or lower than the per share value, depending on market sentiment.

Closed-end funds are purchased through brokers or discount brokers. If they are listed on an exchange, the shares may be margined, allowing you to borrow 50 percent of the market value. The shares may be registered in your name or held by the broker. By comparison, when you own open-end funds, the shares are usually held by the fund's custodian bank and you receive regular statements of your fund account.

Investors pay a commission on the initial offering of shares in a closed-end fund, or when existing shares are subsequently purchased through a broker. The fund management company takes its annual expenses and fees out of the assets of the company, as described in the prospectus.

Generally, you'll find closed-end funds used for investments in particular foreign countries (see chapter 25) or investing in a specific type of bond (see chapter 23).

Terry's Tip:

$$$ For more information on closed-end funds that invest in stocks, bonds, tax-free bonds, and international stocks and bonds, the *Closed-End Fund Digest* (800-282-2335; monthly, $200/year) is one of the most comprehensive newsletters on the subject.

Morningstar Closed-End Fund Survey (800-876-5005; $195/yr, $35/3-month trial) offers a complete listing of all major closed-end funds with a full-page description and analysis of each. Categories covered include equity, international equity, income, convertible bond, high-yield corporate bond, general corporate bond, government bond, international bond, and several categories of tax-free municipal bond closed-end funds. This survey should also be available at your local public library in a loose-leaf binder which is updated biweekly.

Chapter 16

How to Buy Mutual Funds

While many people have heard about mutual funds, they are often confused about where to buy them. As noted earlier, funds that charge a load, or sales commission, are most frequently sold by brokers or financial planners or in sales offices located in banks and S&Ls. The broker will handle the purchase of a fund in the same manner as any other stock or bond. No-load funds require the individual to contact the fund company for information, using a toll-free telephone number. Then there are several ways you can conveniently invest your money in a no-load mutual fund, either on your own or using the services of a financial planner.

Mutual Fund Buying Strategy #1: Buying No-Load Funds Direct

No-load fund transactions are primarily done through the mail and by toll-free telephone number. When you call for information, the fund company will send you a prospectus, describing the fund's costs and objectives, along with an application that should be returned by mail with your check. You can open an account in a single name, or in joint tenancy with another person. You can also open an Individual Retirement Account, a custodial account for a child, or a trust account with yourself as trustee.

The application generally requires only the name in which you're opening the account, address, Social Security number, and choice of funds. You will also be asked to check options such as whether you want your dividends reinvested or mailed to you.

If you are investing substantial sums of money, you should inquire about the availability of bank wire-transfer systems both for investing in the fund and for having your money returned to you when you sell shares in the fund. You may also ask for checks that you can use to draw on your mutual fund account.

Any questions about a fund application can be answered by the fund's telephone representative. Some of the larger mutual fund companies have sales and service offices around the country where you can talk to a representative or open an account in person.

You will not receive a stock certificate when you invest in a mutual fund unless you specifically request one. Instead, you should receive a monthly statement from the fund, giving the number of shares you own and their market value. You'll receive a statement every time you make a purchase or sale transaction, and you'll be sent either a monthly or a quarterly statement describing your account activity, current share ownership, and current market value. Most mutual fund companies will also send you a statement with valuable tax information in January of each year, detailing your gains and income distributions for income tax purposes.

Mutual Fund Buying Strategy #2: Discount Brokerage Firms

You can purchase many no-load mutual funds through discount stock brokerage companies. The names and numbers of the largest of these brokerage firms are listed below. They do business through offices around the country and through telephone transactions.

Charles Schwab (800-648-5300)

Fidelity Discount Brokerage Services (800-544-8666)

Quick & Reilly (800-926-0600)

Jack White & Co. (800-216-2333)

Waterhouse Securities (800-934-4443)

These discount brokerage firms offer you the opportunity to buy and sell hundreds of no-load mutual funds. In most instances, you are charged a small fee. The competition for this business is so great that fees are being cut quickly. At most discount firms the fee is expressed as a percentage of the dollar amount being invested, and you can expect to pay about 0.6 percent, or a minimum of $30 per transaction.

Customers of Charles Schwab and Jack White & Co. may buy and sell more than 100 of the most popular no-load mutual funds with no fee. The fund companies that have agreed to participate in this program are underwriting the cost in order to get wider distribution of their mutual funds.

Many investors find it worthwhile to pay small fees to buy no-load mutual funds because when you buy a variety of funds through a brokerage firm, you receive just one monthly statement detailing all of your mutual fund accounts. Also, if you want to buy and sell funds from different fund families, you don't have to wait until you receive a check from the sale of one fund in order to send in a purchase application to another fund. The brokerage firm will handle the transaction for you simultaneously. Finally, holding your mutual fund shares at a brokerage fund may allow you to borrow against your shares when they are held in a margin account. (See chapter 21.)

Mutual Fund Buying Strategy #3: Automatic Investments

Most mutual fund families offer plans that allow you to make automatic monthly investments into your fund accounts. When you're choosing a no-load mutual fund, read the prospectus and application form to see if you can sign up for a program that will authorize the mutual fund company to *automatically withdraw* a certain amount of money from your personal checking account, or even from your company paycheck, to be invested in your mutual fund.

These automatic investment plans are the perfect way to fund an Individual Retirement Account, or college savings program for a child. Plus, you're using the strategy of dollar cost averaging (see chapter 13).

Terry's Tips:

$$$ When starting an automatic monthly investment program, you should deal directly with the fund company instead of working through a

brokerage firm. If you're investing monthly you won't want to pay the brokerage service fees.

$$$ If your fund company does not offer automatic withdrawals from your bank account, consider opening a money market account with the mutual fund company and authorizing the fund to switch a certain amount of money every month into one of the other funds you have chosen.

Mutual Fund Buying Strategy #4: No-Load Funds and Financial Planners

Many financial planners do sell no-load funds. Although they do not receive a sales commission on your purchase, they will charge a small fee—usually about 1 percent of assets—to assist you in choosing a fund, monitoring its performance, and helping you with the paperwork.

In fact, many planners subscribe to computer services that help you choose a no-load fund based on past performance and your own risk profile. The Adam Network (800-753-ADAM) is one such service. It has historical ratings of more than 1,400 no-load funds (as well as 2,200 load funds) over the past 30 years in its computer database.

The Adam program assesses the client's risk tolerance and then creates an asset allocation model to apportion money in different types of funds—aggressive, conservative, or income-oriented. Then the program generates buy and sell signals for specific mutual funds based on a conservative strategy tailored to an individual risk profile. The cost is 1.85 percent above the fees charged by each individual fund. The mutual fund transactions are made through large discount brokerage firms such as Charles Schwab, so there may be a small transaction fee for each purchase and sale. The client receives a quarterly portfolio report listing all mutual fund positions.

Galaxy of Funds (800-942-9441) is another program that manages money in both load and no-load mutual funds for financial planners. Their fees are slightly higher (2.4 percent), but this management service is a market-based, active decision-making process using the major no-load fund families.

Both of these services are available only through selected financial planners and some smaller brokerage firms. If you call their toll-free numbers, they'll give you names of planners in your area using their service. Or ask your financial planner what method he or she uses to select no-load mutual funds for clients.

Chapter 17

Simple Mutual Fund Investment Strategies

Once you understand how mutual funds work, you may decide to get started immediately—or you may want to do some research on your own. Here are three simple mutual fund investment strategies that can get you started right away. The next chapter presents three mutual fund research strategies to use if you decide to do some more investigation before choosing a fund.

Simple Mutual Fund Strategy #1: Buying the Whole Market

This is a mutual fund strategy designed for the investor who doesn't want to spend time and effort choosing funds that will *beat* the market, but instead will be pleased to do *equally as well* as the market—in good times and bad. To simply match the overall market performance all you have to do is purchase an *index fund*—a fund that uses computer technology to purchase stocks that match the Standard & Poor's 500 Stock Index.

According to a Morningstar, Inc. study, index funds have beaten the performance of 75 percent of all managed equity funds over the past three-, five-, and ten-year periods. Doing as well as the market average meant doing better than most mutual fund managers! That's one reason investors have placed more than $6 billion in index funds.

Index funds tend to have lower costs of operation because computers do most of the work instead of portfolio managers. There are no expenses for research or big salaries for fund managers because investing is simply the process of allocating new money to stocks in the S&P 500 Index. Because most of the fund's money stays invested in the same blue-chip stocks, the commission costs of buying stocks are reduced.

There may be some disadvantages to index funds as well. Because the S&P 500 Stock Index represents the largest blue-chip companies in America (median market capitalization $10.5 billion), the funds tend to do better when shares of these larger companies lead the market, as they did through much of the 1980s. In years when smaller company stocks lead the market, index funds could lag in performance.

My favorite strategy is to use the United Services All-American Equity Fund, because this is the only index fund that allows you to open an account for as little as $100—if you join their "ABC" plan. That stands for "automatically building capital." It means you authorize them to automatically take as little as $30 a month (or more if you can afford it) out of your savings or checking account and invest it in the fund. That's equivalent to investing about $1 a day for your future.

You can determine how much money to put into this regular investment program, and which day of the month your account is debited. You may make additional deposits at any time. You can also take money out at any time—but that's not the idea. It's supposed to be a long-term investment plan, which will help you follow one of the keys to building wealth: sticking to an investment strategy.

This is a program that combines all the benefits of dollar cost averaging (see Basic Investment Strategy #2 in chapter 13) with the advantages of a long-term program of equity investments. It's perfectly suited for saving for a child's college education, setting aside money regularly in an IRA account, or simply building an investment account in the stock market—without worrying about which stock or fund to pick to "beat" the market. At least you're *in* the market—and doing just as well (or poorly) as the market itself.

There are several no-load S&P 500 Index funds:

United Services All-American Equity Fund (800-873-8637)

Vanguard Index Trust 500 Portfolio (800-662-7447)

Fidelity Market Index Fund (800-544-8888)

Simple Mutual Fund Strategy #2: One Choice Only— Growth or Income

This is a mutual fund strategy designed for the investor who wants to make *only one choice*—to opt primarily for growth or primarily for income— and to have a simple answer for either or both choices. T. Rowe Price is a no-load mutual fund company managing $36 billion in 41 funds with a variety of objectives. Recognizing that investors might have a difficult time choosing between their funds, they've created two "superfunds": the *T. Rowe Price Spectrum Income Fund* and the *T. Rowe Price Spectrum Growth Fund* (800-638-5660).

Each of these funds invests in a group of seven other no-load mutual funds also managed by T. Rowe Price. There is no additional fee or management charge for investing in these superfunds, which give the investor immediate diversification. The underlying funds are all no-load funds.

The Spectrum Income Fund invests in the following T. Rowe Price no-load funds:

- Prime Reserve Fund: a money market fund
- Short-Term Bond Fund: short- and intermediate-term government and corporate securities
- Ginnie Mae Fund: mortgage-backed and Treasury securities
- New Income Fund: intermediate- and long-term government and corporate bonds
- High Yield Fund: best-quality "junk" bonds
- International Bond Fund: highest-quality international bonds
- Equity-Income Fund: high-dividend stocks, bonds

The Spectrum Growth Fund invests in these T. Rowe Price no-load funds:

- Prime Reserve Fund: money market
- Equity Income Fund: high-dividend stocks, bonds
- International Fund: international stocks
- Growth and Income Fund: high-dividend and "value" stocks, some bonds
- New Era Fund: large capitalization stocks, primarily natural resources
- Growth Stock Fund: mostly large capitalization growth stocks
- New Horizon Fund: small company growth stocks

There are two advantages for the investor in either of the Spectrum funds. First, you can efficiently invest in a large group of funds with a small amount of money. Second, having a diverse portfolio should reduce volatility—the effect of ups and downs in the market.

For instance, in the Spectrum Growth Fund you own both domestic and international stocks, which frequently move in opposite directions. One equity group—small companies, large companies, or natural resources—may be soaring while another is out of favor.

In the Spectrum Income Fund, international bonds may provide a better return when domestic bond yields are low. Or dividend-paying stocks may provide better total returns than money market funds.

The idea is to smooth the volatility while providing better total return and minimizing risk. The Spectrum portfolio manager will decide the balance of investments in funds within the group. The range is basically around 15 percent in each of the underlying funds.

Using these two Spectrum "superfunds" is a perfect strategy for the individual who wants to diversify mutual fund investment without making investment management a full-time business. To get started, call T. Rowe Price Funds at 800-638-5660 and ask for a prospectus describing the Spectrum funds and an application form. The minimum investment in each of the Spectrum funds is $2,500, or $1,000 for IRAs and retirement plans.

Or you can use the Automatic Asset Builder program, which allows you to open any T. Rowe Price mutual fund account with no minimum investment if you agree to have T. Rowe Price deduct at least $50 a month from your checking account, money market account, or paycheck to be invested in your chosen fund.

Simple Mutual Fund Strategy #3: One Fund Does It All

There is one way to simplify your mutual fund decision making: Buy one fund that makes all the decisions for you. This strategy allows you to be invested without making *any* decisions about investment categories or investments within those categories. There are three mutual funds from different companies that will take on all this responsibility for you.

Fidelity Asset Manager (800-544-8888) is a no-load mutual fund with the defined objective of "seeking high total return with reduced risk over the long term, by allocating its assets among stocks, bonds, and short-term instruments."

If the fund were neutral, the allocation would be 30 percent in short-term money market instruments, 40 percent in bonds, and 30 percent in stocks. In actuality, the range may be quite different, but it is never expected to be more than 50 percent in stocks. The fund is allowed to invest in foreign securities and may use options and other instruments to manage risk. A description of all possible investments is included in the prospectus.

Basically, an investment in this fund turns over to the portfolio manager all of the responsibility for diversifying your investment among the widest possible array of choices. In 1992, the Fidelity Asset Manager fund had assets of more than $2 billion.

The minimum amount to open an account is $2,500, or $500 for an Individual Retirement Account. If you open a custodial account for a child as part of a college savings program, the minimum is $1,000.

You can join the Fidelity Account Builder program, which will automatically transfer a minimum of $100 a month from your bank account into your mutual fund account.

Vanguard Star Fund (800-662-7447) is a no-load fund that invests in a diversified portfolio of ten different Vanguard no-load mutual funds. There is no additional management charge above the average management charge of the underlying funds, which has averaged less than ½ of 1 percent each year.

The ten funds in which Vanguard Star may invest are the Windsor Fund, Windsor II, Vanguard Explorer Fund, Vanguard/Morgan Growth Fund, GNMA Portfolio (Ginnie Mae mortgage securities), Investment Grade

Corporate Portfolio, Prime (money market) Portfolio, Index 500 Fund, U.S. Growth Fund, and World Fund. Approximately two-thirds of the Vanguard Star Fund's assets are held in equities, with the balance in fixed-income or money market funds.

The minimum investment required to open an account is $500, with subsequent investments in $100 minimums. However, you can join their "fund express" program, which will automatically withdraw at least $50 a month from your checking or savings account for investment into the Vanguard Star Fund.

Benham Capital Manager (800-472-3389) is a no-load fund that diversified your investment across a wide range of stocks, bonds and money market securities, including international securities and commodity-based investments such as gold and natural resources stocks.

It is a true no-load fund, with no redemption charges or marketing fees. Annual operating expenses are limited to 1 percent of assets. The minimum investment is $2,500 (or $1,000 for IRAs).

Chapter 18

Strategies for Choosing
a Mutual Fund

One of the most popular ways to choose a mutual fund is to pick a fund with a winning record. You can easily check the performance ratings of mutual funds over periods ranging from the past three months to the past ten years. Many of the popular business and financial magazines publish quarterly surveys of fund performance.

There are substantial risks in picking a mutual fund solely on the basis of past performance. As every mutual fund advertisement is required to disclaim: "Past performance is no guarantee of the future."

If you choose too short a time horizon, it may be that your fund performs well only under certain market conditions that prevailed at the time. That is, the fund may perform well in up markets but be risky in declining markets. Or the fund may have benefited from a short-term trend toward one group of stocks in which it had a large investment.

On the other hand, if you choose a long time horizon in evaluating a fund's performance, you may be ignoring the fact that a small mutual fund may be able to reap big percentage gains more easily than a large fund. Perhaps the fund with the best long-term record has attracted so much money it will now be difficult to post large percentage gains.

The person managing the fund is another important factor to consider. Contact the mutual fund to find out how long the portfolio manager has been with the fund. Changes in fund managers may be a signal to sell your shares in the fund. If a new fund manager has just taken over, past outstanding performance may not be repeated. On the other hand, a fund that performed poorly in the past may benefit from a change in fund managers.

By now, you've probably decided you need more than just a listing of funds and their past performance to help guide your mutual fund investment decisions. Listed below are some strategies for getting advice on mutual funds.

Mutual Fund Advice Strategy #1: Mutual Fund Surveys

Morningstar Mutual Funds Service (800-876-5005) is the most comprehensive survey of mutual fund performance. It covers more than 1,240 mutual funds, giving a full-page report and commentary on each. The Morningstar "star rating system" is based on a combination of performance and risk, and it is an excellent way to evaluate potential future performance. The service, which comes with regular updates, costs $395 per year, or $55 for a three-month trial. But it is also available free of charge at most public libraries, and if you call its toll-free number, Morningstar will give you a list of libraries in your area that offer its service.

Standard & Poor's/Lipper Mutual Fund Profiles (212-208-8000) is a quarterly survey of the 800 largest load and no-load mutual funds. Each fund is evaluated for its performance relative to its peer group during the current phase of the market cycle as well as prior up and down phases. The cost is $132 for one year (4 issues), and this publication is also available in most libraries.

The Mutual Fund Encyclopedia, by Gerald Perritt (Dearborn Financial Publishing) is published annually and includes profiles and performance ratings of nearly 1,300 load and no-load mutual funds. The cost is $34.95 and it is available in bookstores or by calling 800-326-6941. It also contains a comprehensive introduction to mutual fund investing.

Mutual Fund Advice Strategy #2: Mutual Fund Investment Newsletters

There are numerous investment newsletters that offer advice to mutual fund investors. They list hundreds of funds by category, and give a wide variety of performance statistics. Most newsletters are issued monthly and some have telephone hotline numbers to update their recommendations. In

general, the newsletters analyze funds by objective and make recommendations in each category. Most also give advice about which funds and
categories they feel offer the most profit potential.

One of the most comprehensive of these newsletters is the *Morningstar
5-Star Investor*. The title refers to their rankings of top mutual funds; this
newsletter includes complete statistics for 500 chosen funds in various
categories. The newsletter is intended to be "a teacher, a reporter, and a
database" and it fulfills all three functions—with special attention given to
building a fund portfolio.

Recommended mutual fund investment newsletters:

Morningstar 5-Star Investor (ed. Don Phillips) 800-876-5005; $65/year

The Mutual Fund Letter (ed. Gerald Perritt) 800-326-6941; $79/year

Investech Mutual Fund Advisor (ed. James Stack) 406-862-7777; $165/
yr, plus telephone hotline

No-Load Fund Investor (ed. Sheldon Jacobs) 914-693-7420; $82/yr

No-Load Fund-X (ed. Burton Berry) 415-896-7979; $100/yr

Donahue's Money Letter (ed. Ralph Norton) 800-445-5900; $109/yr
plus telephone hotline

Mutual Fund Forecaster (ed. Norman Fosback) 800-442-9000; $100/yr

Terry's Tip:

$$$ Be sure to read the monthly newsletters and other investment
information sent to you by your mutual fund management companies.
There are several independent services that concentrate only on the
funds of one management company. For example, *Fidelity Insight*
(800-638-1987) is a monthly newsletter that covers the Fidelity group of
funds. *The Vanguard Advisor* (800-835-2246) is an independent newsletter
written for investors who concentrate on the Vanguard funds.

Mutual Fund Advice Strategy #3: Mutual Fund Timing

There's one step beyond the concept of investing in a mutual fund and
sticking with it over the years. Market timers try to pick an equity fund and
be invested *only* when the entire stock market is rising, and to switch out of

the fund and into a money market fund when it appears the market is going to decline, thereby increasing the overall return.

There's a great deal of debate over the benefits of trying to "time" the market versus a long-term strategy of "buy and hold." A study published by the American Association of Individual Investors assesses the period from 1926 to 1987. During that 62-year period, the average annual return of the S&P Stock Index was 9.44 percent. But the two professors who performed the study reported that if an investor had been out of the market during the 50 best months—6.7 percent of the time—the entire return would have been wiped out! The conclusion: If your timing is off, even by a few months, you can miss the majority of your profit potential. If you're going to try to time your market moves, correct timing is critical. Otherwise you're better off with a buy-and-hold strategy.

To a certain extent, every mutual fund newsletter uses timing techniques to advise subscribers which funds to buy and when. Many newsletters also advise selling certain funds based on market conditions. The *Hulbert Financial Digest* (see chapter 20), which tracks the performance of newsletters that recommend mutual fund portfolios, concludes that "the number of timers beating the market is extremely low." And Hulbert points out that when taxes are taken into consideration it becomes increasingly difficult to beat the market. Therefore, mutual fund timing techniques are better used in a tax-deferred portfolio such as an IRA, Keogh, or pension plan.

One mutual fund newsletter has created a timing strategy that relies strictly on technical signals to generate buy and sell recommendations. *Fabian's Investment Resource,* formerly called the *Telephone Switch Newsletter* (800-950-8765; $137/yr), has an outstanding track record in telling subscribers when to be in—and when to get out of—general equity funds, gold stock funds, and international equity funds. This newsletter has been ranked among the top few by *The Hulbert Financial Digest* in market timing for the past ten years, and is the only one of the top performers to concentrate exclusively on mutual funds.

Following this newsletter's recommendations over the past 15 years, from April 1977 through March 1992, would have resulted in a 17.58 percent compound annual rate of return. Putting that in terms of dollars and cents, a $10,000 investment on April 1, 1977, grew to $113,556 by April 30, 1992 (not counting income taxes). During the same period the Standard & Poor 500 Stock Index showed a 14.42 percent compound annual return, so $10,000 invested in S&P 500 would have grown to $75,467 in the same period of time.

Fabian's Investment Resource relies strictly on technical signals (such as a 39-week moving average) to tell subscribers when to be invested in various groups of mutual funds and when to switch out into the money market funds. Within each category there are at least ten recommended no-load mutual funds. There is a 24-hour hotline to advise subscribers when a switch signal is given. When the indicator for any group is within 5 percent of a buy or sell signal, subscribers are told they are in an "alert" mode and should check the hotline for an actual signal. The way to use this newsletter is simply to choose one or more of the recommended funds and discipline yourself to follow their buy and sell recommendations immediately without second-guessing the reason.

Mutual Fund Advice Strategy #4: Ask the Fund Family

Many large families of mutual funds offer help in deciding which of their funds you should be investing in, and how much of your assets should be invested in each fund. For instance, Fidelity has a "fund match" program, which helps you analyze risk tolerance, length of time for your investments, and other variables so you can better choose among its funds. If you have more than $100,000 to invest, Fidelity offers Portfolio Advisory Services, which will manage a portfolio of Fidelity funds for a maximum annual fee of 1 percent of assets.

Similarly, T. Rowe Price has an "asset mix worksheet" which, combined with its fund guide, will help you decide how to allocate your assets among this family of funds. Dreyfus also has an asset-allocation program which will advise on a mix of funds after the investor has completed a worksheet describing his or her personal financial situation, risk tolerance, and financial goals.

One advantage of choosing a fund management company with a wide variety of no-load mutual funds is the opportunity to use several different funds to reach your goals and to switch between the funds.

Mutual Fund Advice Strategy #5: Selling Funds Short

This is a strategy that carries high risk and should be used only by sophisticated and alert investors. But in the interests of explaining all the uses of mutual funds, it should be pointed out that just as you can sell individual stocks short (see chapter 13 for an explanation of short sales), you can also short-sell certain mutual funds under various circumstances.

Usually, but not always, the Fidelity funds will allow short sales of their "sector funds," which deal with single industries such as biotechnology, healthcare, gold, energy, environmental services, telecommunications, and several other sectors. The mutual fund shares must be held in a margin account at Fidelity Discount Brokerage. You can also sell short the shares of certain mutual funds if you hold your funds in a margin account at Jack White & Co, the discount brokerage firm (see chapter 16).

It should be noted that SEC rules prohibit most mutual funds from making short sales *within* fund portfolios with more than 30 percent of their assets—and then only under stringent guidelines. However, some no-load funds do get actively involved in short sales up to the maximum guidelines—including several Dreyfus funds: Dreyfus Strategic Investing, Dreyfus Strategic Growth, and Dreyfus Strategic World Investing (800-654-6561). The no-load Rydex Ursa fund uses short-selling and put options to profit from bear markets (800-820-0888).

Mutual Fund Advice Strategy #6: Funds and Taxes

Buying and selling shares in mutual funds is easy. Calculating the taxes is another matter. If you buy your funds in a tax-sheltered retirement account you don't have to worry about sorting out capital gains and dividend payouts. Otherwise, pay special attention to Form 1099 sent to you in January by your mutual fund company. It will detail the previous year's distributions and how they should be allocated on your tax return.

Eventually, you will sell some of your fund shares—hopefully at a profit. Generally your capital gains taxes will be based on the "first in, first out" (FIFO) method, unless you specify otherwise. That is, the IRS presumes that the shares you sell are the ones you purchased first. Using that method will create the biggest tax bill if your shares have appreciated.

Another choice is to average the purchase price of all shares (including reinvested dividends) to calculate your cost basis for taxation. Or you may average short- and long-term holdings separately. In some cases (usually when trading funds through a discount brokerage firm) you can specifically request that sales of fund shares be labeled on the confirmation against specific previous purchase dates. This requires careful record keeping.

No matter how you intend to calculate your taxes, be sure to keep all your fund purchase, sale, and reinvestment statements in your files.

Chapter 19

The Stock Market

There's one simple rule for making money in the stock market: Buy low and sell high! To date, no one has come up with a foolproof method of putting that rule into action! That's what makes the stock market so fascinating—and potentially profitable.

The stock market, with all its trading floors and computer marketplaces around the world, is simply a place where money agrees to disagree about value. For every share you decide to purchase, someone else has decided to sell. Where you see future value, another person has decided to relinquish ownership of that stock. That's a humbling perspective on investing.

The stock and interest rate markets of the world are also the place where "money puts its mouth." Politicians can talk, and pollsters can take surveys, but the stock market is perhaps the most accurate and informed barometer of sentiment about world issues. For instance, from the day the Gulf War started in 1990, the U.S. stock market rallied sharply. You didn't need briefings from generals or television news reports to predict the outcome.

When it comes to investing in the stock market, you enter a vast world of choices and decisions. The value of all publicly traded equities (stocks) in the United States is about $4.2 trillion. Stocks traded in Japan have a market value of more than $2 trillion. The London markets add another $1 trillion. And there are active stock markets around the world, from Mexico

126

to Hong Kong. Investing in these markets can be intimidating if you don't have a strategy and expensive if you don't understand currencies.

Just as there are many different stock markets around the world, there are many segments of the stock market within the U.S. markets. The New York Stock Exchange and the American Stock Exchange have trading floors where securities listed for trading are purchased and sold at prices set by *specialists*—designated market makers who trade for their own accounts while striving to create an orderly pricing mechanism. There are also several regional stock exchanges which trade in the same manner.

The over-the-counter market is a telephone-linked market in which dealers make competitive bids and offers for securities. The prices of many OTC securities are listed daily in the newspapers through the NASDAQ (National Association of Securities Dealers Automated Quotation System). Stock prices of other, smaller companies traded in the huge over-the-counter market can be found in daily listings at brokerage firms called "pink sheets."

Just as there is no one marketplace for trading stocks, it is also a mistake to believe that the entire market can be characterized by one word: up or down, bullish or bearish. At any point in time, one group of stocks may be performing well, while another is in general decline. In chapter 13 you read about some of the more popular averages or indexes that are used to track market performance. But those indicators do not always move in tandem—or with the same momentum.

For instance, in the period between midyear 1983 and the end of 1992, the Standard & Poor's 500 index had a 15.6 percent compound annual rate of return. But a diverse portfolio of small capitalization stocks (smaller, newer companies) returned only 6.6 percent annually during that same period. That's no reason to avoid small stocks, though; it just means they were generally out of favor during the 1980s. In 1991 and 1992, the situation was reversed and the Russell 2000 index of small cap stocks outperformed big companies—gaining 44 percent in 1991 versus 29 percent for the S&P 500 in 1991, and rising 16.36 percent versus 7.6 percent for the S&P 500 in 1992. In 1994, the S&P 500 gained 1.32 percent, including dividends.

Economic conditions can cause divergences in stock performance, or different trends can simply be caused by fads in the markets. For instance, stocks of oil and gas and natural resources companies would do well in an inflationary period, while manufacturing company stocks might lag. Technology stocks might rise as a group when one company makes a scientific breakthrough. Computer stocks may rise or fall as a group when it is perceived that business is growing or slowing for the industry. Of course, not all stocks in an industry group have the same business and management, so when choosing stocks the idea is to pick the one special company, or anticipate a trend for an entire industry.

In fact, the ability to pick stocks has always been considered a sort of "art form"—and many have endeavored to turn it into a science.

Books, indeed entire libraries, have been written about how to invest in the stock market. Perhaps the easiest way to participate is through mutual funds and the strategies I've outlined in the preceding chapters. But if you decide to purchase individual stocks, you need to know how to do so with the most efficiency and least cost, how to evaluate investment ideas, and how to get advice you can trust.

Stock Purchase Strategy #1: Stock Brokerage Firms

Stock brokerage firms spend millions of dollars advertising their services and how they can help you build financial security. They try to differentiate themselves, yet in most respects they are quite similar.

All full-service stock brokerage firms have a few things in common. They are members of the major stock exchanges. They charge commissions on every transaction, although they may negotiate the amount of commission you pay, based on the size of your account and the frequency of your transactions. They will give you research reports generated by their stock analysts and will send you basic informational reports such as those created by Value Line or by Standard & Poor's research service on most stocks.

Brokerage firms will either hold your stocks for you (in "street name") or have the shares registered and send the certificates to you. They will collect dividends and interest on your investments and credit those amounts to your account. Many brokerage firms offer comprehensive money management services that include credit cards.

Brokerage firms frequently underwrite initial offerings of shares in companies seeking to raise capital in the stock market. Or they offer products that they develop, such as limited partnerships. All major brokerage firms are members of SIPC—the Securities Investor Protection Corporation. That means cash and securities in your brokerage account are insured up to $500,000.

Your primary contact at a full-service brokerage firm is the individual stockbroker (often called a *registered representative*) who is handling your account. This is the person who will be making specific recommendations to buy and sell securities. (If you already know what you want to buy or sell, you should be using a discount brokerage firm. See Stock Purchase Strategy #2 below.)

While you may want the comforting presence and investment research of a well-known brokerage firm, choosing the individual stockbroker is most important and should not be left to chance. You might walk into a shoestore and take the first available salesperson, but that's not how you should choose a stockbroker. Instead, ask someone who has been a successful investor in the market for an introduction to his or her broker.

Remember, it's always worth paying full commissions to a stockbroker who gives you money-making advice. But also know that a broker is compensated only by commissions generated when you make a purchase or sale. That can be a powerful incentive to make recommendations when you might be better off on the sidelines in a money market fund. Never give your broker a power of attorney to act without consulting you.

If you have a dispute with your stockbroker, it's important to resolve it promptly and in writing. Always notify the branch manager of a brokerage firm if a problem is not solved immediately. When you opened your account with the brokerage firm, you were probably required to sign a form agreeing to submit any disputes to arbitration, instead of filing a lawsuit.

Arbitration proceedings are conducted by the individual stock exchanges, and you may choose where to take your action. If your complaint is for less than $10,000 you can usually have your claim handled by mail; amounts over that limit require a personal appearance at the proceedings, which are usually scheduled in the large city closest to your home. You don't need to have an attorney present, but if the amount is substantial you should remember that the brokerage firm will have its own legal talent to represent it.

Remember, decisions by arbitration cannot usually be appealed. Also, arbitration proceedings do not usually award punitive damages. Your best protection is to understand exactly what is happening in your account at all times.

If you are unhappy with the performance of your stockbroker, you should either sell all your securities and request that a check be sent to you, or else open an account at a different brokerage firm and ask that your securities be transferred. Too many people feel they have no alternatives once they've opened an account. It's *your* money, and you have the final word on your investments.

Terry's Tips:

$$$ Many large brokerage firms are now offering something called "wrap accounts" in which they charge as much as 3 percent of the value of your account to introduce you to a professional money manager who will make buy and sell decisions. The fee remains the same, regardless of the number of transactions in your account. The sales pitch stresses "professional" money managers who will treat your account with individual attention. In most cases, you'd be better off just buying a no-load mutual fund and saving almost 2 percent a year.

$$$ Be aware that many brokerage firms now charge an "account maintenance fee" just for giving you the privilege of doing business with them. For example, Merrill Lynch charges $40 a year for customers with basic accounts. Dean Witter charges $50 for customers who generate less than $100 in commissions in a calendar year, and Shearson Lehman charges $3.85 in postage and handling for each transaction.

Stock Purchase Strategy #2: Discount Brokers

In 1975, the world of stock brokerage firms was changed dramatically. Instead of all firms charging the same fixed-rate commissions, the brokerage industry was deregulated. Each firm could determine its own cost of doing business, the kind of services it wanted to offer customers, and its own commission schedules.

The result was the creation of *discount brokerage firms*, which in 1991 accounted for 11 percent of all retail commissions. About one in five retail trades now goes through a discount brokerage firm. Commissions charged by discount brokers may be more than 60 percent less than the rates charged by full-service brokerage firms. And some deep-discount brokerage firms reduce commissions even more for large, active trading accounts.

For example, 100 shares of a $30 stock will cost you about $85 in commissions at a large retail brokerage firm like Merrill Lynch or Dean

Witter. But at Charles Schwab or Fidelity Discount Brokerage (see below for phone numbers), the same transaction will cost you about $55.

For larger transactions, the disparity is even greater. Commissions on 500 shares of a $20 stock will run about $230 to $240 at a full-service firm. But you can pay $110 at the two largest discounters, and as little as $61 for the trade at Waterhouse, one of the deep-discount firms.

If that kind of savings attracts your attention, you should also understand what you do *not* get at a discount brokerage firm. Basically, you don't get advice and hand-holding that a full-service broker provides. You probably won't speak to the same person each time you place an order. You won't get free research reports recommending stock purchases, although you may request fact sheets on individual stocks. Some discount brokerage firms now offer lengthy research reports for an additional fee. (See Stock Research Strategy #3 in the next chapter.)

On the other hand, most discount brokerage firms can confirm your order execution while you wait on the telephone. And most will accept your orders 24 hours a day, seven days a week. They will hold your stocks and collect dividends for you, and they will accept open and limit orders. They will help you establish IRA or Keogh accounts or custodial accounts for your children.

Some of the larger discounters like Schwab and Fidelity offer free checking and Visa or MasterCards keyed to your account so you can access your money market account or borrow on the value of your marginable securities. The major discounters are also members of SIPC, which insures your account up to $500,000.

Most discount brokerage firms have offices around the country, although accounts can be opened by phone and mail.

SOME DISCOUNT BROKERAGE FIRMS

Charles Schwab	800-435-4000
Fidelity Discount	800-544-7272
Quick & Reilly	800-221-5220
Olde Discount	800-USA-OLDE
Waterhouse	800-765-5185

Stock Purchase Strategy #3: Direct Purchase/Dividend Reinvestment Plans

There is actually a way to purchase stocks without going through any type of brokerage firm. More than 900 companies and closed-end funds allow shareholders to reinvest their dividends, and even purchase additional shares, with no commission cost. In fact, many of these plans allow shareholders to purchase stock at discounts of from 3 to 10 percent below current market price of the stock. There are even a few companies that allow investors to make initial purchases directly from the company, bypassing brokerage firms completely. Some companies may charge a small fee for this service, but it is far lower than brokerage commissions.

While these dividend reinvestment plans are typically used to purchase a few shares at a time instead of taking a cash dividend, the plans can be used to accumulate substantial positions in a company's stock without paying commissions. The upper limit for additional cash purchases of shares is $60,000, or more in some plans.

One of the difficulties with buying and selling shares of a company through a dividend reinvestment plan (DRP) is that you have little control over the timing of your transaction. The company purchases stock for those in its plans only on certain dates, usually once a month or every quarter. So you should use dividend reinvestment plans for long-term investment programs.

Some companies will not sell or redeem shares accumulated through dividend reinvestment plans unless they are fractional shares. They'll send shareholders a certificate for full shares that must be sold through a stockbroker.

One other thing to keep in mind when purchasing stock through DRPs is the hassle of recordkeeping. Most companies will send you annual statements of your purchases. You must pay taxes on the money that is invested in additional shares even though you don't receive the cash. Plus, each share purchased through the plan has a different cost basis, making tax calculations a nightmare when you go to sell the stock. That's why many people use DRPs for shares held in their Individual Retirement Accounts or Keogh plans.

Terry's Tip:

$$$ For information on whether a company has a dividend reinvestment plan, look at the company report in the *Value Line Investment Survey*, which is available at most brokerage firms and most public libraries. If you want to get seriously involved in acquiring shares through DRPs, you should read *Buying Stocks Without a Broker*, by Charles Carlson (McGraw-Hill, 1991), or subscribe to Carlson's monthly newsletter, *The DRIP Investor* (800-962-4369; $49/yr).

Chapter 20

How to Choose Stocks

Once you understand the process of purchasing a stock, you're still faced with the most important question: *which* stock to buy. There is a seemingly endless variety of strategies for choosing individual stocks. They range from buying a "hot tip" given to you by a friend who "knows something" (a process that can be truly dangerous if the friend has inside, nonpublic information) to spending your days poring over investment data and charting stock prices. Some investors look for stocks selling at prices lower than the company's intrinsic value; others purchase stocks based on predictions of future earnings growth. Listed below are a variety of strategies best suited to the individual investor, and sources for more information.

Stock Research Strategy #1: Look Around You

One of the most overlooked stock research strategies is simply opening your eyes to the businesses that are growing around you. Whether you're involved in corporate America, shopping at the grocery store, or raising a child, you'll find potential investments in the products you buy and the services you use.

One of my favorite investment stories came about as the result of my teen-age son's change in preference for shoes. When I tactfully suggested to him that it might be time for a new pair of Reeboks (his could have walked to the trash can on their own), I was greeted with disdain. "Mom, Reeboks are *out*; Nike Air Jordans are *in*!"

After several trips to various stores in search of the then-new Nike Air Jordans, I realized we were onto a truly hot commodity. I immediately called my broker to sell the Reebok stock I owned and purchase Nike. It was an excellent trade that more than paid for the new shoes! I've missed a few winners, too, by not keeping my eyes open. I only wish I'd purchased stock in Toys " Я " Us years ago, instead of all the money I spent buying toys there!

Whether you notice that your company is using a new computer technology or you find a new product on the store shelves that seems to be selling well, you should take time to investigate whether the company producing the product is publicly traded. That's easy to do, simply by taking the manufacturer's name and address and contacting the company itself. Or you can ask your broker to check it out for you.

A few holiday seasons ago one of the hot gift items was Presto's "Salad Shooter." The stock of the company, National Presto Industries—a small, publicly traded appliance manufacturer—doubled in price in just a few months. And it might have been a better idea to purchase the stock of CML Corporation instead of the Nordic Trak exercise machine the company manufactures. Most of those machines gathered dust after New Year's resolutions were forgotten, but the stock soared.

The moral of this story is: The best investment research starts at home.

Stock Research Strategy #2: Brokerage Firm Reports

A more conventional way to pick up investment ideas is to look at the research reports produced by stock analysts at brokerage firms. Most major brokerage firms employ a large number of analysts who cover specific industry groups. If you're interested in drug stocks or automobile manufacturers, chances are the analyst has created reports on most of the major companies in that group. It's an excellent way to compare stocks within an industry and get a picture of that group relative to the entire market. And it's one reason to have a stockbroker at a major investment firm.

Brokerage firm reports are typically based on either *value* or *growth* analysis, or a combination of both. You'll get the brokerage firm analyst's estimate of future earnings and an evaluation of the company's balance sheet and assets.

The current price of the company's stock relative to its current year's earnings (or next year's estimated earnings) is its P/E, or *price-earnings ratio*. That's a convenient way to compare stocks in the same industry group and see which are overpriced or underpriced compared to the group as a whole, or the entire market.

When acting on the basis of brokerage firm reports, it's important to keep a few things in mind. These reports are widely followed, and if you're not one of the first to read the report it may have already had an impact on the price of the stock. Many times you'll read that a stock fell a few points because a stock analyst for a major brokerage firm downgraded his earnings estimates or took the stock off his "buy list."

The second thing to remember is that brokerage firms issue far more "buy" recommendations than "sell" signals. In fact, there have been a few well-publicized cases where brokerage firm analysts have been fired because they were too bearish or negative on the market. If you do purchase stock on a brokerage firm recommendation, you should be aware that you'll have to be more active in deciding when to sell.

Terry's Tip:

$$$ When a brokerage firm downgrades its rating from "buy" to "hold," you should be thinking of selling. If you don't think the stock has enough upside potential to buy at this price, is it worth holding?

Stock Research Strategy #3: Stock Report Services

When you're making an investment decision or listening to a broker's recommendation, it helps to have the basic facts and figures about a company. There are two easily available services that provide this information.

Nearly every brokerage firm and most public libraries carry the *Value Line Investment Survey* reports and the *Standard & Poor's Stock Reports*. These are one-page reports on most publicly traded companies. The reports are updated regularly and kept in loose-leaf binders. Each gives you information about the company's business, earnings, and dividends. Each report has a small chart of past price performance. If you want to contact the company directly, the report gives the address and phone number of the corporate headquarters.

If you're looking for opinions, the Value Line report rates each company based on safety, timeliness, and beta (a measure of volatility in comparison to the entire market). The last paragraph names the Value Line analyst and gives his or her opinion for each stock. The Standard & Poor's one-page report sticks primarily to factual information but does give a brief summary and opinion of performance outlook.

Standard & Poor's (800-642-2858) also offers a comprehensive, in-depth individual stock report on more than 4,000 publicly traded companies. The reports are updated daily to reflect the latest company news and earnings. Each seven-page company report contains a survey of brokerage analysts' opinions and earnings estimates on the stock, as well as the industry outlook, charts, and information on purchases and sales of the stock by company insiders. The reports cost $10 each, which can be charged to a bankcard, and are sent by first-class mail. Overnight express or fax service is available for an additional charge.

Clients of Fidelity Brokerage Services (800-847-0342) can order the same seven-page Standard & Poor's report through this discount brokerage firm. When you order through Fidelity, the cost is $9.95 for the first report, and $7.95 for additional reports ordered at the same time. Fax and overnight service are also offered.

Stock Research Strategy #4: Technical Analysis

Most investment research reports issued by brokerage firms are based on *fundamental analysis*. That is, the analyst looks at the company's business outlook, earnings prospects, and general economic conditions when making a recommendation.

Another method often used to decide whether to buy or sell a stock is called *technical analysis*, and it has nothing to do with the company's business. Instead, it is based on statistics such as trading volume and price, often as portrayed on charts and graphs of the company's past stock price performance. Technical analysts do not care if they are looking at the price chart of a big company stock or soybean prices. They believe the trading patterns that show up on the chart give them an advantage in deciding whether to buy or sell. And they may look not only at recent price charts but also at very long-term patterns or cycles to predict market action.

"Charting," or technical analysis, can be a fascinating and all-consuming pastime. Numerous books have been written on the subject, and many investment newsletters use technical analysis as a basis for investment recommendations. But in this age of computers you don't have to do the actual charting yourself.

If you want a stock price chart on any stock on the New York Stock Exchange, American, or NASDAQ listed stock, contact *Daily Graphs*, the chartbooks published by William O'Neil & Company. They publish a weekly chartbook for each exchange, plus one that relates stock and option prices. They also publish a chartbook of long-term values, tracking 4,000 stocks with charts extending 15 years. You can subscribe on a weekly, biweekly, or monthly basis, or they'll send you one issue of any book for $17 (310-448-6843).

Stock Research Strategy #5: Investment Newsletters

One practical way to get investment advice is to subscribe to an investment research newsletter. You may have already received mailings from some of these services, advertising their past successes and promising fantastic insights into future investment profits. Or you may have seen their ads in financial newspapers offering tantalizing peeks into the "best" stocks to buy or sell in current market conditions.

Some investment newsletters can be a real asset in picking stocks and mutual funds. Others may mislead you. You should know that these newsletters do not necessarily have to be registered with the Securities and Exchange Commission or any other government agency. The newspapers in which they advertise do not screen their performance claims.

Past performance is important, but it is not the sole consideration when choosing an investment newsletter. You should also make sure the newsletter's style is compatible with your own trading and risk attitude. Some newsletters make frequent trading recommendations, requiring you to call their hotline numbers for daily recommendations. Others have a longer-term outlook on the market. Some newsletters recommend more volatile stocks or options, while others have a more conservative stance. And, frankly, some newsletters are just easier to read and understand.

Terry's Tips:

$$$ There is one highly respected service that keeps track of newsletter recommendations and their performance over the years. *The Hulbert*

Financial Digest is published monthly (703-683-5905; $135/yr, or $37.50 for a five-issue trial subscription). It rates the performance of 130 newsletters over several periods: the past 11 years, the past five years, and the period from January 1987 through the most recent quarter.

If you would like a directory (including phone numbers, addresses, and costs) of the newsletters rated by Hulbert, the cost is $20, and it is available through the phone number listed above. Hulbert's directory includes all of the most popular names in the newsletter industry, and his monthly newsletter is a good way to sort out the veracity of the promotional literature you'll receive.

$$$ You might want to take a shorter-term trial subscription to a few services to find out if you're comfortable with the style of the newsletter. Select Information Exchange (212-247-7123) is a company that offers a package of 20 trial subscriptions for $11.95. You can choose your trial from a list of more than 50 of the most popular newsletters. (This trial package makes a great gift for market watchers.)

$$$ I'm frequently asked to name my favorite newsletter, and that's a difficult choice to make. I read dozens every month and have mentioned a number of the more useful ones in the chapter on mutual fund investing. But if forced to choose only one market letter every month, I'd pick *The Wellington Letter*, published by Bert Dohmen (800-992-9989; $450/yr includes telephone hotline access and market warning bulletins). This 20-page monthly letter covers a broad range of topics, including the domestic and international economic outlook, plus investment recommendations in both domestic and international stocks and mutual funds. And I look forward to reading Dohmen's commentaries.

Stock Research Strategy #6: Investment Clubs

Starting an investment program in the stock market does not have to be a solitary venture. Nearly 25,000 people belong to investment clubs, and there are more than 8,000 of these clubs in America, according to the National Association of Investors Corporation (810-583-6242).

This organization is dedicated to helping groups form investment clubs and start an investment program. Dues are $30 a year per club plus $10 per member, which covers the cost of their monthly *Better Investing* magazine. They'll send out materials on how to form a club, create a partnership agreement, and set up accounting procedures.

The purpose of investment clubs is to enable group members to meet regularly and share investment ideas. Many clubs require members to invest as little as $100 to start and an additional $25 a month. They often invite brokers to their meetings or just present research reports that members have gathered from various brokerage firms. Investment choices are made by a vote of the group. There are surprising success stories from many of these clubs, which are started by people with very little knowledge of the stock market.

Stock Research Strategy #7: The American Association of Individual Investors

If you prefer to create your own investment program, you might want to seek out a support group created especially for amateur individual investors. The American Association of Individual Investors based in Chicago, Illinois (312-280-0170) has more than 120,000 members in the United States, Canada, and Europe. For annual dues of $49 members receive ten copies of the *AAII Journal*, containing articles about investing, plus a copy of the excellent annual *AAII Guide to No-Load Mutual Funds*. Each member also receives an annual update of the personal tax and financial planning booklet. This organization conducts seminars around the country for its members.

Stock Research Strategy #8: Initial Public Offerings

Many people prefer to buy shares in a company when they are first being offered to the investing public. It's called an initial public offering (IPO). Depending on market conditions and the price that is put on the shares, this can be a profitable strategy to make investments with growth potential— or you can be caught owning shares that insiders want to dump at unconscionable prices.

Initial public offerings are one way companies raise capital to fund growth and expansion and create new jobs. Generally, an IPO will be a smaller company that has been privately owned. However, many larger companies were "taken private" in the leveraged buyout craze of the 1980s. After a company has been revamped and streamlined, shares in this privately held company may be reoffered to the investing public—usually at a price far higher than was paid to take the company private.

In an initial public offering you'll almost always find that the current private owners of the company have a far lower cost of ownership of their shares than the public is being asked to pay. Sometimes this is justified, if the private owners have invested their capital and hard work to make the company profitable. At other times it appears unconscionable that once the shares are publicly traded, the remaining shares that continue to be owned by the insiders now command a huge market value.

When a company sells stock to the public, the proceeds of the sale go into the company's coffers to be used for expansion or to repay debt. But when you read the offering circular, or prospectus, you'll sometimes see that in addition to the shares being offered by the company itself, some of the original shareholders are cashing in a portion of their stock at a substantial profit.

The price of stock being offered in an IPO is determined by the underwriting brokers. Theoretically, it is based on the company's business history plus current and future earnings prospects. All too often, this initial price is based on a calculation of "what the market will bear." If other companies in the same industry are trading at a very high relationship of price to earnings, then the IPO will come out at a relatively high price-earnings ratio. If there are no current earnings, the price is based on speculation about what the company might be worth in the future.

On occasion, you may be offered shares in a *secondary offering*. That takes place after the stock has been trading for a while and either the company, or the inside shareholders, or both decide to sell more stock to the public. When a company has a secondary offering, the price is based on the current market price of the already outstanding shares. You won't see a commission charge printed on your sales confirmation for an IPO or secondary stock offering. That's because the commission is built right into the price of the stock and is being paid by the selling company.

Terry's Tip:

$$$ Some IPOs are "hot" new issues. After the offering, the stock price will soar to a premium in the trading market, creating instant profits for those who are allocated shares in the public offering.

Here's a rule of thumb: If you're not a big trader or an important client, and your broker offers you shares in an IPO, decline the offer. Shares in hot new issues are generally reserved for important clients as a way of saying thank you for past commissions. If you can get stock very easily, it means the price may well decline after the initial public offering.

Stock Research Strategy #9: Market Timing

Many of the investment newsletters you will read attempt to "time" the market. That is, they give you buy and sell signals based on overall market performance. As noted on page 122, very few market timers are consistent winners. And as you can see from the graphic below, the cost of missing market turning points can be expensive.

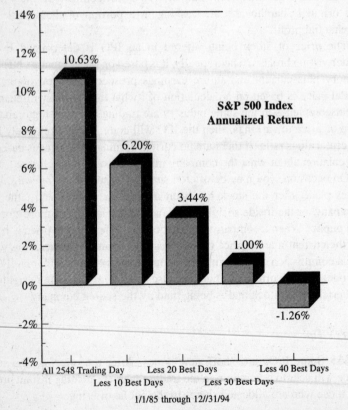

S&P 500 Index Annualized Return

All 2548 Trading Day — 10.63%
Less 10 Best Days — 6.20%
Less 20 Best Days — 3.44%
Less 30 Best Days — 1.00%
Less 40 Best Days — -1.26%

1/1/85 through 12//31/94

SOURCE: INVESCO

Chapter 21

Investing Using Leverage

The concept of *leverage*, explained in chapter 13, allows you to get "more bang for your buck" when it comes to investing. Leverage also multiplies your risk. Some investments, such as commodity futures, are designed to take maximum advantage of leverage. Other leverage strategies, such as margin accounts, simply magnify the risk of fairly conservative investments.

If you decide to use an investment strategy that employs leverage, be careful to understand the downside as well as the increased potential for gain.

Leverage Strategy #1: Use a Margin Account

A margin account is simply a loan account, with stocks or other securities pledged as collateral. Current Federal Reserve rules (under Regulation T) set the margin that may be loaned on stocks at 50 percent. The margin on corporate bonds is currently 70 percent (meaning you can borrow 70 percent of the current market value, not the face value). You can borrow 75 percent on municipal bonds and 90 percent on government bonds.

No bank or broker may legally lend you more than that percentage on any security. The price, or interest rate, of the loan can be determined by the lending institution. Generally speaking, brokerage firms charge the *broker loan rate* (about the same as the bank prime rate, which is charged to the best banking customers). Interest rates are charged on a sliding scale, with lower rates for higher amounts borrowed. Starting in 1994, margin interest can be used to offset interest and dividends, but can only offset capital gains when they are taxed at the investor's personal income tax rate.

Margin accounts can be a source of quick cash (see chapter 34), or they can be a way to leverage your investment dollars. If 100 shares of XYZ stock cost you $10,000 in a cash account, you can buy the same amount of stock for $5,000 in a margin account. If the stock then rises $4 a share, you have a 4 percent return on your money in the cash account, but an 8 percent return on your investment if you purchased the stock in a margin account.

Margin accounts also allow you to make use of accumulated profits in stocks, without selling the shares and incurring a capital gains tax. Borrowing money through use of a margin account does not trigger a taxable event. So if you purchased the XYZ stock at $70 a share and it has risen to $100 a share, you can now make use of some of the increased cash value through your margin account.

The downside of buying stocks in a margin account is that you must always keep at least 50 percent equity in the account. So if your stock drops, the brokerage firm can call and ask for more shares, or more cash. The shares do not have to be the same as the ones on which you are borrowing money. You could put up stock in any other company as collateral for your purchase.

The concept of margining mutual fund shares was mentioned in chapter 18. Since you do not receive a certificate when you purchase a no-load mutual fund, it is easiest to open a margin account when you purchase no-load fund shares through a discount brokerage firm.

A few major brokerage firms have formed dealer agreements with some no-load mutual fund companies, allowing their fund shares to be margined. In this case, the brokerage firm will ask you to sign a transfer agreement and it should take a few weeks for the paperwork to be completed.

Leverage Strategy #2: Use Options and "LEAPS"

What if you could purchase that 100 shares of XYZ for only $650 instead of $10,000? Well, not exactly purchase the stock, but buy the right to own it at the current price for the next six months—and also the right to any appreciation in the stock that takes place in the next six months.

That's real leverage, and that's exactly what a call option gives you. When you purchase an option on a stock, you put up a relatively small amount of money for the right to purchase that stock at a fixed price during a specific time period.

If the value of the underlying stock goes up, the value of your option rises as well. If XYZ stock rises to $120 a share and you purchased an option giving you the right to buy XYZ at $100, then your option is worth at least $20. If the option cost you $650, then you have a $1,350 profit. You've doubled your money! In percentage terms, that's a much larger gain than the 20 percent you would have made on the stock.

If the stock goes down, your option will also decline in value. But if you owned XYZ at $100 and the stock suddenly fell to $80, you would lose $2,000. When you own an option, all you can lose is the amount the option cost you.

Options limit your loss in dollar terms, but don't forget that your option can become worthless—costing you 100 percent of your investment. That's hardly likely to happen when you own the stock, unless the company goes bankrupt.

Options are listed for trading on major exchanges. The price of an option at any moment is dependent on several factors: (1) the price of the underlying stock, (2) the time remaining until your option expires, and (3) the relationship of the current stock price to the striking price (or purchase) price guaranteed by your option.

An option is a combination of time and money. You have to be right about both to make a profit. XYZ may rise, but if you own an option instead of the stock, it must rise within the short lifetime of your option. If the stock just sits at $100 a share for six months, your option expires worthless—a total loss. If you'd owned 100 shares of the stock, all you would have lost is the potential interest you could have earned on the money you had tied up in owning the stock.

In addition to purchasing options on individual stocks, you can purchase options on the market itself; that is, you can buy options on the S&P 500 and 100 stock indexes. This is really the leveraged version of buying an *index mutual fund* (see chapter 17).

The person who *sells* an option on stock he owns receives the payment or *premium*, from the option buyer. In effect, he earns extra income on the stock. The option seller accepts some risk. If the stock goes up, the buyer will call the stock away. In that case, the seller receives the previously agreed-upon price, plus the option premium, but forfeits any additional gains on the stock. If the stock price falls, the extra income will at least partially compensate the option seller for the price decline on the stock he owns.

Before getting involved in options you should understand exactly how they work and the risks you are assuming. Basically, the risks are as follows:

Option *buyers* risk losing their entire investment if the stock does not rise and make the option more valuable during the fixed period of time. The option could expire worthless.

Option *sellers* risk limiting their profits on the upside if the stock rises and is called away. And option sellers also risk losses if they hold on to a declining stock because they're worried that it might rise again and be called away in the future.

Options are generally listed in three- and six-month maturities, but in recent years the Chicago Board Options Exchange created a product called LEAPS (Long-term Equity Anticipation Securities). These are really long-term versions of ordinary call options, with original maturities of up to three years (or two years for LEAP index options). Naturally, the prices are higher because of the longer-term nature of these options, but they still offer a substantial amount of leverage.

Options are not limited to U.S. markets. The American Stock Exchange trades Nikkei put warrants—an option used to speculate on a decline in this major Japanese stock index.

There are many sophisticated options strategies, including *writing* or granting options, buying or writing *put options*—in which the buyer profits when a stock declines—and combining put and call options. You should consult your broker and read the options prospectus and related materials before entering into any of these strategies. You should also read *Understanding Options*, a pamphlet available from the Chicago Board Options Exchange, 400 S. LaSalle Street, Chicago, IL 60606.

Leverage Strategy #3: Commodity Futures and Funds

Commodity futures are the ultimate form of leverage. Not only can you lose everything you originally invested, but you can lose more than you started with! Great fortunes can be created in commodity futures—and even greater fortunes can be lost.

When you buy a futures contract, you make a very small margin down payment, usually less than 10 percent. In fact, it's not even officially called margin; it's considered a "good-faith" deposit or performance bond. This small investment can control a futures contract in soybeans or Swiss francs or pork bellies worth tens of thousands of dollars.

The combination of a small initial investment with the volatility of most futures markets creates the most powerful form of leverage. In one trading day, an entire margin deposit can be wiped out—or doubled. Even more dangerous, the markets can get "locked in" to a trading limit, either up or down. That means no more transactions can be executed that day. The following day the market can again jump the allowable daily limit. If no one is willing to sell (or buy) at the limit price, those who are on the wrong side of the market have lost more money, with no chance to exit.

Then the brokerage firm will issue a margin call—requiring the trader to put up more money. If markets get "locked limit" several days in a row, the trader can lose his or her entire initial investment—and owe the brokerage firm much more money!

In recent years, managed commodity funds have been promoted as a way for investors to minimize the risk in trading futures. Most funds guarantee that the investor cannot lose more than the initial investment in the fund. And some funds trade with only a small portion of the money, investing the balance in Treasury bills or other short-term money market instruments.

Commodity funds have grown so popular that it's estimated their trading accounts for as much as 30 percent of the volume in some futures contracts on some days. In fact, the actions of the funds, and the floor traders trying to anticipate the funds, can move markets in ways entirely unrelated to fundamental financial information.

Commodity funds can be an expensive way to get involved in the futures market. The average fund takes as much as 20 percent of the profits for the management company, as well as brokerage fees and sales commissions. And, in spite of professional management and leverage, the average fund has not had an outstanding record in recent years. In 1994, the average of return on publicly traded commodity funds was a loss of 7.7 percent, while the S&P 500 Stock Index gained 1.32 percent.

Managed Account Reports (212-213-6202; monthly, $265/yr) is a newsletter that tracks the performance of commodity pools and funds.

Chapter 22

Understanding Interest Rate Investments

Many investors decide to invest for income instead of striving for gains in the stock market. Traditionally, interest rate investing has been considered a more conservative approach to managing your money.

If there's one thing the American public has learned over the last decade, it's that interest rates on even the safest investments such as money market funds can move sharply higher or lower, causing big swings in the interest checks that many people use for living expenses. And changes in interest rates cause big swings in the market value of fixed-rate bond investments.

In 1980, the prime rate that banks charged their best borrowers reached a high of $20\frac{1}{2}$ percent. But as fears of inflation subsided and the Federal Reserve eased credit availability, the overall trend of interest rates in the following 12 years has been sharply lower. People who worried about future inflation and were afraid to lock up their money in 30-year government bonds at *only* 15 percent in the early 1980s, were scrambling to reinvest bank certificates of deposit at rates around 3 percent in 1993!

Higher interest rates tend to help lenders; lower interest rates are viewed as helpful to borrowers. But not all people are happy about lower interest rates because even in this era of debt, not all people are borrowers. Falling interest rates have cut billions of dollars out of household income in the years between 1990 and 1992. When you think of a lender, you typically picture a bank making loans to a customer. But *you* become a lender when you decide where to invest your money to earn interest.

If you're searching for the place to earn the highest interest rate on your money, there's one basic rule to keep in mind:

The higher the interest rate you receive, the greater the risk you are taking!

There are simply no exceptions to this rule in a world where there is immediate access to information for borrowers and lenders. Interest rates on everything from bank certificates of deposit to longer-term bonds are determined by free market perceptions of the risk of lending money over a short or long period of time to a particular type of borrower.

Generally speaking, in spite of its huge budget deficits, the United States government is considered the most creditworthy borrower. Interest rates on its borrowings—whether short-term Treasury bills or 30-year Treasury bonds—are viewed as the standard for interest rates against which other, riskier bonds are measured.

You can find higher yields with long-term bonds. You can find higher yields with low-quality bonds. And you can find the highest yields when you're willing to accept a combination of a long-term bond from a borrower with a poor credit history—a junk bond. But you're taking a lot more risk with your money.

UNDERSTANDING BOND TERMS

Before you consider making any bond investments, you should understand some of the specialized terms used in discussing fixed rate investments. Let's start with the term "fixed rate." *Fixed rate* refers to the fact that most bonds carry a set interest rate that is paid at regular intervals—usually six months—until the bond reaches *maturity*—the date on which the face value of the bond is repaid.

The amount of the original investment is called the *face value* of the bond. Most bonds have a face value of $1,000. You may purchase a bond for more or less than the face value. The price you pay for the bond on any given day is the *market value*. The market value depends on how much investors are willing to pay to earn the interest rate paid by the bond.

The *coupon rate* is that fixed interest rate the borrower agreed to pay to buyers of the bonds. There may be a difference between the *coupon rate* of your bond, and the *current yield* of a bond. The coupon rate is fixed, but the market price of the bond can move up and down. (See Interest Concept #2 in this chapter.) So if you buy a bond with a $1,000 face value and an 8 percent coupon at a price of less than $1,000—perhaps for only $900—your investment yield is higher than 8 percent. Your current investment yield is 8.9 percent on the $900 you invested to purchase the bond.

But current yield is not the only way you can make money on a bond. Let's suppose the price of your bond moves back up to $1,000 (because of market conditions described below). Then you have a $100 gain on the market price of your bond. The *total return* on your investment depends on a combination of your current yield plus any market gains (or losses). That's how to really measure the performance of your bond investment.

It's also important to understand the concept of *yield to maturity*. That is the actual return you will get if you hold the bond to its maturity date. It takes into account the coupon rate, the market price at which you purchase the bond, and the number of years left until maturity. If you purchase a bond sometime after its initial offering, you'll need to be aware that the yield to maturity will be different from the coupon yield by virtue of the fact that the bond has fewer years left until maturity and probably is not trading at its original offering price.

Finally, you should be aware of the *call provision* in any bond you purchase. You may think you're locking in a high interest rate for 30 years, but the issuer may have the right to *call*, or redeem, the bonds early, which often happens when interest rates drop. You receive the face value of the bond, but you are faced with the problem of reinvesting your money at lower rates. *Yield to call* is the calculation of your return if you assume the bond might be called in by the issuer at the earliest possible date.

Interest Concept #1: Rates and Risk

When lenders feel there is risk involved, they will demand a higher interest rate for the use of their money. There are many different types of risk. The most obvious risk is the credit quality of the borrower. A risky borrower, such as a new business, will have to pay a higher interest rate to borrow money than a company or state with a triple A credit rating.

Lenders also take into account the risks that can occur over time. Usually, you'll demand less interest if you're lending your money for only a few months. But if you're making a longer-term loan, you'll demand higher interest rates to compensate for all the unexpected things that could happen during the long run. For example, inflation could return during the period of your loan, making the money you eventually get back worth far less. The greater the uncertainty about the future, the greater the differential between short-term and long-term borrowing rates.

On rare occasions, short-term rates move higher than long-term interest rates. That usually happens when the Federal Reserve is tightening up on the availability of credit, and desperate borrowers are willing to pay very high rates for a few months just to keep their heads above water. Usually, though, long-term rates are higher because lending for the long term involves more risk.

You may hear the term *yield curve*. That's simply the graphic representation of the different interest rates being paid as maturities lengthen.

Interest Concept #2: Risk and Price

Bonds have traditionally had the reputation of being safe and even stodgy investments for widows and orphans. But the interest rate swings of recent years have taught a much different lesson. Investing in bonds carries a substantial price risk.

If you hold a long-term bond and interest rates move higher, the market value of your bond will decline. If you plan to hold the bond to maturity, you won't take a price loss; you'll simply receive lower than current market interest rates. But if you should want to sell that bond before maturity, you could be facing a loss.

Here's an example. You purchase a triple A-rated $1,000 bond that is scheduled to mature in 30 years and pays an 8 percent interest rate. A few years later you decide to sell your bond. If interest rates have moved higher in the meantime, perhaps to 9 percent, you will not receive $1,000 when you try to sell your bond. Because an investor could now receive 9 percent on a $1,000 bond investment, your old bond is worth only about $890 right now if you decide to sell it. (The lower price makes the 8 percent yield equivalent to the yield on a new 9 percent bond.)

The loss you'll take has nothing to do with the quality of the bond or its likelihood of continuing to pay interest. If you decide to hold the bond for 30 years, you'll receive your full $1,000 back at maturity. But in the meantime, current interest rates can have a dramatic effect on market price.

Here's the rule to remember:

Bond prices move in the opposite direction of interest rates.

This rule applies to *all* bonds—those issued by the U.S. government, bonds issued by corporations, and tax-free bonds issued by cities and states (municipal bonds). And the rule applies to "packages" of bonds such as closed-end bond funds, unit investment trusts, and pools of fixed-rate mortgages such as Ginnie Maes (more about all of these later). In all of these cases, when interest rates go *up*, market value goes *down*, and vice versa.

The longer the maturity of the bond, the greater the swing in price. Chart III-2 illustrates the relative price swings of short-, intermediate-, and long-term bonds if interest rates move either one percentage point higher or lower. As you can see, price fluctuations are relatively small with short-term bonds, but much larger with long-term bonds.

CHART III-2

How Changes in Interest Rates Affect Bond Prices
Assuming a $1,000 bond paying 8% interest

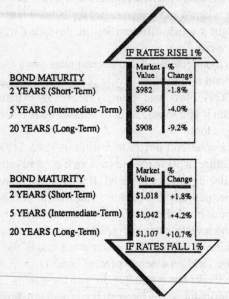

IF RATES RISE 1%		
BOND MATURITY	Market Value	% Change
2 YEARS (Short-Term)	$982	-1.8%
5 YEARS (Intermediate-Term)	$960	-4.0%
20 YEARS (Long-Term)	$908	-9.2%

BOND MATURITY	Market Value	% Change
2 YEARS (Short-Term)	$1,018	+1.8%
5 YEARS (Intermediate-Term)	$1,042	+4.2%
20 YEARS (Long-Term)	$1,107	+10.7%
IF RATES FALL 1%		

This example shows market value changes uninfluenced by any other fluctuations in market conditions.

SOURCE: Charles Schwab & Co., Inc.

Interest Concept #3: Benchmarks for Measuring Yields

How do you find out at any given time what current interest rates are for different risk categories of bonds? Well, just as the stock market has the Dow Jones Industrial Average and the Standard & Poor's 500 stock average as benchmarks, there are also lesser-known bond indices to give you a perspective on yields. You'll find each of these bond indexes listed every day in the *Wall Street Journal* "Market Diary" section, which is usually on page 1 of Section C in that section.

The *Lehman Brothers Long Treasury Bond Index* measures the daily performance of all outstanding U.S. Treasury bonds with remaining maturities of ten years or more. It's a market-weighted index, meaning that prices of larger bond issues affect the movement of the index more than issues with fewer bonds outstanding.

The newspaper listing for this index reflects *total return* (a combination of interest paid and price gains) and gives you comparisons from the value of the index one year ago. It also gives the yearly high and low and the current yield of this index. While the index itself is not something you're buying, it does give you a feel for the price movements of long-term Treasury bonds.

The *Dow Jones 20 Bond Average* is an arithmetical average of price and current yield for ten large industrial and ten private utility bonds. All of the bonds in the index are considered "investment grade," meaning they are rated at least Baa or higher by Moody's rating service and BBB or higher by Standard & Poor's. This index is useful for approximating current corporate yield changes, although it is less useful for measuring specific yields since it includes such a diverse group of bonds.

The *Salomon Brothers Mortgage-Backed Index* is a market-weighted index that includes all outstanding Ginnie Mae, Fannie Mae, and Freddie Mac bonds. These are bonds backed by mortgages which are guaranteed as to repayment of principal and interest by the U.S. government or a government agency. It's a useful benchmark for measuring how long-term mortgage-backed securities are performing in terms of price compared to other types of bonds.

The *Bond Buyer Municipal Bond Index* is a group of 40 bonds representing the long-term, tax-exempt municipal bond market. Like the other indexes, it's a benchmark giving a perspective on the price behavior of long-term tax-free bonds.

Chapter 23

Strategies to Increase Yields

If you're looking for higher yields, it's important to understand *all* the risks you might be taking.

Make this wise old saying your motto:

"I'm not so concerned about the return on my money as I am about the return of my money!"

With that philosophy in mind, the strategies outlined here are designed to earn a higher return with commensurate additional risk.

Higher-Yield Strategy #1: Build a Bond Ladder

Building a bond "ladder" is simply a strategy of investing your money in bonds scheduled to mature sequentially over the years. This strategy increases yield while limiting the risk of tying all your money up in longer-term bonds. If rates move even higher, you'll always have some bonds maturing in any given year so that you can reinvest the proceeds in higher-yielding instruments.

For example, if you have $50,000, you divide the money into five parts and purchase $10,000 of U.S. Treasury bonds maturing every two years—

with the longest maturity being ten years. Or you can purchase $5,000 of Treasury bonds maturing yearly over the next ten years.

Using Treasury bonds eliminates credit risk, and limiting your ladder to only ten years allows you to take advantage of the steepest part of the yield curve, since the greatest spread of interest rates is usually in the first ten years of maturities. When creating a bond ladder with corporate bonds, you should use only the highest-quality bonds to minimize risk of default.

If you use corporate bonds to create a ladder, you must also be aware that some higher-yielding bonds could be "called in" by the issuer before maturity. That means you receive full face value but do not continue to get the higher yields you had anticipated. After the bonds are called, you must reinvest the money at lower interest rates.

The strategy of creating a bond ladder only works if you stay on the ladder. That is, you must plan to hold each bond to maturity and then reinvest it at the then-current rates. That way you'll always be earning interest—and always be able to take advantage of the latest interest rates with a small portion of your funds.

You won't lock in the highest rates, but you'll escape the risk that rates will move higher if you invest all your money at current rates. The real drawback occurs if rates continue to move downward and you have to reinvest each year at lower rates. Still, your average return would be higher than if you'd invested it all at the current low rates.

Higher-Yield Strategy #2: Bond Funds

Bond mutual funds work just like stock market mutual funds: Your investment dollars are pooled with those of other investors to purchase bonds selected by a professional money manager. The manager watches the markets closely, buying and selling appropriate bonds for the fund. In addition to the advantage of professional management, diversification over many different bonds should reduce risk.

Just as with stock market mutual funds, there are load bond funds sold by brokers and planners, on which you may pay from 2 to 8 percent commission. Or, if you're willing to do your own homework, you can purchase no-load bond funds from the same companies that manage stock market funds. (See Appendix A.)

Fund Prices and Yields

Every day at the close of business, the price of your shares in the fund is determined by the market value of all the fund investments divided by the number of shares outstanding. You can check the share price in most daily newspapers or by calling the fund. In the same manner, you can also check the current yield of the fund.

The *yield* on these bond mutual funds will change as the general direction of interest rates changes. As new money is invested in the fund, the manager must purchase new bonds. That changes the current yield of the fund. The *total return* of the fund includes the current yield plus any increases in the value of your fund shares. Unlike money market funds, which have a stable net asset value per share, longer-term bond funds have fluctuating share prices, which tend to move in the opposite direction of interest rates.

Fund Profits

You can make money in a bond fund in one of two ways. First, the interest earned on the bonds owned by the fund is passed along to shareholders to be reinvested, or spent. Most bond funds declare interest dividends every month; some pay interest dividends twice a year. If the portfolio manager has sold bonds during the year, any profits are distributed at year-end as a capital gains distribution.

Or you may make money by selling your shares in the fund at a profit. If you purchase your shares when interest rates are high and decide to sell when interest rates have dropped, the price of each share will be higher. That profit may be taxed as a short- or long-term capital gain, depending on how long you have held your shares.

Government Bond Funds

These bond funds invest only in U.S. government securities, or "full faith and credit" obligations of the U.S. government, which could include IOUs of government agencies.

Longer-term no-load government bonds funds include:

Fidelity Government Securities Fund (800-544-8888)

Dreyfus 100% U.S. Treasury Long-Term (800-648-9048)

Twentieth Century U.S. Government Fund (800-345-2121)

Value Line U.S. Government Securities Fund (800-223-0818)

Vanguard Long-Term U.S. Treasury (800-662-7447)

Some funds purchase shorter-term (but not money market) U.S. government securities, with correspondingly lower yields. They include:

Benham Treasury Note Fund (800-472-3389)

United Services Intermediate Treasury Fund (800-873-8637)

Vanguard Short-Term Federal Bond Portfolio (800-662-7447)

Corporate Bond Funds

When choosing a corporate bond mutual fund, read the prospectus carefully. There you'll find out the goals of the fund and how much risk the fund managers are willing to take to achieve those goals. If the main goal is highest yields, be sure to note the quality rating of the bonds in which the fund is allowed to invest. The highest yields will come from the lowest-quality bonds—junk bonds. Professional management and diversification may lower the risk of junk bonds, and in some years these funds have turned in an outstanding performance, but they are no substitute for the secure income to be earned by higher-quality bonds.

International Bond Funds

Sometimes it pays to invest in the bonds of foreign countries and companies. Because of different economic conditions, bonds or even short-term IOUs denominated in a foreign currency may have higher yields than domestic debt securities. Many of those foreign bonds carry a guarantee from the government of that country.

While higher yields abroad can be tempting, you should also be aware of an important risk inherent in any foreign investment: changing currency values. For instance, if you can earn 9.5 percent on British bonds at a time when U.S. bonds are paying only 8 percent, the overseas yield will be tempting. But if the British currency falls only about 3 percent against the dollar, the yield advantage will be wiped out.

In chapter 25, you'll learn how to invest in international funds.

Higher-Yield Strategy #3: Ginnie Mae Funds and CMOs

Ginnie Mae funds and other mortgage-backed securities such as collateralized mortgage obligations (CMOs) are basically ways for an investor to receive the higher yields that people pay on their home mortgages. Ginnie Maes are packages of mortgages that are themselves insured as to principal and interest payments by an agency of the federal government. (The fund units themselves are not insured, only the mortgages within the units.) CMOs are "pieces" of packages of mortgages, and they may carry a correspondingly higher risk.

With mortgage-backed securities, your monthly income check often includes a portion that is repayment of principal—a return of your original investment. Be sure that you know how much of your return is interest and which portion is principal. Interest income from these funds is taxable.

Like all bonds, the price of these mortgage securities moves in the opposite direction of interest rates. Mortgage-backed securities do have the advantage of paying slightly higher interest rates than on comparable maturity government bonds. But they also have some disadvantages: When interest rates fall, people tend to refinance their old, high-rate mortgages. Then the principal is repaid early to owners of the mortgage securities. Instead of locking in higher yields, investors are left to reinvest at lower rates.

Terry's Tips:

$$$ When you buy mortgage-backed securities from a broker, you are, of course, paying a commission. Listed below are several no-load Ginnie Mae mutual funds that allow you to invest in the same securities at a lower cost and with managers who reinvest fund earnings and mortgage prepayments. You can elect to reinvest your dividends or have them paid to you monthly.

Benham GNMA Income (800-472-3389)

Dreyfus GNMA (800-645-6561)

Fidelity Ginnie Mae (800-544-8888)

Franklin U.S. Government (800-342-5236)

Scudder GNMA (800-225-2470)

T. Rowe Price GNMA (800-638-5660)

Vanguard Fixed-Income GNMA (800-662-7447)

$$$ When buying a CMO, ask the broker about the projected impact of rising or falling interest rates on this particular piece, or *tranche*, of mortgage security. Usually the most volatile tranches are sold to individual investors, with institutions buying the more stable parts of the package.

Higher-Yield Strategy #4: Adjustable-Rate Mortgage Funds

Adjustable-rate mortgage funds work very much like longer-term Ginnie Mae funds, but with much less price risk, albeit slightly lower yields. That makes ARMs a good investment for those who want to earn more than the rates offered in money market mutual funds without taking on substantial principal risk. They are an alternative for "chicken money" investors when rates are dropping.

The reason there is less price fluctuation in ARM funds, even when interest rates change, is because the rates on the mortgages the fund owns are changed ("adjusted") every one to three years, depending on the general level of interest rates. Since the lender is taking less risk because the rates adjust frequently, there are far smaller swings in price.

An ARM fund is not the same as a money market mutual fund because share prices of the ARM fund can move up and down within a narrow range. But if you're willing to hold on to your ARM fund for a year or two, to smooth out those fluctuations, you may be rewarded with yields as much as 250 basis points (2.5 percent) higher than those in money market funds.

Terry's Tips:

$$$ Stick with ARM funds that buy only government-insured adjustable-rate mortgages. The yields will be slightly lower because the government insurance eliminates the risk of a homeowner defaulting on a mortgage that is owned by the fund.

$$$ Once again, you can save substantially on commissions by purchasing one of the three no-load, adjustable-rate mortgage funds. They are:

Benham Adjustable Rate Government Securities Fund (800-472-3389)

T. Rowe Price Adjustable Rate U.S. Government Fund (800-638-5660)

Value Line Adjustable Rate U.S. Government Securities Fund (800-223-0818)

Higher-Yield Strategy #5: U.S. Savings Bonds

Don't overlook Series EE U.S. savings bonds as a higher-yielding strategy. When bank CDs are yielding far less than 4 percent, savings bonds, with their minimum guarantee of 4 percent interest if held for five years, become a very attractive investment. Of course, if the general level of interest rates rises, savings bonds holders are protected on the upside. Although rates on savings bonds cannot drop *below* 4 percent if held for the full five years, rates do adjust upward every six months in line with U.S. Treasury securities. (See chapter 14 for a complete explanation of U.S. savings bonds.) Note: Saving bonds purchased after May 1, 1995 do not have this minimum 4 percent rate guarantee if held for less than 17 years.

Higher-Yield Strategy #6: Zero Coupon Bonds

Don't let the name scare you away from an interesting investment. Zero coupon bonds work much like U.S. savings bonds. You purchase them at a discount from their face value, and the interest you earn each year increases the value of the bond. At maturity, the bond is worth its full face value.

Unlike savings bonds, with zero coupon bonds you are required to pay income tax on the interest income every year, even though you don't receive a check. That's why zero coupon bonds should be purchased in tax-sheltered accounts such as IRAs or Keogh plans. Then you don't have to worry about taxes. Or you can purchase zero coupon municipal bonds that pay tax-free interest.

Zero coupon bonds do carry a fixed rate of interest, just like regular coupon bonds. The rate is fixed at the time you purchase the bond, and the rate determines the dollar amount of interest that will accrue to the value of your bond every six months.

Because zero coupon bonds do have a fixed interest rate, the market value of the bond is affected by changes in the general level of interest rates. The value of the bond may be increasing because of the interest buildup, but falling because the general trend of interest rates moves higher. Of course, if you purchase zero coupon bonds when rates are declining, your bond will increase in market value.

The longer the maturity of the bond, the lower the price you will pay to purchase it, because there is more time for the interest to build up to face value. However, longer-term zero coupon bonds are also subject to wider swings in price when interest rates change direction.

Zero coupon bonds do not give you a higher yield than standard bonds of the same quality and maturity; in fact, the yield may be slightly lower because you do not have to worry about reinvesting your interest checks at potentially lower rates over the years. Your interest is always building up at the promised rate, making zero coupon bonds advantageous for those who do not need to receive regular interest payments to cover living expenses.

Terry's Tips:

$$$ Many types of zero coupon bonds can be purchased through brokerage firms. They offer zero coupon bonds issued by the federal government and some corporations. However, this is a relatively illiquid marketplace, and you may pay a premium price to purchase a small lot of zero coupon bonds or have a difficult time getting a good price when you sell.

Instead, consider buying zero coupon bond mutual funds: Benham Capital Management (800-472-3389) offers a series of Target Maturity Funds. Each is a no-load mutual fund containing U.S. government zero coupon bonds that will mature in a particular year: 1995, 2000, 2005, 2010, 2015, or 2020.

As with other no-load mutual funds, you can sell your shares any day, requesting that the check be sent to you or that the proceeds be transferred into another Benham fund, such as the Capital Preservation money market fund, which buys only U.S. government Treasury securities. Or you can decide to hold your shares in the zero fund to maturity, at which time you'll receive the full face value.

$$$ Many state governments offer college tuition savings programs using zero coupon tax-free bonds. See chapter 37 for more information on these programs.

Higher-Yield Strategy #7: Convertible Bonds

The easiest way to describe convertible bonds is to say that they are part stock and part bond. Convertible bonds carry a fixed rate of interest that makes them attractive to investors looking for higher yields, but the feature that makes them particularly attractive is the holder's right to convert the bond into a fixed number of shares of common stock at a preset price.

Convertible bonds, like all bonds, share the ups and downs of market price based on changing levels of interest rates. But if the underlying stock moves higher, the price of the bond will also increase because of the conversion feature. If the stock price falls below the fixed conversion level, the bond will still be attractive because it pays a regular amount of interest. In fact, you'll find that convertible bonds frequently trade at a premium to the conversion price because of the interest they pay.

Convertibles are attractive to the companies that sell them because they are a less expensive way for the company to raise money. With the stock "kicker" the company can pay a lower interest rate than it would on standard bonds.

Terry's Tips:

$$$ Companies often call in their convertible bonds to refinance and take advantage of lower rates or better terms. Be sure to purchase a convertible bond that offers "call protection" for at least three years.

$$$ If you want to read more about convertibles, there are several newsletters that specialize in these issues:

Value Line Convertible Strategist (ed. Allan S. Lyons) (212-687-3965; 48 issues/yr, $475)

RHM Convertible Survey (ed. Mark Fried) (516-759-2904; weekly, $350/yr)

\$\$\$ If instead of picking individual convertible bonds you decide to invest in a convertible bond fund, you'll be faced with a wide variety of choices that are not always easy to compare. Some convertible bond mutual funds specialize in bonds of top-grade companies; others invest in convertibles of lower-rated issuers. Some funds also use strategies involving futures and options, which may increase yield but do not necessarily minimize risk.

When comparing convertible bond funds, it's important to read the prospectus and to compare total return for the previous years. In the first nine months of 1992, convertible bond funds returned an average of 16.3 percent—more than six percentage points ahead of the average stock fund for the first nine months of 1992.

Some no-load convertible bond funds:

Dreyfus Convertible Securities (800-645-6561)

Fidelity Convertible Securities Fund (800-544-8888)

Value Line Convertible Fund (800-223-0818)

Vanguard Convertible Securities (800-662-7447)

Higher-Yield Strategy #8: Convertible Zeros—LYONs

What do you get when you combine a convertible bond with a zero coupon bond? A LYON, or Liquid Yield Option Note. The corporate finance departments at Merrill Lynch and First Boston claim credit for creating this hybrid form of investment.

Like all zero coupon bonds, these are sold at a substantial discount from face value—based on the time until maturity and the inherent interest rate. When you purchase a convertible zero, you get the advantages of a fixed interest rate but the disadvantages of paying taxes on interest you don't actually receive. As with other zero coupon bonds, these are better purchased in tax-sheltered accounts so you don't have to pay taxes on interest checks you won't receive until later.

With convertible zeros you get the advantage of being able to convert into stock, which adds value to the investment. You also have the option to put the bond back to the company in return for the original offering price plus accrued interest. This put option can be exercised by the bondowner at one or more specific future dates.

Companies like to issue zero coupon bonds because even though they do not pay out the interest, the company can deduct the amount as if the interest had been paid.

Terry's Tip:

$$$ The market for convertible zeros can be very thinly traded, so bonds may be expensive to purchase and difficult to sell. Use limit orders and proceed with caution.

Higher-Yield Strategy #9: Preferred Stocks and Utilities

Many companies pay high dividends to shareholders instead of plowing their earnings back into growing the business. Some companies even create classes of *preferred stock* that carry a higher dividend than common stock. Dividends on preferred shares must be paid in full before any dividends are paid on common stocks.

Preferred stocks may not offer as much potential for gains, but they do have a basic price stability as a result of their higher yields. For more potential appreciation, you'd choose a *convertible preferred stock*, which can be switched into common stock at a specific price level.

Utility stocks—both common and preferred shares—are often used to increase investment yield. Utility earnings are regulated by the states in which they do business. But generally speaking, state regulators allow the companies to set rates that cover the cost of operations, a reasonable profit, and a fixed dividend to be paid to shareholders. Regulators usually recognize that a utility company cannot raise capital for new generating capacity and repairs unless it can guarantee a good return to its investors.

When the general trend of interest rates is down, many investors seek out high-yielding utility stocks to increase their returns. That demand causes prices of those stocks to move higher, reducing the relative yield. Rising interest rates on other investments can cause the price of utility stocks to drop. But the biggest worry with utility companies is the willingness of state regulators to allow the companies to increase the rates they charge their customers, as well as increasing competition because of deregulation.

For more information on buying utility stocks, contact:

Utility Forecaster (800-832-2330; monthly, $87/yr)

Argus Research Utility Spotlight and Rankings (212-425-7500; monthly, $225/yr)

Some no-load funds that specialize in utilities and/or preferred stocks:

Fidelity Utilities Income Fund (800-544-8888)

Financial Strategic Utilities (800-625-8085)

Lindner Dividend Fund (314-727-5305)

(See also the category of equity/income funds in the Morningstar directory, Mutual Fund Advice Strategy #1 in chapter 18.)

Higher-Yield Strategy #10: Closed-End Bond Funds

Another way to invest in bonds to lock in higher yields is to purchase closed-end bond funds. When these funds are created, they offer shares to investors at a fixed price to raise a specific amount of money—perhaps $30 million or more. The money raised is invested in bonds, and a portfolio manager is responsible for buying and selling bonds within the fund to earn profits and interest.

Once the fund is launched, no additional money is accepted for investment into the fund. The only way the fund can grow is to make profits on its investments. Investors who want to purchase shares in the fund must buy them from existing investors. Usually these closed-end bond funds are listed on a major stock exchange. (See chapter 15 for a complete explanation of closed-end funds and the terms used below.)

The trading price of the shares is determined by two factors: the value of the investments in the fund and the demand for the shares. That means the price of the fund shares does not necessarily reflect the exact value of the underlying assets. Sometimes the shares may trade at a premium to the per-share value of the investments in the fund, and sometimes the shares may trade at a discount. If the fund owns a lot of high-yielding bonds at a time when investors are hungry for yield, the demand may push shares to a premium over their true (net asset) value.

When you buy a closed-end fund that is selling at a discount to net asset value per share, you can win in several ways if the fund becomes more attractive because of its investment performance:

- The shares will rise in price.
- The discount will narrow.
- Your true yield is increased.

However, if you buy a closed-end fund that is selling at a premium to net asset value, you have three ways to lose money if the process is reversed.

Higher-Yield Strategy #11: Strategic Income Funds

In recent years a new category of mutual funds has emerged with the objective of increasing income by diversifying investments. Strategic income funds invest in U.S. government debt securities, foreign bonds, and high-yield bonds of lower quality. Those three markets rarely move in tandem. A strengthening dollar may help Treasuries, but hurt foreign bonds. An improving economy may boost prices of high-yield bonds as issuers are viewed as more likely to be able to maintain interest payments, while Treasury bonds might fall in price in the same scenario.

Diversification of asset quality is a prime characteristic of a strategic income fund. It's the portfolio manager's job to balance the mix of assets to minimize risk and improve returns. Of necessity, however, investing in a strategic income fund involves more risk than investments in a money market fund.

Some strategic income funds:

Blanchard Flexible Income Fund (800-458-8621) (no-load)

Colonial Strategic Income Fund (800-248-2828) (load)

John Hancock Strategic Income Fund (800-225-5291) (load)

Putnam Diversified Income (800-225-1581) (load)

Terry's Tip:

$$$ To minimize risk in a strategic income fund, choose one whose overall portfolio is rated *investment grade*. To find this information, look in the prospectus or ask the fund representative.

Chapter 24

Tax-free Investment Strategies

It makes sense to shelter your investment earnings from ordinary income taxes, particularly if you are in a high tax bracket. As you can see from chart II-7 on p. 72, money grows and compounds more dramatically if you do not have to deduct a portion of your earnings to pay federal and state income taxes.

But it's important to understand the two different (legal) ways in which you can obtain tax-free income. One strategy involves *deferring* taxes until some time in the future. The other strategy involves purchasing investments that are legally free from income taxes on the interest you earn.

Tax deferral must be done within *qualified* plans that allow you to buy investments that generate interest which would ordinarily be taxable—corporate bonds, federal government bonds, preferred stocks, for example—and then to place those investments in tax-sheltered accounts such as Individual Retirement Accounts, Keogh plans, and annuities. The interest or profits earned on the investments within such a plan are not taxed until you take the money out, usually at retirement. Eventually you'll have to pay taxes, and that's why this type of plan offers what is called tax *deferral*. (We'll explain more about those plans in chapter 44.)

The second way to shelter income from taxes is to buy investments that pay interest on which you are *never* required to pay income taxes. The interest-bearing IOUs of cities, states, and some local taxing districts are collectively called *municipal bonds*. By law, the interest they pay is free from federal income taxes, and may also be free from state income taxes if you buy municipal bonds issued by the state in which you live. For example, a New York City bond owned by a New York City resident is exempt from city, state, and federal taxes—triple tax-exempt.

Buying municipal bonds is not an automatic bargain, though. Since the bonds are free from federal income tax, they pay a commensurately lower rate of interest. That allows cities and states to raise money at a lower cost in order to fund necessary projects. The marketplace is very efficient, and the lower interest rates on tax-free bonds generally reflect the after-tax return you could earn on taxable bonds if you're in a high tax bracket.

It does not pay to invest in tax-free bonds unless the lower rate of interest you earn on them is better than the after-tax return on a taxable bond.

For example, if a 30-year, tax-free, AAA-rated, insured municipal bond is paying 6.25 percent interest, and a 30-year U.S. government Treasury bond is paying 7.35 percent interest, which is the better investment?

If you're in the 31 percent tax bracket, the after-tax yield of the government bond is 5.07 percent—far less than the yield on the municipal bond. So it makes sense to buy the tax-free bond. If you're in the 15 percent tax bracket, the after-tax yield on the government bond is 6.24 percent. The real advantage of municipal bonds becomes apparent if tax rates rise to 40 percent. Then the 6.25 percent tax-free bond yield is equivalent to a 10.42 percent yield on a taxable bond.

When it is expected that tax rates will rise, demand for municipal bonds pushes their yields lower in relation to taxable bonds. So you need to do the math every time you're deciding between a taxable and a tax-free issue. If you're in the 15 percent tax bracket, it usually will not be advantageous to purchase tax-free municipal bonds.

Don't purchase municipal bonds just because you can avoid paying taxes on the income.

Instead, ask your broker or accountant to figure out whether you'll come out ahead or behind when you compare the yield to similar quality and maturity taxable bonds. The following graphic (chart III-3) will give you

CHART III-3

In These Tax Brackets	A Federal Tax-Free Yield of:							
	3.5%	4.0%	4.5%	5.0%	5.5%	6.0%	6.5%	7.0%
	Is Equivalent to a Taxable Yield of:							
15%	4.12%	4.71%	5.29%	5.88%	6.47%	7.06%	7.65%	8.24%
28%	4.86%	5.56%	6.25%	6.94%	7.64%	8.33%	9.03%	9.72%
31%	5.07%	5.80%	6.52%	7.25%	7.97%	8.70%	9.42%	10.14%
36%	5.47%	6.25%	7.03%	7.81%	8.59%	9.38%	10.16%	10.94%
39.6%	5.79%	6.62%	7.45%	8.28%	9.11%	9.93%	10.76%	11.59%

an idea of the relative yield you'd need to earn in a taxable bond to earn as much as in a tax-free bond or bond fund. The rates quoted are for federal income tax rates. If you live in a state that has high income taxes, you might do even better if you purchase double tax-exempt bonds.

Terry's Tip:

$$$ Remember that while the interest you earn on tax-free bonds is not subject to federal income taxes, any gains on the sale of these bonds is indeed taxable, and losses may be used to offset other gains or to offset a portion of your ordinary income, depending on tax laws.

Tax-Free Income Strategy #1: Municipal Bonds

If you've decided to buy municipal bonds issued by a particular city or state, you'll have to do your homework. Among the questions you'll want to ask before purchasing a bond:

What is the *rating* of the bond? As with all bonds, municipals are rated for quality by several independent rating services, the largest of which are Moody's and Standard & Poor's. The highest rating is AAA.

Is the bond a *general obligation* of the issuer, or is payment of interest dependent on *revenue* from a particular public works project? Revenue bonds are considered slightly more risky than those bonds which are backed by the full credit of the issuer. Remember, even general obligation bonds are backed only by the ability of the state or local authority to collect or increase tax revenues.

Is the bond *insured*? Some municipal bonds are insured by third-party guarantors as to timely payment of principal and interest. An insured municipal will pay a slightly lower yield. Questions have also been raised about the ability of some bond insurers to make good on their commitments.

Is the bond protected from being *called*? In the early 1980s, many investors thought they had locked in high, tax-free yields for 30 years, but they forgot to examine the *call provision* of the bonds they purchased. When interest rates dropped, many bond issuers decided to call in their old, high-rate bonds and refinance them with lower-cost debt. The bond-holders received full face value for their bonds, but they also faced the dilemma of reinvesting at a time when yields had dropped.

Terry's Tips:

$$$ It's hard to know if you're truly getting the best price when buying individual municipal bonds because these bonds are not listed on any exchange. Instead, they are traded among bond dealers. That means you must place a lot of faith in your broker, check prices for the same bonds through several brokers, or else buy bonds only on their initial public offering, and not in the secondary trading market.

$$$ There is no fixed commission when buying bonds; in fact, you may never see a commission marked separately on your purchase or sale confirmation. When brokers hold bonds in their inventory, they include a mark-up in your actual purchase price of the bond.

Tax-Free Income Strategy #2: Municipal Bond Mutual Funds

If you want to avoid the work of buying individual issues of municipal bonds, you can easily purchase a municipal bond mutual fund. As with all mutual funds, you'll get professional management and diversification. Your interest income can be automatically reinvested in the fund or sent to you on a monthly basis.

There are both load and no-load municipal bond funds. Some examples of no-load tax-free bond funds include:

AARP Insured Tax-Free General Bond Fund (800-253-2277)

Dreyfus Insured Municipal Bond Fund (800-645-6561)
   (also Dreyfus Intermediate Municipal Bond Fund and Dreyfus Tax-Exempt Bond Fund)

Fidelity Insured Tax Free (800-544-8888)

T. Rowe Price Tax-Free Income (800-638-5660)

Scudder Managed Municipal Bonds (800-225-2470)

For more aggressive investors seeking higher tax-free income, the following funds invest in lower-quality bonds:

Fidelity Aggressive Tax-Free Bond Fund

Fidelity High Yield Tax-Free Portfolio

T. Rowe Price Tax-Free High-Yield Fund

Stein Roe High-Yield Municipals (800-338-2550)

While municipal bond interest is free from federal income taxes, there are also a variety of state-specific municipal bond funds that are attractive to residents of those states who are seeking exemption from high state as well as federal taxes. The *Morningstar Mutual Fund Survey* (800-876-5005) lists a number of these funds, especially useful for residents of high-tax states such as New York and California. Some funds are triple-tax-exempt, by virtue of only holding bonds issued by one high-tax city such as New York City.

Terry's Tips:

$$$ Read the prospectus of any municipal bond fund very carefully to understand the quality of bonds the fund buys and the risks you are taking.

$$$ Don't forget that although the interest income you earn is tax-free, any gain on the sale of shares in the municipal bond fund is a taxable event.

As with all bonds, fund shares increase in value as the general level of interest rates declines.

$$$ Bonds issued by Puerto Rico, Guam, and the Virgin Islands are tax-free in all states, but their bonds have low credit ratings.

Tax-Free Income Strategy #3: Closed-End Municipal Bond Funds

As explained previously in the section on closed-end taxable bond funds (see chapter 23), closed-end funds have a money manager whose job it is to buy and sell bonds for the fund. Shareholders who want to invest in the fund after the initial offering must purchase shares from current holders, because these funds do not accept additional investments once they are formed.

Closed-end municipal bond funds will trade at a discount or premium to the net asset value of the investments, depending on the demand for their shares. Shares of some of these funds are traded on major stock exchanges. Tax-free interest is paid out to shareholders on a monthly basis, and that interest may be automatically reinvested in the fund. At year-end, there is a capital gains distribution of any profits made from buying and selling bonds within the fund.

When closed-end funds are originally offered, the first investors pay a sales load of from 6 to 8 percent as part of the purchase price. Subsequent buyers pay the daily trading price on the exchange, plus a brokerage commission.

Some examples of closed-end municipal bond funds include:

Allstate Municipal Income Trust (NYSE)

Colonial Investment Grade Municipal Trust (NYSE)

Dreyfus Municipal Income (American Stock Exchange)

Dreyfus Strategic Municipals (NYSE)

Each fund may have a different investment strategy, and concentrate on bonds with different risk profiles, so it's important to read and understand the portfolio orientation. For the most complete information, check the *Morningstar Closed-End Fund Survey*, which is available in your public library or by subscription (800-876-5005).

Terry's Tips:

$$$ It may be wise to purchase a closed-end municipal fund *after* the initial offering, when shares may be trading at a discount. Those who purchase shares of most closed-end funds on the original offering will find that only about 93 cents of every dollar spent to buy the shares is invested in bonds. The rest goes to the brokerage firm that sold the shares.

$$$ Recently some closed-end funds have been offered on a no-load basis. Instead, the funds charge a larger annual management fee—as much as 1.5 percent (which is about twice what you'd pay on an open-end municipal bond fund). A portion of that annual expense is used to reimburse commissions paid to the brokers who sell the shares on the initial offerings. However, unlike standard closed-end funds that charge an initial load, the entire proceeds of the initial offering of the fund are invested in tax-free bonds. In this case, those who buy after the initial offering may pay heavier annual expenses than with a standard closed-end municipal bond fund.

Some examples of these closed-end, no-load, tax-free bond funds listed on the New York Stock Exchange:

Van Kampen Merritt Municipal Trust

Shearson Lehman Managed Municipals Fund

Smith Barney Intermediate Municipal Fund

Tax-Free Income Strategy #4: Unit Investment Trusts

Unit investment trusts are fixed packages of municipal bonds. Of the nearly $1 trillion outstanding in municipal bonds, it's estimated that about $100 billion has been placed in unit investment trusts, which allow investors to purchase a diverse portfolio of municipal bonds.

Unlike closed-end funds, unit investment trusts have no manager deciding when to buy and sell the bonds held within the fund. The bonds that are purchased when the unit trust is formed remain in the unit until they mature or are called in. All income from the unit investment trust is paid out to shareholders, including any early principal repayments.

Unit investment trusts are generally packaged and sold by securities dealers in units of $1,000. The purchase price will include a sales charge. The units can subsequently be traded freely in the marketplace, where prices depend on the yield of the fund and the current trend of interest rates.

The most well-known unit investment trusts are offered through brokers and sponsored by:

John Nuveen & Co (800-621-7227)

Van Kampen Merritt (800-341-2911)

If you contact these fund sponsors, they will put you in touch with a brokerage firm that sells their unit investment trusts.

Terry's Tip:

$$$ When buying a unit investment trust in the marketplace, and not on the original public offering, check carefully to see that all of the original bonds making up each original $1,000 unit remain in the trust. After a trust has been public for a while, it is possible that some of the bonds in it may have been called or redeemed, and the principal paid back to shareholders. You don't want to purchase a unit that will not repay its original $1,000 at maturity unless you are aware of the situation and pay an appropriately lower price for that unit.

Tax-Free Income Strategy #5: Short-Term, Tax-Free Income

If you think interest rates are going to rise, you'll want to avoid all investments in longer-term bonds or bond funds. But you may still seek short-term, tax-free income. In that case, you'll want to buy municipal bonds with a very short remaining lifetime until maturity, or something called tax anticipation notes that are often issued by municipalities to raise money until annual taxes are collected. These investments can be purchased through a broker specializing in municipal issues.

You can simplify the process by purchasing an intermediate-term municipal bond fund, or a tax-free money market fund. In these funds, the portfolio managers make the selections of short-term, tax-free issues, and you pay a small management fee. Just as with other mutual funds, you have access to your money at any time.

Most of the mutual fund companies listed above as having long-term municipal bond funds also offer short-term, tax-free money market funds.

If you are worried about investing in longer-term municipal bonds, but want slightly higher yields than tax-free money market funds offer, consider intermediate-term tax-free bond funds.

Some examples of medium-term tax-free funds:

T. Rowe Price Tax-Free Short-Intermediate Fund (800-638-5660)

Scudder Medium Term Tax-Free (800-225-2470)

SteinRoe Intermediate Municipals (800-338-2550)

United Services Near Term Tax Free Fund (800-873-8637)

Chapter 25

International Investing

In the 1990s, our daily lives give proof that we work and invest in a giant global economy. Many of the products we buy are imported; many of our jobs are in industries that export products to the rest of the world. You might be surprised at how many of America's top companies derive a substantial part of their profits from investments and sales in other parts of the world. For example, Coca-Cola derives as much as 79 percent of its operating income from abroad.

Economies of countries around the world may be in different stages: A strong economy in the United States may coincide with a recession in Europe or Asia. There is no fixed relationship between economies because each country has its own domestic policies regarding interest rates, taxes, and money growth. International trade is financed by each country's currency, and those currencies do not always bear the same relationship in value to each other. Depending on domestic interest rates and inflation, the currency of a country may become "stronger" or "weaker," affecting its purchasing power in the international arena (see chart III-4).

Just as economies and currencies may be in different stages, the stock markets that represent the business economies of countries around the world may also be in different stages. A bull market may be surging in one part of the world while stock markets in other countries are declining.

In a world so interdependent it would be a mistake to ignore the

Chart III-4
Dollar Exchange Rates in the Futures Market

Dollar Price of the Deutschemark

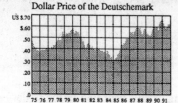

Dollar Price of the Japanese Yen

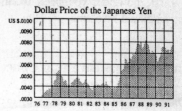

Dollar Price of the British Pound

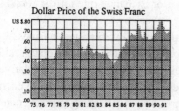

Dollar Price of the Canadian Dollar

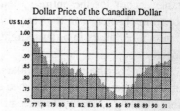

Dollar Price of the Swiss Franc

Dollar Price of the Australian Dollar

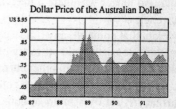

These graphs plot the currencies' dollar exchange rate in the futures market.
They all reflect "American terms" (dollars per unit of currency). Prices are
month-end settle of front-month contracts.

SOURCE: International Monetary Market/Chicago Mercantile Exchange.

opportunities to invest abroad—especially since mutual funds and other techniques make international investment strategies so much easier.

First, however, you need to understand some basic concepts about international investing.

International Investing Concept #1: Currency Risk

Once upon a time, all currency exchange rates were tied to the dollar—and the dollar was tied to gold. As long as foreign central banks could exchange dollars for gold, the system worked fairly well. Gold created a stable anchor for the entire system of exchange rates. But as we mentioned in chapter 4, in the early 1970s the United States started creating many more dollars in order to fight the Vietnam War and build the Great Society.

Foreigners who received dollars as the United States started purchasing their products grew concerned about the real value of the dollars they were holding. Finally, French premier Charles de Gaulle decided to exchange the French central bank's holdings of dollars and demanded payment in gold. That occurred in 1971. President Nixon promptly closed the "gold window." No longer would dollars be redeemable in gold. No longer was there a fixed anchor or exchange rate for the world's currencies.

From that point on, any time a central bank or international business—or even a tourist—held currency of a foreign country, the conversion rate back into dollars or into other currencies would be determined by relative economic conditions in the two countries. The relative daily value of each currency is set by a multi-billion-dollar worldwide trading market, conducted primarily by large international banks.

That's the concept of *currency risk*. If you're a business that is selling products in Germany, you worry that all your profits might be lost when you convert the German Deutschemarks back into dollars. If you're an American tourist in Germany, you quickly learn that the number of German marks you get for $100 may be different tomorrow than it is today. And even if you do not travel or do business in other countries, you may look around and see that the price of imported products you purchase—everything from German or Japanese cars to French wine—may increase or decrease because of currency fluctuations.

International Investing Concept #2: A "Strong" or "Weak" Currency

When you start learning about international investments, you'll quickly hear the terms *strong dollar* and *weak dollar*. Or you may hear that the Japanese yen is rising or falling. Just like other freely traded markets, the value of a currency can rise or fall (see chart III-5).

When the dollar is strong, it will buy more of other currencies. For example, one dollar may buy 140 Japanese yen. If the dollar is weakening, it will buy fewer Japanese yen—perhaps 120 yen.

Now look at it from the opposite point of view. If the dollar is strong, it means that a Japanese investor who wants to buy a business or a piece of real estate in the United States must scrape together 140 of his Japanese yen to purchase $1 of U.S. real estate. If the dollar weakens to 120 yen (which means the Japanese yen is getting stronger), the Japanese investor needs to use only 120 yen to purchase $1 of U.S. real estate.

What makes a currency strong or weak? Domestic economic policies affect the relationship between currencies. If a country has higher interest rates, its currency generally will be stronger because foreigners will want to switch into that currency to deposit money there and earn the higher rates.

Sometimes a country has high interest rates because it has a domestic inflation problem. Then its currency might weaken in spite of high interest rates. Foreign investors don't want to be caught in a currency that is quickly losing value—and that's the definition of inflation.

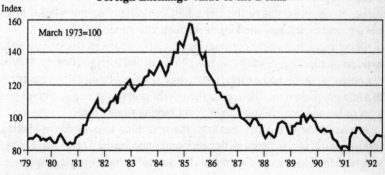

CHART III-5
Foreign Exchange Value of the Dollar

Index

March 1973=100

160 — 140 — 120 — 100 — 80

'79 '80 '81 '82 '83 '84 '85 '86 '87 '88 '89 '90 '91 '92

SOURCE: Federal Reserve.

If a country has low inflation, reasonable interest rates, relatively good economic growth, and a stable political condition, its currency will be viewed as strong. If a country is troubled with inflation, or a recession, or political instability, investors will avoid switching into that currency, and the currency will be considered weak.

International Investing Concept #3: Currencies and Trade

When a country has a strong currency, the products it imports are relatively less expensive. When the dollar is strong, it buys more of another country's currency—and that makes it less costly to purchase that country's products. So, for example, a strong dollar encourages imports into this country.

At the same time, when the dollar is strong it makes U.S. exports more costly to foreigners. They have to scrape together more of their currency to buy $1 of our merchandise. So when the dollar is strong, exports fall and imports into the United States rise. When the dollar is weak, foreigners easily buy more of our products. Our exports increase—but our imports become more expensive.

International Investing Concept #4: Currencies and Stocks

The same principle applies to investments. A strong dollar will buy more shares of stock in another country. In fact, when the dollar is strong, foreign stocks might look quite attractive. Similarly, when the dollar is weak, foreigners come to the United States and buy up our stocks, businesses, and farmland—making investments in America.

Of course, when you're considering purchasing foreign stocks, you want to do so on the basis of the business outlook in that foreign country. Maybe the dollar is strong and a foreign currency is weak because that country is in a terrible recession. Then, even though the dollar is strong and gives you a lot of buying power, you might avoid buying stocks there.

Just as in the U.S. stock markets, the first thing to consider in making foreign stock investments is the economic and business outlook for the shares of that company. That means doing research—or paying someone, such as a mutual fund, to do the research for you.

If you do decide to buy foreign stocks, and if you make a profit on the sale of the stock, you face one more problem that does not come into play if you invest only in U.S. stock markets. Your profits could be diminished if the value of the dollar has increased since you switched your investment into the foreign currency. It would take more units of that country's currency to switch back into a rising dollar.

If you bought the Japanese yen at 120 to the dollar, made a profit in your stocks, and then repurchased dollars at 140 yen to the dollar, much of your yen profits would be lost in the process of rebuying dollars.

The same problems of currency risk occur when Americans send their money abroad to deposit into foreign accounts at times when foreign interest rates are higher. All that extra interest may be lost when it comes time to transfer the money back into dollars, if the exchange rate differential has moved against you.

The key to international investing: Only switch out of your own currency when you think it is falling in value—or when you are optimistic that the profits to be made overseas will more than compensate for any currency risk.

International Investing Concept #5: Hedging Currency Risk

Hedging—or offsetting—currency risk is a multi-billion-dollar international process involving the use of futures and forward contracts and options to try to offset the volatility of international exchange rates. The largest international banks and the futures markets have developed sophisticated strategies—swaps, caps, cross-hedges, forwards, and more—to dampen the risk of making international transactions in different currencies.

For the ordinary investor simply seeking to profit from opportunities in worldwide stock and interest rate markets, it is enough to note that many mutual fund managers utilize some of these techniques in an attempt to minimize the currency risk for fund investors.

International Investing Concept #6: Currency Quotes

One of the most confusing aspects of foreign currencies is understanding how prices are quoted. Sometimes you'll see prices quoted in European terms. For example, the relationship between the dollar and the Deutschemark might be called 1.49 DM. Those are the terms you'll find when you're traveling and decide to switch from dollars into a foreign currency. But when you're trading the futures markets, the quotes are reversed. You'll see that 1 DM is worth 67 cents. That is, 67 cents is the *dollar price* of one unit of the German currency.

Like any other marketplace—cash or futures—there's a bid price and an offer price, depending on whether you're selling or buying the currency. The difference—the *spread*—is the amount of potential profit to the person making the market, such as a company or bank. As an investor or trader, you'll want to look for the marketplace with the narrowest spread. It will be the most efficient market.

Chapter 26

Strategies for International Investing

The United States has the largest equity (stock) market in the world, but it is not always the place to make the most money. In fact, going back to 1975, the United States has not once been the top performer among the world's nine largest stock markets; it has been in the top three only four times. That's a pretty good incentive to diversify your investments internationally. (See chart III-6.)

It also means that you have to keep a sharp eye on economic conditions around the world, and on general stock market performance trends in various countries. Fortunately, each of those countries with a major stock market has its own index, similar to our Dow Jones Industrial Average or S&P 500. Chart III-7 lists those international stock indexes.

When it comes to fixed-income investments in foreign countries, most investors are better off sticking with mutual funds that invest in high-quality foreign government and corporate bonds. In 1992, while short-term U.S. Treasury bills were yielding less than 3.5 percent, comparable German government IOUs were yielding 8 percent. Investors in long-term international bond funds could earn returns of 9.5 percent (compared to about 7.5 percent on U.S. Treasuries). Clearly, it pays to look at international investments—if you understand the risks.

When you use mutual funds to invest in foreign securities, you'll see two

CHART III-6
Performance of Major Stock Markets
(average annualized return in U.S. dollars: 3 years ended May 31, 1992)

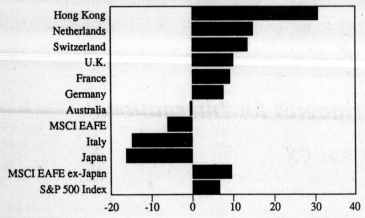

* The EAFE Index reflects 18 major foreign stock markets, but is heavily dominated
by Japan.

SOURCE: T. Rowe Price Associates, Inc. Data supplied by Morgan Stanley Capital International
Perspective and County Nat West.

terms: *global* and *international*. Global generally means that the fund may
make investments in foreign markets but also may have some of its
investments in U.S. markets. International funds, on the other hand, have
all or almost all of their investments outside the United States.

CHART III-7
World Market Index Characteristics

Country	Index	No. of Stocks
Japan	Nikkei Average	225
United Kingdom	FT-SE	100
Germany	DAX	30
France	CAC	40
Canada	TSE	300
Hong Kong	Hang Seng	33
Mexico	I.P.C.	40
Australia	All Ordinaries	320+
United States	Dow Jones Industrial Average	30

International Investing Strategy #1: Global Income Funds

It is worth considering global income funds for a portion of your assets when interest rates are higher outside the United States. Global income funds invest in the short-term, highly rated securities of foreign governments and some foreign countries. These global income funds are *not* substitutes for U.S. money market funds because there is some risk to principal.

Because they invest in securities with maturities of up to three years, unlike money market funds, which must buy securities with a maximum maturity of 180 days, there is some volatility in the share prices of these global income funds. Global income funds also carry a certain amount of currency risk even though the fund managers try to hedge against this risk. The hedging process cannot eliminate all currency risk, and it does come at a cost to the total return of the fund.

When comparing the returns on global income funds to any other investment, it is particularly important to look at the *total return*, not just the yield. Total return includes any gains or losses from currency transactions, plus the cost of hedging the currency risk. There have been times when the interest rate yield of these funds was very attractive, but the overall total return barely exceeded that of less risky U.S. short-term income funds.

Many of the largest brokerage firms offer global income funds: Merrill Lynch Short-Term Global Income, PaineWebber Short-Term Global, Kemper Short-Term Global, Inc., and Shearson Short-Term World, Inc., are a few examples. These brokerage firm-sponsored global funds generally carry a sales load of about 3 to 3.5 percent.

There are also some no-load global funds for those investing independently. They include:

Scudder Short-Term Global Income Fund (800-225-2470)

Fidelity Short-Term World Income Fund (800-544-8888)

Blanchard Short-Term Global Income (800-922-7771)

International Investing Strategy #2: Longer-term Bond Funds

Global diversification of assets and higher overseas yields are reasons to consider investing in longer-term bonds issued by foreign governments and corporations. Bond investors have many of the same concerns whether they're investing in the United States or internationally:

The first concern is *quality*: You can always get higher rates from lower quality securities.

The second concern is the *economic outlook*: You don't want to buy long-term bonds if you think interest rates are going to move higher.

When it comes to buying international bonds, there is a third consideration: *currency risk*. You don't want to invest in foreign bonds if you think that country's currency will weaken, causing you to lose money when you switch back to dollars.

You *do* want to consider foreign bonds when the following considerations are on your side:

Interest rates are higher in a foreign country than in the United States.

You expect that interest rates in the foreign country are near their peak and might decline, giving you profits on the prices of your foreign bonds. (High interest rates will slow the foreign economy and cause rates to decline at some point. Of course, lower rates might cause the currency to weaken, offsetting your profits.)

You expect the value of the dollar to weaken against that country's currency, giving you profits on the currency and diversifying your investments out of the weakening dollar.

When those considerations are met, most investors will choose international bond funds. Again, many of the larger brokerage firms offer their own long-term international bond funds. For investors seeking no-load funds, see the following list:

Benham European Government Bond Fund (800-472-3389)

T. Rowe Price International Bond Fund (800-638-5660)

Fidelity Global Bond Fund (800-544-8888)

Scudder International Bond Fund (800-225-2470)

International Investing Strategy #3: Stock Market Funds

When investing in foreign stock markets, most investors choose the diversification and professional management of mutual funds. It is possible to open individual accounts with some large domestic or foreign brokerage firms to buy individual foreign stocks, but that involves exchange rate risk and complicated tax considerations. Plus, it may be difficult to evaluate foreign securities because different taxation systems result in earnings that are not easily compared to U.S. companies.

Americans can also buy foreign shares through ADRs, American Depository Receipts. These are shares of foreign companies that are issued by American banks and are substitutes for the actual shares held in their foreign branches. The ADRs are listed for trading on American stock exchanges, making purchase, sale, and tax considerations much less complicated. You can buy ADRs through your regular brokerage firm account.

Open-end mutual funds are probably the easiest way for Americans to own a diversified international portfolio. In recent years, so many of these funds have been created by mutual fund management companies that it is now possible to pick an international fund that specializes in the shares of just one region or one country, or to diversify between the larger or smaller growth companies of a particular geographic area. There are even index funds that track the performance of major geographic regions.

As with all major mutual fund categories, you may pay a sales commission to a broker or planner to help you choose the right fund investment, or you may concentrate on no-load international funds. Many of the best performing international funds do charge sales commissions, usually less than 6 percent. The following are some no-load international fund categories:

International Stock Funds
Fidelity Worldwide Fund (800-544-8888)
Kleinwort Benson International (800-223-9164)
T. Rowe Price International Stock Fund (800-638-5660)
Scudder International Fund (800-225-2470)
Twentieth Century International Equity (800-345-2021)
Vanguard World International Growth (800-662-7447)

European Region Funds
Fidelity Europe Fund (800-544-8888)
Financial Strategic European (800-525-8085)
T. Rowe Price European Stock (800-638-5660)
Vanguard International Equity Index European (800-662-7447)

Pacific Region Funds
INVESCO Strategic Pacific Basin (800-525-8085)
Japan Fund (800-535-2726)
Fidelity Pacific Basin (800-544-8888)
T. Rowe Price New Asia (800-638-5660)
Vanguard International Equity Index Pacific (800-662-7447)

Latin America Region Funds
Scudder Latin America Fund (800-225-2470)
INVESCO Latin American Growth Fund (800-525-8085)

International Investing Strategy #4: Closed-End Country Funds

Closed-end mutual funds have been some of the most favored ways to create investment opportunities in foreign countries. As explained in chapter 15, closed-end funds have a fixed number of shares trading publicly, and the shares are usually listed on major stock exchanges. The daily share price of a closed-end fund bears some relationship to the value of the investments in the fund, but the shares may trade at a premium or discount to the net asset value, depending on demand for the limited shares in the fund itself.

When demand is high, closed-end funds may sell at substantial premiums to their intrinsic per-share value. For example, in 1989 the Spain Fund sold at a price more than 130 percent above the value of its underlying securities. It was one of the few ways to easily invest in Spanish securities, which were booming in anticipation of the 1992 Olympics and World's Fair. Shares in the fund subsequently dropped to a 3 percent discount in mid-1992. During that entire period, however, the share price ranged roughly between 8 and 14, and the fund was trading at 11½ when the price dropped to a 3 percent discount from net asset value.

The Spain Fund is a graphic example of how you can make or lose money in a closed-end fund. Not only can the value of the fund investments rise or fall, but the premium or discount can change dramatically, offsetting or enhancing your profits. Similar changes in premium occurred when investors rushed to buy closed-end German and European fund shares after the fall of the Berlin Wall.

Buying these funds at a discount to their net asset value can be considered a sort of "insurance policy" against the volatility and currency risks involved in international investing.

There are closed-end country funds ranging from Mexico to India, Brazil to Indonesia. Most are listed on the New York Stock Exchange.

Terry's Tips:

$$$ For more information on closed-end international funds, see chapter 15 for information on subscribing to the *Closed-End Fund Digest* and the *Morningstar Closed-End Fund Survey*.

$$$ When purchasing a closed-end fund, look at a chart comparing price performance with the spread between premiums and discounts. The Morningstar service offers this chart in each report. Even though the share price may not have moved dramatically, the premium or discount may have changed significantly. Purchase shares when discounts are historically high, and sell when shares go to a premium.

International Investing Strategy #5: Buying Currencies— Cash and CDs

Although some people invest in foreign securities for capital gains, and other investors are searching abroad for higher yields, there are people who simply want to diversify their investments out of the U.S. dollar, and to purchase currencies of foreign countries that appear to be growing stronger against the dollar.

Foreign Currency—Cash and Traveler's Checks

One way to switch out of the dollar is simply to walk into any international bank and exchange your dollar bills for a foreign currency or for traveler's checks in a foreign currency. However, there are costs associated with this process that make it impractical to exchange large amounts of money.

First, there is the spread between the bid and the asked price for the currency. Unlike futures markets, the cash retail market will nick you for a spread of 4 percent or more, and you'll pay a high service fee. Second, once you translate your money into actual foreign currency bills or traveler's checks, you won't be able to earn interest. That also adds to the cost of switching out of dollars.

Terry's Tip:

$$$ When traveling, always buy traveler's checks in dollars, unless the dollar is falling rapidly. Remember, if you convert traveler's checks in foreign currencies back into dollars, you'll once again pay the differential. Always exchange traveler's checks in banks, not at local hotels.

Foreign Currency Bank Accounts

It's not illegal for Americans to open foreign bank accounts, but the process can be complicated and expensive, and it may catch the attention of the IRS. As an alternative, some banks in the United States allow you to open certificate of deposit accounts denominated in foreign currencies. You may earn higher interest on these CDs, but you are exposed to the currency risk. These accounts are designed for people who want to take that currency risk by actually converting their dollars to interest-bearing accounts denominated in another currency.

Mark Twain Bank in St. Louis, Missouri (800-926-4922), offers a program called World Currency Certificates of Deposit. These are FDIC-insured certificates of deposit denominated in more than 20 foreign currencies, in minimum amounts of $20,000. Investors can choose among maturities of from three months to one year.

Conversion rates are determined by the current foreign exchange markets, with a very narrow spread between bid and offer (although not the same rate given to multi-million-dollar exchange transactions). The interest rate on the CD is based on rates offered for similar maturity CDs in each country.

The interest rate is fixed when the CD is purchased. The investor's return is equal to the foreign interest rate earned, plus or minus any difference in currency exchange values between purchase date and maturity date. The interest earned is taxed as interest income, and any currency gain or loss must be treated separately.

At maturity, the CD may be rolled over into another CD, in the same or a different currency, or exchanged for dollars at the then-prevailing rate. Or you can take actual possession of the foreign currency by bank draft or wire. This CD may not be refunded or redeemed before maturity date, so unless you use some other hedging technique to lock in your profit or limit your losses, you're exposed to the currency risk until maturity.

These CDs can be purchased by personal check, bank wire transfer, or delivery of a foreign currency. They are approved for IRA accounts.

International Investing Strategy #6: Currency Mutual Funds

An easier way to diversify your dollars directly into foreign currencies is to purchase a mutual fund designed expressly for that purpose. Huntington International Currency Portfolios offers this service, allowing individual investors with a minimum investment of $2,500 to participate in the movements of 16 foreign currencies against the dollar. These funds do not hedge against currency risk; they are designed to allow investors to profit from currency risk.

There are three separate Huntington currency funds—and a U.S. dollar money market fund into which the other portfolios can be switched. Each portfolio carries a 2.25 percent sales charge, although there is no fee to switch between the funds. Investments are made through financial planners, brokerage firms, or directly through the fund management company (800-354-4111), which will send you a prospectus.

Huntington Global Currency Portfolio
(FOCUS: TOTAL RETURN)
Invests in money market instruments denominated in at least three major currencies; may include dollar investments, seeking a combination of yield and currency gains.

Huntington High-Income Currency Portfolio
(FOCUS: YIELD)
Invests in top-quality, high-yielding foreign securities with average maturity of 120 days. Chooses securities from only three to five countries; if foreign yields are not deemed high enough, may also invest in U.S. or Canadian dollars.

Huntington Hard Currency Portfolio
(FOCUS: CURRENCY MOVES)
Invests in money market instruments denominated in three to five of the
  lowest inflation currencies, determined semiannually; no dollar investments, seeks protection against dollar depreciation.

In addition to the original sales charge, these funds have total annual
fund expenses of about 1.6 percent (read the prospectus to get the most
recent figures). Even so, that's a relatively small price to pay for the
convenience of switching out of dollars and into foreign currencies either
for yield, currency profits, or a combination of both.

International Investing Strategy #7: Currency Futures and Options

Foreign currency futures are the most leveraged way to profit (or lose!) on
changing currency values. Futures contracts on Swiss francs, Deutschemarks, Japanese yen, Canadian dollars, British pounds sterling, and
Australian dollars are traded on the International Monetary Market of the
Chicago Mercantile Exchange. A relatively small margin down payment
can control contracts worth hundreds of thousands of dollars worth of a
foreign currency.

For more information on currency futures, write: Chicago Mercantile
Exchange, 30 S. Wacker Drive, Chicago, IL 60606 and ask for their free
booklet: *Using Currency Futures and Options*.

The Philadelphia Stock Exchange allows individual investors to purchase options on cash currency contracts on eight major currencies, including the European Currency Unit (ECU). Each contract is worth
approximately $45,000, but the option prices allow individuals to control
that amount of the currency for a small fraction of the cost. For example, a
one-year option on the Deutschemark contract might cost about $1,250 to
control the profits (or losses) on that $45,000 of DM.

The Philadelphia Stock Exchange trades about $2 billion a day in
foreign currency options, or about 45,000 contracts. For more information
on these options, call the Philadelphia Stock Exchange at 800-THE-PHLX
and ask for their booklet: *Understanding Currency Options*.

Chapter 27

Investing for Financial Self-Defense

In the late 1970s, the United States experienced a bout of inflation unprecedented in this century. Cash was losing value at a rate of 13.5 percent a year. People rushed to buy anything that they thought would "beat" inflation: gold, real estate, oil, soybeans, and farmland, to name a few hot investments of that era.

In the 1930s, banks failed and there was no federal insurance to protect depositors. The money scare was so great that people stood in long lines to get actual currency that could be stashed under a mattress or in tin cans buried in the backyard. There was a real fear that the system would collapse.

In 1984, Chicago's Continental Bank—at the time one of the ten largest banks in the world—faced an international run on deposits. A good portion of its deposits were in "jumbo" CDs—over $100,000—and not covered by federal deposit insurance. The Federal Reserve and the nation's banking system hastily organized a bailout that included even the uninsured deposits. That rescue headed off potential disaster for hundreds of smaller U.S. banks and even the multinational banks that had deposit and trading relationships with Continental.

On October 19, 1987, I stood on the floor of the Chicago Board Options Exchange and watched as the racing ticker tape showed the Dow

Industrials down more than 500 points on volume that grew to more than 500 million shares. The numbers were impossible to believe—and world-wide stock markets were taking their cue from the United States. For a few moments I felt the chill of watching the possible disintegration of the world's financial and banking system.

If there is one lesson to be learned from the few times our modern financial system has moved to the brink, it's that there's no way to hedge, insure, or protect against a complete collapse of the worldwide financial system. Rental real estate won't protect you if your renters can't pay. Money in a Swiss bank will not protect you, even if you can get a seat on the last plane for Switzerland. By then, the banks there will be closed too. Gold will not protect you because you can't eat gold—and no one will trade that last loaf of bread for a gold coin. And even if you store food and fuel, as some doomsayers have advised, will you be willing to barricade yourself against hungry neighbors?

So while tales of international financial collapse may make interesting theoretical talk, you'll do much better financially by seeking protection against the possible and profits from the probable. Within this context, investments in gold and silver, real estate, foreign currencies, and natural resources all have a potential place in your investment portfolio.

Defensive Investment Strategy #1: Gold and Silver

There are several ways to buy gold and silver: coins, bullion bars, stocks, options, and futures. But there is only one safe way to purchase them, and that is from a reputable dealer. In the last twenty years, huge amounts of money have been lost in scams involving precious metals. People tend to invest in those commodities when they're scared, and that makes the investor a prime target for manipulation.

This warning comes before any other investment advice: Always buy from reputable banks and brokerage firms—and not from telephone sales pitches.

Coins

There are two types of gold and silver coins:

Numismatic coins are valuable because of their rarity. They tend to be very old, or part of a series in which very few coins were minted. Their value depends not only on their rarity, but on their condition. It's important to buy numismatic coins that have been certified as to authenticity and quality. Even a small difference in grade, or condition, can make a big difference in price. When purchasing collector's coins, ask for a certificate from a grading service approved by the American Numismatic Association (719-632-2646).

Bullion coins are valued strictly for their precious metal content. They tend to be coins that are minted in huge numbers, and may even be currently minted—such as Canadian gold Maple Leaf coins or U.S. gold Eagle coins. Some currently minted coins may be offered in "proof," or collector's sets, which are supposed to add to their value. It may take quite a few years for those proof sets to have much incremental collector's value over the metal content. Always take possession of your bullion coins and store them in your own bank safe deposit box.

Bullion

Gold and silver come in bullion form, which is usually used for industrial purchases. After all, a suitcase full of gold bars is quite heavy. (The suitcase doesn't get any lighter even when the price of gold rises!) One other detriment to owning precious metals in bullion form is the fact that you don't earn interest on the money you have invested in the bullion. Plus, you'll probably be paying storage costs in a vault. So you have to believe that gold or silver prices will rise dramatically to offset the opportunity cost of buying bullion.

There are smaller-size bars, and even "wafers" of gold and silver that have been minted for collectors and as jewelry. They may come in weights as small as one-tenth of an ounce. However, the manufacturing costs for these small bars are so high that the price you pay will be difficult to recoup unless precious metals prices soar.

Futures Contracts and Options

Futures contracts on both gold and silver are traded on major commodities exchanges, the most liquid contracts being traded on the COMEX in New York. Futures contracts are based on the concept of leverage—a small margin down payment to control a huge amount of the commodity. That makes futures the most volatile way to participate in the precious metals markets. A small decline can wipe out your investment and result in a call for even more money to settle your losses.

Options on futures contracts can limit your losses, but they can be very expensive. What you're buying is *time*, not the precious metal itself. You're hoping that the price of the metal will rise (or fall, in the case of a put option) within a very short period of time. If you're directionally correct, but run out of time and your option expires, you've lost your entire investment.

Gold and Silver Stocks

There are a number of individual gold and silver mining stocks and mutual funds that specialize in the precious metals and other natural resources. One advantage of buying stock of a gold or silver mining company instead of the bullion is that the stocks tend to pay significant dividends.

Many gold mining companies are based in foreign countries. Shares of many of these foreign companies are listed on U.S. stock exchanges in the form of ADRs (American Depository Receipts). That makes them easy to purchase and allows margin loans on the shares. Quite a few North American silver mining companies—both U.S. and Canadian—also have shares listed on Canadian and U.S. stock markets.

Precious Metals Mutual Funds

Perhaps the easiest way to participate in stocks of metals and mining companies is through a specialized mutual fund. Listed below are some of the larger no-load funds in this category:

Benham Gold Equities Index (800-472-3389) (buys only North American gold stocks, large cap)

Bull & Bear Gold Investors (800-847-4200) (worldwide stocks, substantial assets in bullion)

Financial Strategic Gold (800-525-8085) (primarily American companies, 20 percent nongold metals such as copper)

United Services Gold Shares (800-873-8637) (only South African gold shares, some platinum)

United Services World Gold (800-873-8637) (North American, Australian stocks, smaller producers)

Some closed-end gold funds are also listed for trading on the exchanges:

ASA, Ltd. (NYSE) (shares of South African gold mining companies)

Central Fund of Canada (AMEX) (owns actual bullion)

Defensive Investment Strategy #2: Real Estate

When you start talking about investment real estate, the first thing to do is rule out the family home and the dream vacation home. Those are not investments; they are shelter and pleasure. For more on acquiring and mortgaging those dreams, see chapter 42.

Real estate investment had its heyday in the 1980s when the combination of tax laws, inflation, and low fixed-rate mortgages combined to create incentives for buyers. All of that has changed in the 1990s. Current tax laws make real estate less attractive as an investment; we are in a period of *de*flation, not inflation; and the demographics have changed in the residential real estate market. Many of the baby boom generation have already purchased their first home, taking some of the upward demand pressure off of the residential real estate market.

So while real estate may offer investment opportunities in the nineties, it would be unwise to believe that the investment success stories of the previous 15 years will be easy to repeat. As noted previously, the nineties are a different game.

Rental Property

While tax laws have changed, it may make sense to own and actively manage investment real estate, if your income level allows you to use the deductions such as depreciation and mortgage interest generated by your investment property. If your adjusted gross income (AGI) is less than $100,000 per year, you can deduct up to $25,000 worth of real estate losses per year. As your AGI moves over $100,000, your allowable deduction declines to zero at $150,000. If your income is above $150,000, you can still deduct some losses if they're used to offset "passive income" such as income from another real estate project.

Smaller real estate investment projects are facing the constraints that hit big developers in the early 1990s. Bank financing is difficult to get for those properties, even when values are sound and cash flows appear reliable. Make sure you have a likely mortgage commitment before you start shopping for property.

There's one other problem to consider when you own and actively manage real estate: what to do with the profits when you ultimately sell. If you've depreciated the property over the years, you'll be faced with a huge tax bill when you sell, even though your profits will likely be taxed as capital gains.

There are two possible alternatives if your property has appreciated over the years. First, simply don't sell. If you want to realize some of the appreciation, you can try to refinance the building and take out some of the profits tax-free. Or you can try to organize a "like-kind" exchange of property. You don't actually have to trade exactly similar property with another owner. In fact, you have 180 days to sell your property and close on another purchase of a similar piece of income property. Check with an experienced real estate attorney for guidance on like-kind exchanges.

Real Estate Investment Trusts (REITs)

One of the better ways for individuals to participate in real estate investments is through publicly traded real estate investment trusts. REITs are like closed-end mutual funds in that they raise money from investors and purchase a diversified portfolio of properties. Some REITs purchase equity ownership of properties, and others use their cash to make mortgage loans. The advantage of investing in a REIT is that it passes on the rent or mortgage income from these properties to its shareholders. The REIT itself is not taxed as long as it pays out at least 90 percent of its income.

After the initial public offering, you'll find the shares of these REITs listed on the major stock exchanges. Since the shares are listed and publicly traded, REITs offer liquidity along with participation in the real estate marketplace. Investors searching for higher yields may find the generous payouts of REITs make them attractive.

For a complete listing of real estate investment trusts and where they are traded, write to the industry trade group: National Association of REITs, 1129 Twentieth Street N.W., Washington, D.C. 20036.

Terry's Tip:

$$$ There is a no-load mutual fund that specializes in investing in shares of REITs as well as equity shares and debt securities of companies

involved in construction and management of real estate in the United States and abroad. For more information and a prospectus, contact:

United Services Real Estate Fund (800-873-8637) (minimum $1,000)

Fidelity Real Estate (800-544-8888) (minimum $2,500)

Defensive Investment Strategy #3: Real Estate Mistakes

Dangers of Buying Distressed Property

In spite of the Saturday morning television infomercials that promise a fortune to be made in investment real estate, I'd be willing to wager that the general public has been a big loser on investment real estate. The premise of most of those courses on acquiring real estate is that somewhere there is a distressed seller or foreclosed property waiting to become your bargain.

Indeed, in recessionary times there are such bargains, but they are frequently entangled in legal complications such as the need to evict a current tenant. Then be prepared to invest time and money in renovating such a property. There is no guarantee that inflation will come along and result in a higher-priced sale in a few months. In the meantime, the investor is left to pay the property taxes and interest on the money borrowed to finance the purchase.

The promoters are making money selling the real estate investment *courses*—not the real estate. As with all investments, it's important to understand what you're getting into *before* you get started.

Real Estate Partnership Woes

The other way investors have been burned in the past decade is through participation in commercial real estate syndication partnerships. The 1986 tax law changes destroyed the investment value of most of those deals. As commercial real estate values plummeted, investors were left with illiquid and worthless partnership interests. Worse, when the properties within the partnerships were foreclosed, IRS rules said the action triggered a taxable gain in the amount of the mortgage on the property, even though no proceeds were realized. Investors were forced to lay out cash to pay taxes on gains they did not receive.

It's very difficult to sell a unit of a limited partnership (LP). You can contact the original brokerage firm sponsors of these LPs to see if they will repurchase the units or if they offer to match sellers with buyers. A number of companies have created a trading market for resale of these units:

Chicago Partnership Board, Inc. (800-272-6273)

National Partnership Exchange (800-356-2739)

Liquidity Fund (800-227-4688)

If you're interested in finding out more about the current state of the limited partnership market, *Partnership Profiles* (817-488-6115) is a newsletter that publishes a directory of partnership units and updates on taxes and other news related to limited partnerships.

Keep in mind that if you are trying to "scavenge" among the outstanding units to find a bargain, there are usually more sellers than buyers. If you already own a limited partnership that has little current market value, you have two choices: You can sell it, take the tax loss, and try to forget your mistake; or you can hang on to it and hope that the properties will one day regain value and liquidity so you can realize some return on this (very) long-term investment.

Low-Income Housing Tax Credits

In an attempt to encourage investment in rental housing for lower income tenants, Congress created federal tax credits to be allocated to investors in buildings which have between 20 and 40 percent of units occupied by renters with no more than 50 to 60 percent of the area's median household income. Low income housing tax credits were made a permanent part of the tax code in the 1993 Tax Bill. These dollar-for-dollar credits against income taxes are one of a few remaining tax "shelters"—and therefore, the limited partnerships which invest in these projects have attracted investors' attention. There are some caveats.

The amount of credit an individual can take is limited to a deduction against ordinary income of $25,000 a year. For an investor in the 36 percent tax bracket, that works out to a tax credit of about $9,000 per year—limiting the amount you should invest to get the maximum usable tax credit each year. These partnerships must last at least ten years, during which time the building must maintain its required percentage of low income tenants. If the building falls out of compliance, current and past tax credits may be lost.

While most deals promise the investors will receive more than 100 percent of their investment in the form of tax credits over the years, there is still some question about the future market value of a low income housing development after it is held for the required 15 years. Ask for the internal rate of return—without expecting any return of your original investment down the road. Also note that these partnerships tend to be illiquid, and often have hefty internal fees for the promoters and developers. If you're buying into a new partnership, ask how much net capital of the total raised will actually go to pay for building these units, and how much is overhead and sales fees.

Vacation Time Shares

Time sharing in resorts had a huge boom in the 1980s. It was a concept designed to appeal to a generation that had a desire for travel and vacations—and figured that inflation would make that desire increasingly expensive every year. In theory, the buyer would purchase the right to a specific week every year in a particular resort apartment complex, locking in vacation reservations and costs for years to come. Also in theory, it would be easy to sell or trade your week at that resort for another person's time-share interval at a different resort.

In practice, it worked quite differently. The time shares were overpriced in the first place, and many intervals remained unsold. Little money was set aside for renovations, and many time-share owners were asked to ante up additional money for needed repairs. It was difficult to sell or trade units, even though brokers offered to list them on various "time-share exchanges" for a fee. And there was—and is—no shortage of these time-share units to push values down.

Defensive Investment Strategy #4: Natural Resources

One theory of defensive investing turns to natural resources as a hedge against inflation and uncertainty. There is a limited supply of land, industrial metals, petroleum resources, natural gas reserves, and forest products. Several mutual funds specialize in these areas, or subsets of the natural resources category. They tend to perform poorly in times of low inflation, with the exception of some industrial raw materials companies that see their stocks rise in times of economic recovery.

The Fidelity Fund group has a number of natural resource specialty funds, including Fidelity: Select Energy, Select Energy Service, Select Paper and Forest Products. Each of these carries a 3 percent sales charge.

Among no-load natural resource funds are:

Financial Strategic Energy (800-525-8085)

T. Rowe Price New Era (800-638-5660)

United Services Global Resources (800-873-8637)

Vanguard Specialized Energy (800-662-7447)

If you see energy prices starting to rebound, these are the funds you should turn to for profits.

Terry's Tip:

$$$ Do not confuse investing in *natural* resource stocks and mutual funds with purchasing *strategic minerals and resources*. The latter have been a fertile field for scam artists in recent years. In fact, many of these minerals are rare and found in their natural state only in the former Soviet Union and South Africa. Metals such as titanium, magnesium, chromium, and others are indeed vital to national defense and many domestic industries. But there is no legitimate way for most individuals to invest in stockpiles of these minerals, so when a salesperson calls, just hang up.

Chapter 28

Tax-deferred Annuities as an Investment Strategy

You've already seen how tax-deferred compounding of your investments can make your money grow dramatically over the years. That's the main reason to take advantage of opportunities to invest in your Individual Retirement Account, Keogh plan, or company savings plan such as a 401(k). All of those accounts offer the double benefit of deducting your contribution from current income, plus tax-deferred investment growth.

There is one other way you can create your own tax-deferred investment account—with no limitation on the amount of after-tax dollars you can invest. It's done by using insurance company products called *tax-deferred annuities*. Don't let the words scare you. These are simply the same investments you've already learned about—no-load mutual funds or fixed-rate CDs—placed inside an insurance company envelope.

A tax-deferred annuity is like creating an unlimited IRA account. Although you cannot deduct your investment into the annuity on your current income tax return, there is no limit to the amount of money you can invest in the annuity on an after-tax basis. And all your investment profits and interest income earned in the annuity will grow and compound tax-deferred—until you take the money out. Even better, unlike an IRA which requires you to start withdrawing money at age $70\frac{1}{2}$, you are *never* required to take money out of your annuity account unless you want to.

You get the benefits of tax deferral simply because the powerful insurance industry has managed to get Congress to approve these programs that allow people to create their own retirement funds. Of course, in exchange for the benefit of tax deferral, there are some restrictions on how and when you can take money out of the annuities. So tax-deferred annuities are best suited for long-term investment programs.

First some definitions and rules.

UNDERSTANDING ANNUITIES: THE DEFINITIONS

Annuity

You've probably heard the word "annuity" in the context of "payment for life." That's because you're thinking of *immediate annuities* in which you give a lump sum of money to an insurance company. The insurance company looks at your age, your life expectancy, and current interest rates, and then guarantees that they'll send you a specific dollar amount every month, no matter how long you live. Or you can decide to stretch the payments over the lives of yourself and your spouse—or another person—which will mean you get a smaller monthly check.

Tax-Deferred Annuity

To establish a tax-deferred annuity, you give the insurance company a lump sum of money, which is put into an investment that will grow tax-deferred over the years. Many companies offer flexible-premium deferred annuities, which allow you to add money to your annuity investment in various amounts over time. You don't pay any income taxes on the investment earnings or profits until you take the money out. At some point in the future you can take money out of your annuity in one or several payments, or take only the interest out on a regular basis, or take the money out in regular checks over your life expectancy. You can choose the method of withdrawal.

Guaranteed-Rate Annuities or Variable Annuities

Tax-deferred annuities can be designed to pay either fixed interest rates that are guaranteed for a period of one to ten years at your choice, or to allow the holder to choose among stock market mutual funds, money market funds, and bond funds for purposes of investment. If you choose the latter option, there is obviously no guarantee of what your annuity account will earn. That's why it's called a variable-rate annuity.

UNDERSTANDING ANNUITIES: THE RULES AND COSTS

Once you place your money inside a tax-deferred annuity you must leave it there until you reach age 59½ (with one exception that will be explained later). If you take any of the money out before age 59½, you'll face a 10 percent federal tax penalty on any interest earnings to date, but not on your principal.

Each annuity also sets its own penalty rules for early withdrawals, which are called *surrender charges*. Generally, those surrender charges start at around 5 to 7 percent of your investment in the first year, and decline 1 percent each year until they are eliminated.

There is usually no up-front load or commission on annuity sales, so your money goes right to work for you. Yes, the sales agent is compensated by the insurance company, but the compensation is not taken directly out of your investment. Those costs are built right into the management fees on variable annuities, and the interest rate on guaranteed-rate annuities.

UNDERSTANDING ANNUITIES: TAKING MONEY OUT

When it comes to taking money out of either your fixed-rate or variable-rate annuity, you'll have several choices.

1. You can *annuitize*. That means the insurance company will send you a fixed-amount check every month, quarter, or year at your choice—as long as you live. Or you can set a fixed number of years over which you wish to annuitize and receive a monthly check. The shorter the time period, the larger the check.

The money in the check will be a combination of principal (on which you already paid taxes before you purchased the original annuity) and interest you earned in the annuity over the year. Therefore only the portion of your monthly check that represents interest earnings will be taxed.

There's one advantage to annuitizing: The insurance company guarantees that you'll never outlive your money.

There can also be two big disadvantages to annuitizing:

- If you die, the insurance company gets to keep the balance of your money unless you specify that you wish a refund of the balance to your heirs, in which case you'll receive a smaller monthly check.
- You are stuck forever with a predetermined monthly check based on the account value and current interest rates on the date you decide to annuitize. If inflation returns, you could be sorry that you have such an inflexible income structure. (There are, however, variable-rate annuities that allow you to annuitize using the underlying mutual funds; these could provide growing monthly checks.)

Unless everyone in your family tends to outlive the mortality tables, you will probably be better off with the following annuity withdrawal strategies. With methods #2 and #3 below, when you die, the balance in your annuity account (or the guaranteed minimum) goes to your beneficiary. Plus, you can change your payment amounts whenever you want to fit your needs.

2. You can start a *systematic withdrawal* program that gives you complete control over your investment income. Simply ask the insurance company to send you a check on a monthly, quarterly, or annual basis. The check can be for a specific dollar amount or simply the monthly interest earned on a guaranteed-rate annuity. You can start, stop, increase, or decrease your checks at any time. Many companies will deposit the money directly into your bank account.

3. Your third choice is to take one *lump sum distribution*, or a number of individual distributions as you need the money. You should consult with your accountant, because taking a large sum of money in one year could have significant tax implications.

ANNUITIES AND TAXES

Current tax rules state that the first money taken out of an annuity is considered interest. Therefore, the money you receive under a systematic withdrawal plan will be taxed as ordinary income at the time you receive the check—until you start digging into your original principal.

If you take a lump sum distribution, the money will be taxed as you withdraw it. If you make a partial withdrawal, the interest earnings are paid out before you take out any principal, so you'll owe taxes on the first money you withdraw. Don't forget the 10 percent federal tax penalty if you withdraw interest earnings from your annuity before age 59½.

Many annuities allow withdrawal of up to 10 percent of your original investment each year without surrender charges. Those withdrawals are taxed as income, and you would still owe the 10 percent federal tax penalty if you take this money out before age 59½.

Terry's Tip:

$$$ If you receive substantially equal payments based on your life expectancy, at least one payment a year for a minimum of five years, and at least one of those payments beyond age 59½, you can avoid the 10 percent penalty. That means you can start withdrawing annuity money early, as long as you structure the payments to last beyond age 59½ and to distribute the payments in equal amounts. (The insurance company will do these calculations for you.) It's wise to consult your accountant when using this option.

ANNUITIES—AND CHANGING YOUR MIND

If you want to change from one annuity to another and don't want to face tax penalties, you do have a bit of flexibility with your annuity investment. You can switch your annuity to a new insurance company using the provisions of section 1035(a) of the IRS Tax Code. It's known as a "1035 exchange" and is simply a direct transfer from one insurance company to another. All you have to do is fill out the forms with the new company and then write to your current company requesting they transfer your account to the new company. Transferring your annuity on a 1035 exchange does not eliminate any surrender charges that might be applicable.

Terry's Tip:

$$$ Once you have decided to *annuitize*—take regular monthly payments—you cannot execute a 1035 exchange. You're stuck with the insurance company that is making the monthly payments to you. That's another reason for not locking yourself into regular, annuitized payments.

ANNUITIES AND INSURANCE COMPANY SAFETY

When you give your money to an insurance company to purchase an annuity, you create an important relationship with the insurance company itself. Unlike banks and S&Ls, there is no federally guaranteed fund to bail out insurance companies that fail. Instead, there are state funds that depend on assessing other insurance companies doing business in the state in order to bail out customers of failed insurance companies.

These days, with all the concerns about insurance company solvency, it's very important to understand the financial condition of the insurance company before you invest. You don't have to understand financial balance sheets, but you must carefully check the insurance company's safety rating.

There are several well-known services that rate insurance companies for safety and solvency. They are: A.M. Best, Moody's, Standard & Poor's, and Weiss Research. Their phone numbers for obtaining ratings are listed in chapter 54.

While past experience is no guarantee of legal decisions in the future, in recent insurance company failures people holding *guaranteed-rate* annuities have been considered general creditors of the company. That means withdrawals have been restricted and interest rates lowered.

When you purchase a variable-rate annuity, it appears you may not have the same exposure to insurance company failure. There is still some debate about whether a variable annuity account is totally separate from the assets of the insurance company in case of its failure.

When you purchase a variable annuity, you only get the tax-deferral benefits because you actually own a *subaccount* of a *separate* account in the mutual fund, through the insurance company. Regulators such as the SEC, IRS, and National Association of Insurance Commissioners have at times stated that variable annuities are "separate accounts" from the general portfolio account of the insurance company. Indeed, the assets of variable annuity accounts are segregated on insurance company balance sheets, which means you own your account and it is not subject to claims of insurance company creditors.

In recent cases of insurance failure, such as Mutual Benefit Life in New Jersey and Monarch Life in Massachusetts, the variable annuity contracts were *not* part of the conservatorship and accounts remained open to withdrawals. That sets a precedent for considering variable annuity accounts separately in cases of future insurance company failure.

Still, you should ask about the safety rating of any insurance company with which you do business.

Terry's Tip:

$$$ Several rating services have been late in noticing the problems of insurance companies that subsequently failed—most notably, the case of Executive Life of California. One rating service follows a much more stringent analysis of the publicly filed information on insurance companies. I strongly suggest that you get a safety rating on any insurance company from:

Weiss Research (800-289-9222) Cost: $15 (can be charged to your bankcard)

Chapter 29

Variable-rate Annuities

Using and choosing no-load mutual funds is the basis for some outstanding investment strategies. Wouldn't it be wonderful if you could invest in those mutual funds and shelter all your profits and dividend income from income taxes?

There *is* one way you can invest an unlimited amount of money in no-load mutual funds and be allowed to shelter all the capital gains and interest income from income taxes. You can have all those benefits when you invest in your mutual funds through a *tax-deferred variable-rate annuity*.

TAX-DEFERRED VARIABLE-RATE ANNUITIES: A DEFINITION

Here's how variable annuities work. They're really no-load mutual fund accounts (called subaccounts) placed inside the envelope of an insurance company's annuity wrapper. The laws say that money invested in this type of product offered by insurance companies is allowed to grow and compound tax-deferred, while the owner of the contract—you—direct the investments among a group of selected mutual funds available within that annuity contract.

You can choose among mutual funds offered by some of the best-known names in the industry, including Fidelity, Vanguard, and Scudder. In addition, many insurance annuities allow access to load funds that have outstanding performance records—without paying the usual sales load. And, as you'll see, you're not limited to just one family of funds; many annuity plans offer choices among a dozen or more mutual funds specializing in growth, income, high-yield securities, international stocks and bonds, index funds, and more. You're allowed to switch your annuity investments between funds and fund families offered by your annuity, so you become your own money manager within this tax-sheltered envelope.

MUTUAL FUNDS IN VARIABLE ANNUITIES: PLUS AND MINUS

There are some costs and limitations to this tax-deferral opportunity. First, as with all annuities, you must keep the money in your annuity until you reach age $59\frac{1}{2}$ or else pay a 10 percent federal tax penalty for early withdrawal.

Second, most of these annuities have *surrender charges*—penalties for withdrawal of your money in the first few years.

Third, it will be slightly more expensive to buy your mutual fund within the insurance company. That's because in addition to the standard management fees for no-load mutual funds, the insurance company takes mortality and expense fees.

But out of those insurance company annual expenses you get one great advantage: *a guaranteed death benefit*. Even if the mutual funds within your annuity have lost money, the insurance company guarantees that at your death your survivors will receive at least as much as you invested in the annuity originally, or the current account value—whichever is greater. In fact, if your account inside the annuity grows very large, you can *step up the death benefit* to guarantee an even larger amount at death. (That may cause a new surrender period to start.)

The real benefit of a variable annuity, though, is the tax-deferred compounding feature. You have to balance that benefit against the fact that your money is tied up—illiquid—for a number of years, and that you're paying slightly higher fees when you buy mutual funds inside an annuity. You must have a long-term time horizon when purchasing tax-deferred variable annuities.

MUTUAL FUNDS IN VARIABLE ANNUITIES: THE COSTS

Almost all variable annuities are sold with no up-front sales commission or load. If you deal with an annuity salesperson, he or she is compensated directly from the insurance company, without any money taken from your investment. The cost of commissions that are paid to the salespeople comes from the annual management expenses described below. In fact, the surrender charges for the first several years are designed to recoup the fees that the insurance company fronts to its salespeople when you open your account.

There are two sets of costs combined into one overall expense figure when you purchase mutual funds through variable annuities. First, there is the annual management fee charged by the mutual fund itself. These management fees may be lower than if you invested directly in the fund itself because the insurance company negotiates a lower fee for its variable annuity accounts and because the fund does not charge 12b-1 fees to cover marketing expenses. The average fund expense is 0.74 percent, deducted from your account by the fund management company.

The second charge is the annual expenses of the insurance company for providing the guaranteed death benefit and to cover marketing and administrative expenses. Those expenses average about 1.26 percent a year. When combined with the mutual fund management expense, the total expense of owning a fund inside a variable annuity averages about 2 percent or more per year.

It's wise to consider the total expense of owning your mutual fund inside an annuity. It can take a while for the fund's performance to offset high annual expenses, especially if you choose conservative income funds inside your annuity account. That's one incentive to choose aggressive funds for your variable annuity account.

MUTUAL FUNDS IN VARIABLE ANNUITIES: HOW TO CHOOSE A PLAN

Almost every insurance company or stock brokerage firm, and many banks, offer variable annuity programs. Usually the annuity program is designed by one insurance company, making it difficult to compare the products' costs, expenses, and mutual fund performance record. You can confer with several agents representing different insurance companies or follow the annuity buying strategies listed below.

No matter how you choose your annuity, here are some questions you should ask:

1. What choice of funds do I have within this annuity, and how have they performed in recent years?

2. What is the total expense, including all fees, for maintaining this account every year?

3. What are the surrender charges?

4. Can I add more money to this annuity, and in what minimum amounts? Will this additional money extend the period of surrender charges?

5. Is there any charge for switching between the funds you offer, and is there any restriction on the number or timing of switches I may make?

6. Do you have an automatic investment program so that you can take money out of my checking account every month and deposit it into my annuity? (Another way to avoid the "see it—spend it" syndrome.)

7. Can I increase the guaranteed amount of my death benefit if my investment account increases in value? Will this trigger a new period of surrender charges?

Variable Annuity Buying Strategy #1: Annuity Shopping Service

If you're look for advice in choosing a mutual fund variable annuity program, contact Independent Advantage Financial Services (800-829-2887), an annuity shopping service representing 40 top-rated companies. Their representatives only respond to inquiries about annuities; they do not make sales calls. They represent dozens of annuity programs, so they can sell the annuity that best suits your needs.

Independent Advantage concentrates on their "honor roll" of what they consider best annuity choices. They will send you that list of annuities, comparing features like costs, surrender charges, minimum investments, and choice of funds. Among their current favorites as of this writing:

Best of America IV
    Offers 19 funds managed by seven advisors
        including: Fidelity, Neuberger & Berman, Oppenheimer,
        Twentieth Century Funds, Van Eck, Nationwide, and
        Strong

Franklin Value Mark II
    Offers 14 funds managed by Franklin Advisers
        including: Utility Fund, Rising Dividends,
        Overseas, and other Franklin funds

Lincoln National American Legacy II
    Offers 7 funds managed by American Funds (Capital
        Research and Management)

Variable Annuity Buying Strategy #2: Buy Direct from Fund Managers

In recent years, several of the larger mutual fund management companies have either purchased their own insurance companies or made arrangements with existing companies to offer variable annuity products directly to mutual fund buyers. There are several advantages to buying variable annuities directly from the mutual fund management companies (via their insurance companies).

First, the overall expense charge tends to be lower by about one-half percentage point per year. Second, some of these annuities may not have a surrender charge, primarily because they do not have the expense of paying commissions to salespeople. On the other hand, when you purchase one of these variable annuities you are limited to the funds offered by this one management company, while other annuity programs may allow you to switch your account between several fund managers.

Note that not all of a fund company's funds will be included in its annuity program. Also, the funds that are offered may not be the original funds, but "clones," or funds patterned after those offered to the retail investing public but designed strictly for annuity separate accounts. These well-known mutual fund management companies also participate in variable annuity programs offered by other insurance company sales forces.

Mutual fund companies offering direct annuity sales include:

Vanguard (800-522-5555) Minimum investment: $5,000; no surrender charges

Fidelity (800-544-0140) Minimum investment: $2,500; surrender charges: 5 percent first year, none after 5 years

Scudder (800-225-2470) Minimum investment: $2,500; no surrender charges

The fund choices may be fairly limited in these direct sale annuity programs. You may find it worthwhile to participate in an annuity program such as the previously mentioned "Best of America" plan that offers a wider variety of fund managers and individual funds.

Chapter 30

Guaranteed-rate Annuities

If you want to shelter your money from taxes, but don't want to take on the job of deciding which mutual fund to choose, you can purchase a guaranteed, fixed-rate annuity. This is very much like purchasing a certificate of deposit, within the insurance company envelope. One big difference is that the guarantor of this CD is the insurance company itself, not the FDIC. That's why it's particularly important to purchase guaranteed-rate annuities only from the strongest insurance companies.

There are some other things you should know about purchasing guaranteed-rate annuities.

GUARANTEED-RATE ANNUITIES: A DEFINITION

A guaranteed-rate annuity is a promise by an insurance company to pay a fixed rate of interest on your after-tax deposit for one or more years. The interest grows and compounds inside the annuity, tax-deferred, until you take the money out.

The interest rate may be guaranteed for the first year or for as many as ten years. After that initial period, the insurance company will annually tell you what it is going to pay for the following year. This is a very competitive market, which guarantees that rates in later years will be attractive relative to then-current market conditions.

Each insurance company will offer its own interest rate, and those rates may differ by several percentage points. But as you'll see below, interest rates are not the only factor in choosing a guaranteed-rate annuity.

GUARANTEED-RATE ANNUITIES: THE RULES

The rules on guaranteed-rate annuities are the same as for variable-rate annuities: You must leave your money inside the account until age 59½ or face a 10 percent federal tax penalty on interest earnings.

Also, you will be charged a surrender penalty by the insurance company if you take your money out in the first few years. Generally, you can expect to be charged about 7 percent of your investment if you withdraw in the first year. The penalty declines each year until it disappears completely after seven or eight years.

Although these products are sold by insurance company agents, there is no commission immediately taken out of your deposit. All of your money goes to work for you, earning the promised rate. Instead, the commission is built right into the interest rate you earn over the years. That's the reason for the surrender charges if you withdraw your money in the early years.

A very few guaranteed-rate annuity products do charge a front-end load. Ask your agent if *all* of your money starts earning interest. Do not purchase an annuity with a front-end load.

GUARANTEED-RATE ANNUITIES: HOW TO CHOOSE

Guaranteed-rate annuities have a different checklist from variable-rate annuities when it comes to making an investment choice. Because these annuities have always been considered assets guaranteed by the insurance company itself (unlike variable annuities that are in mutual funds), insurance company safety must be at the top of your checklist.

Insurance company safety: Buy guaranteed-rate annuities only from the top-rated companies. Contact Weiss Research (800-289-9222) for the safety rating of the insurance company.

Current interest rate: You want to choose the highest guaranteed rate from the safest insurance company. Some companies will offer a fairly high rate and guarantee it for three years. Others may offer a high rate but guarantee it only for one year. You have to make the choice, depending on your interest rate outlook.

Guaranteed minimum rate: All annuities will also guarantee a minimum rate below which the annual rate cannot fall once you purchase the annuity. Recently, many companies have set this minimum at around 4 percent, making these tax-deferred annuities an even better deal when regular bank CD rates dropped below 4 percent. The minimum rate is the rate the insurance company must pay you after the guarantee period, and for the life of the policy. However, most companies are paying far more competitive rates than the guaranteed minimum.

Bailout rate: Many policies also have a bailout rate that may be set about one percentage point below the initial rate, or on some other basis. It allows you to transfer your annuity to another company with no surrender charge if rates fall below this level.

Surrender charges: Look carefully at the way the surrender charges are designed for your policy. Most policies design the charges to decline year by year, but some do have a fixed charge of as much as 5 percent of your investment for a six-year period.

Minimum deposit: Each insurance company will set its own minimum amount for opening a guaranteed-rate annuity. Many of the best plans will let you open an account for as little as $2,000.

Free withdrawals: Many of these guaranteed-rate annuities will allow you to take as much as 10 percent of your accumulated value out in one withdrawal each year, without paying surrender charges. Such withdrawals are taxed as interest income and are subject to the 10 percent penalty for those under age 59½.

Add-ons: Some, but definitely not all, guaranteed-rate annuities will allow you to add additional money after your initial deposit. Other plans require you to start a new account for additional money. If your plan does allow add-ons, check to see if that triggers a new surrender period.

Free look: Recognizing that purchasing an annuity can be a complicated process, many of these companies offer a "free look" period of between ten and 30 days, in which you can purchase the annuity and then change your mind and get a refund of your money with no penalty or surrender charge.

Annuity Purchase Strategy #1: Annuity Shopping Service

Don't be intimidated by this long checklist of guaranteed-rate annuity features. It's worth taking the time to find a guaranteed-rate annuity from a secure insurance company because your money can work even harder for you when it is tax-deferred.

Your choice is to call several insurance companies, sales agencies such as those located in banks or S&Ls, or to use an annuity shopping service. Again, my recommendation is to call Independent Advantage Financial Services (800-829-2887) and ask for its "honor roll" list of guaranteed-rate annuities. This list compares all of the above categories side by side for about six plans from top-rated companies.

PART IV

Everyday Living Strategies

No ONE has *extra* money! It's a fact of life that we can all spend as much as we earn. There always seems to be something more we "need" to purchase to make life complete. So the task of finding the additional money to put aside for the future requires some reorganizing of the money that's coming in and going out today.

This does not require a program of self-denial. I've often said that more people stick to their diets than to their budgets! But there are many strategies you can use in everyday life that will free up money to fund your investment program. The real secret is to take the savings and gains from these strategies and employ them in your investment program—instead of spending the savings now.

And don't overlook the most significant way to extricate yourself from debt and fund your investment strategies. It's simply to *make more money*! That's the primary strategy—and it's really the easiest way out of your money problems.

Most people set their own limits—and wind up in jobs that match their expectations. One trait of all successful people is that they never accept the limits other people set for them. Making more money does *not* mean asking the boss for a raise, nor does it mean dreaming about winning the lottery. It means assessing your talents and time—and making better use of them.

In these days of corporate downsizing and job eliminations, it takes great courage and self-discipline to imagine that you can create a better financial future for yourself and your family. But being pushed out of the secure job nest has often proved a great opportunity for unlocking potential success.

Companies can take away your job, but they can't take away your talents and abilities. You may start your own business, or apply your talents to a weekend or evening job to earn extra money. You may find a way to provide a service that others need and will pay for, or use your experience to counsel those starting out.

A goal without a plan is just a dream. Whether your dream is to be financially independent or just free from debt, whether your dream is to build an investment portfolio or just pay for everyday necessities, the opportunities exist. Knowledge helps you make a plan, and positive thinking helps that plan succeed. Here are the important financial steps:

1. *Get out of debt as soon as possible.* Debt will bury you in the 1990s because the interest rates are so high and because consumer debt (except for home mortgage debt) is no longer tax-deductible. Carrying consumer debt is like digging yourself into a deeper hole every day.

2. *Use credit wisely.* Understand the real cost of the credit cards you are carrying, and if you must carry a balance for a while, choose the lowest rate card with the fairest billing practices. Always check your credit report yearly to make sure there are no errors.

3. *Pay yourself first—and regularly.* Throughout this part of the book you'll learn how to set aside everyday money for future needs. The money you generate from these strategies can be used in the investments described in Part II.

4. *Be a smart shopper.* Whether you're purchasing and financing a home, car, appliance, or even your wardrobe, understand that the real status in the nineties is in getting a "good deal."

5. *Be forward thinking.* Compare the benefits of satisfying today's "needs" with the potential benefits of making your money work for the future. Reorient your perspective from today to tomorrow.

Chapter 31

Strategies for Everyday Money Handling

It's difficult to manage your money if you don't know where it's going. That means keeping track of your small cash outlays as well as your big monthly expenses. You can make this a high-tech process, using a computer program, or spend a few dollars at the local office supply store and purchase a family budget book. The strategy is to identify where your money is going—and see if you can redirect some of those expenditures to pay yourself first.

Here are the everyday strategies you'll need just to keep your ordinary expenses organized.

Everyday Money Strategy #1: Direct-Deposit Your Paycheck

Ask the payroll department at your company to deposit your paycheck directly into your checking account. You may have to change banks to one that will accept direct deposits from your company—usually the bank on which the company draws its payroll checks.

There are two advantages to this strategy. First, you can earn interest on the money if you have your paycheck deposited into a money market account—and then transfer needed money to your everyday checking account. Second, direct deposit avoids the temptation of withdrawing "just a few dollars" when you cash or deposit your paycheck personally at the bank.

If both spouses work, consider depositing paychecks in separate accounts. With real self-discipline, you may be able to save the entire paycheck of one spouse and live on the earnings of the second. Keeping the deposits separate will facilitate that effort.

Everyday Money Strategy #2: Pay Yourself First Using Automatic Deductions

The best way to avoid the "see it—spend it" syndrome is to have money automatically taken out of your paycheck before it gets into your hands.

1. If your company allows automatic deductions for a 401(k) savings plan, have the maximum contribution deducted from each paycheck (see chapter 44).

2. If your company has a payroll deduction plan for U.S. savings bonds, arrange for a regular deduction from your paycheck (see chapter 14).

3. If your paycheck is deposited directly into your bank checking account, ask the bank to take a fixed amount out of your paycheck every month and deposit it in your bank money market account.

4. Open an account at a no-load mutual fund and have a specific amount withdrawn automatically from your checking account each month and invested in a stock or money market mutual fund (see chapters 16–18 and Appendix A).

Everyday Money Strategy #3: Establish a Banking Relationship

If possible, open your checking account at a bank with which you can establish more than one financial relationship. For instance, the bank or

S&L that originated your mortgage, or your home equity loan, or your auto loan is a good place to establish your personal checking or money market account, if it is convenient.

You never know when you'll need one of those other loans, and a longer-term relationship with a bank might make the difference in quick processing for your other banking needs.

Everyday Money Strategy #4: Establish an Overdraft Account

Here's a suggestion that can be both expensive and dangerous if not used properly. At a time when you *don't* need money, ask your banker for an automatic overdraft line of credit for your checking account.

The advantage is that you'll never "bounce" a check—even if you made a subtraction error. The automatic overdraft feature will kick in. And this is an easy place for a quick "loan" if an unexpected repair or tax bill must be paid immediately.

The disadvantage of an automatic overdraft line of credit is that it can be very expensive—and habit-forming. Interest rates on these borrowings run to more than 18 percent at most institutions, and it is nondeductible consumer interest. Banks frequently offer the overdraft only in round numbers such as $100 or $500, so you may wind up paying interest on additional money you didn't really need to borrow. In order to repay the overdraft, you may have to issue specific instructions when you make your next deposit, asking for the overdraft line to be repaid immediately.

Worst of all, an automatic overdraft can make your checking account seem like a bottomless pit. You can get dependent on this feature, and if you carry your overdraft from month to month, it is as bad for your finances as carrying a balance on your credit cards.

Everyday Money Strategy #5: Choose Your Checking Style

The actual style of your checking account system can make a big difference on how easy it is to keep track of your money. If you have a problem with impulse buying, take your checkbook out of your briefcase or purse and use a large, desk-style checkbook system.

Make it your most important habit to enter the amount of every check in the check register as soon as you write the check. Also make sure you immediately enter all withdrawals from automatic teller machines.

All desk check registers are not the same. Some have three checks to a page, with a stub for each check. The most useful check registers have all your checks and deposits listed on one page, instead of checks with stubs or carbon copies as a record. If you use this full-page type of executive check register, you'll find it easier to keep track of your balance and any unreturned checks, and to get the big picture of your spending habits.

Terry's Tip:

$$$ Start a new check register on January 1 each year. File the old register away with your tax return and canceled checks, making it much easier to prepare your taxes in April, and keep records organized year by year.

Everyday Money Strategy #6: Balance Your Checkbook Regularly

Your checkbook doesn't have to balance to the penny, or even to the dollar, although you'd be surprised at how many people will spend hours trying to reconcile a bank statement. But you should get into the habit of opening your bank statement every month, and checking off all the returned checks in your checkbook register. Also make sure your deposits have been credited properly. Use the reverse side of the bank statement to do a rough calculation, to make sure you and the bank are in fairly close agreement about the amount of your balance.

Everyday Money Strategy #7: Establish a Bill-Paying System

Next month, put all your bills in a pile. Locate the due date on each bill. It's important to set up a system to match your paycheck deposits with the money you need on hand to pay your bills on time. You may decide to pay bills twice a month—on the 1st and 15th. Set aside a special place, usually your desk or kitchen drawer, to put the bills as they come in. Then stick to your bill-paying schedule.

If you're really organized, you might want to pay bills in the same order in your checkbook each month. First the mortgage, then the electricity, then the insurance bill, etc. Keep the paid bills in a separate drawer, making it easy to enter the amounts in your budget book or to deal with any bill-paying disputes.

Everyday Money Strategy #8: Use a Cash Management Account

As the financial services industry has grown more competitive in recent years, it seems everyone wants to help you manage your money. Brokerage firms offer checking accounts and debit cards. Banks offer stock brokerage services and perhaps insurance. And mutual fund companies offer a combination of banking and credit services.

Consolidating your financial operations with just one or two institutions is an appealing thought. The paperwork should be less confusing, and your entire financial picture will be consolidated. But there are costs to these services, and you should evaluate them carefully before using a cash management account.

It may be that by using separate services, you can save money. Stocks can be purchased through a discount brokerage firm. Why buy them where you bank and pay a larger commission? You may get free checking at your local bank, or a no-fee credit card. Why pay for those services at a brokerage firm?

Here are two examples of cash management accounts:

Fidelity Ultra Service Account (800-544-6262)
　　No monthly or annual fees
　　Minimum $5,000 to open account (in cash, securities, or marginable mutual funds)
　　Unlimited free checking
　　Daily interest on cash balances at money market rates (or tax-exempt money market rates)
　　Free Gold Visa debit card, with ATM access
　　Consolidated statement of all checking, debit, stock, and mutual fund holdings, including year-end summary

Discount stock brokerage
No-load mutual funds
24-hour service availability

Merrill Lynch CMA Account
Cost: $100 per year, plus $25 for Gold Visa debit card
Minimum account size: $20,000 in cash or securities
Unlimited free checking
Daily interest on cash balances at money market rates
Free Visa debit card (or additional $25 for Gold Visa debit card)
Automatic direct deposit of payroll, pension, or Social Security checks
Merrill Lynch stock research
Merrill Lynch stock brokerage (discounts may be negotiated)

Everyday Money Strategy #9: Computerize Your Records

It may sound like an impossible task to transfer the mess in your desk drawers to a computer program, but that is one of the great advantages of computers: Everything has a well-organized place in the system.

You can use your computer to pay your bills electronically, write your checks, track your budget expenditures, follow your investments, prepare your taxes, and plan your retirement. In the first dimension, a good computer program will simply organize your financial life. In the second dimension, the program will keep you instantly updated on your spending and investment performance. Beyond these basic levels, your computer program can make forecasts and projections based on the assumptions you choose, thereby encouraging you in your savings and investment goals.

If you want to figure out how much you should be saving for a college education for your children or for your retirement, you'll have to make some assumptions which you'll learn in the coming chapters. Then you can use your computer program to actually see if those assumptions will give the desired results, based on the investment amounts and returns you predict.

My favorite software is *Andrew Tobias' Managing Your Money*, but there are other useful programs on the market, such as *Quicken*. I promise that you do not have to be a "computer genius" to make these programs work for you.

In Debt? You're Not Alone!

Read on for more information about strategies to help you get out of debt and use credit wisely.

Chapter 32

Using Credit Wisely

Americans owe a *lot* of money. In 1994, we owed $919 billion in consumer debt, which included $342 billion on credit cards and a matching amount in auto loans, plus a variety of other consumer loans. Our mortgage debt totals nearly $4.3 trillion. Our corporations have $2.7 trillion in debt on their books. State and local governments owe another $964 billion. And our National Debt owed by the federal government—by us, the tax-payers—now exceeds $4.6 trillion!

The federal government pays about $200 billion a year in interest on the debt; the burden on consumers is even greater because consumer loan interest is higher than the average rate the government pays to borrow. And, of course, if the burden of debt gets too great for the government, it can always resort to "printing" more money! Millions of debt-laden Americans don't have that alternative.

Whose fault is all that debt? It's hard to assess blame. Going into debt has been a socially accepted practice in the past 30 years—and was even considered a wise strategy when inflation was pushing prices higher. The idea in the 1970s was to buy now on credit and repay the debt with "cheaper" dollars as inflation made each dollar worth less.

Today, the lenders behind all that debt are worried. The burden of debt forced more than 1 million Americans into bankruptcy in 1992—double the number who filed in 1987, and triple the number who filed during the

1981 recession. Bankruptcies caused nearly $6 billion in losses to credit card issuers in 1992.

In a related problem, credit card fraud is estimated to have cost the industry more than 1.5 billion—including fraud in bankruptcy losses. That kind of loss ratio contributes to the high cost of credit cards. It's also making lenders pay much closer attention to credit reports before making loans on homes, autos, and even before issuing new credit cards.

Credit Strategy #1: Get a Copy of Your Credit Report

There are three national credit bureaus: TRW Credit Services, Trans Union Credit, and Equifax. If you've ever borrowed money, received a credit card, purchased a home, or applied for life insurance, the odds are that one or more of these credit bureaus has a file on you. Each of these bureaus has a file on nearly 200 million Americans. Their computers accept information about your payment habits from all of the major companies with which you do business.

Credit bureaus do not deny credit or issue credit ratings. They merely report your payment history to business subscribers, who then make their own credit decisions, based on your credit report. It's your right to see what's in your credit report, and you should check it for errors every year. You can contact the major credit bureaus at the following addresses:

Trans Union Credit
  Trans Union National Consumer Disclosure Center
  25249 Country Club Blvd
  P.O. Box 7000
  North Olmstead, OH 44070

TRW Credit Services
  TRW Consumer Assistance Center
  P.O. Box 2350
  Chatsworth, CA 91313

Equifax
  Equifax Information Service Center
  P.O. Box 740241
  Atlanta, GA 30374

Include your name (and any variations of your name that you use), your address, and your Social Security number, and sign the request personally. If you've recently been turned down for credit, there is no charge for getting a copy of your report.

What's in your credit report? Your credit report tracks payment history of any purchase you made using credit. Whether you make extended payments on credit or you always pay your bills in full every month, your payment record is reported to the credit bureau. The printed report uses a series of codes to identify your payment habits, but the credit bureau is required to give you a clear explanation of its reporting terminology. If a lender has recently inquired about your credit, that inquiry will be noted on your credit report.

Your credit record does *not* include information about your salary or wages, your bank accounts, or your assets. However, if you apply for a large insurance policy or mortgage, the lender can request an "investigative" report, which could contain the above information as well as information gathered from business associates and neighbors about your personal living habits. (In 1992, Equifax signed an agreement limiting investigative reporting questions.)

Although the three major credit bureaus do have overlap files on many people, the information in each company's file may be different. To check thoroughly on your credit, you should contact the three major agencies and read each report.

If you don't have a file with the credit bureaus, we'll show you how to establish one in Credit Card Strategy #4 in the next chapter. You'll probably need a record with the credit bureau to buy a home or car, or to get a credit card. (Since the 1990–91 recession, most financial institutions have stopped sending unsolicited credit cards to college students and dogs!)

Terry's Tip:

$$$ Check your credit report for accuracy—as well as for positive information that should be included but is not. For example, make sure the report includes all charge cards and recently repaid loans.

Credit Strategy #2: Correct All Errors Immediately

If you feel there is an error in your credit report, be prepared for a long fight. Although the credit bureaus are under pressure to deal more quickly with consumer complaints, erasing errors from your credit report can be a nightmare.

If you feel a reporting error was made by a company you do business with (a department store, gasoline company, mortgage company, etc.), contact that company directly, asking for a written statement of the error to be sent to the credit bureau. Many businesses send credit information to more than one credit bureau, so be sure to ask them to contact *each* credit bureau to which they previously made reports.

The business making the original error can have the most direct influence on changing an item in your credit report. You should follow up with all three credit bureaus to make sure the erroneous information has been corrected.

If there is an inexplicable error, such as confusion with another person of a similar name, you'll have a more difficult time clearing your credit report. Stolen credit cards and mistaken identities can cause long-term credit problems.

You are entitled to submit a brief statement to the credit bureau explaining your side of any credit dispute. Your statement will be mailed out along with the credit report when anyone checks your credit status.

Terry's Tips:

$$$ The major credit reporting bureaus recently settled lawsuits with the Federal Trade Commission and 19 states regarding their credit reporting practices, the way they deal with errors on consumer credit reports, and how they respond to consumer questions.

If you feel that a credit bureau has not responded promptly and fairly to your situation, contact the attorney general of your state or the Federal Trade Commission in Washington, D.C.

$$$ Ask for a copy of your credit report *before* you apply for an auto loan or home mortgage, so you can clear up any errors before you are denied a loan.

Credit Strategy #3: Get Credit in Your Own Name (Especially for Women)

Request a copy of your credit report—the report that lists you separately in your own name, not in the name of your spouse, or as a "signer" on a joint account. Many married women carry credit cards with their name imprinted on the card (or Mrs. *John* Jones, instead of *Susan* Jones) but find out only later that the credit card itself was issued to a spouse. In this case, regular monthly payments are credited to the spouse whose financial information was used to establish the credit account. Make sure the credit bureau lists you as "jointly responsible" for the credit, not as an "authorized signer" on the card.

The Equal Opportunity Act guarantees that a married woman is legally allowed to apply for credit separately in her own name. The same act says that the account must be reported without the use of titles such as Mr., Mrs., Miss, or Ms.

Credit bureaus do not have joint credit reports; if you have credit in joint name, transactions on that account are reported separately under individual names. Joint accounts opened since 1977 are generally reported separately to the credit bureau.

If a credit grantor has not been reporting payment history separately, you should request a change in writing. Then check back a few months later to see if the change was made. You do not have to have a job or income to have credit in your own name. You do have to have your payment history reported separately to the credit bureau on joint accounts in order to have credit in your own name.

Mortgage payments on property held in joint name must be reported separately, even if the income of only one spouse was used to apply for the mortgage.

If you are legally separated or divorced, you should close all joint accounts, open new ones in your own name, and then check with the credit bureaus in a few months to make sure your old account is reported closed. (See chapter 36, "Dollars and Divorce.")

If you don't already have, and can't seem to get, credit in your own name, see Credit Card Strategy #4 in the next chapter.

Credit Strategy #4: Get Help *Before* You Ruin Your Credit

Negative information stays on your credit report for seven years, except for bankruptcy, which will stay on your report for ten years. You should do everything possible to avoid ruining your credit record. That means facing up to credit and debt problems as soon as they occur.

In the 1990s, creditors understand the difference between credit problems caused by profligate spending and those caused by unexpected situations such as illness and job loss. You will be surprised at how many creditors are willing to work with you—if you face up to the situation early and fully.

If you feel the situation will be temporary, you can try to talk to your creditors about arranging an extended payment plan or an interest-only payment plan. If creditors are not responsive, or if you have too many creditors, it's time to seek help.

Warning: Avoid credit repair "clinics" and "specialists" who promise to solve your problems.

This is another big opportunity for scam artists who charge a few hundred dollars, saying they'll talk to your creditors and arrange a repayment schedule. Or they may ask for $1,000 to make payments on your "consolidated" loans. The money goes straight into their pockets.

There are two legitimate places to turn for credit assistance:

The National Foundation for Consumer Credit
8611 Second Avenue
Silver Spring, MD 20910 (800-388-2227)

Family Service America, Inc.
11700 West Lake Park Drive
Milwaukee, WI 53224 (800-221-2681)

Each of these agencies will put you in touch with a local office that will provide consumer credit counseling. These nonprofit organizations will work with you in two ways. They'll contact your creditors and help work out a repayment plan if possible. And they'll help you understand how to deal with a spending problem if you have one, so you can avoid future credit woes.

Terry's Tip:

$$$ Remember, if you have an argument with a merchant over an unpaid bill, the merchant has the power of the credit system as an ultimate weapon. If you refuse to pay a bill while you are arguing about a defective product, the merchant will report your delinquency to the credit bureau,

thereby jeopardizing your future borrowing ability. It's better to hire a lawyer, or file a suit and represent yourself (*pro se*) in court to get the dispute resolved.

Credit Strategy #5: Bankruptcy Is *Not* an Easy Out

As noted above, an estimated 1 million Americans filed for bankruptcy in 1992—a record number. With that many individuals and a great many public corporations filing for protection under the bankruptcy laws, much of the stigma has disappeared. But bankruptcy should only be considered as a last resort—when the mountain of debt is so great and the creditors so unrelenting that no other accommodation can be reached.

A bankruptcy stays on your credit report for ten years, making it difficult to reestablish your credit. But a bankruptcy may also affect your ability to get a job in the future, as many employers pull a credit report when assessing job applications.

There are three forms of bankruptcy for individuals. Chapter 7 is a straight bankruptcy liquidation plan. It requires the swift sale of any assets to satisfy creditors. How much will you be allowed to keep of your personal possessions? Each state has its own set of rules, and there is a set of federal exemptions.

The federal exemptions to a Chapter 7 bankruptcy allow the debtor to keep $7,500 in personal property used as a residence or in a burial plot, $1,200 equity in a motor vehicle, $4,000 in total value of household goods (with no individual item worth more than $200), $500 in personal jewelry, $750 in professional books or tools of a trade; and a few other exceptions.

Bankruptcy does not impair a debtor's right to receive Social Security, veteran's benefits, disability or unemployment benefits, alimony, or most pension payments. On the other hand, some debts such as alimony, child support, and most taxes survive bankruptcy and will still be owed.

Chapter 13 bankruptcy is a court-supervised program that reorganizes your debts and supervises a monthly repayment program over a period of three to five years. But Chapter 13 can be used only by those who have a regular income and debts under $100,000. While you are under supervision of the bankruptcy court, your creditors cannot take additional steps to attach your property, giving you time to work out your problems.

In 1991, the Supreme Court ruled that individuals may file to reorganize their finances under Chapter 11 of the federal bankruptcy law—the same chapter that is most used by businesses. The advantage of Chapter 11 is that the business or individual remains in possession of assets during the reorganization period.

A final word: You definitely need an attorney to counsel you before declaring bankruptcy and to guide you through the bankruptcy process if that is the only alternative. Do not, however, fall prey to the advertisements promising that bankruptcy is an "easy out." Use only a reputable specialist in the field of bankruptcy, and do not hesitate to interview several lawyers before choosing one.

If you know that bankruptcy is inevitable, do not charge up your credit cards or obtain cash advances. And do not pay off one favorite unsecured creditor within 90 days of declaring bankruptcy. Your lawyer can help you with the rest of the details.

Chapter 33

Credit Card Strategies

Americans hold 1.13 billion credit cards of all types. In 1994, Americans charged $611 billion to the five types of general purpose credit cards issued by Visa, MasterCard, American Express, Discover, and Diners Club. If you add in the spending on credit cards issued by retail stores, gasoline companies, telephone companies, airlines, and auto rental companies, the total charged in 1994 was $731 billion.

As you're certainly aware by now, not all credit cards are the same. There is a difference between charge cards issued by retail businesses, bankcards, and travel and entertainment cards. The primary differences between these cards relate to the payment requirements—and the differences can be significant. Rules vary from issuer to issuer. Even though a card may belong to the Visa or MasterCard association, the institution that issues the card sets the rules regarding annual fees, interest charges, and billing practices.

That makes it very important to choose—and use—only the cards that meet your personal needs. As you select the few cards you need, be sure to cut up and cancel any other cards you may hold, thereby avoiding the temptation to use them unwisely.

In the nineties, a whole new type of credit card has emerged. Traditionally, Visa and MasterCards have been issued by banking institutions, but in recent years other companies have been getting into the business—from AT&T to General Motors. Nonbank credit card issuers had a 24 percent share of the credit card market in 1992—up from 5 percent in 1986.

Although the General Motors card is actually issued by a financial services company, this affinity card offers a credit toward the future purchase of a GM car. Similarly, the General Electric card offers rebate checks that can be used on purchases at major retailers. The AT&T card doubles as a telephone calling card.

Airlines offer Visa and MasterCards that give "miles" for every dollar charged. Many charities also offer affinity cards that result in donations for each purchase charged to the card. And large retailers are starting to offer their own branded Visa and MasterCards, largely because typical store charge balances average about $250, while Visa and MasterCard average balances are about $1,400.

It's up to you to decide whether you're getting value in these cards. Many of the affinity cards promise no annual fees, very competitive interest rates, and extra benefits. It makes sense to shop around and compare credit card features.

One strategy you might consider is using a credit card that offers additional benefits such as air travel miles to make major purchases that you would have otherwise paid by check. College tuition bills or medical expense bills can often be charged to your credit card—and then paid in full at the end of the month. I know of several people who have even paid for automobiles using a credit card that earned mileage in a frequent flier program.

Of course, it helps to have a large credit limit on your card! But you may also ask providers of some services to bill you over a three-month period, enabling you to earn the bonus points or miles on your card. Check with your card issuer about expanding your credit limits and about the limits many card issuers are placing on the number of bonus points or miles you can earn in one year. Above all, don't get involved in this strategy unless you know you can pay your bill in full at the end of the month.

Terry's Tips:

$$$ Don't apply for more than one or two credit cards at a time. Each inquiry about your credit is included in your credit report. If too many credit grantors inquire at once, they'll all be suspicious of your intentions.

$$$ Make it a personal rule not to charge "disposable" items such as gasoline and food on your credit card. These items are long gone by the

time you receive your credit card bill. Unless you need the records for a business deduction, pay cash for food, restaurant meals, and gasoline.

Credit Card Strategy #1: Choose Your Credit Card Carefully

If you regularly carry a balance on your credit card, then choose a card with the lowest interest rate. If you pay your balance in full every month, don't worry about the interest rate on finance charges. Look for a card with no annual fee and a full grace period that allows you time to actually pay in full.

Here are two organizations that offer a list of bankcards with the lowest finance charges or no annual fees:

Bankcard Holders of America (703-389-5445) (cost $4)

CardTrak (800-344-7714) (cost $5)

Chart IV-1 shows the breakdown of interest rates paid by consumers on bankcards as of mid-1992, according to *The Nilson Report*, the industry's largest newsletter.

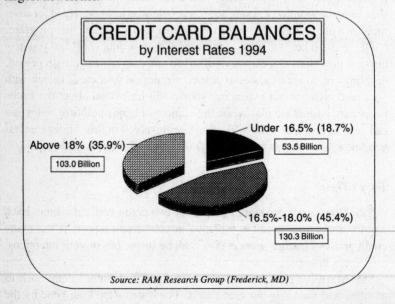

CREDIT CARD BALANCES
by Interest Rates 1994

Under 16.5% (18.7%)
53.5 Billion

Above 18% (35.9%)
103.0 Billion

16.5%-18.0% (45.4%)
130.3 Billion

Source: RAM Research Group (Frederick, MD)

Terry's Tips:

$$$ You may not have to change card issuers to get a lower-rate finance charge. Many card issuers will lower your rate if you have a good credit record. The first step is to call the toll-free number on your bill and inform your current card issuer that you're planning to switch unless you get a lower rate, and then see if they'll offer you a better deal.

In 1992, nine of the top ten card issuers offered lower rates, either on all cards issued or to selected customers with good repayment records.

$$$ One of the newest scams involves companies that promise to get you a low-interest-rate credit card—for a fee. Avoid these middlemen. Contact the card issuer directly, using the lists available from the sources listed above. Do not pay a fee unless the card is actually issued to you, at which time the fee will be added to your account balance.

Credit Card Strategy #2: Transfer Your Balance to a Lower-rate Card

If you apply for and are accepted for a low-interest-rate card, immediately transfer the outstanding balance from your old, higher-rate card. That can be done in one of two ways.

Either take a cash advance from your new card and use it to repay the charges on your old card. Or ask the issuer of the new card if they have actual payment "checks" that can be sent directly to the old card issuer to pay off your balance. This method can avoid costly cash advance fees. Make sure the low rate applies to transferred balances.

Credit Card Strategy #3: Avoid Cards with Costly Billing Practices

Beware of billing practices that can cost you more, in spite of advertised lower rates. Avoid the following:

- Cards that charge interest from date of purchase with no grace period.
- Cards that charge interest immediately on a cash advance, *plus* charge a fee for each cash advance.
- Cards that charge late fees and over-the-limit fees.

If you carry a balance from month to month, even a small balance, you will be affected by a common billing practice. Most cards charge interest on the "average daily balance." With this type of billing, consumers lose two ways. Even if a portion of the balance is repaid during the month, interest is charged on the average balance for the entire month. And interest will be charged on new, larger purchases from the date of purchase, forfeiting the grace period.

Credit Card Strategy #4: Apply for a Secured Credit Card

People who have no credit history, or those who can demonstrate that they have taken steps to repair a poor credit history, should apply for a *secured credit card*. Secured cards may be the first step in building a credit history for students, divorced women without their own credit history, or widows who face the same lack of individual credit.

Secured cards are offered by a number of banks and S&Ls around the country. The banking institution takes your deposit of from $500 to $5,000 and places it in an interest-bearing deposit account. The amount of your security deposit becomes your line of credit on the card.

The bankcard you receive looks and works just like a regular Visa or MasterCard. There is a standard annual fee for a secured card, and you will generally be charged a slightly higher than average rate on unpaid balances. But you shouldn't carry an unpaid balance when you use a secured card. The idea is to pay your charges in full every month. The card issuer will report your prompt payment history to the credit bureau. Before long you'll have established a good credit history, allowing you to get other cards or loans.

Again, a warning: Do not apply for your secured card through a "card shopping service" or any other type of middleman. Apply directly to the financial institution itself.

Some recommended secured card issuers:

Key Federal Savings Bank (800-228-2230)

Citibank (South Dakota) (800-743-1332)

American Pacific Bank (800-879-8745)

American Pacific Bank even offers a secured card for small businesses, with a minimum $1,000 security deposit required. This is a good way for a small business that does not yet qualify for a bank loan to establish credit and purchase needed start-up equipment.

For a complete list of secured card issuers, contact either Bankcard Holders of America or CardTrak at the toll-free numbers listed above in Credit Card Strategy #1 in this chapter.

Credit Card Strategy #5: Keep an Updated List of All Your Cards

Make a list of *all* the credit cards (and other cards such as insurance, driver's license, etc) you keep in your wallet. Note the account number, and next to it place the toll-free phone number that you have been given to call in case of loss or theft. (You'll find that number on your monthly bill.)

Know your liability if your cards are lost or stolen:

- If you report the loss of your credit cards *before* they are used, you have no liability for any charges.
- If you report the loss of your credit cards, but they have already been used, you are liable for the first $50 charged on each card.
- If a lost or stolen card is used for a mail order purchase and is not presented directly to the merchant, you are not liable for any of the purchase.

Terry's Tip:

$$$ There are some credit card registration protection services that offer to limit your entire liability in the case of lost or stolen cards. While these service can be expensive, they do offer a convenience for frequent travelers. If your cards are lost or stolen, you can make just *one* phone call to report the loss, and they will notify all your credit card issuers. Be sure to check your homeowners insurance policy to see if it will cover the $50 deductible on each credit card.

Credit Card Strategy #6: Know Your Credit Card Rights

Merchants sign their own agreements with card issuers such as Visa, MasterCard, and American Express. According to those agreements, merchants:

- Cannot ask for your phone number, address, or driver's license in order to accept your card.
- Should not ask for your credit card number in order to accept a check, and you should not allow your credit card number to be written on the back of your check. Also, merchants are not allowed to charge the cost of a bounced check to your credit card, even if they have your card number.
- Visa and MasterCard prohibit merchants from requiring a minimum dollar amount purchase in order to use your card. American Express has the same policy in most states.

Credit Card Strategy #7: Handle Credit Card Disputes Properly

Many people mistakenly believe that using a credit card to make a purchase automatically protects them in case of a dispute. While some premium cards do offer buyer protection plans that guarantee products which are lost, stolen, or defective, using a standard card does not absolve the shopper of the need to use discretion in purchasing.

A credit card is not like a check, in that you cannot "stop payment" for a purchase. You cannot notify your credit card issuer to decline payment once you have signed the charge slip. Instead, you must wait until the disputed charge appears on your bill. Then you have 60 days to notify your card issuer—*in writing*—that you dispute the charge.

Your card must notify the merchant's processing bank, which then contacts the merchant. If the merchant declines the chargeback and insists the charge stay on the bill, *you must pay*. Then your only remedy is to take the merchant to court.

A strong warning: If you are in a dispute with a merchant, you must continue to make payments on your charge or credit card account. If you don't, the damage to your credit report will be worse than any gains you feel you can get by harassing the merchant. Do not let your credit account become delinquent.

Credit Card Strategy #8: Avoid Credit Card Fraud

Credit card fraud is a $1.5 billion problem in the United States. You can avoid being a victim by using your credit card carefully:

- Do not make mail order purchases or give out your credit card number to individuals or companies that solicit you over the phone.
- Use credit cards for mail orders only with well-known companies, and only when you instigate the purchase.
- Do not write your credit card number on your personal check.
- Take possession of all carbons used in credit card transactions.

Credit Card Strategy #9: Apply for a Debit Card

If you can't seem to get your credit card spending under control, but you need the convenience of a credit card, apply instead for a *debit card*. They're issued by many major banks around the country, and they look just like a standard Visa or MasterCard. The only difference is that when your "charge" slip is processed, the amount of the purchase is deducted directly from your personal checking account. If there's no money in your checking account, the transaction won't go through.

With a debit card you no longer have to worry about receiving a big credit card bill every month and paying interest. Instead, you have the convenience of a credit card and the discipline of a finite spending limit: the amount of your checking account balance.

Chapter 34

Quick Cash and Bigger Borrowing Strategies

Everyone needs to have some funds available for emergencies or simply to negotiate bargains on purchases. Sometimes just a small amount of "quick cash" will do; at other times you might need a larger loan.

An individual or family should try to have at least six months' living expenses readily available in case of job loss or a medical or financial emergency. With so many people living at the edge these days, that's not always possible. So you want some strategies for when you need money fast.

Sometimes you'll find you need actual currency in an emergency. Although you can even pay for traffic tickets with credit cards these days, you should have access to instant cash. Automatic teller machines may limit you to withdrawals of $300 a day, but you might need even more cash on short notice.

At other times you may need a larger sum of money—although not necessarily cash. You may be unwilling to cash in your certificates of deposit and pay the penalty, or sell your stock and face the tax consequences. It's difficult to get a personal loan these days without putting up any collateral. But if you have assets—such as a house or stock certificates—you can raise cash without selling them. It's always easier to raise money when you don't need it, so many of these strategies require that you plan ahead.

Quick Cash Strategy #1: Authorized Overdrafts

One way to have immediate access to your cash is to prenegotiate a checking account *automatic overdraft* that will allow you to cash a check for more than your balance. It's a handy feature, but you'll be paying a steep rate of interest to get the extra money, so you should not get into the habit of using the overdraft on a regular basis. The same principle applies to cash advances on your credit card. They can come in handy, but they're no substitute for savings.

Terry's Tip:

$$$ Find out and compare the interest rate on your bank overdraft line of credit and on cash advances on your credit card. See if either type of account also charges a fee for each transaction. Also check to make sure that the overdraft on your checking account will be repaid automatically out of your next deposit. If not, you may have to notify the bank to repay your overdraft so that interest does not continue to accrue.

Quick Cash Strategy #2: Cash Advance from Your Credit Card

Your credit card can become an easy—but expensive—source of quick cash. Most Visa, MasterCard, Discover, and American Express cards work in global networks of automatic teller machines (ATMs). Depending on the type of card, you can access cash in various amounts. There is always a fee for each withdrawal, and finance charges may start from the day of withdrawal. That can make credit cards a particularly expensive source of quick cash.

MasterCard and Visa

If you have a Visa or MasterCard in your wallet, turn it over and look for the little logo on the back: it will have either a Cirrus or a Plus logo.

Cirrus and Plus are the bank-owned computer networks that have ATMs around the United States and in many other countries. Your card will work in any machine that carries the same logo. In fact, many of those terminals are now being shared, so it's quite possible that you'll find both logos on an ATM.

In order to get a cash advance on your Visa or MasterCard, you'll need the personal identification number (PIN) that you created when you first opened the account. If you didn't establish a PIN number, contact your card issuer.

The card-issuing bank sets any fees for cash advances, and the interest rate—which will probably be charged from the date of the withdrawal. Each card-issuing bank also sets its own limits for withdrawals, ranging from about $300 to more than $1,000. However, you may stop at an ATM which has its own, lower transaction limit. If you are allowed a larger cash advance than the machine limit, you'll have to use your card to make two or more withdrawals.

Discover

If you carry a Discover card, it will work in any ATM carrying the Discover logo. If you want to use your Discover card for a cash withdrawal and can't find a nearby machine, call 800-347-2683.

Fees for cash withdrawal on Discover cards are charged on a sliding scale: up to $500, you'll pay 2.5 percent; between $500 and $1,000, the fee is 2 percent; and it drops to 1.5 percent for withdrawals over $1,000. If you pay your entire card balance, including the cash advance, within 30 days, there are no finance charges.

American Express

American Express has its own "Express Cash" program. It allows you to use your American Express card either to access your own personal checking account or a line of credit at the American Express Centurion Bank through automatic teller machines, or to cash a personal check at any American Express Travel Service office.

You must sign up for the Express Cash program in advance of needing the cash. As part of the process, you create your own PIN number, allowing you to use your card in regular bank ATMs. Not all ATMs accept the American Express card, but there is a 24-hour, toll-free number that will give you the nearest ATM location: 800-CASH-NOW.

Using a standard green American Express card in an ATM, you can access $1,000 every seven days in the United States (or every 21 days abroad). Using a American Express Gold Card, you can access $2,500 every seven days in the United States (or every 21 days abroad). The ATM may have a lower limit on withdrawals, so you will have to use your card to make multiple withdrawals if you want a larger amount of cash.

The fee for the ATM access is 2 percent of the amount withdrawn, with a minimum fee of $2.50 and a maximum fee of $10. If the money is being withdrawn from your checking account, there is no interest charge. If you are withdrawing cash against your line of credit at American Express Centurion Bank, the interest rate depends on your credit history.

If you use your card at an American Express Travel Service office to cash a personal check, the limits are $1,000 for a green card and $5,000 for a gold card, with the same restrictions as to dates.

Terry's Tip:

$$$ You may find that you have four or five PIN numbers—one for your bank ATM card and one for each of your credit cards. Most card issuers allow you to choose your own PIN. It's perfectly all right to use the same PIN number for each card. Just make sure you don't use your address, birthdate, or phone number. If your wallet is stolen, those are the first numbers a (thinking) thief would try!

Quick Cash Strategy #3: Turn Stocks into Cash Without Selling

If you ever need a large sum of cash quickly, don't forget about the money you have invested in stocks. While you might not want to sell your stocks, either because of your market outlook or because of tax considerations, you can easily borrow money against most stock certificates. Simply bring or send the stock to a broker, and sign a stock power and a margin agreement.

Under current Federal Reserve rules, the brokerage firm can lend you up to 50 percent of the market value of the stock. The interest rates charged on margin accounts are among the lowest anywhere, since they're based on your fully secured asset. Usually that means you'll pay interest at the broker's loan rate, which is usually only one point above the prime rate.

You can also borrow against the market value of your mutual fund. To do this, you must have purchased your shares through one of the discount brokerage firms, such as Charles Schwab or Fidelity Discount Brokerage, that allows mutual fund margin accounts. (See Mutual Fund Buying Strategy #2 in chapter 16.) Or you can purchase shares directly from the mutual fund, and ask the brokerage firm for a transfer-of-asset form instructing the mutual fund custodian to transfer your shares to the discount brokerage firm.

Terry's Tips:

$$$ Be careful when borrowing against volatile stocks. If the market price of your stock drops, the brokerage firm could ask you to send more shares as collateral or replace some of the money you borrowed from your margin account. Mutual fund shares, even those of stock market mutual funds, tend to be less volatile.

$$$ The interest you pay on your margin borrowings is deductible— but only against other investment income, such as dividends and interest.

Quick Cash Strategy #4: Your Home Equity

If you have equity built up in your house, it may be tempting to take out a home equity line of credit for an emergency. This strategy starts out with a word of warning: Be careful when tapping into the equity you've built up in your home. If you miscalculate and cannot make repayments, they're not just repossessing your car or refrigerator; this time they can take your home!

Although homeowners have always had access to second mortgages to tap the equity in their homes, the real marketing of home equity loans and lines of credit started after the 1986 Tax Reform Act, which phased out the deductibility of consumer interest—except for mortgage interest. Suddenly, banks and S&Ls started making it simple to borrow against the equity in your home.

Interest on home equity loans is deductible on borrowings of up to

$100,000 over the initial amount of the first mortgage. By year-end 1991 there was $131 billion in outstanding home equity lines of credit—more than one third of all second mortgage debt.

As we pointed out in chart I-6 (chapter 4), the percentage of equity controlled by homeowners has fallen to 55 percent—the lowest ever. But the combination of fairly low interest rates—usually about 2 points over prime—and tax deductibility of the interest have made home equity loans a real magnet for borrowers.

The traditional second mortgage was used for home improvements or for major expenses such as sending a child to college. But fewer than one third of today's home equity borrowers use the money for home improvements. The equity in homes is financing vacation trips, business start-ups, and debt consolidation. In a slowing economy, that will spell trouble for borrowers.

Some suggestions if you insist on using home equity loans as a borrowing strategy:

1. Understand the difference between a home equity *loan* and a home equity *line of credit*. If you take out a home equity loan, you'll be paying interest from the time you sign up for the loan. To secure a line of credit, you might have to pay an up-front appraisal and loan fee, but you don't start paying interest until you draw down the line of credit, usually by writing yourself a check.

2. Understand the repayment terms of your loan or line of credit. Many of these programs require *interest-only* monthly repayments. That can make the loan seem more affordable, but could leave you with a big balance, sometimes called a "balloon payment," when the loan comes due in five or seven years.

3. Understand how the interest rate is set on your loan or line of credit. Some rates are tied to prime rate, plus three or more percentage points. If interest rates start to rise again, the monthly payments could weigh heavily on your budget.

4. Do not be lured by very low interest rates offered for the first six months or one year on a home equity loan or line of credit. If the advertised rate is substantially below the indexed rate, which will take

effect in a matter of months, you could be surprised by a big jump in required payments.

5. Don't use a home equity loan or line of credit to refinance consumer debt without getting professional credit counseling. Once you have paid off your credit cards, the temptation is great to use them again. That puts you right back in the jackpot—but this time your home is on the line.

Quick Cash Strategy #5: Personal Loans

If you don't have some asset to use as collateral, it will be very difficult to get a personal loan. One of the first places to turn is your company credit union. There is a common misconception that you cannot get a loan at your credit union in excess of the amount you have on deposit. Yes, you do have to be a member of the credit union, meaning you have to have an account there, but the loan amount is not related to your balance on deposit.

Finance companies frequently advertise that they will make unsecured personal "signature" loans, but the rates are very high. That's what makes those loans so profitable for finance companies—and pawnshops (which in the 1990s have taken on the title: consumer loan banks!).

Quick Cash Strategy #6: Borrowing on Life Insurance

If you have cash value life insurance, it should be fairly easy to take out a loan. No one will ask to see a credit report or check your ability to repay. After all, you're borrowing your own money. But there are some drawbacks to borrowing against your life insurance.

First, the death benefits of your insurance are reduced by the amount you borrow. So if you die with a loan outstanding, your heirs will receive less than you had intended when you purchased the policy.

Second, the real cost of borrowing against your life insurance is not always apparent. The stated interest rate may be fairly low, but you are not actually borrowing the cash *out* of your policy; instead, you are using the cash value as collateral against a loan. The interest rate you are supposed to be earning on that cash value is reduced on the portion that is used as loan collateral. So your overall earnings on the policy are reduced, plus you are paying interest on the loan.

On some policies, such as universal life policies, the amount you take out is not considered a loan but a policy withdrawal. So you will not owe interest on this type of withdrawal. But, in a worst-case scenario, borrowing against the cash value in this type of policy could so deplete your insurance policy that you won't have enough money to continue paying the premiums, and your insurance will lapse (see chapter 52).

Before borrowing against a life insurance policy, always ask the agent to illustrate what might happen to the death benefit, the cash value, and the annual premium payments if you do not quickly repay the loan.

Chapter 35

Marriage and Money

Many people find it difficult to get a grip on their own money. Marriage doesn't just double money problems, it multiplies the pain of dealing with financial issues. As I've often noted, there are two types of people in this world: the savers and the spenders. For better or for worse, they often wind up marrying each other! That's the root of most money problems in marriage.

Most couples discuss religion, children, sex, and politics while they're dating. Yet most couples avoid talking about money, even though it's the cause of some of the biggest fights within marriage. In spite of all the humor about spendthrifts and shopping sprees, if you have a basic difference in money attitudes within your family, it is no joke—and it won't go away without discussion.

Every financial decision and many other family decisions—where to vacation, which car to buy, whether to give the children an allowance, which restaurant to choose—will be impacted by money attitudes. The only solution is to sit down, talk about, and reconcile your money attitudes. The best time to talk about marriage and money is *before* the wedding ceremony. In fact, talk might not be enough. As you'll see, it might be important to actually structure a legal agreement that covers the money issues during and after a marriage.

Some of these strategies require legal advice, and a few require *separate* legal advice for both parties to the marriage. Other strategies require only the self-discipline to confront the financial issues that crop up in most first and second marriages.

Just as some couples need the advice of a marriage counselor, you might also decide to seek the advice of a money counselor—a financial planner, accountant, or attorney with experience in the field. Or you can take your own common-sense approach to dealing with everyday money matters within marriage.

Marriage/Money Strategy #1: Discuss Money Before Marriage

Obviously this advice will come too late for many people reading this book. But you are the ones who can validate this strategy and speak openly about it to your friends or children who are contemplating marriage.

Here is a checklist of some of the major money issues that should be discussed—and perhaps committed to writing—*before* the ceremony:

1. How much money each party earns—last year and this year.

2. What *assets* each party owns, and what *debts* each party currently owes.

3. How income will be handled after marriage:
   One joint checking account.
   Each contributes to a joint account, but keeps a separate account for personal expenses.
   Each contributes an equal amount to a joint account, or an amount proportionate to earnings.
   Each draws a fixed weekly "allowance" from a joint account, or spends personal money from a separate account.

4. How debt will be handled after marriage:
   Each responsible for paying debts incurred prior to marriage.
   Premarital debts paid out of joint marriage account.
   One party pays the other's debts in full.

5. How credit will be handled after marriage (and the related question of whether one person changes name):
   Couple has a joint credit card account (each person having a card and credit reported in both names).

One party changes name but keeps credit separate.

Individuals keep previous names and separate credit (check with your attorney to see how state laws regarding community property and debt responsibility affect your ability to keep credit separate after marriage).

6. How you will save for major joint purchases, such as a house, car, or vacation:

Create a separate money market account with variable or regular contributions from each party.

Make purchases whenever one or both have enough cash.

7. How you will structure investments—especially if you have different risk tolerances:

The one who contributes most makes all decisions.

The one with past experience makes all decisions.

Decisions are made jointly, with both parties required to understand risks and investment concepts.

8. How you will divide your assets if one spouse dies, and how you want to structure your estate plan and life insurance policies.

9. How you will divide assets, future income, and property in case of divorce.

and, perhaps most important,

10. Who will have the monthly responsibility for paying the bills, writing the checks, and balancing the checkbook:

Bills are divided as previously agreed and paid out of separate checking accounts.

One person is always responsible for bill-paying chores.

Responsibility rotates from month to month (the other person gets to do an equally rewarding job such as washing dishes, doing laundry, or cleaning the gutters!).

Marriage/Money Strategy #2: Title Assets Correctly

It's important to consider how any assets you acquire should be titled—for purposes of estate taxes, potential divorce, and to protect assets in case of a lawsuit. Many of these considerations are determined by state law, especially in community property states where it may be difficult to title (or dispose of) marital property in one name. Still, these are important issues to consider in conjunction with your attorney.

There are a few basic ways you can title property jointly:

Joint tenancy with right of survivorship means each partner owns an equal share of the property and can sell or otherwise dispose of it without asking the other partner(s). On death, that partner's share is left to the one remaining partner, or divided equally among other partners.

Joint tenancy in common means co-owners can dispose of their shares of the property independently, but on death one partner's share goes to heirs named in a will, or next of kin, instead of going automatically to the remaining partner(s).

Tenancy in entirety is allowed in some states. It is similar to joint tenancy with right of survivorship, but each partner must have the permission of the other to sell his or her share in the property.

No matter how property is titled, if you live in one of the nine community property states (Arizona, California, Idaho, Louisiana, Nevada, New Mexico, Texas, Washington, and Wisconsin), the property may be considered to be owned equally by both marriage partners. You will probably need attorneys and a prenuptial agreement to keep property ownership separate in those states.

In chapter 55, you'll learn that under current federal inheritance taxation law, any spouse can pass an unlimited amount of assets to a surviving spouse—free of all estate taxes. But when the second spouse dies, then there could be a huge estate tax burden. That's why it may be a good idea to title property in the name of a living trust. You can't avoid estate taxes, but you can structure the trust to shelter $1.2 million from these taxes, which run as high as 55 percent. Plus, you can avoid probate fees, which can be significant, and transfer assets more easily and privately. Be sure to read chapter 56 before you title your major assets.

There is one other thing to consider in titling your property and investment accounts: One spouse may be more vulnerable to litigation than the other because of his or her profession. That's something to take into account when titling major assets such as a home. If a transfer of property takes place *after* one spouse is sued, or files bankruptcy, the conveyance of title can be attacked as an attempt to defraud. That's why you might consider a strategy such as the *family limited partnership*, described in chapter 57.

Marriage/Money Strategy #3: Understand Prenuptial Agreements

Prenuptial agreements are just what the words imply—financial and other arrangements made *before* marriage. The importance of making such an agreement before the ceremony can't be stressed enough. *Postnuptial* agreements can cover the same topics, but the motivation of the two parties is different at that point, and the legal considerations may also be different.

Prenuptial agreements can cover:

Arrangements for disposition of assets acquired during the marriage in case of death, or divorce;

Arrangements for disposition of assets owned by either party before the marriage in case of death or divorce;

Arrangements for one party to pay (or not pay) maintenance or other benefits in case of divorce;

Arrangements for care of children from previous marriages, in case of death of the custodial parent.

As you can see, prenuptial agreements are not just for the wealthy, or those with disparate incomes. This type of agreement is becoming standard in second marriages, where the parties want to protect the assets and children of previous marriages. But prenuptial agreements are also becoming more prevalent in first marriages—where both parties have careers and may have built up some financial assets.

There are two key ingredients required for a prenuptial agreement to hold up in court:

1. Each party must be represented by a *separate* attorney.

2. Each party must make *full disclosure* of all assets.

Don't wait until the week before the wedding to contact an attorney. If you're going to have a legal agreement, make it a part of the advance planning. You can discuss the basic agreements together before meeting with your attorneys. Recognize that it might seem painful to have the details of a death or split-up outlined on legal paper, just at the time you're feeling most optimistic about the success and longevity of your relationship.

The time to solve any disputes or problems is in a loving setting—not in a court during divorce or by arguing with family members after a death. You buy life insurance when you're healthy. Consider this prenuptial agreement in a similar way—as marriage insurance to be purchased when your prospective marriage is healthy.

Chapter 36

Dollars and Divorce

Although the divorce rate has been falling in the nineties, there's still a one-in-three chance that your marriage will fail. If you have a prenuptial agreement, many of the financial arrangements of your divorce will have been worked out in advance, thereby saving expense and stress.

People intuitively know that divorce is expensive. What they fail to recognize is just where those expenses are incurred. Of course, it will cost more to keep two separate households, especially if there are children. But one of the largest costs of divorce is in the legal fees.

In many cases a couple will have reached a basic agreement about how assets and future income will be split, and then consult attorneys. Then each attorney may assure the client that a better settlement could be reached through the legal process. That begins a process of bitter wrangling between spouses while the legal meter is running. Assets that could have been divided are used to pay legal bills.

Each party should have a competent attorney in a divorce proceeding and should respect the attorney's legal advice. But as in the case of investments, this is still your (failing) marriage and your future life at stake. Maintaining control of the process is critical.

While divorce is an emotional family issue, it is also an important financial situation. As in all financial matters, knowledge is the key to a positive financial result. Check to see if your state bar association has publications that deal with the financial issues of divorce discussed below.

DIVISION OF PROPERTY

Understand how property is legally divided in case of divorce in your state. Some common forms of property division are:

Equitable distribution: Each spouse is recognized as a partner in the marriage and the marital assets. If you can't agree on a distribution of marital assets, the court will decide on an "equitable"—not necessarily equal—distribution of marital property based on criteria such as need, potential earnings, previous financial contribution, etc. *Fault* is not a consideration in distribution of assets.

Community property or "marital property": All property acquired during the marriage is considered community property, to be divided by the parties. The only exception is property acquired separately: before the marriage, inherited, or specifically excluded from the community property by legal agreement.

Common-law: This concept of property is used only in a few states, such as Mississippi. Distribution of property is based solely on who holds title to the property, without any considerations of equity.

SPOUSAL MAINTENANCE AND CHILD SUPPORT

Understand how spousal support and child support are decided under the laws of your state. Does your state have certain minimum requirements such as a percentage of income to be paid in establishing support? Are there standards for duration of spousal support?

Many states require child support to be paid through the courts, and they offer a procedure for garnishing wages if support is not paid. That may add a few days to the receipt of a check each month, but it can be an important guarantee of regular payments.

CREDIT AND DIVORCE

Start immediately to establish separate credit after divorce. During the period of separation, contact the three major credit bureaus (see chapter 32 for addresses) and any local credit bureaus in your town which can be found under "Credit Bureaus" in the Yellow Pages.

Request a copy of your current credit report and check the report carefully for outstanding balances and accounts that have been registered in joint name. Immediately pay off and close all joint accounts—unless there are outstanding balances that you are asking the court to allocate for payment. In the case of an account opened using only one spouse's financial statement, that spouse may request that the account be closed or that the other signer's name be removed from charging privileges on the account.

After the divorce is finalized, inform the credit bureaus in writing of your new marital status. Request that your credit information be reported in your name only after the divorce. A creditor cannot close your account simply because you have been divorced. However, the creditor can require you to submit a new application if the original application was based on only one spouse's financial information. During this process, you must be allowed to use the account.

If you were only a card user on your previous credit accounts, and not jointly responsible for the credit, you may find yourself with no separate credit history after divorce. You may try to prove that you were equally responsible for the payments by submitting a personal financial statement, but most credit bureaus will not alter the original credit status of the account unless new financial information is submitted.

Without a credit history, it's almost impossible to get new credit. When applying for a new credit card in your own name after divorce, you can request that regularly received child support and alimony or maintenance payments be considered as part of your income. If your credit record and income are not convincing enough, a *secured credit card* is a perfect solution (see chapter 33).

Even after a final divorce decree is granted, both spouses may be considered liable for outstanding bills on joint accounts. One exception may be in the case where one spouse ran up huge bills in anticipation of divorce. Even though the court may decide that one party is responsible for certain debts, both spouses are liable for the entire outstanding amount on joint credit cards.

TAXES AND DIVORCE

When you agree to a divorce settlement that includes division of property and future support payments, it is imperative that you understand the tax considerations. While your divorce attorney should be well versed in tax considerations, you might also want to consult an accounting authority before signing any settlements.

Some basic considerations:

Alimony and maintenance payments are usually taxable income for the receiving spouse and tax-deductible for the paying spouse.

Child support is generally not considered either taxable to the receiving spouse or a deduction to the paying spouse.

Transfers of assets such as a house or property may be tax-free at the time of a divorce settlement, but will be subject to taxes when the house is eventually sold. Consult your accountant to find the tax basis of the portion of the property received in a divorce settlement.

The spouse who is receiving taxable alimony or spousal maintenance will have to start filing quarterly estimated tax returns because no withholding taxes are deducted from these payments. Consult an accountant immediately to determine the proper amount of quarterly payments, and get the estimated tax forms that must be filed.

Generally, the custodial parent may use the dependent exemption for tax-reporting purposes. In cases of joint custody, the divorce agreement should specifically state which parent may take the exemption.

Check with your accountant to see if as custodial parent you qualify for "head of household" status, and thus pay lower taxes.

Alimony or spousal maintenance may be considered "earned income" to the receiving spouse and thus qualify for contributions to an Individual Retirement Account.

The Retirement Equity Act (1984) allows divorcing spouses to share in the benefits in all qualified pension and retirement plans without penalty or loss of tax advantage, as long as the money is kept in the plan or rolled into another IRA. Consult your attorney and accountant about these provisions.

If you incur childcare expenses, you may be eligible for the childcare tax credit. Ask your accountant or local IRS office for the rules and forms.

Some attorney fees may be deductible as "tax advice," so get an itemized bill for divorce attorney services.

DIVORCE AND FINANCIAL FAIRNESS

While there are reams of case law in the field of divorce, no set of laws has yet decreed that divorce will be "fair." In fact, much of the case law has been made in disputes over what is financially fair and equitable. One judge commented that he knows his decision is most "fair" when both parties seem to be equally unhappy with his ruling!

Plenty of help is available in dealing with the emotional aspects of divorce, but there has been relatively little focus on financial counseling— especially in the case of women who do not have as much financial experience as their spouses.

What may look like an equitable division of current assets—the wife gets the home, the husband the stocks—is not necessarily a balanced division of property. The home will require upkeep and annual property taxes; the stocks will declare dividends and offer liquidity. Frequently, the future earning power of one spouse is far greater than the potential of the other spouse. These things are hard to quantify and are not necessarily measurable in dollars and cents.

That's when an independent, qualified financial planner can come in handy. Although it's important to seek financial advice to reorganize your financial advice *after* divorce, it may be equally beneficial to consult a financial professional *before* you agree on terms of a final settlement.

Chapter 37

Money Strategies for College

Among the largest investments you will ever make is a college education for your children. If you have several children, the cost will be at least as expensive as buying your home. The only difference is that you purchase a home with a relatively small down payment—and keep paying it off over the years. When college comes along, it will be a huge expenditure that has to be paid in a very short period of time. That's why it's so important to start saving early for those college expenses—and to use the same discipline that you use for paying your mortgage every month.

There's no doubt that a college education is one of the best investments you can make. Studies have shown that an individual with four or more years of college will earn approximately $500,000 more (in today's dollars) over a lifetime than a person with only a high school education. In fact, in 1990 the average earnings of a male with a college education were approximately 44 percent higher than a fellow with only a high school education. For women, the disparity was greater; in 1990 a woman with a college education earned, on average, 54 percent more than a woman who had only completed high school.

While a college education certainly pays off in the long run, the cost of higher education has become a greater and greater burden on the average family. That's no surprise, because college cost inflation at private schools during the 1980s grew at more than twice the rate of the increases in the consumer price index during that decade (see chart IV-2).

CHART IV-2

The Cost of a College Education Is Rising Faster than Inflation
(Cumulative rise in college costs compared to the Consumer Price Index, 1982–92, years ending July 31)

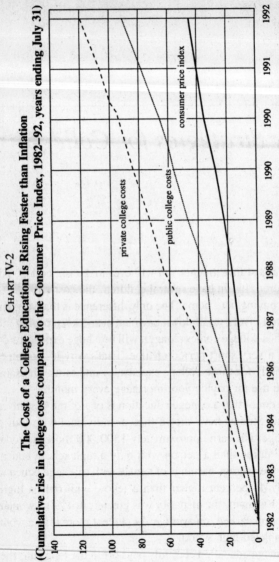

SOURCES: Source of college costs: Digest of Education Statistics, 1992, U.S. Department of Education; 1991, 1992 costs estimated. Source of Consumer Price Index: Department of Labor, Bureau of Labor Statistics.

As you can see from chart IV-3, the cost of one year of private college education soared throughout the 1980s and now absorbs nearly 47 percent of the annual income of a median-income family. While public college costs have also been rising, state colleges and universities remain much more affordable (see chart IV-4).

During the 1992–93 school year, public universities cost an average of $6,500, and the average cost of one year at a private university was $18,700. Projecting the recent rates of increase until the year 2007, when today's toddlers start college, gives a forecast of nearly $80,000 as the cost of a four-year education in a public university; four years at a private institution would cost more than $260,000!

But that may not necessarily come to pass. First, although tuition costs will continue to increase at public colleges and universities as states struggle with budget crunches, state schools will continue to enjoy a tremendous cost advantage over private schools. More and more middle-income parents, faced with job uncertainty and declining real estate values, may opt to send their children to excellent, but less prestigious, in-state schools. That trend will help keep in-state tuition down.

Second, demographics will start to work against private universities. Those schools get the majority of their students from upper-income

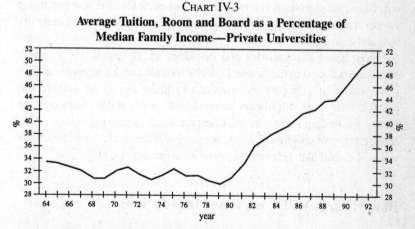

CHART IV-3
Average Tuition, Room and Board as a Percentage of Median Family Income—Private Universities

SOURCES: Source of college costs: Digest of Education Statistics, 1992, U.S. Department of Education; 1991, 1992 costs estimated.
Source of median family income: U.S. Department of Commerce, Bureau of the Census; 1992 figure estimated.

CHART IV-4

**Average Tuition, Room and Board as a Percentage of
Median Family Income—Public Universities**

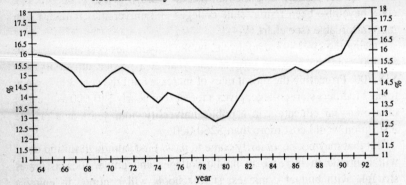

SOURCES: Source of college costs: Digest of Education Statistics, 1992, U.S. Department of Education; 1991, 1992 costs estimated.
Source of median family income: U.S. Department of Commerce, Bureau of the Census; 1992 figure estimated.

families—where the baby boom became a baby bust in the 1970s. There will be pressure to limit runaway fee increases before the few remaining paying students defect to public schools. In other words, economic reality will arrive at college campuses.

You've heard the statistics and estimates about how much a college education will cost in the future. Don't be intimidated; be determined. The strategies in this chapter are designed to make saving for college less painful. Plus there will always be ways that resourceful families can find money for student loans. So don't despair about ever being able to afford college for your children. College for your children is the best investment you will ever make. Get started on an investment plan, right now.

How Much It Will Cost, How Much to Save

You can either save as much as you can and hope it will be enough, or try to get a handle on what college will cost when your child is ready. Of course, the trends could change. If you'd like a forecast of costs at a specific college or university for a particular year in the future, several investment firms offer that service free of charge:

The INVESCO Funds Group (800-525-8085), based in Denver, Colorado, tracks college costs and projects future costs at 3,000 colleges and universities around the country.

T. Rowe Price (800-638-5660), the no-load mutual fund management company, has an excellent college planning package, which projects not only college costs, but also the amounts required to be saved to meet those costs.

The College Savings Bank (800-888-2723), which sells a certificate of deposit designed to assure future funding of college costs (Strategy #3 in this chapter), also provides a planning package which includes worksheets to help you determine how much you will need to save. Charts IV-5 and IV-6 are provided by the College Savings Bank.

BEFORE YOU START YOUR COLLEGE SAVINGS PLAN: Important Tax Rules Related to Children and College Savings

The first step is to be aware of some of the basic tax rules that could affect your savings plan:

1. *The "Kiddie Tax"*.

Under current tax laws, the first $650 that a child under the age of 14 earns in interest or dividend income is completely tax-free. The second $650 of income is taxed at the child's rate, currently 15 percent. Any interest or dividend income over that amount is taxed at the parents' rate until the child is 14. Once the child reaches age 14, the income is taxed at the child's rate. The limits are indexed upward every year. These are the rates if a separate tax return is filed for a child, and the filing includes Form 8615.

If a child has only interest and dividend income that is greater than $500, but less than $5,000, parents may choose to file Form 8814 with their own tax return instead of filing a separate return for the child. In that case, the child's investment income under $500 is tax-free; between $500 and $1,000 is taxed at 15 percent; and over $1,000 is taxed at the parents' rate. There is no annual inflation adjustment.

CHART IV-5
College Cost Table

This table projects total four-year costs of tuition, fees, room and board (TFR&B) for students entering college between 1993 and the year 2016. It assumes 7.9% annual increases in college costs (7.9% is the average annual increase in private college costs for the ten-year period ended 1992).

Child's Age	Current Grade	Year Child Will Enter College	Projected Future Cost of 4 Years TFR&B Private College	Projected Future Cost of 4 Years TFR&B Public College
		1993	$ 78,999	$ 31,600
16	11	1994	85,240	34,096
15	10	1995	91,974	36,790
14	9	1996	99,240	39,696
13	8	1997	107,080	42,832
12	7	1998	115,539	46,216
11	6	1999	124,667	49,867
10	5	2000	134,516	53,806
9	4	2001	145,142	58,057
8	3	2002	156,609	62,643
7	2	2003	168,981	67,592
6	1	2004	182,330	72,932
5	KG	2005	196,734	78,694
4		2006	212,276	84,910
2		2007	229,046	91,618
1		2008	247,141	98,856
0		2009	266,665	106,666
		2010	287,731	115,093
		2011	310,462	124,185
		2012	334,989	133,995
		2013	361,453	144,581
		2014	390,007	156,003
		2015	420,818	168,327
		2016	454,063	181,625

Note: Annual increases are estimated. Actual college costs may vary.

SOURCES:
Source for 1992–1993 private college costs: The College Board's Independent College 500 Index.
Source for 1992–1993 public college costs: U.S. Department of Education.

CHART IV-6

Two Ways to Build Your Child's College Fund

(Assumes 6% annual return compounded monthly before any applicable taxes)

Value After	Planned Savings Program Monthly Investment			Lump Sum Gift* Amount of Gift		
	$50/ month	$200/ month	$500/ month	$10,000	$25,000	$50,000
2 Years	$1,278	$5,112	$12,780	$11,272	$28,179	$56,358
5 Years	3,506	14,024	35,059	13,489	33,721	67,443
10 Years	8,235	32,940	82,349	18,194	45,485	90,970
20 Years	23,218	92,870	232,176	33,102	82,755	165,510

* Annual lump sum gifts over $10,000 per recipient ($20,000 for a married couple) are subject to federal gift taxes.

2. Gift Tax Rules

Each parent may give $10,000 every year to each child, tax-free to the child and without any estate or gift tax consequences to the parent. But, as you'll see below, you should think twice about putting money for college in a child's name. If the family is going to apply for financial aid, assets held in a child's name, or in custodial accounts for the child, count more heavily against the family in the aid formula.

If grandparents are thinking of using their $10,000 each annual gift to create a college fund, they should give the money to the parents instead of the child if the family is going to apply for financial aid. Or better yet, the grandparent can write a check in any amount directly to the college for tuition and fees, with no gift tax consequences. (See an explanation of this strategy in chapter 57.)

3. Uniform Gifts to Minors

When you transfer money or assets to children or grandchildren, the usual way to title the assets is through a custodial account established under the Uniform Gifts to Minors Act. The account is opened using the *child's* Social Security number, with one parent as custodian. Thus, the account should read: "Mrs. Betty Smith, custodian for Billy Smith." You can open several accounts with each parent as custodian of a different account.

Setting up a custodial account does not jeopardize your ability to claim the child as a dependent on your return. The child is still a dependent as long as you furnish half his or her support, and he or she is either under age 19 or a full-time student under age 24.

Once you have transferred money to a custodial account, you cannot use that money for normal parental obligations such as food, clothing, or shelter. If you do so, the money spent out of the account is taxable to the parent. If you want to transfer real property—including real estate, collectibles, and paintings—you will use the forms for the Uniform *Transfer* to Minors Act. See your attorney for proper transfer of title to these assets.

Terry's Tips:

$$$ If one parent makes the gift of money or other assets, the other parent should be named as custodian for the child. In that case, if the gifting parent dies, the assets cannot be included in that parent's estate.

$$$ In many states, when little Billy turns 18, the money is his (in 22 states, the age of majority is 21). You may have had it set aside for college; he may want a sportscar. That's something to keep in mind when making gifts to children under the Uniform Gifts to Minors Act.

4. Trusts for Minors

If you want to transfer a substantial amount of money to a child, you may want to establish a separate trust with yourself or your spouse as trustee. The legal cost of setting up this kind of trust can be significant, and gift tax rules apply on all transfers of assets to this type of trust. Plus, the trust must file its own tax return annually.

There may be serious disadvantages to putting money in trust for a child if you ever apply for financial aid. All the assets of the trust may be considered as the child's assets (which are more heavily assessed in the aid process), even if the trust documents do not make all of the trust assets available for college.

5. Financial Aid Rules

This subject will be referred to in greater detail in the next chapter, but you should be aware that assets held in the child's name will weigh six times more heavily against your family than assets held in the parents' names when it comes to assessing need in relation to financial aid and need-based scholarships. (College aid formula counts 5.6 percent of parents' savings, but 35 percent of child's savings when figuring loan amounts.) So if you think you might be applying for financial aid, it would be unwise to put considerable assets in your child's name.

College Savings Strategy #1: Buy a Stock Market Mutual Fund

To take advantage of the "kiddie tax" rules, you might want to put growth stocks or mutual funds in an account for your children. If you commit to this plan early enough, you'll have the advantage of investing for growth, historically getting better returns over the long run than fixed-income investing. Plus there are some tax advantages to investing for capital gains instead of current income:

With interest rates at 5 percent, your child could have $12,000 in a savings account, earn the $600 interest, and pay no taxes. With $24,000 in that savings account, the second $600 in interest would be taxed at the child's rate—currently 15 percent.

Putting any more money in the child's name to earn interest does not give you a tax break, although it does build a college fund. That's one reason it makes sense to invest a young child's college account in a growth stock mutual fund. The fund will pay relatively low dividends and capital gains, avoiding taxation at the parents' higher rate.

But the best reason to put a college account for a young child into equity investments is the greater opportunity for growth of assets. My favorite strategy for this situation is Simple Mutual Fund Strategy #1 in chapter 17. With the United Services All American Equity Fund, you can open a custodial account for your child with as little as $100—and have them automatically withdraw from your checking account as little as $30 a month or more to add to your mutual fund account. You're buying the S&P index of the 500 largest companies in America—a good basis for saving for a college education in the long run.

If you don't want to put your entire savings into the stock market fund, United Services also has a U.S. Government Securities Savings Fund, which was the highest-yielding Treasury money market fund for most of 1992. You can divide your regular monthly investment between the stock index fund and the money market fund, with the same automatic monthly investment limits. For information and prospectus, 800-US-FUNDS.

You can also choose from the dozens of no-load growth stock funds and related money market funds featured in the Morningstar service (see Mutual Fund Advice Strategy #1 in chapter 18).

Terry's Tip:

$$$ This strategy will only work if you keep making that regular monthly investment through all the ups and downs of the stock market. However, at some point a few years before college starts, you should transfer a substantial portion of your college money out of the stock market and into a money market fund. While equity investing is a good idea over the long run, you need lower volatility as college approaches. Many funds will set up an automatic plan to transfer a specific dollar amount out of the stock fund each month as college approaches and into a money market fund where there is no risk of loss.

College Savings Strategy #2: Series EE U.S. Savings Bonds

As explained in chapter 14, U.S. savings bonds have been recast as an excellent variable-rate, tax-deferred investment—with a special deal for parents who purchase savings bonds and use them later to pay college tuition. Subject to certain restrictions, as detailed below, all the interest earned on those savings bonds will be tax-free if the bonds are cashed in and used to pay tuition in the same year.

Here are the rules to make the interest on Series EE savings bonds completely tax-free.

The Series EE bonds must have been purchased in 1990 or at any time since then.

The bonds must be purchased in one or both *parents'* names. They cannot be owned, or co-owned, with the child.

At the time of purchase, the parent must have been at least 24 years old.

The bonds must be cashed in and used *in the same year* to pay tuition for a child (or yourself or your spouse).

Note: This provision applies only to tuition and fees, not to room and board at college.

You must meet certain income restrictions for the year in which the bonds are redeemed. Those income limitations are increased every year:

For 1995, the EE bond interest is tax-free for married couples with adjusted gross incomes below $63,450, and singles with incomes below $42,300.

Above those levels, the tax break is gradually phased out until there is no tax break at all for married couples with adjusted gross incomes above $93,450 and singles with incomes above $57,300.

Terry's Tip:

$$$ For the year in which you cash in the bonds, your reported income for determining the tax break includes the profit you made on the bonds. So it is wise to cash in only a small amount of the bonds for tuition each year if you are close to the income limits.

College Savings Strategy #3: College Savings Bank

An enterprising banker came up with the idea of creating a certificate of deposit with the interest rate linked to the rising cost of higher education as measured by the College Board Index of costs for 500 independent colleges. That was the start, in 1987, of the College Savings Bank in Princeton, New Jersey, and the CollegeSure CD.

The unique concept is that the interest rates paid on this FDIC-insured certificate of deposit are guaranteed to meet the rising cost of college. For example, in 1994–95, the College Board found that one year's tuition, fees, and room and board totaled $18,186 at the average private college, up from $17,247 in the previous year. That was a 5.44 percent increase, and that was the basis for the interest rate credited on the CollegeSure CD. Over the ten-year period ending in 1994, private college costs increased an average of 7.27 percent per year versus an increase of 3.61 percent in the CPI.

The CDs are sold in units, or portions of units. One full unit at maturity is equal to one full year's average cost for tuition, fees, room, and board at a four-year private college. Each unit is guaranteed to pay at maturity one full year of average college costs—even if costs soar.

The CDs are sold in maturities of from one to 25 years, and all CDs are timed to mature on July 31. If you purchase four units, you'll want to time them to mature each summer when tuition will be due. When you buy a unit CD, it is priced slightly above the current index value for one year of college, but at a deep discount to the estimated cost of one year of college at maturity. Each year interest is credited to the CD, bringing it to full face value (the cost of one year of college) at maturity.

Some colleges and universities cost more than the average, while others cost less. Chart IV-7 lists current costs at selected schools and the number of units required to pay those costs each year. If you think your child will attend one of the more expensive colleges, you'll have to set a goal of purchasing more units in order to completely fund a more expensive education.

If you cannot afford to purchase a full unit at one time—and certainly most parents cannot—you can purchase a partial unit. Most people start with the minimum $1,000 investment in one of these CDs, and add money regularly in the minimum additions of $250. The College Savings Bank even has a payroll deduction program that allows for amounts as little as $25 per pay period. If you tell the College Savings Bank which university or college you'd like your child to attend, they'll calculate approximately how many units, or partial units, you'll need for each year of college and how much money you'll need to save every month, depending on the school of choice.

Interest on these certificates of deposit is credited on July 31 each year and is calculated retroactively for money on deposit during the previous year. The interest compounds annually. There is a minimum guaranteed rate on the CD of not less than the college inflation rate, minus 1.5 percent. But there is also a floor of 4 percent interest in any year in which the rate would have dropped lower.

Just like a zero coupon bond, the cost of each unit is lower for the more distant maturities. The interest is credited each year toward the guaranteed value at maturity. You do pay income taxes on the interest earned each year, which is one reason for opening the CD in a custodial account for your child. As noted above, the first $650 of interest is tax-free, the second $650 is taxed at the child's (15 percent) rate, and interest above that amount is taxed at the parents' rate until the child reaches age 14 and files his or her own tax return.

If for some reason your child decides not to attend college, or gets a full scholarship, you still get all of your principal and interest back when the CD matures. The money can be used for any purpose.

These certificates of deposit are FDIC-insured up to $100,000 per depositor, and the bank itself has top ratings from Veribanc and other bank

CHART IV-7
Selected College Costs and Unit Value
1994–95 Academic Year

	(D) Total Charges*	(E) Units Required Per Year†
Average Private College	$18,186	1.0000
Average Public College	7,274	0.4000
Baylor University	11,658	0.6410
Boston University	25,500	1.4022
Brigham Young University	5,920	0.3255
Duke University	25,020	1.3758
Loyola University of Chicago	17,160	0.9436
Pennsylvania State University	9,123	0.5016
Princeton University	25,810	1.4192
Rice University	16,495	0.9070
Southern Methodist University	19,474	1.0708
Spelman College	13,855	0.7618
Stanford University	25,464	1.4002
Temple University	10,786	0.5931
University of Arizona	5,817	0.3199
University of California at Los Angeles	9,697	0.5332
University of Chicago	25,616	1.4086
University of Delaware	8,330	0.4580
University of Illinois	8,017	0.4408
University of Michigan	9,876	0.5431
University of Notre Dame	21,440	1.1789
University of Pittsburgh	9,976	0.5486
University of Virginia	8,432	0.4637

* Total charges include tuition, fees, room and board. State college costs are for in-state students.

† Each full unit of a CollegeSure (Plus) CD will pay upon maturity a sum of money at least equal to the average cost of one year's undergraduate tuition, fees, room and board at selected 4-year independent colleges in the U.S. Fractions of units pay upon maturity proportionately the same amount.

SOURCE: The College Board

safety rating services. There is no fee or commission to purchase the CollegeSure CD.

The minimum required to open an account is $1,000, but deposits of $10,000 or more earn up to one-half percent higher interest rate. You can add to your CD units at any time in minimum $250 amounts, and can even arrange to have a minimum of $250 transferred from your own bank account on a monthly or quarterly basis, or a payroll deduction program for amounts as little as $25 per pay period.

There is a substantial penalty for early withdrawal from these CDs: 10 percent of principal if money is taken out in the first three years, and 5 percent thereafter until the final year, when the penalty declines to 1 percent.

For complete information, call the College Savings Bank at 800-888-2723.

College Savings Strategy #4: State College Savings Programs

A number of states have instituted some creative programs to help parents save for college tuition.

Tax-Exempt College Bonds

These are tax-free, general obligation municipal bonds sold by the state in which you live. They are sold at deep discounts, like zero coupon bonds (see chapter 23), and priced to mature at face value, usually $1,000 per bond, in the year your child will need the money for college.

When you purchase the bonds, there is an implied fixed-interest rate that will add to the value of the bond each year. The interest rate is set by market conditions at the time the state sells the bonds. For instance, if you purchase a bond in 1992, set to mature in 2003, with an implied interest rate of 5.7 percent, your purchase price will be $2,726. Each year the value of the bond will increase, until the state redeems it for $5,000 in 2003. (This is an actual example taken from a State of Illinois College Bond offering made in September 1992.)

Many states add a tuition "kicker." If the proceeds of the bond are used to pay tuition at an in-state school, you'll get a discount of a few hundred dollars on tuition. But even if your child decides not to attend an in-state school, or decides not to go to college at all, at maturity the cash can be used for any purpose. Because these are zero coupon *municipal* bonds, there is no federal or state income tax due either annually or when the bonds mature.

Prepaid Tuition Plans

A number of states have offered programs that allow parents to prepay tuition for a state school. Depending on the child's age, parents make a payment now, which is substantially discounted from expected tuition when the child will attend college. Then that child is guaranteed full tuition payment, no matter what the cost in the future.

There are some drawbacks to this plan. When the student enrolls in school, he or she will have to pay income tax on the difference between the parents' original deposit and the current cost of tuition. Another problem arises if the child decides to attend an out-of-state school. Each state has a different refund policy, and most are costly. If there is any doubt that your child will attend an in-state school, it might be better to invest the original tuition deposit money in a mutual fund, Series EE savings bonds, or a CollegeSure CD. To find out more about your state's participation in one of these programs, contact the financial aid office at your state university.

College Savings Strategy #5: Beware of Life Insurance for College Savings

Many life insurance companies produce literature illustrating the use of their products as a savings vehicle for college. But it doesn't make sense to pay the mortality expenses of life insurance in order to build a savings fund. Life insurance certainly has a place in your financial picture, but it is not the way to save for college.

Life insurance on a parent is expensive, reducing the amount you can save. Life insurance on a child is less expensive, but totally unnecessary. (I know of no parent who would want to spend the proceeds of such a policy.) As an incentive to buy life insurance policies for college savings, you'll be told that you can withdraw premiums that have been paid into the life insurance policy with no tax consequences. But why pay for the insurance itself? Instead, put the money into one of those strategies outlined above.

One other note: Annuities are also being sold as a savings vehicle for college. But using an annuity to save for college assumes that in spite of paying the 10 percent penalty when money is withdrawn (because the student will be under age 59½), there will be an advantage in that the savings will grow faster because of the tax deferral inside the annuity.

Only parents who know they will be age 60 or older when their child goes to college should consider using annuities for this purpose. If the annuity is purchased in the child's name, there's no guarantee of what income tax rates will be when your child reaches college age; it's entirely possible that the child's tax rate, plus the penalty on the annuity withdrawal, will more than offset the tax-deferred growth of the annuity investment.

Chapter 38

Financial Aid for College

Recognize that in spite of your best efforts, you simply may not be able to save enough money to pay for college for all your children. There are many places and ways to borrow money for college, and listed below are some strategies for obtaining those loans. No matter what your family income level, don't give up on the possibility of getting financial aid from the school your child will attend, or from a number of federal student aid programs.

The secret to finding all this money is getting organized in your search. The first thing you have to figure out is how much money you need to supplement your college savings fund. That question is not easily answered. What you think you need is not necessarily what the standardized need analysis forms will agree you need. First things first: the forms.

College Aid Strategy #1: Understand Need Assessment

The first step in applying for financial aid is to pick up the standardized need analysis forms that are available at your child's high school college guidance office. The forms must be filled out in January of the student's senior year, but you might want to get a look at them earlier.

All students applying for financial aid should complete the FAFSA (*Free Application for Federal Student Aid*), available in the high school guidance office or the college financial aid office. Some colleges will request a supplement, which is called the FAF (*Financial Aid Form*), or another supplement that the college may create for its own use. Some states also have their own forms to apply for aid from state scholarship and grant programs.

Don't be surprised at what you're asked to reveal on these forms! They're a lot like income tax forms—by design, so that the information can be corroborated by your tax return. In fact, some colleges ask you to authorize release of your income tax forms to the college aid office. In addition to information about your income, these forms also ask you to reveal everything about your assets and liabilities. The college financial aid officers will know your family finances better than your tax accountant!

The completed form is sent in to the needs analysis agency that created the form. Each uses the same federally mandated formula to assess the income and assets of both parents and student to come up with a critical number—the EFC (expected family contribution). That's the amount they judge your family should be able to pay. The service then sends out this evaluation to every college you designate.

The college financial aid officer takes a look at the EFC and compares it to the cost of a year of college tuition, room and board, and fees at that school. The difference is your "need"—the amount the college aid office will try to help you make up with a combination of scholarships, grants, and loans. There's no guarantee that the college of your choice will be able to come up with a complete package of aid. That depends, in part, on how badly they want your child as a student, and in part on the total funds available at that school.

It may be possible to negotiate with the school's financial aid officer to get more money or a different structure for the aid package. Be aware that you must go through this process again every year, filling out new financial aid forms, until your child has completed college.

College Aid Strategy #2: Adjust Your Finances to Increase Aid

The information you submit on the financial aid forms about your assets and income must be truthful and accurate or you run the risk of losing all chance of financial aid. Still, there are several ways you can adjust your financial picture in the "base" year being reviewed in order to increase your chances for assistance.

Remember: Parents' income may be assessed up to 47 percent in determining need for financial aid; parental assets (not including home equity) are assessed at 12 percent.

1. If possible, avoid taking pension distributions, bonuses, or large income tax refunds in the base year that is being audited for aid because these items all increase your income level.

2. If you are going to sell some stocks for a profit to pay for college, don't sell them in the year before you are applying for aid. Yes, the cash from the sale is an asset, just as the shares were. But you have to report the gain from the sale as *income*, which weighs more heavily against you in financial aid formulas. Consider borrowing on the value of your shares to raise money for college. Instead of selling your stock, use a margin account (see chapter 21) because margin loans can be deducted against the total value of your assets.

3. Money built up in retirement plans such as IRAs, Keoghs, and 401(k) plans does not count against you as assets when financial aid is calculated, and it is not reported on financial aid forms. So it makes sense to contribute to these plans in the early years. However, money deferred into these plans in the base year will still be calculated as current income.

4. Starting in fall 1993, home equity was eliminated from the calculation of parental contribution to college costs. That means more families qualify for federal student aid based on need. However, colleges may still require additional data from parents before making scholarship decisions. Therefore, consider replacing outstanding credit card bills with a home equity loan. Credit card debt is not counted in the totals, but a home equity loan reduces the figure for equity in your home, adding to your chances for aid if the college or university uses more stringent calculations.

5. In fact, use your cash to pay down all possible consumer debts, and even prepay your property tax bill. Cutting down on available cash assets increases your need for aid. (Don't, however, go on a spending spree!)

College Aid Strategy #3: Choose College Based on Financial Aid Offer

As noted above, even though each college receives a statement of expected family contribution, not every college will be willing to come up with an aid package to make up the difference. For that reason the student who needs financial aid should apply to several schools, instead of asking for "early decision" at just one school. If several offers of aid are received from different schools, the student can always go back to his or her first choice and try to negotiate a better package.

To find out more about the specific aid profiles of individual colleges, start with your high school guidance office. You might also want to check the library for the annual edition of *Peterson's College Money Handbook* ($19.95 in bookstores), which gives cost and aid profiles for most U.S. colleges and universities.

College Aid Strategy #4: Apply for Available Aid

You should have a basic idea of the kind of aid that is available. Some financial aid comes in the form of grants or scholarships that do not have to be repaid—outright gifts from the federal or state government or private sources. Some aid comes in the form of loans, either to students or parents, and may or may not be based on need. There is also a federal work-study program for college students. Many of these aid programs are applied for automatically when you submit your financial aid form.

As of July 1, 1993, the annual maximum loan limits have been expanded. The interest rates were set on October 1, 1992, for the loan programs, and are subject to change based on the indexes described below. (For answers to any questions about federal loan and grant programs, call the Federal Student Aid Information Center at 800-433-3243.)

Government Grants

Pell Grant
  From: U.S. government
  For: low-income, undergraduate students
  Application: automatic when FAFSA is filed
  Size: between $200–$2,300 per year, based on need

SEOG (Supplemental Educational Opportunity Grant)
>   From: U.S. government, but awarded by schools
>   For: low-income, undergraduate students
>   Application: automatic when FAFSA is filed
>   Size: between $200–$4,000 per year

State Grants
>   From: individual states
>   For: resident students attending state schools, or students from states with reciprocal agreements, based on need
>   Application: automatic with need forms (but check with your state to see if additional forms are required)
>   Size: depends on state

Loan Programs

Stafford Student Loan Program
>   From: guaranteed by federal government, but made through a bank
>   To: students, based on need
>   Terms: government pays interest during college years and subsidizes interest differential between loan rate and market rate during re-payment years after graduation; no repayment required until six months after graduation
>   Amount: up to $23,000 total for undergrad years
>   Current rate: 90-day Treasury bill rate, plus 3.1 percentage points in first four years of loan, with a cap of 9 percent

>   (Note: anyone who received a Stafford loan before October 1, 1992, is locked into the old rates of 8 percent with a 10 percent cap.)

>   Application: direct to college for approval, then application at any major participating bank

Stafford Nonsubsidized Student Loan Program
>   From: federal government does not pay interest during college years
>   To: students, regardless of need
>   Terms: no deferral of interest payments
>   Amount: $23,000 total for undergrad years
>   Rate: 90-day Treasury bill plus 3.1 percent; 6.5 percent origination fee
>   Application: forms available at college, application made at banks

Perkins Loan Program

From: awarded directly from college as part of financial aid package

To: students, based on need

Terms: government pays interest while student is in school; repayment starts nine months after graduation, ten years to repay

Amount: $4,500 for first two years; $9,000 for four years total

Interest rate: 5 percent

Application: automatic when FAFSA is filed

PLUS Loan Program

From: local banks, S&Ls, credit unions

To: parents, *not* based on need—but requires good credit report (similarly: SLS loans direct to grad students)

Terms: immediate start to repayment, or deferred until student graduates

must be repaid within five to ten years of graduation

fee of up to 5 percent paid to bank

Amount: up to total college costs, less financial aid

Rate: 52-week Treasury bill rate, plus 3.1 percent; adjusted annually on July 1; rate capped at 10 percent

Application: direct to financial institution

Private Scholarships

You might be amazed at how much money is available for college—even to students who do not qualify for financial aid based on family income. Among the best known non-needs-based scholarships are athletic scholarships. Any student athlete should contact his or her high school coach or guidance counselor, as well as the college athletic department.

It is estimated that significant amounts of private scholarship aid go unused every year, simply because students do not know it exists. Fewer than half of these privately funded scholarships, fellowships, and grants are based on need. Local Rotary clubs, boosters groups, and many other civic organizations give out scholarships. Companies often have scholarship programs available for children of their employees. And many colleges and universities have scholarships left by alumni, with criteria such as sharing the same last name, or hometown. You can research these scholarships in the library by consulting *The College Scholarship Book: A Complete Guide to Private Sector Scholarships, Grants and Loans for Undergraduates* (Prentice-Hall, $19.95).

The College Board has created a software program called the *College Cost Explorer Fund Finder* which is available in many high school guidance offices and college financial aid offices. It creates customized lists of potential aid packages from a data base of thousands of private sources of scholarships and loans for both undergraduate and postgraduate students. If your school does not offer this service, contact the College Board Publications Office at (212) 713-8165.

Or there are private groups with computer databases that will research the information for you—if you're willing to pay the cost. The following two services have been in business for a number of years and have a good reputation (unlike some newcomers to the business that are expensive and do not have such large databases):

The National Scholarship Research Service (800-432-3782) is based in Santa Rosa, California. They have an extensive database, and will send a free brochure and application form which must be filled out with basic information in order to search for applicable scholarships. The cost is $75, and the student may get annual updates for $45. This company has worked with Prentice-Hall on its annual college scholarship books.

National College Services, Ltd. (800-662-6275), markets its database primarily to high school and college guidance departments, although it will provide individual consultations for $30. This is the one service that also tracks federal aid programs and athletic scholarships. Check to see if your high school guidance office subscribes to this on-line database of more than 200,000 student aid resources, or contact the service directly.

Chapter 39

Children and Money

If you don't teach your children the value of money, you can hardly expect them to appreciate the importance of all the dollars you have invested in their education. Our entire economic system is based on free enterprise and an understanding of the rewards of working hard—and working smart. It's never too early to start teaching those lessons to a child.

Children and Money Strategy #1: Saving Money

My own child had a savings account when he was barely old enough to reach over the bank counter. He understood that if you give the bank your money to keep, "the bank pays you rent—called interest." Watching the interest posted to his account kept him motivated to save—for a while.

Children need to have money so they can make the decision whether to spend or to save. That means if you're paying an allowance, you have to leave enough room for those alternatives, not just cover the basic cost of school lunches and bus fare.

Children and Money Strategy #2: Making Investments

A child who goes to the movies or has learned to read is old enough to know that people pay for things—and that companies make products and earn money from people who buy the products. That's when you can introduce a child to the concept of stock ownership in companies he or she recognizes.

Identify the company that makes the toys you buy, or owns the fast-food restaurant you patronize, or makes the movies you watch. All of these are recognizable brand names and would make good stock gifts for your child. But at the same time you might want to explain the stock tables in the newspaper, or the tickertape on the financial TV station—showing that when more people buy the stock, the price goes up, and little Billy or Susie makes money! Of course, people buy the stock only when a lot of people are buying the products the company sells. If the company pays a dividend, it can be invested in more shares of stock. (See chapter 19 on dividend reinvestment plans.)

This is also a good age to open a stock market mutual fund for your child. Then some birthday gifts, or holiday gifts from grandparents, can be used to purchase shares in the fund. (See chapter 17 on mutual fund strategies.)

The Securities Industry Association (212-608-1500) sponsors a 10-week Stock Market Game for students around the country. More than 500,000 students in grades 4 through 12 participate in several divisions. The students are "given" $100,000 to create an investment portfolio. Their stock "purchases and sales" are registered through a central computer program. Teachers attend workshops to learn the basics of the game, and local stockbrokers often attend class to assist them. Student participants are encouraged to watch the nightly business television shows and read the business section of the newspaper. If your school does not participate in this excellent business experience, you should contact the Securities Industry Association for more information.

Children and Money Strategy #3: Financial Hobbies

Hobbies like collecting stamps or coins can teach a child about the value of money, as well as invaluable lessons about history and geography. Not every child will have the temperament to become a collector, and some may opt for baseball cards instead of stamps. But no matter what the collection, it requires judgments as to value and trade-offs, and those are important financial lessons.

Children and Money Strategy #4: Economic Education

If your school doesn't have a Junior Achievement program, help to get one started; you can contact the national JA office (717-540-8000). You may remember Junior Achievement as an after-school club that made and sold products in an effort to teach the workings of business. Today, Junior Achievement reaches 1.4 million children each year through a variety of in-school programs that start as early as the primary grades. All teach the value of the free enterprise system and give a practical business education. One of the most rewarding programs is taught to high schoolers: "The Economics of Staying in School."

By the way, I make it a rule never to pass a lemonade stand or a children's business venture without making a purchase. Any young person who shows an entrepreneurial spirit today deserves to be rewarded.

Children and Money Strategy #5: Children and Taxes

If you're filing a tax return for your child, show it to him or her. If the child is earning interest or dividends, it's certainly time to explain how the government gets a piece of everything you earn by way of taxes!

Consult your accountant about the special rules for children and taxes, often called the "kiddie tax." Currently, a child must file a tax return if he or she has at least $650 in unearned income such as dividends, interest, or capital gains. If the child had earned income from a summer job, he or she must file a tax return if the earnings from work totaled $650 or more *and* if the child had *any* unearned income.

If the child did not have any unearned income but did have a job, he or she is not required to file unless earnings from work totaled more than $3,900. If federal income taxes were withheld from the child's paycheck, then a return must be filed to claim a refund.

The first $650 of a child's *unearned* income is tax-free; the next $650 is taxed at the lowest rate. Earnings above that amount are taxed at the parents' marginal rate. Above age 14, a child's earnings are taxed at the child's own rate—which is probably lower than the parents' rate. In that case, you'll want to file a separate return for the child. If the child has earned income of more than $650 in addition to unearned income—at any age—a separate tax return must be filed for the child.

Children who file their own returns may still be taken as dependents on their parents' return if they are under age 19, or are full-time students under age 24 and the parents contribute more than half their total support. When parents include investment income of a child on the parents' return, they must also file form #8814, Parents' Election to Report Child's Interest and Dividends.

Chapter 40

Strategies for Getting, Keeping, and Leaving a Job

The foundation for all the money you plan to spend, save, or invest is the income you earn from your job. In the 1990s, the words "job security" have become an oxymoron. There is very little security in your association with a business; your real job security is in your own talents, education, and experience.

In the 1990s, a wave of corporate restructuring and downsizing has left American workers—both blue-collar and white-collar—with a pervasive insecurity. Of course, every business cycle in the past 40 years had provided layoffs and unemployment, but those were largely cyclical. Factory workers knew that eventually they'd be called back to the assembly line. Today's workers are finding that their jobs have been eliminated permanently.

In a different era, workers' lives were intertwined with the company that provided their income. It was not uncommon for an individual to work for only one company throughout a lifetime. A wristwatch and a handshake on retirement were the subject of jokes then; now, many employees wish they had that much to look forward to.

Many pension benefits were negotiated 40 years ago by unions—never believing that one day companies would try to take back those hard-won retirement guarantees. Yet today, major corporations are asking retirees to take cutbacks in health insurance, and other promised retirement perks.

It's a fact of life in the nineties that loyalty to a company and its products has been overshadowed by the need to be loyal to one's personal financial needs. Even IBM, which had always proclaimed a policy of "no layoffs," found itself transferring workers to lower-level jobs, offering incentives for early retirement, and announcing outright layoffs.

Workers in the nineties are faced with terms like "severance" and "buyout"—and they're forced to make decisions on whether to retire early with lower benefits or face the possibility of being fired. So, before we get to the chapter on retirement planning (chapter 44), it's time to take a look at job planning: strategies to find, keep, and, if necessary, leave in the most financially beneficial way. Plus a few words on creating your own job if you're laid off.

Job Strategy #1: Finding the Best Job

Generations of workers followed their parents into traditional jobs. Sons of steelworkers became steelworkers themselves; coal miners' sons went into the mines; teachers' daughters became teachers. Each of these was an admirable and high-paying job—but because of changing economic conditions, today most of those jobs are gone, or paying far less in terms of family living standards.

The lesson is: Start early to look around and see where the need for employees will be in the next decade—and find out what kind of training will be required.

That's not a foolproof strategy. Thousands of engineers have been laid off in the defense industry. But at least they have the basic education to be retrained in growing fields like environmental engineering.

Where will the demand be in the future? We have an aging population that will need care. Some of that care will be given by custodial workers. But there will be a great demand for those skilled in medical technology, physical rehabilitation, nutrition, and medical facility management. Our world is running out of places to store its trash. Not only will the demand for garbage collectors increase; there will be a need for those trained in environmental care and waste disposal.

The technology revolution will continue. Not only will there be jobs in creating technology, but there will be highly paid people who train and retrain others to use new technologies.

There are hundreds of millions of untrained workers entering the workforce worldwide. As countries like China open up to modern Western influences, there will be a surplus of unskilled labor—bringing with it a decline in the wages that will be paid for this type of work. The high demand—and higher wages—will be for educated, skilled workers in every field. Make yourself—and inspire your children to be—among them. The more you read and the more education you have, the more valuable you become as an employee.

The most secure job you ever have will be the one you create for yourself.

Identify a need and fill it as an employee, or start your own business to profit from your vision. Be alert to job possibilities with a business that is offering a new, and needed, service or product. Don't confuse the existence of a job with the "need" for an employee. Only unneeded employees are being laid off. The secret to job security is inside yourself.

Job Strategy #2: Evaluating a Buyout Offer

In the 1990s, buyout offers became not only an acceptable but a prevalent way of thinning the ranks of middle management and office workers—primarily those age 55 and older. According to a study by Hewitt Associates, the pension and benefit consulting firm, 43 percent of the companies they surveyed had offered a buyout or early retirement window to employees in 1991. That's up from an average of 27 percent of companies making similar offers in the previous five years.

This was a survey of approximately 700 companies, most of them among America's largest employers. The average number of employees offered an early retirement window was 900. The average acceptance rate was 30 percent. The following were the incentives typically offered in buyout plans and the percentage of surveyed companies offering these incentives:

Cash payments outside the pension plan (45%);

Liberalized pension eligibility (waiving number of required service years) (30%);

Improved pension benefits (such as elimination of early retirement payment reductions) (67%).

What should you do if presented with a buyout offer? You'd like to work several more years, but when faced with a proposal you fear that if you turn it down, the next step could be severance—with far lower benefits.

Here are some questions to consider:

How close are you to retirement—and what will this do to your ultimate retirement benefits?

You are fully *vested*—entitled—to your company benefits after a maximum of seven years, and in many companies after five years. But the level of retirement payments will be based on a formula determined by the number of years you worked and your salary in the last few years you worked.

The company should do a projected retirement benefits statement, comparing the benefits you'd receive if you worked to full retirement age (or the earliest retirement age) and the benefits you'll be entitled to if you take the buyout offer.

How does this offer compare to others made in your industry recently?

It's difficult to get an industry average on buyout or severance benefits. As you can see from the Hewitt survey, many companies are creating buyout plans.

At the senior executive level (those earning more than $150,000), it is generally accepted that a severance package will receive a minimum of nine months' salary—and as much as 18 months or more for top executives. Office workers earning in the $35,000 to $45,000 annual range may get two to three months of service, plus vacation pay. Severance at that salary level is also affected by years of service.

Will your company sweeten its offer to bring you up to full retirement benefits?

The only way to find out is to ask. If the company is making an offer to an entire group, it is unlikely they will make exceptions for one individual—unless you can point out unusual circumstances. Most, but not all, of these retirement "window" packages have some formula for bridging the layoff years before retirement so that retirees receive full benefits.

Do you think you can go back into the workforce and have time to earn additional pension benefits?

Your first worry may be simply finding another job. But you should also consider the possibility of working at another job long enough to qualify for a second pension. Obviously, since pension payouts are based on years of service as well as salary, the combination of small pension from your old company and small pension from your new company is unlikely to equal what you would have been paid if you had worked at the first company until retirement.

Job Strategy #3: Financial Considerations in Leaving a Job

Whenever you leave a job—either because you're fired, accept a buyout, or decide to change jobs—there are a number of financial issues to consider.

What will this do to your health benefits?

Usually, when you receive your last paycheck, your health benefits will no longer be paid by the company. If you work for a company with 20 or more covered employees, you will have the option (called COBRA) of picking up the cost of your health insurance at the same rate the company pays, plus a small administrative fee. That extension must last at least 18 months. Then you're on your own.

Most state laws require that you be allowed to "roll over" from the company plan into a private policy at the end of the COBRA period. In fact, you'll have very little choice if you or a dependent have a preexisting medical condition that would be excluded from coverage if you transfer to another plan. But the individual policy will be very expensive. If your company is self-insured, then only the 18 months of COBRA coverage will be offered.

Will your severance be paid out in one lump sum or over a period of months?

There are advantages and disadvantages to each method. Taking a lump sum will give you the cash to start a new business or make an investment. And you no longer have to think about your old company on a weekly basis when your check arrives.

On the other hand, a lump sum received at the end of the year will result in a large tax liability the following April. (Or the company will withhold taxes.) If you receive weekly or monthly severance payments, your health insurance coverage will probably be extended as well. That means you don't move into the 18-month COBRA period until much later.

What will happen to your pension benefits?
If you're not being offered early retirement and additional pension benefits, you have to consider the alternatives for the pension benefits you have accumulated as defined by the documents in your company's plan.

The first step is to find out how much you have in *vested* (owned) benefits. The most likely choices are that you can either take the money out and roll it over into an IRA, or that you will be required to leave the money with the company until you reach a specified age and can take it out as retirement payments.

Terry's Tip:

$$$ Find out if your company pension plan is "fully funded" and whether it has made huge investments in the company's stock through an Employee Stock Ownership Plan. If the company itself is on shaky financial footing, these two indicators may be a clue that you should take your money out and roll it into an IRA if you are given that choice.

If you are required to leave your money in the corporate pension plan, you have some reassurance in knowing that your basic benefits are insured by the Pension Benefit Guaranty Corporation. But read chapter 44 to learn the limitations of this coverage.

What will happen to your 401(k), company savings plan?
You may have to take your entire 401(k) plan in a lump sum distribution. Then you'll be faced with the choice of rolling it over into a new IRA and maintaining tax deferral, or spending all or part of it. *Don't spend it!* You will never again have this opportunity to let your money continue to grow tax-deferred for retirement.

And remember, under the new tax rules, you must have your company deposit the money directly into your IRA rollover account at your new custodian—a bank, brokerage firm, or mutual fund. If you take possession of the check, even for a few days, the company must withhold 20 percent for income taxes.

Some companies will allow you to keep your 401(k) investment in the company savings plan. That eliminates having to make decisions about investing the money. But do you want to leave your money with the company you just left?

What happens to company stock options you hold?

You will have 90 days from your last date of work to exercise stock options, if they have any value. However, if your severance calls for a 12-month payout, you may have more time to make the decision on exercising the options (and the stock may move to a level that makes the options profitable within that period of time).

Will the company offer other benefits such as outplacement counseling?

If you want to go back into the workforce, you may need help with a résumé, an evaluation of your talents, and job interview and networking counseling. Outplacement is a benefit that must be purchased by the company on behalf of its severed employee. Alternatively, many companies will set up a separate assistance center if it is terminating many employees at one time.

Can you negotiate?

Once the company has decided to terminate you, or your job, it is unlikely that you can negotiate to remain employed. You may be able to "sweeten" the severance package—unless an entire class of employees is being terminated at the same time with the same level of benefits.

If you feel you are being discriminated against because of age, race, sex, or physical disability, you have remedies with the Equal Employment Opportunity Commission. Remember, this is the time when the company will be having the greatest guilt feelings about letting you go. So this is the best time to negotiate a better settlement for yourself.

What should you sign?

You may be asked to sign a waiver when you agree to accept the severance package. By law, you have 21 days to consider before signing anything if you are individually laid off, and 45 days to consider if this is a group offer. Don't sign anything without consulting an experienced labor attorney. If you change your mind, you have seven days to revoke your agreement after it is signed.

Job Strategy #4: Deduct Legitimate Unreimbursed Business Expenses

Whether you're job-hunting, working for a company, or starting your own business, you should keep careful track of deductible business expenses. For instance, if you're searching for a new job in your present occupation you can deduct employment and outplacement agency fees you pay. Similarly, you can deduct the amounts you spend for typing, printing, and mailing copies of your resume to prospective employers.

If you travel to another city or state and spend time looking for a new job in your present occupation, you may be able to deduct travel expenses. It's important to be able to substantiate that the primary purpose of the trip was to look for a new job. And that job must be in your current occupation, not a new line of business. You can also use the standard mileage rate to deduct transportation expenses of looking for a job in your hometown.

If you're employed, keep a record of business expenses that are not reimbursed by your company. If you subscribe to business-related magazines or pay professional club or union dues (the portion that is membership, not pension-related), you should deduct these items as business expenses. Even a portion of private club dues may be deductible if you can demonstrate that your use of the facilities more than 50 percent of the time is for business reasons.

Similarly, if you pay tuition to take courses or seminars that improve your business skills, or buy books or supplies related to your business, and these items are not reimbursed by your employer, you can deduct these expenses unless they are taken for purposes of receiving a degree. These expenses are itemized deductions that are subject to the 2 percent limit on adjusted gross income.

If you buy equipment that is used exclusively for your own business, you can deduct its cost. For example, if you purchase a home computer, it will be deductible up to certain limits—unless your child also uses it for homework and games. (Don't ask how the IRS will find out!) If you use your business equipment for both personal and business uses, check with your accountant about taking a portion of the cost in depreciation over a fixed number of years.

Travel and entertainment expenses are some of the most carefully scrutinized items on your income tax return. If possible, it is best to use a company credit card or make arrangements to have these business expenses fully reimbursed. Make sure your employer does not report these reimbursements as taxable wages, but instead sets up an official reimbursement account. If you are not reimbursed, you can deduct only 80 percent of the business-related meal and entertainment expenses, although 100 percent of hotel lodging and transportation costs is deductible.

Keep all receipts, and write on them the names of the people involved in the entertainment and a note about the nature of the business discussion. You don't have to talk business during the entire meal, but the main purpose of the gathering must be to conduct business, or the meal must be in conjunction with a business meeting.

When it comes to use of your personal car for business reasons, check the rules carefully. You may not deduct the costs of commuting to and from your regular place of business. But if you use your car for allowable business reasons such as making sales calls or selling real estate, you may be allowed to deduct 27.5 cents per mile or a portion of your actual annual automobile expenses. See IRS booklets #463 and #917 for details on automobile business usage deductions.

Terry's Tip:

$$$ It may appear that you can take a substantial amount of business-related expenses. Employee business expenses should all be listed on IRS Form 2106. Those that exceed 2 percent of your adjusted gross income are deductible. If you file Schedule C, the expenses are listed on that form instead.

Even if you can list and prove all of your business-related expenses, there are limits to the real benefit of these deductions. You must combine the total on Form 2016 with all your other itemized miscellaneous deductions on Schedule A of your income tax return.

Currently, only the amount of miscellaneous deductions that exceeds 2 percent of your adjusted gross income can be deducted. Additionally, if your AGI is over $100,000 you will lose some of the benefit of your itemized deductions. That can put a real cap on the benefit of your business deductions. Still, it's worth keeping track of all those expenses because every dollar of deductions helps your tax picture.

Chapter 41

Strategies for Creating Your Own Business

Whether you call it entrepreneurship or simply the desire to be your own boss, a growing number of Americans have decided to start their own business. While nay-sayers point to the high failure rate of new businesses, there are millions of success stories, and yours could be one of them.

If you decide to start your own business, you'll run into many financial issues, and you should have good legal and accounting advice. Of course, your goal is to make money in your business. But even if you don't make money for the first few years, you may be able to generate some valuable tax deductions—in effect, putting money in your pocket that would have gone to the IRS.

Your first financial decision will be the legal form your business should take. You can set yourself up as a sole proprietor, a partnership, a Subchapter S corporation, or a regular business corporation, known as a C corporation.

Your Own Business Strategy #1: Sole Proprietorship

Most businesses start as sole proprietorships, or partnerships. If you form a partnership, it will need its own tax ID number. But if you just want to start your own small business, you can use your own Social Security number as long as you have no employees. If you do have employees, you'll need an employee identification number (EIN) to file your payroll tax returns. You can get an EIN from the Internal Revenue Service by completing Form SS-4. You can even get the EIN issued over the phone by calling 816-926-5999.

As a sole proprietor, you don't have to file a separate tax return for your business. All you will do is attach a Schedule C (Profit or Loss from Business) to your next personal income tax return. You'll need to examine your tax situation several times during the year because you'll probably have to make quarterly estimated tax payments to the IRS to cover income and self-employment taxes. Get IRS booklet #505 for more information on the filing requirements.

If you have a regular job as an employee, FICA is being taken out of your paycheck. But if you establish a business as a sole proprietor, you will still have to pay self-employment tax at the 15.3 percent rate to the extent that your wages as an employee did not reach the maximum covered levels (see Chapter 11). You can easily compute this amount on Schedule SE, which you will attach to your Form 1040 and Schedule C.

Here's the immediate financial advantage of creating your own business: If you have business expenses that are greater than your earnings from the business, you can deduct the difference from any other income. So if you start your own business on the side, while you are still earning a salary from your regular job, your business losses can lower your personal income tax obligation.

There are rules about taking those losses, and you should consult your accountant especially about how the "passive loss" rules may affect you. Basically, you must demonstrate that you are operating in a businesslike manner and are attempting to make a profit. You cannot keep deducting business losses forever! In fact, for most types of small businesses you must show a profit in three out of five years (slightly longer for some small businesses that involve livestock and natural resources).

If you do not show a profit in this period of time, the IRS will probably reclassify your business as a hobby. Then you can deduct the expenses related to your hobby against the income you earn from your hobby, but you cannot offset additional losses against other income. If you believe you will make a profit in the fourth or fifth year, you can ask the IRS to delay a decision on whether you are, indeed, engaged in a potentially profit-making business.

If your business is successful and you make a lot of money, you'll want to consider setting up some type of tax-deferred retirement plan. If you're not covered outside your business by any other corporate pension plan, you'll be able to deduct up to $2,000 for an Individual Retirement Account or you can set up a Keogh plan.

You can still set up a Keogh plan for your self-employment earnings even if you have coverage in a corporate retirement plan from your full-time job (see chapter 44). No-load mutual fund families have the simple forms to fill out and will take care of all the paperwork for you, as will most banks and stock brokerage firms.

Terry's Tip:

$$$ Remember that when you start your own business as a sole proprietorship you are liable personally for lawsuits against your business. That means your personal assets such as your home could be attached by the court or creditors. So be sure to take out a business liability insurance policy large enough to cover any potential personal liability arising out of your business.

Your Own Business Strategy #2: Subchapter S Corporation

The reason usually given for incorporating a business is to limit the liability of the corporate shareholders. A Subchapter S corporation is one of the two types of corporations you might consider for your business. A Sub S corporation is limited as to the number and type of shareholders and classes of stock that may be offered. There can be no more than 35 shareholders, and no partnerships or corporations can be shareholders.

A Subchapter S corporation operates like a regular business corporation—except for one significant area. The corporation itself does not pay taxes on its income; instead, the business earnings (and losses) flow directly through to the owner of the corporation, to be taxed at the owner's individual tax rate. Rules for the deductibility of losses are complex and also depend on whether you are active in your business or a passive investor. See your tax advisor for specifics.

You'll use a different income tax form if you incorporate your business as a Sub S corporation. The Sub S corporation will file Form 1120S to report its earnings, with Schedule K-1 attached to it. The income (or losses) reported on Schedule K-1 will be transferred to your personal income tax return. You get similar tax benefits from a Sub S as from a sole proprietorship. That means any losses can be deducted from your other personal income, subject to the three-out-of-five rule.

If you do make a profit in your Sub S corporation, you have several alternatives for creating your own pension plan. You can have a simple IRA if you have very little salary, or you can set up a regular pension and/ or profit-sharing and 401(k) plan. A profitable small business can be a way to create a significant retirement plan for yourself and your employees. Just remember to get proper legal advice so you follow all the nondiscrimination rules if you have employees.

Your Own Business Strategy #3: Regular C Corporation

Many small businesses have chosen to incorporate as Subchapter S corporations instead of regular C corporations because after 1986, for the first time, personal income tax rates (at 31 percent) were lower than regular corporate rates (at 34 percent). That created an incentive to use a SubS corporation in which income is passed through to the owner.

Regular C corporations pay taxes on all net earnings, after deducting the salaries paid out to their owners and employees. The money a corporation pays out in dividends to its shareholders is taxed twice—first to the corportation, and then to the recipient. In additon, when owners of a C corporation decide to sell the business there is a larger capital gains tax to be paid if the business has been profitable.

If you're incorporating a new business, you'll have to look at the current relationship between personal and corporate tax rates. If individual rates are increased over corporate rates, then a regular C corporation might become advantageous. But before switching your current business from a SubS corporation to a C corporation, consult your tax advisor. Any appreciation in corporate assets carried into the new C corportation would be subject to double tax if the assets are sold or the company is liquidated. And SubS status, once revoked, can't be reinstated for five years unless there is a major change in company ownership.

When you set up a regular C corporation, you will be subject to rules, and sometimes taxes, in the state in which you are incorporated. That's why you should check with an attorney about these additional expenses before deciding to incorporate. With a regular C corporation you must follow specific rules in setting up a defined benefits or defined contribution retirement plan. If you need an attorney, accountant, and actuary to monitor the changing rules for such plans, you can run into quite an expense.

One alternative to an expensive, qualified retirement plan is a Simplified Employee Pension Plan (SEP). It is basically a single retirement plan made up of separate Individual Retirement Accounts (IRAs) for each employee. In fact, the employees each set up their own IRA accounts at any financial institution they choose. The employer makes each employee's contribution directly into his or her own IRA account.

The paperwork required for a SEP-IRA is far less complicated and less expensive than for a qualified retirement plan. Many banks, brokerage firms, and mutual fund companies will handle the paperwork for you. This type of retirement plan is well suited for the owner who wants coverage at a low cost and is willing to equitably cover eligible employees.

Your Own Business Strategy #4: Working at Home

A growing number of Americans will work at home in the nineties— although many of those workers will still be employed by major corporations. Recognizing the need to attract skilled workers, and understanding the costs of commuting, more and more companies are allowing flexible time, or even letting full-time employees work from their homes.

Working from a home office is also an inexpensive way to start a company or business. In fact, there is even a networking organization for home-based businesses. The National Association for the Cottage Industry is a far more modern group than the name implies. It lobbies on public policy matters affecting home businesses, offers two newsletters, seminars, and even a group health insurance policy for its members. This is also a place to seek advice on homeowners insurance policies that have special coverages for home-based businesses. Membership is $45 a year; they can be contacted at Box 14850, Chicago, IL 60614.

There are some important financial considerations when working at home. Most revolve around taking tax deductions for business expenses. There are several IRS requirements for deducting home office expenses:

- You use the office to meet with customers or suppliers; or
- the office is your principal place of business (and you do not have use of an office at your employer's place of business); or

- the office in your home is a place that you use regularly and exclusively to conduct your employer's business and it is for the employer's convenience.

In 1993, the Supreme Court issued a new ruling that further defines the circumstances under which expenses for home offices can be deducted. The ruling affected some of the 1.6 million taxpayers who claimed home office deductions of more than $8 million in 1992. The new test for deductibility of home office expenses requires that:

1) The home office must be the place where the most important function or service of the business is provided.

2) The amount of work time spent in the home office must be greater than the amount of time spent outside of it.

Home office deductions must be claimed on a separate form, #8829, which is used for itemizing home office expenses. Those expenses might include a portion of your rent or mortgage payment, utilities, and other maintenance costs. The home office should have a separate business telephone line. If you own your home, you may take a fixed depreciation amount each year for your home office, but you'll have to recapture that deduction if you sell your home. Check with your accountant about the special provisions that go into effect when your home office deduction creates a loss on your Schedule C.

Your Own Business Strategy #5: Health Insurance and Medical Costs

One potentially significant tax benefit of owning your own small business is your ability to deduct more of your medical expenses. Of course, if you were working for a large company, you probably would receive medical insurance as one of your benefits. But as an individual or family you cannot deduct unreimbursed medical expenses unless they exceed 7.5 percent of your adjusted gross income. That limits your deductions significantly.

If you have your own business as a sole proprietorship, or as a Sub S corporation, you can deduct 25 percent of all health insurance premiums you pay each year. In the case of a Sub S corporation, the company may be able to deduct payments for uncovered medical expenses for employees; however, that amount would be considered taxable income to the employee.

And if you own your own regular C corporation, the company can deduct costs of a medical insurance program as an ordinary business expense, and the benefit received is not taxable to the individual. Plus, the corporation can create a medical reimbursement plan that will repay employees for any uninsured, out-of-pocket medical expenses. Consult your attorney to make sure you set up a plan that meets all the required standards—especially those that relate to discrimination requirements and to single owner-employee companies.

Your Own Business Strategy #6: Employing Your Family

One of the potential advantages of owning your own small business is that you can pay family members to work in your business. Because they are earning income, those family members can start their own tax-deductible IRA accounts (if they are not covered by a pension fund elsewhere), or they may be eligible to participate in your company's retirement plan.

Usually family members do pitch in to help when a small business is started. All you have to do is formalize this assistance by creating a regular paycheck for the family members who work in your business. Ordinary chores such as having the children take out the trash do not qualify as business reasons for paying your children. But if they help with the filing or make deliveries of product, then they can certainly earn a paycheck. The child can invest the money in a no-load mutual fund and start a college account. You get to deduct the wages as a business expense.

If you pay your spouse on a regular basis, he or she can (if not covered elsewhere) take $2,000 of that income and open a deductible IRA account. In fact, even if your family employee is covered by a company pension plan at a full-time job, up to $2,000 a year in earnings from your company can still be put into a nondeductible IRA to grow and compound tax-deferred.

If your dependent children work for you, they can earn up to $3,900 each in 1994, without having to file an income tax return. Children must, however, file a tax return if they earned at least $650 at work, plus have *any* unearned income such as interest, dividends, or capital gains. (See Children and Money Strategy #5 in chapter 39.)

Don't worry that you will lose your child as a dependent if he or she files a tax return. You can always claim children as dependents if they are under the age of 19 and are living at home (unless a divorce decree states otherwise), or if they are full-time students under age 24 to whom you contribute at least half of their support. However, children who are claimed as your dependents cannot take their own personal exemption ($2300 for 1992) when they file their own tax returns.

If you are a sole proprietor, wages paid to a child under age 18 are exempt from Social Security taxes. If you are incorporated, Social Security taxes must be paid on a child's income, just as for any other employee.

Remember, the first $650 of a child's investment earnings is currently tax-free; the second $650 is taxed at a 15 percent rate. Above that amount, investment earnings of children under age 14 are taxed at the parents' higher rate. To avoid that problem, simply create an IRA for the child with money he or she earns. That money will grow and compound, completely tax-deferred.

It's always wise to avoid taking money out of an IRA before age 59 ½ because of the 10 percent federal income tax penalty. But, given the chance to grow and compound tax-deferred over the years, it might be worth paying the penalty if you decide to use your child's IRA to fund a college education.

Chapter 42

Mortgage Strategies

The 1990s have already seen big changes in home values and financing costs. Lower mortgage rates made homes more affordable to potential homebuyers. But in many areas of the country, the same economic slowdown that brought mortgage rates down also brought home prices down. For homeowners who made the mistake of considering home equity a substitute for a savings or investment plan, this was a rude awakening.

Lower home prices and lower mortgage rates created opportunities for first-time homebuyers early in the decade. In 1991, the average mortgage payment for first-time buyers was $1,046. On average, this monthly payment represented 35.7 percent of household income. The average down payment for the first-time homebuyer was 14.7 percent in 1991—with about 12 percent of that down payment money coming from relatives.

The combination of lower mortgage rates and housing prices that can go down as well as up leads to some creative new strategies for buying and financing the family home. Ever since the depression, 30-year fixed-rate mortgages have been the most common way for Americans to finance their homes. Today there are some sensible alternatives.

Home Mortgage Strategy #1: *Where* to Get Your Mortgage

When you're buying a house, you'll have to decide where to get your mortgage loan. If you already live in that city, start with the local bank where you already have a banking relationship. If you're new to town, you may rely on the advice of your real estate broker. In any case, you should know that it's not just a question of rates and points when choosing a mortgage lender.

Not all mortgage lenders are the same, and you should be aware of differences. The time to start considering mortgage sources is before you start to look for a house, not when you're excited about having your offer accepted. By arranging mortgage financing before you start your house search, you know in advance how large a mortgage you will qualify for, and if your credit is acceptable. And you'll have a pretty good idea of comparative costs—rates and points—and other charges for completing the mortgage process. (Each *point* is 1 percent of the loan amount.)

Many financial institutions make mortgage loans: banks, savings and loans, savings banks, and mortgage banking companies. All of them can offer a wide variety of mortgage programs: 15-, 20-, or 30-year fixed-rate mortgages, adjustable-rate mortgages with different options, and other creative financing plans. But not all of them can make the same loan commitment.

In some cases, you'll want to have some leeway. You can get the mortgage commitment now—and fix the rate just before closing. If you think rates are trending downward, that could be a good idea. But most people prefer to "lock in" the rate at the time the loan commitment is made.

Your loan commitment is an important document. Read it carefully. Does it *guarantee* that you will get the promised mortgage amount at a specific rate and points, subject only to appraisal of the property? Or does it say that the loan commitment is "subject to the availability of funds"? In that case, you are probably dealing with a mortgage *broker* who is acting as an intermediary between lenders/investors and borrowers/homebuyers.

Failure to understand the difference has caused many homebuyers a great deal of anguish. In recent years when rates moved higher between the time of commitment and the date of closing, some mortgage lenders reneged on their promises. The investors who finance those loans would not provide the money at the lower rates promised earlier.

You always want to deal with a reliable lending institution—and check the written promises carefully. If you're dealing with a mortgage broker, understand the difference between a firm agreement and an agreement that is "subject to availability of funds."

Home Mortgage Strategy #2: When to Refinance

It may seem a bit strange to start a discussion of mortgage strategies with some advice on refinancing. That presumes you've already had at least one experience with taking out a mortgage. In 1992, mortgage refinancings for the first time outweighed mortgages made on original home purchases. The steep decline in interest rates meant that most homeowners who bought in the past ten years would benefit from refinancing at a lower rate.

When does it pay to refinance? There used to be an old rule of thumb stating that it paid to refinance your mortgage only if the rates dropped by two percentage points. You can throw that rule out because if you're planning to stay in your home for a while, and if you find a very good deal on refinancing costs, it might pay to refinance with only a 1 percent lower rate.

To figure out whether it pays to refinance, you must do some simple arithmetic.

1. Ask the lender what amount you would have to pay monthly under a new lower-rate mortgage. Subtract the new payment from your old payment to find out the *monthly savings*.

2. Ask the lender the amount of the *total cost to refinance*: loan fees, new appraisal, title search, etc.

3. Divide the *total cost* by the *monthly savings*. That will tell you how many months it will take you to break even and then start coming out ahead on a refinancing.

For example, if the total costs of refinancing are $2,400, and your monthly payments on the new loan are $200 lower, it will take you 12 months to break even. If you plan to stay in the home for at least that much time, it will pay to refinance.

Note: Points and fees you pay to refinance a mortgage loan are not immediately tax deductible as they are on a new financing. Instead, they must be amortized over the life of your refinanced loan.

Not everyone qualifies for refinancing. In the late eighties, many homeowners bought with only 10 percent down. Now that rates are lower and they're seeking new financing, they find that the appraisals on the home have dropped by more than 10 percent. In other words, they have no equity left in their homes. To qualify for a lower-rate mortgage, they would have to make a new equity down payment on the home in which they're already living. If they can't come up with the cash, they may be stuck with the old, higher-rate mortgage. Another group in a similar bind: Homeowners who accumulated credit card debt and no longer qualify for financing are stuck with old high-interest-rate mortgage loans.

If you do qualify for refinancing and the numbers make sense, start your search for a new mortgage commitment. The best place to start may be your current lender, who might not require a new appraisal. But before you decide to refinance to a new 30-year mortgage, consider Home Mortgage Strategy #3 below.

Home Mortgage Strategy #3: 30-Year vs. 15-Year Mortgage

Most of the mortgage rates you'll see quoted are for the traditional 30-year mortgage. But if you're willing to take a 15-year mortgage, you should be able to get a rate that's one-quarter to one-half percent lower. That's not the main reason for considering a 15-year mortgage.

When you take out a 15-year mortgage, you can save a fortune in interest over the life of the loan. Suppose you decide to refinance your $100,000, 30-year mortgage that carried an 11 percent interest rate. Your monthly payments look like this:

Current mortgage: 30 years at 11 percent = $952.33/mo

New mortgage: 30 years at 8 percent = $733.77/mo

Refinancing to a lower rate saves you $218.56 every month. But instead you decide to switch to a 15-year mortgage at 8 percent. Your monthly payment actually rises a few dollars:

New mortgage: 15 years at 8 percent = $955.66/mo

But here's the amount of interest you'll save over the life of the loan:

$170,820

You've already budgeted the old, higher monthly payment into your family finances, so it should be fairly easy to manage the payments on the 15-year mortgage. And you'll own your home—free and clear—just about the time the children are ready for college, or you're ready for retirement.

Even if you're not refinancing from a higher-rate loan, the savings on a shorter-term mortgage can be dramatic. Chart IV-8 shows the amount of total interest you would save on loans with terms of 20, 15, and even 10 years, compared to a standard 30-year mortgage. You'll note that you will also pay a slightly lower interest rate on a shorter-term mortgage because there is less risk to the lender.

There's a lot of debate about switching to a 15-year mortgage. Those who are still thinking with an eighties mentality are quick to point out that you'll lose a huge income tax deduction if you don't pay all that interest. And they note that if you put that extra monthly amount on a 15-year mortgage into a stock market mutual fund with an after-tax return of 10 percent over the 15 years, you would have more than enough money to pay off the mortgage balance in 15 years, with some left over for a vacation.

If you have the discipline to use one of the regular mutual fund investment strategies in chapter 17, and *if* the stock market rewards investors with a 10 percent average annual compound growth rate in the 1990s, you might be slightly better off with the 30-year mortgage, investing the difference.

But no matter what the marginal dollars and cents and tax deductions

CHART IV-8

Shorter the term, lower the interest

Here's how much shorter mortgage terms can save you in interest, based on a loan of $100,000. Rates are fixed, and monthly payments show principal and interest only.

Loan Term	Rate	Monthly Payment	Total Interest	Interest Savings*
30 years	7.75%	$716.41	$157,908	---
20 years	7.50	805.59	93,342	$64,566
15 years	7.19	909.48	63,706	94,202
10 years	7.00	1,161.08	39,330	118,578

*versus 30-year mortgage

SOURCE: 100 Highest Yields, N. Palm Beach, Florida 33408.

involved, there's an immeasurable but tremendous psychological edge in knowing that you own your own home—free and clear. That makes a 15-year mortgage worth giving up a portion of the tax break.

Home Mortgage Strategy #4:   Adjustable-Rate vs. Fixed-Rate Mortgage

In the early 1980s banks and S&Ls around the country were stuck with long-term, low-interest-rate mortgages in their portfolios. Yet depositors were demanding high interest rates on their savings, or they'd pull their money out of the bank and put it into higher-yielding Treasury bills. To help counter this problem, a mortgage-backed securities market was created. Now the banks could sell off those low-yielding mortgages—at a big discount—and have some cash to make new mortgages.

The banks were determined not to be caught again with long-term fixed-rate assets matched up against deposits whose rates changed weekly. Thus was born the adjustable-rate mortgage (ARM)—out of the bankers' desire to protect their balance sheets. Within a few years, there was a trading market for adjustable rate mortgages as well as fixed-rate mortgages. The banks could take the fees for making and servicing the loans but not worry about holding on to even these adjustable-rate mortgages.

Who bought the mortgages? You did—when you bought a Ginnie Mae or adjustable-rate mortgage fund in an attempt to earn higher interest rates than you could on bank certificates of deposit (see chapter 23). But if you're buying a home or thinking of refinancing, the big question is, should you be on the *paying* end of an adjustable-rate mortgage?

Adjustable-rate mortgages can carry rates as much as 40 percent lower than comparable fixed-rate mortgages, at a time when mortgage rates are falling. That makes them very tempting to home buyers. But having an ARM also carries a great deal of uncertainty: What if rates rise again? That's why more than 75 percent of homeowners still opt for fixed-rate mortgages.

In order to make an intelligent decision about choosing an ARM over a fixed-rate mortgage, you have to ask some questions—of yourself and your lender—and do some arithmetic.

1. How long do you plan to stay in the house?
If you're only going to be living in the house for a few years, it would make sense to take the lower-rate ARM, especially if rate adjustments are made only every three years.

2. What do you think is the general direction of interest rates?
In recent years the trend has been down, making ARMs a good deal for homeowners. Instead of seeing increases in their monthly payments, they've seen declines—and without the cost of having to refinance to a new, lower-rate mortgage.

3. How high could your monthly payment go if interest rates rise?
Do the arithmetic *before* you decide on an ARM. For example, take an ARM that has a maximum annual increase of two percentage points and a lifetime maximum increase (cap) of six percentage points in total. The mortage amount is $100,000.

If the opening rate is 5 percent, your initial monthly payment is $536.82.

Take a worst-case scenario in which rates rise sharply and your ARM adjusts the maximum 2 percent increase each year.

In the second year, your monthly payment would jump to $662.21.

In the third year, your monthly payment would jump to $795.40.

Assuming rates continue to rise sharply, you would reach the 6 percent lifetime cap in the fourth year, and your monthly payment would jump to $934.38.

This is a most extreme scenario, but could you afford the highest possible payment in that very unlikely event?

4. Would you be better off taking this ARM with a starting rate of 5 percent, or taking a fixed-rate mortgage with a higher rate of 8.25 percent?
Again, it's a question of arithmetic:

In our example above, you would have 12 monthly payments of $536.82 in the first year, or a total of $6,441.84.

In the second year, your monthly payments would total $7,946.52.

In the third year, your monthly payments would total $9,544.80.

And in your fourth year, your 12 monthly payments would total $11,212.56.

Altogether, you would have paid $35,145.72 on your ARM in the first four years of the worst-case scenario.

If you had taken the fixed-rate, 8.25 percent mortgage, your total payments over the four-year period would have been $36,060.

Even in a worst-case scenario, the ARM is $914.28 less expensive over the first four years. And if rates are steady or rise more slowly, it would take even longer for the ARM to become more costly than the fixed-rate loan. It all depends on the trend in interest rates and the spread between the initial low ARM rate and the rate on the fixed-rate mortgage. (In each of these examples we've omitted the up-front costs of the mortgage, which could include points, application and appraisal fees, and closing costs.)

If you're planning to stay in your home for many more years, you might want to opt for the fixed-rate mortgage anyway. In a period when interest rates are lower than they've been in a decade, you can consider the slightly higher cost of a fixed-rate mortgage the price you pay for peace of mind!

When considering an ARM, there are some additional variables you should consider:

1. What index is used to set the rate?

Most ARMs are tied to the one-year Treasury bill rate. This is slightly more volatile than other bases such as the *cost of funds* index in your Federal Reserve District. What is the *spread*—the number of percentage points above the index—that you will be charged? The spread should be no more than three points, and you may find an ARM with only a two percentage point spread.

2. How frequently does the ARM adjust?

The most popular ARMs adjust every year. Some ARMs adjust every three years, based on yields on three-year Treasury securities. While the initial rate on a three-year ARM may be slightly higher, you have a longer time period before you have to worry about an adjustment.

3. When is the ARM adjustment made?

Most ARMs adjust every year, on the anniversary of the mortgage. The new rate is actually set about 45 days before the anniversary, based on the index at that time.

4. Is there a provision in the loan for converting to a fixed-rate mortgage without going through a new application and appraisal procedure?
How much are you paying for this conversion feature, in the form of a slightly higher initial interest rate?

Terry's Tip:

$$$ You can't always count on your bank to make the correct adjustment in your monthly payment. There have been many cases where, either because of incorrect computer programming or error in the input of data, homeowners have found they were paying far too much after their ARMs were adjusted for rate increases.

Several commercial services offer to check on the accuracy of your ARM payment. They claim that it is worth their fee because as many as one-third of the mortgages they research result in refunds from the mortgage company:

Consumer Loan Advocates (800-767-2768); fee: $99.50

LoanCheck (800-477-6166); fee: $74

Loantech (800-888-6781); fee: $69

Mortgage Monitor (800-283-4887); fee: one-third of amount refunded
   by lender

Home Mortgage Strategy #5: Making Additional Principal Payments

You don't have to refinance to a 15-year mortgage to save on the interest payments. You can simply decide to pay an extra amount every month, or every quarter, to reduce your mortgage balance. In the first few years of mortgage payments, you are primarily paying interest on the loan, and very little principal is repaid. In fact, if you ask the bank for a mortgage statement every year, you might be surprised at how little of your initial monthly payments goes toward principal. Not until the 22nd year does more than half of your monthly payment go to principal on a 30-year mortgage at 8.5 percent.

Those interest payments really add up. On a $100,000, 30-year loan at 8.5 percent, you'll pay back a total of $276,808.85. The interest cost is far greater than the cost of your home.

If you can make additional monthly principal payments, you can avoid paying interest, and interest on the interest, for that portion of your original loan. The sooner you start the better, although you can make additional payments at any time (unless prohibited by your loan documents, which is very rare).

Even if you can only make an additional monthly payment of $25 or $50 dollars, the savings can add up. And in the process, you'll pay off the mortgage many months early, giving you the security of owning your home without an outstanding mortgage.

It's important to make sure that any extra payments you make are credited against *principal* and not against interest. Your monthly payment slip should have a line where you can designate that any extra payment should go to paying down the principal amount of your loan. It's best to make a regular additional payment, because most banks use computerized systems that may question unusual payment amounts.

Here's the strategy: Decide on a fixed, affordable additional payment and add it to your mortgage payment check each month. You might find it easier to "round off" your check. For instance, if your monthly mortgage payment is $856.92, then simply write your check for $900 each month. It's easier to write, and you'll soon get in the habit of thinking that your mortgage payment is $900. On the payment stub, note that the additional $43.08 is to be credited toward the principal of the loan. (Make a note of the difference on top of your check register, so you don't have to do the subtracting each month!)

If you decide on this regular program of increased payments, ask your lender for a new amortization schedule. That will let you know when the loan will be fully repaid and how much interest you're saving over the life of the loan. Those amounts will be quite an incentive to stick with your plan. But if your financial circumstances change, you can always go back to your original lower monthly payments.

Home Mortgage Strategy #6: Biweekly Mortgage Payments

Some mortgage lenders offer a biweekly mortgage payment program, or accept biweekly payments even if the agreement is not part of the formal mortgage documents. Instead of making 12 monthly payments, the borrower makes 26 biweekly payments—each for half of the amount of the full monthly payment. The arithmetic is obvious. You are making two additional payments each year, and the entire payment process is accelerated. The result is a faster paydown of your mortgage and a large interest savings.

If you have a 30-year, fixed-rate mortgage at 9.5 percent, instead of paying $202,708 in interest over the life of the loan, you'll pay out only $132,931 in interest if you opt for the biweekly payment schedule, and the life of the mortgage will be shortened by eight and a half years.

Biweekly payments make especially good sense for people who receive paychecks on the same basis. It's easier to divide the regular mortgage payment in half and pay one portion every time you receive a paycheck.

Home Mortgage Strategy #7: Understanding Home Equity Loans and Lines of Credit

See chapter 34 for a complete discussion of the rewards and perils of borrowing against your home equity.

Home Mortgage Strategy #8: Reverse Mortgages

See chapter 66 for a complete discussion of this unique opportunity for senior citizens to remain in their homes while taking a fixed amount of money out of their home equity in the form of a guaranteed monthly check.

Chapter 43

Strategies to Save Big Bucks When Buying

One characteristic of the 1990s is an increasing awareness of value—a willingness to shop and, if necessary, negotiate for a good buy. Value should not be confused with low prices; it's really the concept of getting more for your money. The product or service you purchase must be worth the cost. Bragging about getting a "good deal" is replacing conspicuous consumption in the nineties. Therefore, whatever you buy, you will not only need to examine the quality carefully, but also to know some strategies for getting the best deal possible.

Buying Strategy #1: Getting the Best Price on a New Car

Buying a new car may be one of the most expensive purchases you'll ever make, and one in which you, as the buyer, may be at the greatest disadvantage. Car dealers talk about their "deals" and even invite buyers to "make your best deal," but car buyers usually have very little information to guide them. Only recently have some car dealerships such as Saturn dealers announced a "fixed-price, no-negotiation" policy. At most dealers there's a "sticker" price on the car window, but that's just the manufacturer's suggested retail price. You can buy a car for a lot less than that, if you have the right information.

The one number you need to know to make a good deal is the *dealer's invoice cost*. Rarely will a dealer show you his actual factory invoice. But you *can* get the dealer invoice cost on any car, any model, any accessories with just one phone call.

Car/Puter International, based in Ft. Lauderdale, Florida (900-226-CARS), has a telephone service that will give you the true cost on any make or model. The service costs $2 per minute, and the average call costs about $16. You have the information ready about the specifications of the car you are looking at; Car/Puter will give you the dealer's invoice cost.

The system is computerized, so it can be accessed 24 hours a day. But if you call between 8:30 a.m. and 10:00 p.m. eastern time, you can press a button and talk to a personal counselor who will also tell you if there are any special factory cash offers taking place. Dealers aren't obligated to pass these rebates on to customers, so they could add to a dealer's profit— or help sweeten your deal.

If you can wait a day or two for the information, you can call the Car/ Puter toll-free number (800-331-4001) and request that a printout be mailed to you. The cost of a printout of costs for any new car is $20, charged to your bankcard. Car/Puter also has a service that sells cars slightly above invoice price from a network of participating dealers.

Other similar services include:

AAA Auto Pricing Service 900-776-4222 ($1.95/min);

Nationwide Auto Brokers (800-521-7257) $11.95 per quote;

Auto Advisor 800-326-1976 (auto buying and consultation service, cost $339 and up).

Armed with this information, you can walk into any car dealer and negotiate a good deal. What's a good deal? It all depends on the demand for that particular model, whether it's sitting on the dealer's lot or has to be ordered, and the general economic conditions. But it won't be a surprise if you can get the car for $150 to $250 over the dealer's invoice cost.

Don't feel sorry for the dealer if you do make this deal. Dealers who sell domestic models also get what's called a "holdback," which amounts to about 2 percent of the base sticker price of the car. This is a rebate from the manufacturer that's designed to pay the dealer's overhead—rent, lights, and heat. The dealer may also get money from the manufacturer to cover his local advertising costs.

And, the dealer has some other ways to make money on you! See the strategies below.

Buying Strategy #2: Avoid Paying for Unnecessary "Extras"

Yes, the car dealer does have other ways of making a profit—even after you negotiate the price of the car. After you've made your deal with the salesperson, you're sent to the F&I department. That stands for "financing and insurance"—and that's not all. Even though you may not want to finance the car or buy insurance, this "business manager" will probably be involved in writing up the contract. Here's how dealers make more money.

Financing

You may need financing for your car, and the dealer will offer it to you. Dealers make a lot of money on the financing—even when it's done through the manufacturer, such as Ford Motor Credit, Chrysler Credit, or GMAC. So be sure to check other sources of financing such as your local bank or credit union before signing up for financing with the dealer. Sometimes your best financing deal may come from the manufacturer, who may offer low-rate financing just to keep assembly lines operating.

Extended Warranties

Your car will come with a manufacturer's warranty for a fixed number of years and a specific number of miles. One of the biggest profit centers for a dealer is the sale of extended warranty plans. You should understand how they work and what they cover.

First, ask the dealer whose extended warranty plan he is selling. Is it offered by the manufacturer or by another private warranty company? That's an important distinction. Many private warranty companies have gone out of business in recent years, leaving the car owner to pay for repairs. If you're going to pay for a manufacturer's warranty, make sure the manufacturer is standing behind it, not a private company or the dealership.

Then be sure you understand what the warranty really covers. It should pick up where the manufacturer's plan stops. The dealer may be selling you a "five-year" plan, but if the manufacturer covers the first year, then you're really only getting a four-year extension, while paying for five years.

Make sure the warranty is transferable if you sell the car. And, if you think you might sell the car in a few years, do you really need a warranty? Just remember, selling extended warranties is big business. Don't buy one if you don't think you'll need it. (See also Buying Strategy #6 below.)

Credit Life and Disability Insurance

In the car dealership industry it's called "choke and croak" insurance. *Never* buy insurance through your car dealer. The "croak" (life) part of the insurance is designed to pay off the balance you owe on your car if you die. But if you die, who cares? If you do need insurance, you can buy a simple term insurance policy about ten times cheaper (see chapter 51).

The "choke" (disability) part of the policy is designed to continue making car payments if you're disabled. If you're disabled, you won't be able to drive the car. If you're worried about disability, what you really need is a policy to pay the rent and put food on the table (see chapter 49).

Dealer Extras

Before you leave, the business manager will ask if he or she can provide some "extras" for you—special rustproofing, a burglar alarm, or customized striping. Remember, these are pure profit items for the dealer, and you could probably negotiate a better deal elsewhere.

Buying Strategy #3: New Car or Used

You've always heard that the price of your new car depreciates the minute you drive out of the dealership. Do you know how much? Twenty percent! You can always get a better deal on a new car if you wait until the end of the model year. But even that deal will not offset the instant annual depreciation.

Many smart buyers prefer to buy a used car—*if* they know the history of the car's ownership. There's a big difference between buying a car off a used-car lot and buying a car that you know has been driven lightly and taken care of very well. There was a time when many Americans traded in their cars every two years, even though the car had fairly low mileage. Today, those sweet deals have been replaced by either executive-driven or promotional cars on which you can receive a substantial discount. And you should be able to get a complete warranty from the manufacturer. Since warranties may now be transferred with the car, you can contact the manufacturer to verify the history of ownership.

Another large source of used cars is the fleet sales of national rental car companies. Many rental car companies have stopped selling their used cars through the wholesale market. Instead, used rental cars are re-purchased by the manufacturer and then processed through closed dealer auctions in which only the manufacturer's own dealers may participate. The manufacturers screen the cars to eliminate any that have had severe damage or heavy repairs.

The cars purchased at these auctions are shipped directly to the dealers' used car lots. These cars are clearly labeled as "program" cars, and usually have only about 15,000 to 20,000 miles on the odometer. The dealer is able to purchase these year-old cars at about 30 to 35 percent off the original list price, depending on the model of the car, and pass the savings on to used-car buyers. Supported by the manufacturers, the dealers may also be able to offer extended warranties at special prices, and special finance terms.

Whether you're buying or selling a used car, you need to have an idea of what the car should be worth. You can get that information from several printed sources—including the National Association of Auto Dealers' (NADA) *Official Used Car Guide*. It comes out annually and is usually referred to as the "blue book." There are two separate prices listed in the guide. The first is the *average retail price*. This is the amount the car would sell for on the dealer's used-car lot if it were in good condition. That's the price you might ask if you were listing the car yourself in the newspaper.

The second price is the *wholesale price*, which is lower than the retail price. This number is derived from the prices for this type of car at dealer auctions. This is probably the price the dealer is going to offer you when you bring your car in to trade.

If you want an up-to-date estimate of the current value of any used car, Car/Puter International will also give you that information through its telephone service (900-226-CARS). You'll have to give complete information about model, year, mileage, and both mechanical and physical condition of the car.

Buying Strategy #4: Cash or Finance

The economics of financing any major consumer purchase such as a car or appliance changed with the Tax Reform Act of 1986, which phased out the deduction for consumer interest. Now there are only two reasons to pay finance charges on any major purchase: (1) you don't have the cash to pay in full and you definitely need to make the purchase; and (2) you do have the cash, but you could invest the money elsewhere and earn more than the amount of the finance charges.

Since consumer finance charges remain very high on most items relative to the amount you can earn in reasonable investments, you'd have to be a successful professional trader to convince yourself that you can earn more money after-tax than the cost of financing. The one exception occurs when auto manufacturers offer very low-rate or zero-rate financing in an attempt to sell cars.

If you are considering financing a purchase because you can't pay in cash, then your big decision is *where* to do the financing. Before you borrow through the dealer, check alternatives such as your local bank or credit union. Frequently, however, dealers have the least expensive financing. If your credit is borderline, the car dealer may have a more expensive source of financing that will at least allow you to make the purchase.

You may be considering taking out a home equity loan to finance the purchase of a consumer item such as a car or refrigerator. As noted in chapter 34, interest on these loans is usually lower, and is tax-deductible. It is also dangerous: You're putting your most valued asset on the line to purchase an item that can be stolen or destroyed, and will certainly depreciate. Think twice before you do that.

Buying Strategy #5: Buy or Lease

Auto manufacturers have aggressively jumped on the leasing bandwagon in the past few years. In 1992, one out of five new cars was leased. Manufacturers see leases as a way to make cars more affordable—and thus to create demand that will keep their plants running. Leasing a car definitely looks, at first glance, like a less expensive way to drive the car you want, especially since you can no longer deduct finance charges when you buy a car on time. Leasing allows you to drive a more expensive car for less money. But leasing also has its drawbacks.

Leasing a car can be compared to renting an apartment versus buying a home or condo. When you rent, you don't need a down payment and the monthly payments may be slightly less than those required to buy the property. But at the end of your lease you have no equity, just a pile of rent receipts. Similarly, at the end of a car lease, you don't have a car that you can continue to drive, or use as a down payment on your next car.

When you lease a car you don't need a down payment, but you will need at least one or two months' security deposit on the lease, which means you're tying up cash. Although the lessor will pay you interest on the security deposit, it does not give you the advantage of a down payment, which lowers the amount you are financing if you were buying the car.

Many people lease cars for two financial reasons: (1) they think they can deduct the entire lease payment as a business expense; and (2) they think they can lease a very expensive car and avoid certain business rules that limit depreciation on luxury cars.

Before you write off your entire monthly lease payment as a business expense, you'd better be able to justify it. If you drive your car at all for personal reasons, you can only deduct the portion of the lease payment (and operating expenses) that relates to business use. As for beating the luxury car deduction limits, you must add back a portion of the lease payment as income if the value of your leased car exceeds $13,400.

Yes, leasing is less expensive each month. That's because you are only financing the portion of the car—two or three years' worth—that you are using. At the end of the lease term, the car goes back to the dealer who owns the residual value (unless you agree to pay a prearranged price).

You should be aware that even if you get the same purchase price on a car at two different dealers, the monthly lease price may be different, unless it is a promotional lease deal offered and advertised by the manufacturer. Leases made through dealers may differ on the implied interest rates and the end-of-lease value assumptions for the car.

Even though you are leasing, you are still paying finance charges. You are paying a set interest rate on the portion of the car's value—that two or three years' worth—that you are financing. Each dealer may impute a different interest rate to the amount you are "financing" as a leaseholder.

Also, each dealer may come up with a different value assumption for the car at the end of the lease. The result may be a difference in your monthly payments.

Read any lease carefully. There are limits on the number of miles you can drive each year without incurring expense charges. You could wind up paying as much as 15 cents per mile over a fixed limit of about 15,000 miles each year.

There's one other great danger with a lease. If you decide you don't like the car after a few months, you're locked in. You won't be able to get out of your lease without coming up with a large cash payment. So avoid leases with terms longer than 36 months.

Here are some general rules. In a time of low interest rates, you're best off buying a car for cash instead of financing it. Your money in the bank isn't earning much, and the interest you pay on a car loan is not deductible. If you must borrow, the best financial deal is to use a home interest loan because the interest is deductible. As we've already noted, though, tapping your home equity to purchase a wasting asset may be "penny wise and pound foolish."

When a business is considering buying a car, the more expensive the car, the more advantageous leasing is because of the way the IRS leasing tables are computed. For an individual, the question of whether to lease ultimately depends on the terms of the deal—and how many extra costs are buried in the monthly lease payments.

Buying Strategy #6: Major Purchases—Do You Need Extended Warranties?

After you've just spent your hard-earned money on a major appliance or electronics item, your salesperson while writing up the ticket will probably offer you the chance to purchase an *extended warranty*—to protect the investment you've just made. Turn it down. Extended warranties are a huge profit center for retailers, and a huge waste of money for consumers.

According to an article in *Consumer Reports* (January 1991), retailers estimate that for every dollar they take in from selling extended warranties, they will have to spend only between 4 and 15 cents on services! In fact, according to the retailers, only 12 to 20 percent of the people who buy a warranty will ever use it.

Most new appliances already have a manufacturer's warranty. And if you purchase the appliance at a major store, your complaints should get attention even after the warranty period has expired. Plus, if you use certain credit cards such as a gold bankcard, your card issuer may automatically double the manufacturer's warranty on the product. Instead of purchasing an extended warranty, do some research on reliability of the product before you buy it, and save the money you might have spent on the extended warranty.

Chapter 44

Retirement Planning Strategies

This chapter is included as part of your everyday financial strategies, because you can never start early enough to think about and plan for retirement. It should be part of your concern when your children are still young, as you plan your career and make job changes. If you're already retired, or close to that age, you'll find more information about taking money out of your retirement plans, maximizing your income, and deferring taxes in chapter 65. This section is dedicated to those who have the advantage of time when it comes to assessing retirement strategies. This brings us to key rule #1:

The earlier you start saving for retirement, the less you must save to have enough money to live well.

The 50-year-old person who contributes $500 a month to a retirement plan will never catch up with the 30-year-old who has been contributing $100 a month.

If you start saving for retirement at age 35, you only have to put away $1,000 a year in a tax-deferred account in order to accumulate $150,000. But if you wait until you're age 50 to start your retirement program, you'll need to put aside nearly $5,000 each year in that account to accumulate the same $150,000 nest egg.

Here are some basic facts that should inspire you to start planning for and investing for retirement *now*.

To maintain your standard of living after retirement you'll need at least 70 percent of your final preretirement income. But inflation, even at low rates, will increase the amount you need each year. If you retired today on $50,000 annual income, in 15 years you'd need $104,000 to maintain your standard of living!

You'll probably live longer than your parents; plan to live until at least 90. Current actuarial tables in use by the insurance industry say that today's 40-year-old, nonsmoking woman can expect to live until age 86; a nonsmoking, 40-year-old man will probably live until age 81.

Even if Social Security exists in something like its present form when you retire, it will probably only contribute about 18 percent of your retirement income. The Social Security administration estimates that even Social Security and pensions combined add up to less than half the needed income for the average retiree (see chart IV-9). Given the funding problems inherent in the Social Security system, it's reasonable to assume Social Security will become a means-tested program in the next 20 years, becoming even less of a factor for an affluent retiree.

There are so many variables that it's almost impossible to project exactly how much you'll need in personal savings in order to retire and maintain your standard of living. Let's make some assumptions:

CHART IV-9
Social Security and Pensions may not be enough for your retirement.

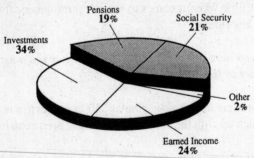

On average, over half of your retirement income needs to come from personal investments and earned income.
DATA: Social Security Administration.
SOURCE: United Services Funds.

You want to retire at age 65;

You will live 15 years in retirement;

Inflation averages 5 percent between now and your retirement;

Your annual income grows at a rate of 5 percent each year;

You want retirement income equal to 70 percent of preretirement income;

You have a company pension that will provide 35 percent of needed retirement income;

You will receive maximum Social Security benefits as projected today.

Chart IV-10 shows how much money you'll need to have on hand in personal savings when you retire at age 65, to maintain your current standard of living. If these numbers don't quite fit your situation, you'll find many financial advisors and mutual fund companies willing to project the numbers for your personal situation.

CHART IV-10
**Retirement Fund Needed at 65 to Maintain
Equivalent of Current Income**

Current Age	Current Income	Personal Funds Needed*
30	$120,000	$2,280,161
	80,000	1,407,087
	40,000	552,839
50	120,000	1,312,274
	80,000	776,278
	40,000	251,842
60	120,000	737,095
	80,000	408,049
	40,000	85,024

* Assumes 15 years of retirement; 5% inflation; 5% annual growth in current income; retirement income equal to 70% of preretirement earnings; maximum Social Security benefit for worker and spouse; a pension equal to 35% of retirement income; 8% pretax return and 28% tax bracket.

SOURCE: Reprinted with permission from SunAmerica Marketing © 1992.

T. Rowe Price, the no-load mutual fund company, has developed an excellent and inexpensive software package and workbook designed to help you figure out just how much money you'll need to put away each year to reach your retirement goals. T. Rowe Price's retirement planning workbook is free; the software costs $15 and is available by calling 800-541-4021. With this software package you can create and change your own retirement scenario in seconds—varying your estimates of inflation, return on investment, tax rates, and other potential challenges to your retirement planning. The program will instantly recalculate the amount of monthly or annual savings needed to fund your projections.

The numbers may be intimidating at first. But some of that fear disappears if you recognize how easy it is to make your retirement funds grow—if you use the correct strategies on a regular basis.

A more reassuring scenario is illustrated in chart IV-11 on p. 338. Just see how a $2,000 annual investment would grow if it earned 10 percent over the next 10, 20, or 30 years. (Remember, 10 percent is about the average rate of return on the stock market over the past 30 years.)

The real impact of this scenario comes when you compare the growth of this investment if it is made in fully taxable investments (31 percent federal tax rate) versus being sheltered in a retirement account where you do not pay any taxes on the dividends or capital gains over the years.

Which brings us to key rule #2:

Take advantage of every opportunity to shelter your retirement funds from current income taxes.

At the same time you're putting money away for a down payment on a house, or for college for your children, you should also be taking advantage of the retirement strategies outlined below. These strategies require you to make some decisions about how you should be investing the retirement funds over which you have control.

That brings us to key rule #3:

Invest your retirement funds for the long run—if retirement is more than ten years away.

As you learned in chapter 10, equities have far outperformed more conservative investments over the long run. While you don't want to speculate with your retirement money, younger people have a tendency to be too conservative. Don't forget that although you may be aiming at retirement at age 60 or 62, you will live for a long time as a retiree, and you will need your funds to continue to grow.

A 1992 survey by Hewitt Associates showed that 59 percent of employee contributions in 401(k) plans are invested in GICs (guaranteed income contracts) offered at a fixed rate by insurance companies. With the concern over insurance company solvency, many large corporations are switching to fixed-rate bonds or long-term bond funds as a conservative alternative in pension plan accounts. Whatever the investment choices offered, the figures show a tendency to trade off growth opportunities for income. That can be a disadvantage for a younger worker.

The strategies outlined below all illustrate opportunities to set aside money for retirement. When you use them, remember to follow the three key rules for retirement savings:

1. Start early and save regularly for retirement.
2. Take advantage of all opportunities to shelter your retirement money from taxes.
3. Invest for the long run.

RETIREMENT SAVINGS STRATEGIES

Some retirement savings opportunities are offered by your company; others require you to set up a qualified program such as an Individual Retirement Account. But every retirement program demands your regular attention and self-discipline in order to make it work for you.

Retirement Savings Strategy #1: Individual Retirement Accounts

There have been so many changes, and proposed changes, to the concept of Individual Retirement Accounts that many people are confused about whether they can make a contribution to an IRA, and whether they can deduct the contribution on this year's taxes.

Let's clear up one thing first:

Everyone, even if covered by another retirement plan, may make an annual IRA contribution of $2,000 or 100 percent of earned income *that year, whichever is less, up to the year in which they reach age 70¹/₂.*

That contribution may or may not be deductible, subject to the rules listed below. But even if the contribution is not deductible, the money you contribute to your IRA each year will grow and compound tax-deferred. That's worth making the contribution even if it is not tax-deductible.

There is one situation in which an individual can contribute even if he or she did not have *any* income:

If you are a couple and one spouse is nonworking, you may contribute an extra $250, for a total of $2,250. (The contributions must be split into two accounts, with no more than $2,000 in the name of one spouse.

For purposes of IRA contributions, earned income is income from salary, wages, or self-employment. Alimony or court-ordered marital support is also considered income. But interest and dividends from your investments are not considered income.

As noted above, your IRA contribution may be deductible on your income tax return if you meet the following requirements. Note that this deduction comes right off the top; you do not have to itemize to claim it.

Who is eligible to *deduct* an IRA contribution on the current year's income tax return?

You may deduct your full contribution if neither you nor your spouse is an active participant in an employer-sponsored retirement plan.

Even if you or your spouse is an active participant in a company retirement plan, you may still be allowed to deduct your IRA contribution, depending on your level of adjusted gross income.

Even if you are covered by a company pension plan, you can deduct your IRA contribution if your adjusted gross income (AGI) falls within the following ranges:

If you are single, you may take a full deduction if your AGI is $25,000 or less. You may take a partial deduction if your AGI ranges between

$25,000 and $35,000. There is no deduction when your AGI exceeds $35,000.

If you are married and filing a joint return, you may take a full deduction if your AGI is $40,000 or less. You may take a partial deduction if your AGI ranges between $40,000 and $50,000. There is no deduction if your AGI is over $50,000.

If you are married and filing separately, there is no deduction if your AGI exceeds $10,000.

Millions of people are still eligible to deduct an annual IRA contribution, either because they have no other retirement plan, or because their income falls within the guidelines listed above.

Deducting your annual contribution can make a difference in your returns over the years, but the same chart shows that even if you cannot deduct your IRA, the tax-deferred compounding can make it a worthwhile forced savings plan (see chart IV-11).

Your IRA contribution must be made by your tax-filing due date (not including extensions), but the earlier in the year you make your contribution, the longer the money has to grow tax-deferred in your behalf. IRS booklet #590 covers the tax rules on IRAs in detail.

For information on IRA withdrawal rules, see chapter 65.

Terry's Tips:

$$$ If you have both deductible and nondeductible IRA contributions over the years (because in previous years even those covered by company pension plans were allowed to deduct IRA deposits), *keep them separate.* One day, when you want to take some money out of your account, you'll find the tax calculations much easier.

The same advice holds true if you leave one job and roll your pension benefits over into an IRA. You must make it a separate account, because one day you might want to put the money into your new employer's plan.

$$$ If you do make a nondeductible IRA contribution, be sure to file IRS Form 8606 with your tax return.

CHART IV-11

**Growth of $2,000 Annual Investment
in Tax-Deferred IRA vs. Fully Taxable
Investments Over 30 Years**

(Assumes 10% annual return and 31% federal tax rate)

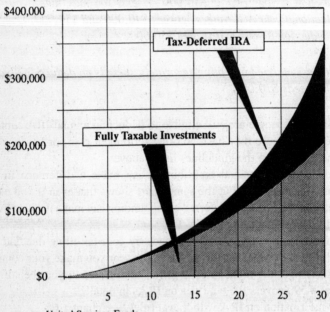

SOURCE: United Services Funds.

Retirement Savings Strategy #2: Keogh Plan

If you're self-employed, you can create your own retirement savings plan
very easily and contribute far more than the $2,000 that is the limit for an
IRA. Even if you work for another company and are covered by a company retirement plan, you can use a Keogh plan to shelter your self-
employment income that comes from consulting, freelancing, or other side
business.

There are two types of Keogh plan: defined benefit and defined contribution plans. You need to understand the differences, but you don't have to
become a legal expert. Just as with IRAs, the paperwork for the most used
of these plans has been done for you by many mutual fund companies,
banks, and brokerage firms. All you have to do is fill in the blanks—and

send in a check. A Keogh plan must be set up by the end of the year, and contributions must be made by the tax-filing due date, including extensions.

In a defined contribution plan, you make the decision about how much you want to contribute to the plan each year. If you choose a defined contribution *money purchase* Keogh plan, you may put in the lesser of $30,000 or 20 percent of net earned income (prior to reduction for the contribution) on a tax-deductible basis. For this calculation, net earned income is reduced by the amount of the deduction for self-employment tax on page one of your tax return.

Or you can select a defined contribution *profit-sharing* Keogh plan. Contributions to this type of plan are discretionary every year, depending on the profits of your business. With this type of Keogh plan, contributions are deductible up to a maximum of 13.04 percent of net earned income (before reduction for the contribution), or $30,000, whichever is less.

If you choose a *defined benefit* Keogh plan, you may be able to deduct larger sums of money each year. That's because contribution limits are based on projected retirement benefits. The annual benefit at retirement for a participant cannot exceed $120,000 in 1995, or 100 percent of the participant's average earned income for the highest three years for which contributions are made, whichever is less. You'll need an actuary to compute the appropriate annual contribution to this type of Keogh plan.

There is an important requirement for Keogh plans. If you have employees in your business, you must include contributions for them as well. The amount of the contribution for employees will be determined by your accountant in accordance with IRS rules. The deadline for establishing a Keogh plan is December 31 of the year for which you make a deductible contribution.

Retirement Savings Strategy #3: Take Advantage of the 401(k) Company Savings Plan

The company you work for may have one or more benefits plans, and it's to your advantage to understand how they work. In most of these plans you have very little to say about the amount of money that is contributed for you and the way it is invested. But if you're fortunate to work for a company that has a 401(k) company savings plan, you should take advantage of your opportunity to contribute the maximum amount allowed. The money will be taken out of your paycheck and you won't miss it—another way to break the "see it—spend it" habit.

The 401(k) plan, named for the section of the tax code that created it in 1981, is one of the best retirement savings deals that employees will ever receive; yet many workers fail to participate, simply because they don't understand how the plans work.

It may be called a "company savings plan" or by another in-house name, but all 401(k) plans work the same way. They allow employees to deduct a portion of their earnings—before taxes—and set the money aside in a plan that has various investment options. The money grows and compounds tax-deferred until the employee takes it out at retirement.

Participating in such a company savings plan is strictly voluntary; after all, the contribution comes out of your paycheck before federal and state income taxes (although it is subject to Social Security taxes). The dollar amount you may contribute each year is subject to a limit set by your company as a percentage of your salary. By law, the contribution can be no higher than 25 percent of salary, or a maximum of $9,240 in 1995.

Some companies even allow you to contribute an additional amount of after-tax dollars to the plan. You don't get a tax deduction, but the additional contribution does grow tax-deferred along with the rest of your account.

The key benefits of participating in a 401(k) plan are:

You don't pay taxes on the money you contribute;

You have control over the investments;

The money grows and compounds tax-deferred;

Any money you contribute is yours—even if you leave the company;

When you leave the company, you can roll over your account into another tax-deferred IRA.

But here's the best part of the deal. Companies are allowed—and most do—to match the employee's contribution, based on a formula. A recent Hewitt Associates study showed that 84 percent of companies match their employees' contributions. The study revealed that half of the matching plans are either dollar for dollar or 50 cents on the dollar. Where else could you get a return of 50 or 100 percent on your money in the first year?

Yet, surprisingly, the same study reveals that only about 72 percent of eligible employees participate in their company 401(k) plans. When asked, some employees said they didn't understand how the plan works; most said they couldn't afford the deduction from their paychecks. An employee who can't afford a small regular deduction will hardly be able to afford retirement.

401(k) Investment Choices

One of the best parts of the 401(k) deal is that you have some control over the investments in the plan. Usually you'll have a choice between a money market account, a fixed-income choice, an investment in your company's stock, and a general growth or equity stock fund.

If you have at least ten years until retirement, take advantage of the opportunity to invest for growth instead of strictly playing it safe. But don't feel pressured into investing the majority of your 401(k) contributions in your own company's stock. It already plays a big role in your financial future.

Most plans allow you to change your investment allocations quarterly; some as frequently as once a month. You should be able to keep track of the investment performance of your funds through the fund investment managers.

401(k) Rules and Restrictions

There are some other rules for 401(k) plans, but they are among the least restrictive of all such retirement plans. You must leave your contributions in the plan, or in a rollover, until age 59½—or face the 10 percent federal penalty for early withdrawal. There are some exceptions for hardship cases, such as emergency medical expenses, college tuition, or purchasing a home. Each plan may set its own rules for hardship withdrawals.

If you can't meet the stringent rules for hardship withdrawals, your plan may allow you to take a loan. Each plan sets its own rules for loans, and you should ask your benefits officer. Most plans state that you can borrow up to 50 percent of your own contributions, including earnings on those contributions. Depending on the rules of the plan, you may have to state the reason for the loan. Interest rates are set by the plan—usually the bank prime rate—and terms of the loan usually require repayment within five years.

403(b) Plans

A 403(b) plan is a pretax savings plan generally offered to employees by tax-exempt, not-for-profit organizations such as schools and hospitals. These 403(b) plans are similar to 401(k) plans, but have slightly higher limits on the amount that can be contributed. If you work for a not-for-profit organization that does not have a 403(b) plan, ask them to consider starting one so that employees can make contributions.

The largest of these plans is sponsored by the TIAA-CREF (Teachers Insurance and Annuity Association—College Retirement Equities Fund), which is the nationwide pension system for higher education, with assets of about $112 billion. Participants in the TIAA-CREF program can make additional pretax contributions by purchasing a Supplemental Retirement Annuity through the program.

Retirement Savings Strategy #4: Take Advantage of Company Plans

If you work for a large company, it probably has a pension plan or some form of retirement savings program. Retirement plan contributions made by your employer are an important part of your total compensation. In order for contributions to such a plan to be deductible to the company, they must meet strict IRS requirements that they be nondiscriminatory and provide for lower-income employees as well as the higher-salaried owners and bosses.

Understand all the benefits you are accumulating under a company benefit plan. Talk to the employee benefits officer. Understand how long it takes for plan contributions made by the company to be owned by you (*vesting*) and how retirement benefits are computed.

Defined Benefit Plans

For generations, the standard company pension plan was a *defined benefits plan*. The plan guarantees the employee a fixed monthly sum at retirement—and for the rest of the employee's life—currently up to a maximum of $120,000 per year in 1995. A defined benefit plan requires the company to make a fixed contribution each year, regardless of profits. That's why many companies are using more flexible plans that will be explained below.

In a defined benefit plan, the monthly pension at retirement will be based on a formula that typically combines a percentage figure based on the number of years you have worked for the company times an average of your earnings. Ask your company benefits officer what the formula is, and what is the earliest age at which you can retire with full benefits. You should also ask how your benefits will be lowered if you decide to retire early.

If you leave the company before you qualify for retirement, or take early retirement, you may be able to take your pension benefits with you and roll them into an IRA rollover account—letting the money continue to grow and compound tax-deferred. But at retirement you won't get that guaranteed monthly check, which is enhanced by the number of years you worked at the company.

There's one caveat: You can only take the money with you if it is vested—that is, owned by you. Each year you work for the company, a portion of your benefits will become vested. By law, your pension benefits must be fully vested in a maximum of seven years. Most companies have full vesting in five years.

Future pension benefits should never tie you to a job you hate, but sticking with a company for 25 years or more does have some rewards.

Terry's Tip:

$$$ Keep informed about the funding status of your company pension plan. Many company plans are "underfunded." Other company plans were replaced with less generous and less desirable programs during the 1980s era of takeovers. In fact, some of those pensions have been replaced with insurance company annuities—leaving your pension at the risk of insurance company solvency.

Your company pension plan is automatically insured by the Pension Benefit Guaranty Corporation unless you work for a professional service corporation (such as a medical or legal office) with fewer than 25 employees. The PBGC protects the pensions of more than 40 million Americans in 85,000 private pension plans. Its guarantees cover retired workers and the vested pension interests of people who are currently working.

However, there are annual insurance protection limits of about $28,000 in benefits per 65-year-old retiree. These limits may not cover all the benefits owed to highly compensated workers. Also, the PBGC has determined that supplemental benefits given to workers who retire early may not be covered. So those who retire early have far lower pension guarantees. And the PBGC does not guarantee other benefits such as life and health insurance benefits that have been promised to retirees.

The Pension Benefit Guaranty Corporation currently estimates that it has exposure to roughly $40 billion of underfunding in corporate pension plans. The PBGC fund had assets of $5.9 billion in 1992, with money coming into the fund at a rate of nearly $800 million a year from premiums paid by employers. But that does not come close to matching the annual payouts to retirees of failed companies. Ask if your pension plan is insured by PBGC—which in 1992 was running a $2.5 billion deficit.

Defined Contribution Plans

When a company sets up a *profit-sharing plan*, it has more flexibility in its contributions. For instance, if the company has very low profits one year, the contribution can be lowered. The benefits in these plans are usually proportional to the salaries of the participants. But these plans may also give a company flexibility to make larger contributions for owners and older employees.

A *money purchase plan* is similar to a profit-sharing plan, but it has basic required contributions based on a fixed percentage of the compensation of those eligible to receive benefits. The trade-off for the percentage requirement is that the owner can make a larger total contribution. Your company may have a combined profit-sharing and money purchase plan. From the closely held company's point of view, the idea is to structure a plan that will allow the owner to put aside the largest amount for his or her retirement. As an employee, you benefit because IRS rules require a certain balance between owner and employee contributions.

Retirement Savings Strategy #5: Create Your Own Retirement Plan Using Tax-Deferred Annuities

Suppose your company doesn't have a 401(k) plan, and you don't think your eventual pension will be enough to fund your retirement. You've already funded an IRA, and you would be willing to set aside a few more dollars each month, if only it could grow tax-sheltered until your retirement years. Or perhaps you've just received a settlement from an accident or lawsuit, and instead of spending the money now, you'd like to set it aside for retirement—letting it grow tax-sheltered in the intervening years.

Retirement Planning Strategies

In chapter 28 you saw how anyone can invest a lump sum of money or make a series of regular payments into a tax-deferred annuity. In effect, this creates a private pension plan, which will let your money grow for the future, subject to many of the same restrictions as your IRA or company pension plan.

There are many good annuity programs that allow you to contribute a minimum of $50 a month to such a plan (although most require that you start with about $1,500). In fact, most of these plans will arrange to have the money withdrawn from your bank checking, savings, or money market account.

Contact your insurance agent or the annuity shopping service listed in chapter 29 for more information about making regular contributions to a tax-deferred annuity.

Retirement Savings Strategy #6: For Government Employees

If you are a federal government employee, you have a chance to participate in a thrift savings program that is the equivalent of a company 401(k) plan. This program is open to government workers who are participants in the Federal Employees Retirement System (FERS)—mostly people hired since 1983—and those in the old Civil Service Retirement System (CSRS).

About 1.8 million government workers already have accounts; and about 1.3 million of them are actually contributing money through payroll deductions. In 1992, there was $12 billion in the plan. FERS workers may put in from 1 to 10 percent of pay and qualify for a matching government contribution of up to 5 percent. Even if FERS workers do not contribute, they still get a 1 percent contribution from the government. One out of three government workers does not make a personal voluntary contribution.

CSRS employees can contribute from 1 to 5 percent of pay. They do not qualify for matching contributions, and retirees cannot join this plan.

Money inside the plan accumulates tax-deferred, as in corporate 401(k) plans, and there is a choice of investments ranging from the G-fund (Treasury securities) to the C-fund (stocks) and the F-fund (bonds).

Government and military employees have a variety of other retirement programs, but this voluntary program is certainly one that deserves attention.

Employees of state and local governments may elect to participate in section 457 plans, which are also similar to company 401(k) plans. They allow pretax deductions from salary to grow tax-deferred. Each state or local government creates a plan for its own employees, so rules and investment opportunities may differ. Check with your government employer about participating in these voluntary savings plans.

Retirement Savings Strategy #7: Rollovers

Rollovers are a general term for any money that you can take out of one qualified (tax-sheltered) retirement plan to move into another qualified plan. It may be money that you have access to at an early age from a defined contribution or 401(k) plan because you leave the company. Or it may be money distributed to you upon retirement from the company.

A "rollover" simply means that you elect *not* to take all or part of the money as current income and pay taxes on it (and the 10 percent federal tax penalty if you are under age 59 ½), but instead decide to continue to keep it growing tax-deferred. So you automatically have it transferred into another tax-sheltered account that is opened in your name with the designation "IRA rollover."

In 1992, a new tax law was passed to encourage IRA rollovers. Previously, you could take the check from your retirement distribution and keep the money for 60 days before making the decision to roll it over into a qualified IRA rollover account. But as of January 1, 1993, all rollover money must be sent directly from your current company custodian to a new qualified custodian, such as a bank, mutual fund, or stock brokerage firm. If you touch the money—even for a day—*you will be subject to a 20 percent withholding for taxes*! You no longer have 60 days to make your decision.

So, if you were to receive $10,000 from your previous employer's pension plan, and the check were sent to you, it would be for only $8,000. The remaining $2,000 would be withholding. If you had $2,000 in another account, you could add it to the retirement funds, investing a total of $10,000 in your IRA rollover—and file for a tax refund.

But if you can't make up the difference out of your own pocket, the $2,000 that was withheld is treated as a distribution—and you owe taxes on it, plus a 10 percent penalty if you're under age 59½. There may be some money left for a refund, but you've lost the tax-deferred use of it forever.

Remember: If you get a tax-qualified distribution from a company plan, it must be rolled over directly into the hands of a new qualified custodian as an IRA rollover account.

This IRA rollover account can be opened at a bank, stock brokerage firm, or mutual fund company—the same places at which you are allowed to open your annual $2,000 IRA. But for various tax reasons, *always* keep an IRA rollover separate from any other IRA account you might have.

If you're under age 59½, the incentive to roll over a distribution is obvious: you'll avoid the 10 percent federal tax penalty. If you're over age 59½, you should consult a qualified tax accountant before deciding whether to take a lump sum distribution or to roll over a distribution. If you don't need the income now, it may pay to continue to let the money grow tax-deferred. But an accountant will advise you if you qualify for some advantageous tax-averaging rules on lump sum distributions.

Terry's Tips:

$$$ Because the rollover law now requires that a company give employees 30 days notice that a withdrawal is subject to tax withholding, the worker will have to wait 30 days for the payment.

$$$ Retirees who elect to have their retirement savings paid to them in yearly installments over several years, but less than 10 years, are also subject to the withholding. Even if those arrangements were made before 1993, retirees will have the 20 percent withholding taken out of checks issued after January 1, 1993.

Retirement Savings Strategy #8: Taking Money Out

The entire subject of how and when you must take distributions from your retirement funds, and the tax consequences of those distributions, is covered in chapter 65. But here, on the subject of investing for your future retirement, it's important to give some thought to how you will manage those retirement assets once you stop working.

As pointed out earlier in this chapter, you may live fully one third of your lifetime in retirement. That means your assets will have to continue to grow during your retirement years, and that you will want to keep the growth of your assets tax-sheltered for as long as possible. When you reach retirement age you'll have to do some careful thinking about how much of your portfolio should be invested for income, and what portion should remain invested for growth.

Those who retire in their sixties might consider a strategy of keeping at least two years' living expenses in a money market fund, and the balance of their portfolio divided between stock and bond funds. When the stock market is performing well, you can sell some fund shares on a regular basis to supplement your Social Security and pension income. If stocks are in a bear market, you can tap into the money market fund for additional living expenses. Bear markets rarely last more than two years, and if that situation should occur you would then dip into bond funds assets before touching your stock funds.

Using this type of strategy, you should be able to withdraw about 3 to 5 percent of your capital each year without cutting into the after-inflation value of your portfolio. For retirees with a twenty-year-plus time horizon, this strategy should keep your standard of living from dropping over the years. It's validated by a look back at Chart II-2 in chapter 9, which shows how much better equities have performed than fixed-income investments—over the long run. Of course, older retirees should weight their investments toward the Safe Money Strategies in chapter 14.

Chapter 45

Everyday Tax Strategies

The changes in tax law resulting from the Tax Act of 1993 have been detailed in chapter 11 and other places throughout this book where appropriate. However, some portions of the tax code appear to be eternal! You may depend on your accountant for specifics, but the general principles explained in this chapter are up to you! It's your responsibility to file a federal income tax return on which you report all taxable income. On that tax return you'll have the option of listing deductions from income that would lower your tax obligation. The deductions you decide to take may be open to debate; the requirement to file a return listing your income is not. The Internal Revenue Service has estimated that 10 million people failed to file tax returns in 1993, and the IRS is devoting an entire task force to finding them. That leads to the first piece of advice about income taxes.

Everyday Tax Strategy #1: File Your Tax Return

Every once in a while you'll read a newspaper story about a public figure or financial executive who has not filed income tax forms, or about tax protestors who have come up with yet another reason not to file income tax forms. Not one of these protests has held up in court. And the odds are great that if you do not file you will be caught. It's your responsibility, and yours alone, to file your tax return. Almost everything else in the tax code is open to a bit of debate; filing is an absolute.

The income requirements for filing vary by marital status (single, married, legally separated, widowed); by filing status (single, head of household, married—joint return, married—single return, qualifying widow[er] with dependent child); by age (under 65 or over); and by gross income. These requirements change annually and are available from the IRS.

For example, in 1994, if you are single and under age 65, you must file if you had at least $6,050 of gross income. But if you are under 65, and your filing status is "head of household," then you must file if your gross income was at least $8,700.

Penalties for *failure to file* are ten times more severe than penalties for those who file tax returns but fail to pay the taxes owed. Even if you cannot pay your taxes, you should always file a tax return. Willful failure to file (that includes tax protestors) and filing a return with fraudulent and false statements can result in criminal penalties, including time in prison. There has never yet been a tax protest based on legal, constitutional, or historic grounds that has been allowed to stand—and there are a number of well-known tax protestors serving time.

Penalties are assessed for a variety of infractions. For instance, the penalty for failure to file for reasons of fraud can be as high as 75 percent of the tax owed. The standard penalty for late filing (failure to file) is usually 5 percent for each month, or part of the month the return is late, up to as much as 25 percent of the taxes owed, plus interest, plus a potential 5 percent negligence penalty.

The penalty for *failure to pay* is $1/2$ of 1 percent a month, or portion of a month, that your tax payment is late. The rate increases after the IRS issues a levy, or demand for payment. The penalty cannot exceed 25 percent of the tax due.

You must pay interest on any tax you owe that is not paid by the due date of your return—even if you get an extension of the time for filing. Interest is charged at a rate that changes each year, but the IRS always charges more (nondeductible) interest on money you owe than you could ever earn in a bank! Pay any taxes promptly to avoid interest charges.

Everyday Tax Strategy #2: Check Your Withholding

Your employer is required to withhold taxes on your income from every paycheck—within certain guidelines. The exact amount of withholding is determined by the information you give your employer on Form W-4, Employee's Withholding Allowance Certificate.

Generally, you'll want to claim withholding allowances based on the number of personal exemptions for yourself and your dependents that you'll be taking on your tax return. If you claim fewer withholding allowances than you are entitled to, extra money will be taken out of each paycheck to pay income taxes. You won't get that money back until you file your tax return and claim a refund. It's like making an interest-free loan to the government. If you received a big federal tax refund last year, you might want to increase the number of allowances.

If you take too many withholding allowances, you might not have enough taxes withheld from your paycheck—and wind up owing money on your next tax return. Worse, you could have to pay a penalty for underwithholding.

You can change the information on your Form W-4 at any time during the year to adjust your withholding amounts. If you get married, divorced, have a child, or take on a second job, you might want to adjust your withholding status.

Everyday Tax Strategy #3: File Your Estimated Taxes

You must make quarterly estimated tax payments if you expect to owe at least $500—beyond any taxes withheld from your paychecks or credits you expect to receive on your income tax return. That is, you must pay in over the year at least 90 percent of the tax you expect to owe on that year's tax return, or 100 percent of the tax shown on your previous year's return. If the previous year's adjusted gross income exceeded $150,000, then 110 percent of the prior year's tax must be paid in. If you fail to make adequate estimated tax payments, you will be charged a penalty. The penalty is an interest charge based on the difference between 90 percent of your tax liability and what you actually paid in estimated taxes.

Generally, if all you have as income is wages, there will be enough taxes withheld from your paycheck to satisfy these requirements. But if you also have income from alimony or maintenance, from your own business, or from interest and dividends, or any other income from which federal income taxes were not withheld, you'll need to make quarterly estimated tax payments.

The Internal Revenue Service wants to make sure it collects all the taxes you owe—along the way during the year, when you're likely to have the money to pay those taxes. The only exception is for U.S. citizens who had no tax liability at all for the previous year, or if you were not required to file a tax return the previous year because you were below the income levels.

Your tax advisor can help you prepare the forms and estimate the amount of taxes you should pay to fulfill the estimated tax requirements. But if you are newly divorced or just starting your own side business from which you expect to have income, you should be aware of the need to file quarterly.

Everyday Tax Strategy #4: Get Qualified Tax Preparation Assistance

Strategies #1 and #2 above may have already convinced you that you'll need professional help in doing your income taxes. If your tax situation is complicated, you may want to have a CPA (certified public accountant) prepare your forms. Or you may choose an *enrolled agent*. Enrolled agents are often former IRS employees or others who have passed a comprehensive series of tests allowing them to represent clients before the IRS.

Many people choose income tax services to prepare their returns. Although these services have the technical expertise, you may be losing out on one of the benefits of using a CPA or enrolled agent: the long-term tax planning that can only be accomplished when the same professional handles your return each year.

For do-it-yourself tax filers, there are also several computerized tax packages available, such as the popular Turbo-Tax, which is available in most bookstores. The drawback with a computerized tax preparation system is that there is no second pair of eyes evaluating your decisions.

Even though a preparer must sign your return, the information included in it is ultimately your responsibility. So read it over carefully, and ask questions of your tax preparer before signing and mailing your tax forms.

One special note: Many qualified preparers can now file your return electronically. You'll still get a paper copy of your filing, but using the electronic filing system will result in a faster refund. Beware of promises of "instant" refunds. These are actually loans made against your future tax refund, and the interest and fees can be very expensive.

Everyday Tax Strategy #5: Keep Good Records

It's important to keep complete and accurate records, not only of your tax-related income and expenses throughout the year, but of previous tax returns you have filed and the evidence that supported those returns.

Records should be kept for a minimum of three years after filing your return. But you should keep your returns even longer if you see the potential for a dispute over your deductions with the IRS. The IRS can reopen returns for six years if they suspect substantial income was not reported. There is no statute of limitations on prosecutions for fraudulent filings.

Copies of past returns can help you file future returns and remind you of carryover items such as capital losses and depreciation. And you'll need past returns in case you have to file an amended return. If you need a copy of a previous year's tax return, apply using IRS Form 4506.

Keeping good records can mean the difference between winning and losing a dispute with the IRS. You'll need not only your cancelled checks, but paid bills, receipts, and other documents to support your argument. Store all these records together in a safe place—the longer the better.

Everyday Tax Strategy #6: Understand Extensions

If you're not able to file your tax return by the April 15 deadline, you will get an automatic extension by filing Form 4868. But this is not an extension of time to *pay* the taxes you owe. When you file Form 4868 you must also make an accurate estimate of the taxes you will owe and include a check in that amount along with your request for an extension. You will be charged interest on any unpaid balance from April 15 until the amount is paid in full. You may also be charged a late payment penalty unless you have paid at least 90 percent of your tax obligation by the April 15 due date. This penalty may be forgiven if you have a reasonable cause for not paying on time.

Everyday Tax Strategy #7: Know Your Rights in an Audit

Nothing can set your nerves trembling like receiving a notice that your tax returns are being audited. Even the written explanation of your rights that accompanies the notice will not calm you. This is where it pays to have your returns done by a professional who is qualified and available to represent you before the IRS. That person can accompany you to the audit, or represent you if you sign written authorization. The notice will explain what portions of the returns are being audited and what information will be needed. Make sure you have all the necessary records and supporting information.

If you do not agree with the results of the audit, you do have recourse. You can request an interview with the auditor's supervisor. But schedule that interview for a future date, not right after the audit that has already upset you. If things get this far, you will definitely want professional representation. For more about your rights in an IRS audit, you should read IRS booklet #556.

Everyday Tax Strategy #8: Be Aware of Special Tax Rules That Affect You

Here's another reason for using a professional to prepare your taxes. You may not be aware of special tax rules and opportunities to reduce your tax obligation. The following are some brief examples which you might discuss with your tax preparer:

1. *Senior citizens get a once-in-a-lifetime tax break*—up to $125,000 of profit from the sale of a home may be completely tax-free. This exclusion applies to those age 55 or older on the date of the sale who lived in the home for at least three of the five years preceding the sale.

Warning: This tax break can only be used once, so remarried seniors may be disqualified if one of the spouses used this exemption prior to the remarriage.

2. The *earned income credit* (EIC) is a refundable tax credit available to working families. In 1994, families with an adjusted gross income of less than $23,753 and having one child may be entitled to a maximum credit of $2,038 against taxes owed. With two or more children, and earnings of less than $25,299, the family might qualify for a credit of $2,527. A family earning less than $9,000 with no children also could get a credit of up to $306.

3. *Casualty losses* that are not reimbursed by insurance may be deductible. If your property was damaged or lost in an area that the president declares eligible for federal disaster assistance, you can deduct the casualty loss either by filing an amended return for the previous year (perhaps triggering a refund), or in the year the loss actually occurred.

4. If you have *declared bankruptcy*, you may still owe prebankruptcy petition taxes and taxes for which no return or a late return was filed. However, if a debtor completes all payments under Chapter 13, the court may discharge all debts, including those for prepetition taxes. The statutory period for collection of taxes (normally ten years from the date of assessment) is extended during the time the bankruptcy court has jurisdiction over a case, plus six months afterward.

5. If you claim expenses for *business use of your home*, you'll have to use a new Form #8829 along with Schedule C.

6. If you are an older or disabled American, the *credit for the elderly or the disabled* may reduce the taxes you owe. It is based on income, filing status, and age. Ask for IRS booklet #554, *Tax Information for Older Americans.*

7. If you *sell your home*, you postpone paying taxes on the gain if you purchase and live in a new home within two years before or two years after the sale, and if the purchase price is at least as much as the adjusted sales price of the old home.

8. If you *win the lottery* or other such contest or a game show, the wheel of fortune has a spot marked taxes! You must report such income on line 22, "other income," of your Form 1040. If you win a large sum of money in a legal gaming casino, you will probably find that at least 20 percent of your winnings will be withheld by the IRS. You may also need to make estimated tax payments.

These are only a few of the special tax issues that may increase or lower your federal income tax burden. And these are only general guidelines to the issues. Your own personal tax situation must be calculated individually. And, of course, these tax laws are subject to change at the whim of Congress.

Everyday Tax Strategy #9: Know How to Get Help

There are some important numbers and services that you should know about when dealing with the IRS.

For telephone tax assistance, you can call 800-829-1040. Always keep the name of the person to whom you talked and a written summary of the information you were given.

To order tax forms or informational booklets, call 800-TAX-FORM (800-829-3676).

To find out if your refund has been sent, wait at least ten weeks after filing and then call 800-829-4477.

If you can't seem to get anywhere with the IRS, call your district office and ask to speak to the ombudsman in the Problem Resolution Office. You may have to file Form 911 (appropriately numbered!) "Application for Taxpayer Assistance Order to Relieve Hardship" to get the ombudsman to intervene in your situation.

PART V

Insurance Strategies

SPENDING MONEY on insurance premiums is like throwing money down the drain—*unless* you find yourself in a situation where you need to collect. Then, you'll probably consider the insurance premiums you paid one of the best investments you ever made!

Life insurance is a bet against yourself. You pay the premiums, but you'll never get to enjoy the benefits; those dollars will be spent by your heirs. Health insurance is another bet you hope you won't collect. Some people complain that you never have enough medical expenses to "beat" the deductible. Of course, the alternative is to have huge medical expenses—and all the problems that go along with those costs! In that case you're a loser, even though you've made the insurance company pay out an amount in excess of your premiums.

The whole concept of insurance from the consumer's point of view is to "waste" your money paying premiums—and hope that you never have to go through the agony of beating the insurance company.

You'll notice that the more valuable your assets become, the more insurance protection you need. You may need to insure your home, your car, your life, or your ability to work. You may choose insurance to protect your assets from lawsuits, medical expenses, and estate taxes. Over your entire lifetime you'll probably spend the most premium dollars on life insurance. Even people who are sophisticated when it comes to other financial matters admit to me that when it comes to life insurance, they rely on an "expert"—the expert who is selling the policy. That can be a most expensive mistake.

There's really no mystery to life insurance. You need to understand only two concepts: the cost of death benefits that can be covered by term insurance; and the cost of arranging for "extra" money to grow tax-deferred inside an insurance policy. The only secret is how much money the insurance agents and companies collect for keeping it all so confusing! We'll unravel the mystery of life insurance and save you money.

The more you have to protect, the more money you'll spend on insurance. The trick is to spend those insurance premiums wisely, paying only for protection you need and getting the best buy for your insurance dollars. The strategies in this section are designed to help you analyze your insurance coverage needs and select the best-priced policies to fill those needs.

Chapter 46

Homeowners Insurance

Before you read this chapter, take out your current homeowners or renters insurance policy. Mortgage lenders require property insurance, but landlords, of course, do not. If you rent and don't have a policy, finish the next few pages and immediately call an insurance agent to buy a renters policy. Read your policy carefully and check it for the strategies listed below.

Your homeowners policy may look like standard "boilerplate" insurance jargon, with a few lines where numbers are typed in to indicate the limits of your insurance. But it's important for you to understand exactly what is covered—and what is excluded from coverage—in the policy that protects the most valuable assets you own.

You'll find the term *perils* used to describe the coverage. Perils are all the things that could go wrong—and there are many. But the best insurance strategies involve not only which items are covered but how much you'll get paid if you need to collect, and how much you pay for the coverage.

Home Insurance Strategy #1: Getting the Right Basic Homeowners Insurance

There are three basic forms of homeowners coverage:

Form HO-1 covers 11 of the most common perils, including:

fire or lightning

smoke damage

windstorm or hail

explosion

riot or civil disorder

damage caused by vehicles

damage caused by aircraft

theft

loss of property that has been removed from house

vandalism

glass breakage

But that's not enough coverage, as dire as all these perils sound, and it is definitely worth paying slightly more for the *broad form* HO-2 policy, which also includes:

damage caused by falling objects

roof collapse because of ice, snow, sleet

collapse of any part of the building

damage caused by hot water pipes or heater exploding

damage caused by frozen pipes or air conditioning system

damage as a result of electrical surges to appliances (except TVs)

In fact, it's worth checking into forms HO-3 (special form) and HO-4 (comprehensive form) to compare the additional benefits they offer and get a price quote. These forms may include:

coverage for personal property (clothes, furniture, appliances) for the perils listed in HO-2

additional risks to the structure—except for exclusions for earthquakes, floods, wars, nuclear accidents and, on some policies, sewer backups

It is worth paying slightly more for complete coverage. Why try to cut corners on the basic coverage of your most valuable assets? But basic coverage is just that—the base on which other coverages stand. See the strategies below for determining amounts, types, and additional coverages required.

Home Insurance Strategy #2: Additional Coverages

Take note of what your policy does *not* cover. Standard policies do not cover earthquakes or floods. That means you have to purchase separate policies to cover those possibilities.

Unless you live in California (or near another earthquake fault line), you may not need earthquake insurance. In California it is expensive, and it carries a very high deductible of as much as 10 percent of the coverage. If you want to insure a $400,000 home against earthquake damage, you'll pay the first $40,000 of repairs.

Flood insurance is available through private insurers but is backed and underwritten by the federal government as part of the National Flood Insurance Program. In order for individual homeowners to qualify for this insurance, your community must have complied with federal flood control building and zoning standards.

Check with your own insurer about the availability of and need for flood insurance. Be aware that the flood coverage is limited and does not apply to items stored below ground level in your basement, except for major appliances such as a water heater or washer and dryer. But a major flood could wash away your entire home and contents, not just fill the basement with water. So if you live in an area where a flood is possible, buy the insurance. If you can't get flood insurance in such an area, don't buy the house!

Depending on the area in which you live, your policy may have specific exclusions for certain types of natural disasters. For instance, certain areas in Washington (near Mount St. Helens) exclude coverage for volcanic eruptions, which are covered in most standard peril policies. The same advice applies here; if you can't get insurance coverage, reconsider your plan to buy the property.

Home Insurance Strategy #3: Coverage for Renters, Condo Owners, and Co-op Owners

Think back to the television reports of Hurricane Andrew in 1992, and countless other natural disasters. Many of those displaced people were renters, not homeowners. And it's estimated that as many as 75 percent of the renters who lost all their belongings to wind and rain were not covered by any type of insurance.

Form HO-4 is the insurance coverage designed for renters; HO-6 is for condo owners, and co-op owners. These two policies cover risks to personal property, as well as structural damage to the building that was caused by the owner or renter. These forms are designed to mesh with the basic building structural insurance that is held by the landlord or owners' association. Remember, the insurance held by the building does not cover tenants' personal property. And if you have a roommate, your insurance policy does not cover his or her property.

Not all HO-4 policies are alike, and some companies will give extra insurance for alterations made to the building structure. That might include built-in bookcases or woodwork, mirrors, and expensive wallpapers and decorating items. When choosing an HO-4 policy, check with your agent as to how these less tangible forms of personal property are covered.

Home Insurance Strategy #4: Getting Enough Coverage

If you have a mortgage on your home, the lender will require you to list the mortgage company on your policy as an "additional insured," and to insure at least 80 percent of the value of your home, or 100 percent of the amount of the mortgage. That's the minimum amount, but this is one area in which it is "penny wise and pound foolish" to settle only for the minimum coverage.

It's not smart to overinsure because you'll be paying premiums for coverage that will never be paid to you. But if you insure for less than 80 percent of the value of your home and contents, and if you suffer a total loss, many companies will place a limit on what they'll pay out, or prorate the coverage based on the percentage by which you are underinsured. If you're covered for 80 percent or more of the replacement cost, most insurance companies will pay for your losses in full—up to the limits of your coverage. If your insurance company doesn't operate on that principle, get 100 percent coverage.

You'll need to check two figures on your policy: the percentage of coverage based on current appraisals and the policy limits for total coverage.

In determining the total amount of coverage you need, there are a few basic things to keep in mind. If you are buying renters insurance, you'll need coverage for the entire value of your possessions. When it comes to insuring a home, you are insuring only the structure and contents, not the value of the land on which the home sits. Even if your home burns to the ground or is blown away by the wind, you'll still have the land.

On the other hand, it can cost more to rebuild than you might think. So don't judge the value of your home (minus the land) by what a real estate agent might appraise it for in the resale market. Instead, it might be worthwhile to have a builder or appraiser evaluate the total cost of rebuilding and replacing the contents.

Home Insurance Strategy #5: Homeowners Contents Coverage and Scheduled Items

Most insurance companies will cover the contents of the home only up to 50 percent of the value of the home itself. A few companies will allow general household goods coverage of 70 percent of the amount of insurance on the structure. If you need more coverage for your furniture and clothing, you will have to purchase additional general interiors coverage separately.

However, if you have valuable items within the house such as silverware, artwork, furs, jewelry, antiques, or a coin collection, you'll need to schedule them separately on a *floater* or *scheduled items* policy. Basic homeowner or renters contents insurance limits coverage on specific items such as these to about $1,000 or $1,500. That limitation applies to *all* jewelry, not each piece; or *all* artwork, not each painting.

In order to purchase a separate floater policy on each of your valued items, you'll need a current appraisal, which may have to be updated each year. Then you'll receive a separate listing for each item and its insurance cost, which can definitely be expensive. You may be able to lower the cost of insuring some of these items by keeping them in a vault and notifying the company when you take out the jewelry, for example, to wear it to a party.

Scheduled coverage will protect valuable items against disappearance, theft, or damage. It's unlikely that the policy will protect you if you break a valuable item while cleaning it, but you can always file a claim. While some of these scheduled items can be expected to appreciate in value (artwork and collectibles, for example), other items such as fur coats will definitely decline in value over the years. The answer to insuring these, and other household items not scheduled separately, is to purchase *replacement cost* insurance as described in the following strategy.

Home Insurance Strategy #6: Demand "Replacement Cost" Insurance

Read your current or prospective insurance policy carefully. Many policies guarantee to pay you the actual cash value for your personal property. That sounds like a good deal, but don't be misled.

You may have purchased your dining room set five years ago for $1,500. Today it is a used dining room set—perfect for your family, but not worth much on the used furniture market. If your home burns down, the insurance company might decide that the current actual cash value is only $500—and that's what they'll pay you. Now try finding a similar table and chairs for only $500.

What you really want is *replacement cost* coverage. That means the insurance company must pay you whatever it costs to purchase a new, similar dining room set. Of course, replacement cost insurance is slightly more expensive, but it's worth the additional money.

Home Insurance Strategy #7: Liability Insurance and Umbrella Policies

The liability section of your homeowners policy covers your personal liability if an accident happens on your property, or is caused by you or your children or pets either at home or on someone else's property.

The standard liability limit is $100,000 per incident, although higher coverages can be purchased. These homeowner liability limits do not cover claims that are related to business or to coverages that are available through automobile insurance. The higher your income and the more valuable your possessions, the more liability insurance you may need in case you are sued.

An alternative to increasing your homeowners liability is to purchase an *umbrella liability* policy. The umbrella kicks in when the basic homeowners or automobile policy liability runs out. In these days of multi-million-dollar lawsuit verdicts, it makes sense to insure against such an event.

Umbrella liability policies come in $1 million amounts and generally cost between $100 and $150 per million. Usually you must purchase this type of policy from the same company that underwrites your basic homeowners or automobile coverage. The underwriter will probably require at least $500,000 liability coverage on those underlying policies.

Home Insurance Strategy #8: Check for Additional Coverages and Exceptions

You should be aware of additional coverages that may be offered by your insurance carrier. Depending on your circumstances, some may be worth paying an additional premium—or you can save money by declining some coverages.

For instance, your homeowners policy may offer $500 of coverage on credit card losses. But you are already limited to $50 in losses per card by federal law. So if you only carry a few cards, it is not worth paying extra for this coverage. On the other hand, your policy should include provisions for "additional living expenses" you might incur if your family has to stay in a hotel or rented apartment while your damaged home is being rebuilt. If you live in an area where you have to pay extra for fire department services, your policy should reimburse those costs.

The medical payments section of most policies will reimburse medical expenses up to $1,000—without regard to fault—for someone injured in the insured home, except the resident family members, or if a member of the insured family injures someone else away from home. This may seem like a small amount, and indeed, if the medical expenses are much higher, the homeowner may be sued for the additional expenses covered under the liability section. But for small injuries to others it is well worth having this coverage in the homeowners policy.

While reviewing these additional coverages, it is also wise to note what is *not* covered. For example, trees and shrubbery may be covered against fire damage but not against wind damage. So if a tree falls on your lawn, you'll be responsible for paying for removal. But if it hits your roof or your neighbor's roof, then the policy will pay for the damages and may pay for removal as well.

Ask your agent if your policy covers damage to any special items in your home, such as a satellite antenna, mechanical items such as your lawn mower, or personal property belonging to guests who are staying with you.

Homeowners Insurance Strategy #9: Cut Your Insurance Costs

There are several ways to cut your homeowners insurance costs without skimping on your coverage for major catastrophes.

1. Raise your *deductible* amount. Every policy has a deductible amount—the amount the insured must pay before the coverage takes effect. If you increase the standard $250 deductible to $500, you can cut your premiums by 5 to 10 percent. And if you're willing to accept a $1,000 deductible, you could save as much as 15 percent on your premiums.

2. Shop around for homeowners insurance. Not all companies charge the same premiums for the same coverage. After all, it's a competitive business. Although you want to be insured by a strong company, it does make sense to do comparison shopping.

3. You may get a discount on your homeowners insurance if you buy your automobile insurance from the same company and have a combined package.

4. You may be able to lower your premiums depending on special circumstances. For instance, if you install a burglar alarm, inform your insurance company and see if you qualify for a discount. Similarly, if you have been insured by one company for several years and have not had a claim, you may be entitled to lower rates. And if you retire, you may qualify for lower rates because retirees tend to spend more time at home, reducing the risk of burglary. Some companies even give lower rates if all occupants of the home are nonsmokers.

5. If you can organize your budget so that you are able to pay your homeowners insurance premiums annually instead of twice a year or quarterly, you should save a few dollars.

Homeowners Insurance Strategy #10: Make Sure Your Claim Will Be Paid

Make a home video of your property. Most major insurance companies will accept your word that you had three television sets and a custom upholstered couch. But in case of total destruction, it is helpful to be able to prove your claims. Finally, there's a perfect use for all that camera equipment you bought.

Take a walking tour of your house, describing all the furnishings and decorating—and making special note of scheduled items such as artwork and antiques. Then store the videotape in a safe deposit box or other location so it can be used if your home is destroyed by fire. If you don't have a video camera you can rent one, or take still pictures and list the contents in an inventory.

The combination of having an accurate inventory plus an adequate amount of replacement cost insurance can take some of the sting out of a natural disaster.

Chapter 47

Automobile Insurance

The potential liability involved with owning and driving a car is horrendous when you stop to think about it. First there's the question of damage done to your car in an accident. Then there's the possible damage that could be done to other vehicles, plus damage to property such as garages, street lights, and storefronts. And that doesn't begin to take in the financial consequences of serious injury, either to yourself or to others involved in an accident when you or a member of your family are driving a car.

In addition to the immediate financial costs of an accident, there is always the possibility that you might be sued by another party to the accident unless you live in a no-fault state. Those lawsuits are not limited to actual recoverable costs; in states where such suits are allowed, an injured party could make claims for "pain and suffering"—amounts that could be stratospheric.

No wonder automobile insurance costs so much. The only people who can do without it (and there are millions who do) are those who have nothing to lose. Unfortunately, as auto insurance premiums keep rising and pricing many people out of the market, it is all too likely that if you are in an accident, the other party will be an uninsured motorist who drives as if he or she had nothing to lose.

NO-FAULT INSURANCE

You've probably heard the term *no-fault* insurance, but you might not know exactly what it means. That's not surprising because no-fault has a different definition in almost every state. True no-fault insurance means that, regardless of who was at fault, each party to an accident is covered by his or her own insurance up to the limits of the policy.

The question of fault is primarily an issue when it comes to suing for medical expenses or pain and suffering. In states without no-fault insurance, a lawyer must sue for compensation. The cost of defending those lawsuits is passed on in the form of higher insurance premiums.

The attorneys who are in this business point out that the ability to sue also means you could receive appropriate compensation if you or a family member become a victim. The lawsuits only work, however, if there is a "deep pocket"—the driver's insurance company, an uninsured driver's personal assets, or perhaps a negligent government that failed to properly locate a stop sign.

In an effort to stop escalating lawsuits and awards, 14 states have passed some form of no-fault automobile insurance laws. In the most strict no-fault states, lawsuits can only be filed when there is severe medical damage such as disfigurement, permanent disability, or death. In cases where lawsuits are allowed to be filed, fault comes back into consideration as the basis for collecting on your suit.

The idea behind eliminating lawsuits for all but the most serious accidents is to lower insurance premiums. But not all states with no-fault laws have such stringent requirements for lawsuits, so it is wise to check with your insurance agent or state insurance regulator as to the exact coverage requirements of your state law.

HOW AUTO INSURANCE IS PRICED

Insurers take into account certain basic economic considerations when pricing auto insurance—and some pricing decisions based on local market considerations.

You'll pay more for insurance if you:

Live in an urban area where traffic congestion results in more accidents, and where there is a greater history of auto theft.

Have a poor driving record. (The insurance industry will check your driving record through the state motor vehicle department.)

Have a record of numerous claims on this or previous policies. (This can be checked by the insurance industry through an Equifax computerized claim record.)

Drive your car for business.

Drive more miles each year than is standard.

Drive a car that is listed among those frequently stolen.

Drive a more expensive or exotic car.

Are a male under the age of 25.

You can decide to minimize some of these conditions. You may be willing to move to the suburbs, for instance, or drive a less expensive car. But you can't do much about most of them, and it is definitely unwise to lie on your application as your coverage could be cancelled.

Sometimes you'll find coverage that costs less because an insurer is trying to build up its policy coverage in one state. Other times you'll find more expensive policies offered by companies that do not want to take on any more insurance risks in your locality. That's why comparison shopping for automobile insurance is so important.

HOW CLAIMS AFFECT PRICING

Your auto insurance premiums can rise if you have a number of *chargeable claims,* which means you were at fault in an accident. Or you may have too many claims for theft on your comprehensive coverage. State laws may forbid your insurer from cancelling your policy because of claims, but when it comes time to renew, the insurance company has the option to drop you.

If you incur a small amount of damage, you might think twice about filing a claim and choose to pay the damages yourself. But if you're in an accident, you *must* report it to your insurance company in case the other driver files a claim. You could be dropped for failure to report an accident.

KEYS TO CHOOSING AN AUTOMOBILE INSURANCE POLICY

There are two key ingredients to any auto insurance policy in any state: coverage and cost. You need to understand the basic coverages: what is required in your state and what's worth paying for. Plus, as you'll see in Auto Insurance Strategy #2 on p. 378, it's also important to check the safety and satisfaction ratings of the insurance company you select.

You may not need all eight of the basic auto insurance coverage categories, but you should understand each one and what it protects before declining any of the coverages. Some may be mandatory in your state at certain minimum levels, but you may decide that the minimum is not enough coverage for you.

The front page, or *declaration page,* of your auto insurance policy will show you the types of insurance and limits you currently have. Chart V-1 shows you what percentage of your annual premium is generally required to pay for each of the basic coverages.

THE EIGHT BASIC COVERAGES

The first two types of coverage are *liability* coverage, which is required in almost every state and is split into two parts:

1. *Bodily injury liability* is the portion of your insurance that pays for the other person's medical costs and loss of earnings if you (or a member of your family) are involved in an accident. This coverage includes passengers in your car, passengers in the other car, and pedestrians. It also protects you and your family members while driving someone else's car or, in most cases, a rental car. In addition to paying medical expenses for those injured, it covers the cost of a legal defense and lawsuit awards up to the limits stated in the policy.

Most states will require a minimum of $25,000 per person and $50,000 per accident in bodily injury insurance. But with expensive medical costs, those low limits could leave you vulnerable to lawsuits for excess costs. If you want to protect your assets, you'll need higher limits on bodily injury liability—as much as $300,000. The increased coverage should add only a small amount to the cost of your policy.

Sometimes bodily injury insurance is purchased with a "single limit," such as $300,000 per accident. Or you may find that your policy offers a "split limit," such as $100,000 per person per accident up to a total of $300,000 per accident. On your policy you'll find it written in this way: $100,000/$300,000.

CHART V-1
Typical Auto Premium Dollar . . . Sliced by the Auto Coverages

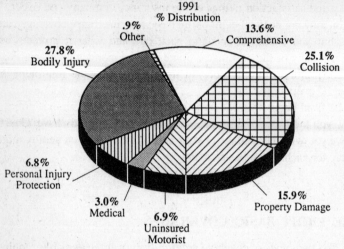

1991
% Distribution

.9%
Other

13.6%
Comprehensive

27.8%
Bodily Injury

25.1%
Collision

6.8%
Personal Injury
Protection

3.0%
Medical

6.9%
Uninsured
Motorist

15.9%
Property Damage

SOURCE: Allstate Insurance Group.

2. *Property damage liability* is the insurance that pays to repair the other person's car or property that is damaged in an accident. While the standard minimum is about $10,000, it won't cost much to upgrade this portion of your liability to at least $25,000 at the same time as you increase your bodily injury liability coverage. It will cover your liability if you are at fault in an accident and totally destroy someone else's very expensive car.

Terry's Tip:

$$$ Ask your agent to coordinate benefits under your auto and home-owners liability insurance with your umbrella liability policy to make sure that you are completely covered against potential lawsuits at the lowest cost. (See Home Insurance Strategy #7 in chapter 46.)

3. *Uninsured motorist coverage* pays off if you or the passengers in your car are injured when struck by a driver with no liability insurance, or if you're the victim of a hit-and-run accident. It may also cover lost wages if you are in an accident. But that's just a form of disability insurance, which could be better covered by a comprehensive disability policy (see

chapter 49). When you buy uninsured motorist coverage, you're paying not only to insure *your* own liability; now you're paying the other driver's premium!

As more and more marginal drivers drop their insurance policies because of high premiums, this is the portion of your policy that you may least afford to drop. And if you live in a no-fault state, this insurance is worthwhile because it will pay benefits beyond your medical expenses if you are injured badly enough to sue. Of course, this time you'll be requesting your *own* insurance company to pay off—and that's another reason to choose an insurance company with a good record of settling claims.

Your uninsured motorist coverage limits may have two parts, similar to your liability coverage. It costs little to upgrade this coverage from the basic $25,000/$50,000 to at least $100,000/$300,000.

4. *Underinsured motorist coverage* is slightly different from uninsured motorist coverage. This part of your policy pays off after the other driver's coverage has been used up. Why leave a chink in your insurance armor? Purchase this insurance in the same amounts as your uninsured motorist coverage.

5. *Medical payments coverage* pays medical, hospital, and funeral bills if necessary for you and members of your family, regardless of who is at fault in an accident. These costs are usually covered by your own medical insurance, which is the primary coverage. In that case, the medical insurance coverage will pay off the deductible and co-payments on your primary insurance. This coverage could be expensive, so if you feel you have good medical insurance for yourself and your family, you may want to decline this portion of the policy.

Medical payments coverage also pays if a nonfamily member is injured while riding in your car—someone who may not have adequate medical insurance. On the other hand, your bodily liability insurance protects you against claims for another person's medical expenses, so you are really paying twice for the same coverage. When pricing policies, check to see how much money you can save by dropping this coverage.

6. *Personal injury protection* (PIP) is similar to the medical payments coverage, but it is a more complete form of medical coverage offered in states with no-fault auto insurance. Like ordinary medical payments insurance, it will pay medical and hospital expenses, and funeral expenses. But

it will also include payments for lost wages and certain services such as housekeeping aid if the accident causes a temporary disability.

Instead of paying for this type of coverage, you'd be better off with a good medical insurance policy and a good overall disability policy (see chapters 48 and 49). But in spite of the fact that no-fault insurance is supposed to reduce premium costs, many states require PIP insurance and you have to pay extra for it.

If you insure in a no-fault state, this PIP insurance portion may be considered the primary medical insurance policy. But your own medical insurance will still be necessary, because medical payments under most no-fault policies are strictly limited for each service and may not cover customary doctor and hospital bills completely.

7. *Collision coverage* is the insurance you probably think of first when considering car insurance. It pays for damage to your car in an accident or replacement of a vehicle that is a total loss. If you have a loan on your car, this type of coverage will be required by the lender. Otherwise, it is optional.

If you have a new car that would cost a small fortune to repair, you'll definitely want to have collision coverage. But as your car grows older, the cost of collision coverage may be more than your car is actually worth to repair.

Terry's Tip:

$$$ You can save almost one-third of your annual insurance costs by dropping your collision coverage. Or, you can save at least 10 to 15 percent of your premium costs by *increasing your deductible* on the collision portion of your car insurance.

The deductible is the amount you must pay before the insurance kicks in. Most policies are sold with a $100 deductible per accident. However, if you increase your deductible to $250, you could cut your costs on this insurance by 10 percent. And if you're willing to pay the first $500 of repair charges in any accident, your cost for collision may be at least 20 percent lower. It is not unheard of to have a $1,000 deductible on a collision policy.

8. *Comprehensive coverage* is another part of your policy that you'll probably want to have. It will be required if you have a car loan. Compre-

hensive covers theft and damage to the car from things like falling trees, hail, vandalism, riots, fire, and flood. On some policies, this portion may also pay for a rental car if yours is stolen.

Comprehensive also comes with a deductible amount, and raising the deductible can save you money on your premiums.

9. *Additional coverages.* Your policy may offer some extra frills that are probably not worth the cost unless you value convenience. Rental insurance will pay only a small amount each day if your car is in for repairs. Towing insurance may already be covered by your auto club membership.

SAVING MONEY ON YOUR AUTO INSURANCE

There are several ways you can save money on your auto insurance: you can lower or eliminate some coverages, you can raise your deductibles, you can qualify for discounts, you can select your car carefully, and you can restructure your auto insurance payments. All of those strategies are explained below. But they pale by comparison to Auto Insurance Strategy #1—comparison shopping to get the most coverage at the best price from a good insurance company.

Auto Insurance Strategy #1: Comparison Price Shopping

The price of similar auto insurance coverage could vary as much as 100 percent from insurer to insurer in your state. That's why it's so important to do some comparison shopping before you buy.

For purposes of comparison shopping, you should check with the largest national insurers in your area. Some policies are sold not through agents but directly from the national office, potentially saving you money if you are willing to do the research. Here are two places to call for quotes that you can use for comparisons:

Amica Mutual Insurance Company (800-242-6422)

United Services Automobile Association (USAA) (800-531-8000) (sold only to members of the military and their dependents)

Auto Insurance Strategy #2: Insurance Company Track Record

Price and coverage are not the only considerations when it comes to purchasing auto insurance. You should also check the reputation and soundness of the insurance company itself before purchasing a policy. It does no good to save on premiums if the insurance company argues about your claims or goes out of business.

You can check the insurance company's financial status and claims-paying history by calling your state insurance regulator. Every year or two, *Consumer Reports* does a study of automobile insurers and their ratings for customer satisfaction as well as general pricing policies.

Auto Insurance Strategy #3: Raise Your Deductible

As noted earlier, you can save a big chunk of premium dollars by raising your deductible on collision and comprehensive insurance. Here's an example of what it costs to insure a single 45-year-old person driving a 1992 Ford Taurus in a city like Chicago. The table shows how much can be saved on premiums for just the collision, and for a total policy, by raising deductibles for both the collision and comprehensive portion:

	Premiums	
	Collision Only	*Total Policy*
$100 deductible —	$440	$1,235
$250 deductible —	$400	$1,167
$500 deductible —	$316	$1,059

Auto Insurance Strategy #4: Make Sure You Get Applicable Discounts

Auto insurance policies offer numerous discounts that can save you money on premiums. Know what the possibilities are—and ask for the discounts that apply.

1. *Combination auto and homeowners package.* You can save from 10 to 15 percent on your total policy expenditures if you have both types of policy written on the same premium. This may be a necessity if you are purchasing umbrella liability insurance.
2. *Multi-car discounts.* If you insure several cars on the same policy, even if one is used for business purposes, you may be able to save as much as 20 percent on your total premiums.
3. *Good driver discounts.* If you have no tickets, you might qualify for a discount of as much as 15 percent on your premiums.
4. *Alarms and antitheft devices.* If you install an alarm or antitheft device on your current vehicle, or when purchasing a new car, advise the insurance agent to see if you qualify for a discount. Similarly, if you always keep the car in a secure garage you might qualify for a lower rate even though you live in a large city.
5. *Antilock brakes, air bags.* Because of recent claims experience, a car with antilock brakes and one or more air bags may qualify for discounts on liability, collision, and medical coverage portions.
6. *Student discounts.* If you have a teenager at home, it is cheaper to insure him or her on your family policy than to list the teen as a primary driver on any one car. Teens may also qualify for discounts based on taking driver training courses or maintaining good grades. If the student attends school more than 100 miles from the family home, there is a large discount on the insurance premium.
7. *Senior drivers.* Some companies offer discounts for mature drivers with good driving records. There is often a discount for retirees.

Auto Insurance Strategy #5: Buy the Right Car

Buy a car that is less expensive to insure. The cost of insurance should enter into your car-buying decision. Check with your agent before you buy that shiny little sportscar to find out just how much it will add to your annual premiums.

Auto Insurance Strategy #6: Pay Premiums Annually

Ask your agent how much you will save on your annual premiums by making one annual payment instead of monthly or quarterly payments. If the difference is substantial, use your automatic savings plans to save enough money to make one annual car insurance payment. While you're saving, you'll earn interest.

WHAT IF YOU CAN'T GET INSURANCE?

You may have a poor driving record that will cause top-rated companies to deny you coverage. If you drive without any coverage, you put all your other assets at risk. That's why many states have "high-risk pools" that offer insurance coverage. In most states, any insurer doing business in the state is obligated to accept a portion of the high-risk pool and insure some of those drivers.

Some companies have separate subsidiaries to insure high-risk drivers. For example, Allstate Insurance Company insures only standard-risk drivers, while Allstate Indemnity provides policies to higher-risk drivers. Other companies specialize only in high-risk cases. Check with your state insurance commissioner about alternatives.

Finally, beware of those late night television commercials promising insurance "no matter what your driving record." These advertisers are often unscrupulous brokers who submit your name to the state risk pool and charge you a high fee for insurance you would have been entitled to anyway.

Chapter 48

Health Insurance

It may be America's greatest national tragedy that so many people cannot find or afford healthcare insurance. While politicians argue over national healthcare programs based on a government-controlled model or on a private insurer-based healthcare system, millions of Americans go without any type of health insurance benefits unless they are completely impoverished and qualify for Medicaid. In fact, given the rising cost of healthcare, serious illness is actually forcing entire families onto the rolls of government assistance.

That's a subject for national debate—and political action. Of immediate concern to you and your family is your own coverage—and how to get the best policy at the most reasonable price.

If you work for a large company that provides medical benefits, you have the best and most cost-efficient coverage available. But you should read your company plan carefully and be aware that many corporations are now requiring employees to contribute to the cost of healthcare benefits. Companies are also employing *managed care* techniques to evaluate treatments and authorize hospital stays. Failure to comply with the rules of your company plan may result in lower benefit payments.

Even current retirees who have been promised free lifetime healthcare are now facing the prospect of paying a portion of those premiums. A recent study found that 80 percent of companies surveyed will alter their retiree benefits plans in the next two years by increasing deductibles, limiting coverage for dental and other conditions, and by requiring retirees to pay more for the coverage.

Many smaller companies also offer group health insurance plans, but these plans tend to be less reliable. Rates rise on an annual basis, and if there is a serious illness within a small group the insurer may cancel the policy completely. Then the employer must search for a new policy that will cover the worker (or worker's family member) with an ongoing serious illness—or provide a separate policy for that worker. Some small employers simply opt out of providing any group health insurance coverage because of rising costs.

If you're self-employed, or work for a company that does not provide benefits, you can plan on a long search and spending as much as $10,000 a year or more to cover your family. Your costs will be even greater and your choices more limited if a family member has an ongoing illness or preexisting condition.

The strategies in this chapter are designed to help you find and price health insurance that meets your needs. But first you should understand some basic types of healthcare policies and choices, and the amounts of coverage you should be seeking.

BASIC HEALTHCARE CHOICES

Comprehensive

A comprehensive policy is the best type of insurance you can purchase because it covers medical and hospital bills up to a very high level of benefits. This is the kind of insurance offered by most company group insurance plans.

In almost every comprehensive policy you'll find an annual *deductible* provision as well as a *co-insurance* provision. The deductible amount is the dollar amount you pay before the insurance kicks in each year. It might be $100 or $200 a year for an individual, or as high as $500 per family.

The co-insurance is the portion you must pay once your insurance benefits start paying the bills. Generally, the insured must pay 20 percent of all bills, while the insurer pays 80 percent of the covered expenses. The best policies have an *out-of-pocket maximum* amount that the insured must pay every year. That limitation might mean that the insurance starts paying *all* covered expenses once the insured has paid the first $2,000 of co-insurance.

There are limits on the total amount of lifetime benefits that most comprehensive policies will pay. Some policies have limits of $250,000— an amount that could easily be exceeded in the case of a serious illness or accident. Your policy should have a lifetime maximum of at least $1 million. If the limits are lower, see below for a description of excess major medical coverage.

Basic Healthcare Policies (Hospital/Surgical)

If you cannot find or afford a comprehensive policy, consider a basic hospital/surgical policy. These policies cover payments only for conditions requiring hospitalization; they do not cover any out-of-hospital costs. Covered expenses typically include the cost of a semiprivate room in a hospital, surgical services and anasthesia, and some outpatient diagnostic services such as X-rays. Specific maximum reimbursement levels may be established for different types of surgery, or else the "reasonable and customary" standard might be used to determine payment levels.

Some hospital/surgical policies may pay every penny of expense, while others require a co-payment of as much as 20 percent of the total services to be paid by the insured. The best policies of this type will cap the co-payment at around $2,000 per hospitalization.

Health Maintenance Organizations (HMOs)

HMOs, as they're popularly called, may be your most efficient choice for health coverage. In fact, they're frequently offered as a choice in corporate medical coverage plans. Joining an HMO privately and paying a monthly or quarterly fee may save a family as much as 60 percent a year compared to premiums for private insurance.

The basic concept of an HMO is that almost every medical cost— including preventive care, checkups, and even prescriptions—is covered by an annual fee. (There may be small additional fees for each prescription or office visit, usually less than $10 each.) The potential drawback to an HMO is that in order to be covered you must see physicians and use hospitals that belong to your HMO network. You may not have an individual physician, but instead be required to see the doctor who is on call at the HMO office. Some HMOs do have groups of individually practicing physicians (IPAs—independent practice associations) that allow you to see the same physician in a private office setting.

Preferred Provider Organizations (PPOs)

PPOs are a cross between an HMO and traditional fee-for-service medical plans. These plans are created by businesses with the help of their insurers to cut down on medical costs. The PPO negotiates with physicians and hospitals to get group rates while allowing employees to choose their own private physician. Hospitals and physicians may become part of many company PPOs merely by agreeing to a set level of fees for service. If the employee goes outside the approved group of PPO doctors and hospitals, treatment costs are covered at a lower rate, requiring the employee to pay more out of pocket for medical care.

SPECIALTY HEALTHCARE POLICIES

Excess Major Medical Policies

As noted above, if you or a family member have an expensive illness or lingering disease, the standard $250,000 lifetime maximum on a comprehensive policy may not be enough. Excess major medical, or *catastrophic*, insurance policies are designed to kick in after your basic insurance covers the first $15,000 or $25,000 of expenses.

Check with your insurance agent or with a business or fraternal organization about the prices for such policies. The deductible amount should mesh with the cap on the lifetime benefits of your basic health policy. Considering the potential financial consequences of catastrophic medical events, the small amount you pay for this type of policy is money well spent.

Disease-specific Policies

You've probably seen *disease-specific* insurance policies advertised on late night television or on the back of a magazine. This policy pays off only if you get a specific disease, usually cancer. Don't waste your money; it's better to insure against *all* medical possibilities than against one.

Hospital Indemnity Policies

Hospital indemnity is another policy that appeals to the uninformed. It promises to pay you a specific amount of money each day you are in the hospital, to be used for any purpose. These policies tend to be overpriced and restrictive compared to a comprehensive major medical program that will pay your daily semiprivate room charges. Most policies have strict limitations on when they apply. For instance, the first three days or first week of hospital care may be considered a deductible. In these times of short hospitalizations, you might never collect on this policy. Most indemnity policies do not pay for extended care facilities, where you are likely to be moved after a shorter hospital stay.

Long-Term Care Policies

This type of policy covers a long-term stay in a custodial care facility. In some situations, with correct coverage and pricing these policies make sense. They will be covered completely in chapter 62.

Health Insurance Strategy #1: Getting the Most from Company Group Plans

One of the advantages of going to work for a company that has a large group health plan is that these plans seldom require evidence that you or your family members are insurable. Preexisting conditions usually do not preclude coverage. A large employer may offer a "cafeteria" of benefits, including disability, dental, and an HMO option, as well as standard group health insurance. Other nonmedical benefits such as childcare may also be included in a cafeteria plan.

Read your company plan carefully, and consult with your benefits officer before choosing among the plan options if there are any. Always be aware of requirements for second opinions and precertification for nonemergency medical care. When an insurer requires a second opinion, it will usually pay the bill in full.

As medical expenses rise, more companies are switching to *salary reduction plans* as a way of sharing the cost burden with employees. This allows employees to pay their share of benefit plan premiums on a before-tax basis. The amount of the salary reduction is not taxable for federal, and most state, income tax purposes. And both the employer and the employee avoid FICA (Social Security taxes) on salary reduction amounts. So the real cost to the worker is minimal both on a current income basis and when Social Security benefits are determined at retirement.

More than 1,400 large companies offer *flex accounts* that allow workers to pay for uninsured medical expenses with pretax earnings. A pretax salary reduction goes into a fund out of which various health, dependent care, and personal legal expenses may be made. The reimbursement for this spending is made on a pretax basis, saving employees the amount of taxes they would have owed on this income. However, if your company does have one of these flex accounts, tax laws require workers to forfeit the unused money at the end of the year. If that is the case, try to plan your use of this account to take advantage of all benefits each plan year.

The *premium only plan* (POP) is another version of the flex plan that allows employees to select in advance from among a list of benefits and pay the premium with pretax earnings. Since workers pay a set premium as an annual contribution, there is no excess contribution to revert to the company. Eligible POP premiums are limited to those for health, dental, vision, group term life insurance under $50,000, disability coverage, hospital indemnity plans, and cancer care coverage.

In some families, both working spouses may be covered under separate group health plans. In that case, benefits are coordinated so that you cannot receive more than 100 percent of coverage for your medical costs. The second plan basically will cover the amount of the deductible on the primary plan.

One spouse might have the opportunity to opt out of a company medical plan. Think twice before making this choice just to save a few premium dollars. The other spouse could lose a job, or there could be a divorce. In order to get back into a company plan, you might have to demonstrate that you are insurable by undergoing a health exam.

Terry's Tip:

$$$ Ask your company benefits officer if the company health insurance plan is "self-insured." That means the company pays health claims out of its own pocket rather than buying insurance policies. It may not be noticeable to employees because the paperwork for processing claims is usually handled by another company.

Supreme Court rulings in 1992 said that self-insured firms are exempt from state and federal rules prohibiting discrimination against gravely ill employees. Self-insured firms have been allowed to reduce or eliminate benefits for employees after those illnesses have been diagnosed.

Health Insurance Strategy #2: Finding a Group Plan

You might still find a way to join a group health plan, even if you don't work for a company that sponsors a plan for its employees. You might get group insurance through your union, or through an association or organization of professionals that you qualify to join. If you own your own small business, even if you have no employees, you'll find some private insurers offer small business group-of-one policies that let you join with other small business owners.

There are two potential drawbacks to these group plans. Rates may rise suddenly if the group is too small and one member develops a serious illness. And rates are generally higher in these association groups than with individual health policies, because people who do not qualify for individual coverage seek out the group plans.

Health Insurance Strategy #3: Finding Individual Health Plans

Individual health policies are available through many life insurance companies, but you'll find them very, very expensive. If you or a family member has a preexisting condition, you may not be able to get coverage from a private insurer at any price—unless coverage for that condition is specifically excluded.

You'll need to compare prices and coverage for several different policies. That may mean contacting different insurance agents, because each may represent only the health plans of one company.

Another place to check is your state Blue Cross/Blue Shield plan. While these companies have a reputation for being a sort of "public utility" when it comes to health insurance, they are actually competitive private insurers whose rates in each locality are based on local cost experience. Blue Cross/Blue Shield may also manage HMO plans or PPO plans.

Your other choices as an individual or family include joining an HMO. Not all HMOs have equal financial strength and the same choices of hospitals and doctors. One way to find an HMO is to check with your private doctor or with the best hospital in your area. You may be able to join an HMO and still remain with your current physician and hospital.

Health Insurance Strategy #4: Coverage with Preexisting Conditions

Having a preexisting condition—one that has required previous healthcare treatment—may disqualify you from many individual and some association group policies. Or the policy may not cover preexisting conditions for the first three to 12 months. Some policies require that you be treatment-free for a period of up to two years in order to cover that preexisting condition. If you have no choice, and if you have other family members who need coverage, you may have to settle for these exclusions on preexisting conditions.

If you simply cannot find health insurance anywhere because of your current state of health, contact your state insurance commissioner's office to see if your state has an *assigned risk pool* for high-risk cases to provide some form of insurance for people who cannot find it elsewhere.

Health Insurance Strategy #5: Coverage When You Lose Your Job

If you work for a company that has a health plan covering 20 or more employees, under federal law (COBRA) the plan must offer continuation of coverage for you and your dependents for 18 months. (The same law provides that in the case of death or divorce of an employee, the family has the right to continue coverage for up to three years.)

Under the COBRA provisions, you must notify your employer within 60 days of leaving the company that you want to continue your group coverage. You'll have to pay the entire premium plus a small service charge—up to a total of 102 percent of the cost of the coverage.

If your company plan has fewer than 20 employees, you will not be covered by COBRA. But your company plan may provide for *conversion* to an individual plan, without requiring a medical examination. If you have a preexisting condition that would make other coverage impossible, this may be your only choice. These conversion coverages tend to be very expensive and may provide limited benefits. You should check out other health insurance options for individuals, as explained above.

Health Insurance Strategy #6: Short-Term Health Coverage

Some private insurers sell short-term health policies meant to last only six months, with perhaps one renewal. These policies generally have comprehensive coverage and may be the solution for those who are in transition between jobs, or for students who graduate from both college and coverage on their parents' policy. A short-term policy provides coverage until they get that first job. Compare prices and eligibility requirements with standard individual policies. It might be a better deal to purchase an individual policy and pay monthly or quarterly, not having to worry about renewal if the next job doesn't come through or doesn't provide health benefits.

Strategies for Cutting Medical Insurance Costs

The first way to cut medical insurance costs is to stick with a job—however unpleasant—if the company provides comprehensive health care as a benefit.

The second way to cut medical care costs is to join an HMO, after doing careful research to make sure it is a financially strong organization with good doctors.

There are some other things you can do to cut costs:

1. When given a choice on an individual policy, *take a large deductible*. If you agree to pay the first $500 or $1,000 of medical expenses annually, you can lower your premiums.

2. *Agree to co-payments*. You can find policies that will pay 100 percent of your medical and hospital costs, but you will save on premiums if you agree to pay 20 percent of the costs—up to a cap. Insist on a cap for co-payments of perhaps $2,000 a year. Otherwise you could owe huge sums of money in case of an expensive illness.

3. *Look for good health or nonsmoker discounts* when purchasing an individual policy.

4. *Get a policy that is guaranteed renewable*. That means the company cannot cancel your individual policy because of claims you make and can

only raise your premiums in line with premiums of all other policyholders. While this type of policy may be a bit more expensive, having a guaranteed renewable policy is certainly worth the peace of mind. (The company could still cancel an entire class or group of individual policies, and many insurers have done so as they abandoned the personal health insurance business.)

5. *Send all claims to the insurer immediately*—even if they are below the deductible amount. The insurance company will keep track of your totals (although you should set up a separate folder with copies of bills submitted). Many insurance companies will not pay claims or consider them against the deductible after one year.

6. *Know the rules for submitting claims* under your policy. Some policies allow 15 months for deductibles to accumulate for any one policy year; some require each family member to reach the deductible before claims are paid for that member, instead of combining claims submitted by the entire family.

Chapter 49

Disability Insurance

Although most people try to insure against the costs of illness and are aware of the need to insure against the loss of income to survivors because of death, it's amazing how few people consider insuring against their inability to work and support themselves.

If you are between the ages of 35 and 65, your chances of being unable to work for 90 days or more because of a disabling illness or injury are about equal to your chances of dying, according to the Health Insurance Association of America. So it makes sense to insure your ability to earn an income.

You may already have some disability insurance through your company benefits plan—either in the form of paid sick leave or actual disability payments in case you are unable to work for an extended period of time. But these company disability programs tend to pay you far less than your weekly salary. You can apply for workers' compensation benefits if you can prove your injury or illness was work-related. And there is civil service disability pay for federal or state government workers.

If you are completely disabled, you can turn to Social Security. But processing disability claims through Social Security can take years, and only the most severely disabled are granted benefits. As a veteran, you might qualify for veterans disability benefits if you can trace your disability to a service-related injury.

None of these programs is intended to come close to replacing your predisability income. The only way you can really be assured of adequate extended payments is to purchase a disability policy designed for your situation. The strategies listed below help you structure the maximum benefits without paying for unnecessary coverage.

Disability Insurance Strategy #1: Decide How Much Coverage You Need

The amount of your income that you can replace through disability insurance depends on how highly paid your occupation is. If you earn $150,000 a year, it will be prohibitively expensive to match your current income through disability payments, and most companies will not cover you even if you can afford it.

The first step in determining how much disability coverage you need is to sit down and figure out what your living expenses would be if you were disabled for six months or more. You'd still have to cover the basics such as rent or mortgage payments, utilities, and food. But many work-related expenses would be eliminated, such as new clothes and commuting costs. On the other hand, you might want to have money to pay for household help with chores you can no longer manage.

Keep in mind that if you pay for your disability insurance policy with after-tax dollars, the benefits will be tax-free. If the disability policy is paid for by your company as a benefit, you will probably owe ordinary income taxes on your monthly check.

If your disability lasts for less than a year, personal savings can fill some of the gaps. But when considering disability insurance, you have to think of the possibility that you'd need an income at least until you reach age 65 when Social Security starts paying you regular retirement benefits.

Disability Insurance Strategy #2: Understand Disability Pricing

Disability insurance is some of the most expensive insurance you can buy. That's because it has to be individually tailored to provide the coverage you need and because there are so many special circumstances.

The cost of disability insurance is determined primarily by the type of job you currently have as well as by the amount of income you want to receive. A highly paid professional might find it easy, although expensive, to purchase a disability policy. But someone in a risky trade, such as a steelworker, a bricklayer, or a window washer, would find it impossible to get coverage at any price (unless through a company or union-sponsored plan). Other key considerations are your age, sex, current state of health (you'll have to take a medical exam), and even the state in which you live. And, of course, the price will depend on how large a monthly check you'll want to receive.

We'll come back to strategies for getting price quotes and lowering costs of disability insurance after looking at some of the variables listed below.

Disability Insurance Strategy #3: Compare Disability Definitions

Definitions of disability vary, and that can affect the type and cost of coverage. It's important to understand the difference before choosing and pricing policies.

Some policies pay benefits if you are unable to perform the duties of your customary occupation; others pay only if you cannot work at any gainful occupation. Others pay only the difference between what you can earn after your disability and what you used to earn. Avoid policies that pay only if you are totally disabled.

The best policy covers you if you cannot return to *your own occupation*. That coverage is especially useful if you are a highly paid professional with a specialty. For instance, a surgeon who lost the use of his or her hands might still make a living by diagnosing patients, but he or she would earn far less money. If the policy had an "own occupation" disability coverage, the surgeon would still receive the full benefits.

An "own occupation" definition guarantees that you will receive the full guaranteed disability payment, no matter what other work you do, as long as you cannot return to your original occupation. As you can imagine, this is by far the most expensive form of disability insurance.

The best disability policies include *residual benefit disability* payments. This type of policy will pay the difference between the income you are able to earn after your disability and the original amount of your guaranteed monthly payments. Check this type of policy carefully to make sure you get the difference whether you return to your old job or to an entirely different type of work. Residual benefits are sometimes automatically included in a policy, or you might have to purchase this coverage through a special rider to your basic policy.

You might choose a *combination* of the two types—electing full benefits for the first five years, even if you return to a lower-paid job, and then taking residual benefits to fill the gap in the remaining years.

Some policies are labeled *income replacement* benefits, and will pay either all your income if fully disabled or the percentage difference between what you earn after disability and what you were earning—up to the limits of the policy. Check the policy definition to make sure that benefits will be paid whether you return to your old job or to a different type of work.

Terry's Tips:

$$$ The wording of a disability policy is very important. If you choose some form of residual benefits, make sure that you do not have to be *totally* disabled before you can claim the residual benefits.

$$$ Also check the wording of your policy to make sure it pays for disability caused by illness as well as by accidents.

Disability Insurance Strategy #4: Choose Term of Benefits

At first thought, you might want to have a policy that pays out benefits for your entire lifetime. But you can save money on the cost of your policy if you only collect benefits until age 65, when you will be eligible for Social Security and any other company pension benefits you might have accumulated.

You can also save money if you agree to accept a longer waiting period before disability benefits kick in. For instance, you might have enough savings to cover the first six months of expenses if you are out of work, or your employer may have a policy of paying six months' salary for sick leave. If your policy states that the disability benefits will start arriving only after six months of disability, then the annual premiums for the policy will be lower.

Disability Insurance Strategy #5: Demand Certain Guarantees

The language of the disability policy can make a big difference in your coverage. You should demand a policy that is *noncancellable* (as long as you keep paying the premiums) and one that has a *guaranteed annual premium* that cannot be increased. That guaranteed premium will be lower if you start purchasing your disability insurance at a younger age—one reason not to put it off.

There are some newer forms of disability insurance that start out to be less expensive and have gradually increasing annual payment requirements—much like term insurance. You count on earning more money every year to keep up with the rising payments. Whatever the illustration you may be shown, there is no guarantee of each year's premium with this type of policy. If you can afford a guaranteed annual premium, you'll have much less uncertainty over whether you can continue to afford your disability insurance.

You also want to have a *waiver of premiums clause*, which guarantees that once you become disabled you no longer have to pay the premiums to keep your disability insurance in force.

Disability Insurance Strategy #6: Keep Up with Inflation and Income Increases

If you do purchase disability income at a relatively young age, two things could create a need for increased monthly payments: Your income could rise (and your expenses, too), and inflation could require larger monthly payments over the years. There are two separate ways to take care of these problems.

If you think you'll want to purchase more disability benefits in the future, choose a policy that allows you to add to your coverage on a regular basis—without taking a physical exam to prove insurability. You'll pay for this option, but it might be worth having. Your other choice is to purchase additional disability policies, which will be subject to medical approval.

To keep up with rising inflation, many policies have a small amount of inflation protection to increase your basic guaranteed benefit. But once you start taking benefits, the only way to increase them is to have previously purchased a cost-of-living rider for your policy. It will guarantee that your monthly check increases either by a fixed percentage or a tie-in to the consumer price index. This type of protection can be expensive, but would certainly be worthwhile if inflation returned to the early 1980 levels.

Disability Insurance Strategy #7: Compare Prices Before Buying

Just as with any other type of insurance policy, the only way to make sure you're getting the best price is to compare. Decide how large a monthly disability benefit you want. Then make a list of the most important features, as discussed in the points above.

Contact at least two insurance agents for quotes. You might also want to contact the USAA Life Insurance Company in San Antonio, Texas (800-531-8000). It is one of the few disability underwriters that sells direct to consumers, without using insurance agents.

Here's an example of costs for a disability policy you might purchase through an agent.

Example: A 42-year-old professional seeking $5,000 per month in disability payments for "own occupation" benefits and residual benefits, with coverage to age 65 and a six-month waiting period, would have to pay about $1,610 a year.

If that same 42-year-old included a future insurability option, allowing an additional $5,000 of coverage without medical evidence of insurability, the cost of the policy would be increased $166 a year. (The option to increase benefits could be activated at any time until age 60.)

Shorten the waiting period to three months and the "own occupation" premium would rise to $1,823 a year.

Insist on lifetime benefits in the first scenario and the premium cost would jump to $2,725 a year.

That illustration should give you some idea of how costs can vary depending on the options chosen.

In order to purchase any disability policy, you'll have to fill out an application, take a physical examination, and may be required to submit proof of income to justify the benefits you're buying. Make sure you answer all the questions on the application honestly, because the insurance company has two years to contest your eligibility—and even longer to sue you for fraud if you lie on your application.

Disability Insurance Strategy #8: Coordinate with Company Disability Benefits

Many people rely on group long-term disability plans provided through employers. Those plans usually provide coverage for 60 percent of an employee's salary. If you have such a plan, you should check its terms carefully. Many of these group disability plans are quite restrictive; they may not offer residual benefits or may limit coverage to only 24 months for some illnesses.

One of the biggest potential problems of relying exclusively on group long-term disability policies is that the benefits are not usually portable upon termination of employment. If you leave a company after a number of years to start your own business and have acquired a health problem in the intervening years, you may not be able to find disability coverage under an individual policy.

One solution to this problem is to have your insurance agent design a disability policy that will complement the one you have at work. This policy does not have to be for a large amount of coverage—as long as it has riders allowing you to purchase further coverage without evidence of insurability.

Chapter 50

Life Insurance

Life insurance is one of the most mysterious financial subjects that people ever consider. It shouldn't be that way because the facts of the matter are very straightforward.

We know that death is a certainty—eventually. We also know that the actuaries—the numbers experts—have figured out the statistical chances of death at any age. As an individual, you just don't know if you will be the exception to those averages and die before your statistical time. To protect against being the exception, you buy life insurance to provide benefits for your survivors in case you die prematurely.

There are only three reasons to buy life insurance:

1. To replace income if the insured person dies prematurely and family members depend on that income.

2. To provide money to buy out a business partner, repay business loans, or hire a successor in case of an owner's death.

3. To provide immediate, liquid money to pay estate taxes.

How much should you pay for life insurance? The amount you pay each year is called a *premium*. After you decide how much life insurance you need in your particular situation, the amount of your annual premium is based on four calculations:

1. Your age (and the statistical chances of death at your age).

2. Your current state of health.

3. How much money the insurance company can earn by investing your premium dollars until your death.

4. The insurance company's expenses for mailing you bills and paying its agents a commission.

You would think a computer could take in all your statistics—such as age, sex, general state of health—do the calculations, and mail you a bill for the amount of life insurance you want to purchase. Simple. Instead, there are 250,000 full-time and 150,000 part-time insurance agents out there—all trying to sell you a policy!

Even simple *term insurance*, where you pay an annual premium just for death benefits, has been complicated by issues like whether the premiums will rise every year or remain level; whether the annual premium prices they show you are guaranteed for one year or as many as 20 years; whether your policy will automatically renew each year; or whether you might have to take a physical again in a year, or five, or ten years in order to keep up the insurance.

If your head isn't spinning already, the agent will introduce you to *whole life* and *universal life* policies whose basic premise is that you contribute more to the policy each year than is needed to pay for the death benefits. The excess money grows tax-deferred inside the policy—and may be used one day to make the premium payments or to build a fund of money against which you can borrow to create a tax-free stream of income.

Actually, that's pretty simple—until the agent starts presenting *illustrations*, which are lists of numbers that swim before your eyes. How do you know that the investment portion of your insurance will grow to the promised size in the future? You don't—and there are very few guarantees. Just a lot of talk about dividends, rates of return, and vanishing premiums. Confused? You're not alone. But read on, because the insurance-buying strategies in this chapter are designed to make life insurance as easy as it should be.

The life insurance industry says you need their agents to explain all the different types of policies they've created and all the various ways those policies are priced. One insurance industry critic says insurance companies spend a lot of money to make sure their policies cannot be compared easily to any other company's policy. But if you are a smart consumer, understand which questions to ask, and how to organize the information you receive, you can make a decision that may save as much as 50 percent of the money you spend on insurance premiums.

There are many reliable, hardworking insurance salespeople who have their clients' best needs in mind. But there are also many salespeople who will sell policies based not on need, but on which policy pays the largest commission. Since commissions on insurance policies are not disclosed, you can't tell the difference. In this chapter, you'll learn more about commissions—and how to buy no-load or low-load life insurance, much as you might use a discount stock brokerage firm—and how to find a fee-only insurance advisor and services that compete to give you the best pricing quotations.

First, though, you'll need to take a look at your personal situation to find out whether you need life insurance and, if so, how much. Then comes a basic understanding of the different types of insurance available—and which types you should be considering. The strategies in these chapters will help you make those decisions, and then show you how to make smart insurance buys.

Insurance Strategy #1: Do You Need Life Insurance?

Refer to the list at the start of this chapter for the three reasons to buy life insurance—any kind of life insurance. Start with Reason #1. If you are a working parent with young children, your income would be sorely missed if you died. Even if you are a homemaker and do not bring in much income, your contribution to a family would be expensive to replace. You need life insurance.

As your family grows older and children move out of the house, your life insurance needs may drop. You're building up assets in your investment program and in your company retirement program. Your children begin to build their own lives. You need less insurance.

Once you retire, there may be no reason at all to have life insurance if its original purpose was to replace your income. After all, you've now stopped working. Your surviving spouse may be covered by Social Security, pension benefits, and your joint investment program. Unless you want to leave a fortune to your children or a charity, leave money to buy out a business partner, or leave money to pay estate taxes when your spouse dies, there's really no need to have life insurance at this stage of life. (We'll discuss those other needs—business liquidation and estate tax liquidity—in the chapters that follow.)

There are some other people who do not need life insurance. If you're young and single and have no one depending on your income, you don't need life insurance. If you're married, both working, and have no children, you don't need life insurance unless you want to leave a present for your spouse. Your health insurance policy at work probably provides about $10,000 in death benefits that will more than cover your funeral expenses. Don't let an agent tell you that you'd better buy now because later you might be uninsurable. Instead, put the money you would have spent on life insurance into a good mutual fund where it can grow into a nest egg for that first house, future children, or even retirement.

Many parents are talked into buying life insurance on their children as a way of saving for college. It's a bad way of saving for college; see chapter 37 for much better strategies. When you set college money aside in an insurance policy, a portion of your "investment" is used to pay for insurance company expenses and mortality charges inside the policy. You'll be in a better position to pay for college if *all* the money you set aside is working for you in your chosen investment. Besides, I know of no parent who would get any joy out of spending the money that comes from the death benefit on a child.

Insurance Strategy #2: How Much Life Insurance Do You Need?

Once you know you need some life insurance to protect your survivors, the next question is, how much? That depends on your stage of life and your perception of how your family will live without your income—and how long that situation might last until your spouse remarries and replaces your income, or until your children are grown. That's tough to estimate, both financially and emotionally, so you'd better use some real-world numbers.

To figure out how much insurance you need, go back to chapter 6 and take a look at your annual expenses. They might even increase if you died and your spouse had to pay additional money for childcare while he or she worked extended hours. How long would it take for your spouse to replace your income, if ever? You might want to leave at least four or five years of your annual income in survivors' benefits. (Remember, life insurance benefits are not taxed as income to the recipients.) Or you might want to leave money for a specific purpose such as a college education.

Until you realistically face the possibility that you might not be around to provide the material things you want for your family, you can't evaluate the amount of life insurance you need. Take your annual budget, figure how it will increase as your family grows, take the percentage of income you expect to contribute, multiply by at least 5, and you'll have an idea of how much life insurance coverage you need.

> *Example:* Annual spending: $85,000
> Projected family budget in 5 years: $_____
> Percent your income contributes: 75%
> 5 years at $_____ × 75% = $_____
> *Total life insurance needed*: $_____

Remember, you're calculating your salary pretax, and the life insurance benefits will come to your family income tax-free, assuming an estate under $600,000, or any size estate that will pass tax-free to your spouse (see chapter 51).

GETTING STARTED

These first two strategies are your own, personal decisions. If you want to get help from a financial planner, that's understandable. But before you turn to the question of which type of policy, and start listening to the sales pitches, you should already have firmly in mind the answers to the first two questions:

1. *Do I need insurance, and if so, how much insurance do I need?*

2. *What kind of insurance?*

This is the place where most people simply throw up their hands and decide it's all too complicated, and they'd better just follow the recommendations of their brother-in-law (boss's son, old college friend, etc.), who has obviously become a very successful insurance salesperson. Wrong strategy.

You can eliminate 90 percent of the confusion if you make one easy decision. You need the simplest form of death benefit: Term Insurance.

Chapter 51

Understanding Term Insurance

Term insurance is the answer to almost every insurance need when it comes to replacing lost income. It is the easiest to compare, the most affordable to purchase when you're young, and will allow you maximum coverage when you need it most. Term life insurance is the policy to buy if you're going to keep your life insurance for about 20 years or less.

Here are the key things to know about term insurance.

1. You pay premiums every year (or semiannually or quarterly) and the insurance stays in force for the entire time the premium is paid. When you stop paying, the policy is cancelled. There is no cash buildup inside the policy because you paid only the cost of insuring your life for that year.

2. With ordinary term insurance, the amount of the premium will increase every year because the likelihood of dying increases statistically every year. That likelihood is called the *mortality rate*.

3. The cost of the term insurance depends not only on age, but on sex (some companies have unisex rates, but since women live longer, their insurance rates are lower at companies that use separate mortality tables) and on general health conditions. You will probably be required to take a physical examination to qualify for term insurance. Smokers may be charged twice as much as nonsmokers for term insurance, even if they only smoke occasionally.

4. The same amount and type of term insurance for the same individual can vary in price by 100 percent, depending solely on which company's policy you purchase.

You might wonder how those price differences can happen. Part of the problem is the obscure nature of insurance pricing. People generally deal with an agent who represents only one company, and don't bother to compare prices from different companies. Marketing decisions and the amount of commissions built into the price can make a big difference in the annual premium payments for term insurance. The way the policy is structured also affects the price. Little differences you might not otherwise notice can add up to a big difference in price.

TERM INSURANCE OPTIONS

All term insurance is not alike in structure. When purchasing term insurance you will have to make choices about whether the premiums remain level and, if so, for how many years. You'll need to know whether those premiums are guaranteed—or just offered for illustration purposes. You'll need to know your options—and those of the insurance company—for renewing your policy each year and for converting it into a cash value policy at some time in the future. The following are some things to consider when purchasing term insurance:

Level Premium Term vs. Annually Increasing Premium Term

Premiums on ordinary annual renewable term insurance policies increase in cost every year. But many companies offer some form of level term in which they project that the annual premium will remain the same for 5, 10, or 15 years. At the end of that period, the policy may revert to one that has premium increases every year, or the premium may then move higher but remain level for another five years, and five years after that. These policies have become very popular because people like to plan in advance how much they'll be paying for their life insurance.

Here are some things to watch out for when purchasing level premium term insurance:

1. Are the premiums *projected* or are they *guaranteed* for five years (or 10, 15, or 20 years)? The difference is important. If the premiums are not

guaranteed, the insurance company is not obligated to meet its projected premiums, even if they are written in the illustration shown to you by your agent.

Read the fine print: policy illustrations are not guarantees.

If you want to make sure your premiums will remain level, get a policy that guarantees its premiums. The cost of a policy with this guarantee will be slightly higher.

2. If you choose a level term policy, *make sure you keep the policy in force for the number of years the premium is level*. Insurance companies know that most term policies stay in force for only about seven years on average. For one reason or another, people will cancel term policies or let them lapse. If you're taking a 10-year or 15-year level premium, the premiums are structured to be a better buy over that longer term. You'll lose out unless you hold on to the policy for the full term.

3. Don't assume that the level premium deal is the best deal. Compare it to a standard term policy that increases every year. Add up the 5- or 10-year outlay projected for the increasing term policy and compare it to the level premium policy over the same number of years.

There's a catch here. Remember when we discussed the time value of money in chapter 13? Well, if you're laying out higher premiums in the early years of a level premium policy, you have to take that into account. The higher premiums in the later years of a standard term policy will be paid in dollars made cheaper by inflation. Ask your agent to compare the *present value* cost of the level term policy against the increasing term policy cost.

4. Beware of short-term level term policies, such as those that last for only five years. The premiums may jump sharply in the next five-year period, and you could be forced to do your insurance shopping all over again in the fifth year—just to make sure you're getting a good deal. Of course, that assumes you're still insurable in the fifth year. If not, you'll have to stick with this policy that just became very expensive in its sixth year.

Reentry Term vs. Annual Renewable Term

A *guaranteed annual renewable term* life insurance policy means that you do not have to requalify by taking a new medical examination every year in order to renew your term policy. Some policies are sold as *reentry term*, which means you must requalify after a certain period—either every year or every five years when premiums are increased on level term policies.

Be careful when reading the language of a policy proposal. Often this reentry term is disguised in language that says: "at the end of ten years the insured may reapply for a new policy of the same type, with evidence of insurability." It sounds like they're doing you a favor, but they're not. In ten years you may not be insurable because of an illness or accident.

If you do have reentry term and are required to take a medical exam to extend your coverage, this time *you* pay for the cost of the physical—and that could be as much as $500 if you get a complete blood work-up and EKG. In that case, even if you are insurable, you might just tell your agent to shop around for the best new policy so the new insurance company will pay the cost of the physical (standard practice when new policies are issued).

Your agent will like that because commissions on new policies will be larger than those on reentry term. But here's a warning:

When you take out a new policy, the two-year period of contestability starts all over again.

That gives the insurance company a chance to renege on payment of death benefits if you made even a minor misstatement on your application. And death benefits are not paid in cases of suicide committed within two years of purchasing a policy.

Most reentry term plans give the illusion of lower cost because the illustrated rates assume you'll always be able to requalify at the lowest preferred rates. If you don't requalify, you'll be stuck with very high renewal rates and the chance that the cost of insurance might become prohibitive.

You should demand *guaranteed annual renewable* term unless you are absolutely sure that you'll only need the insurance for five or ten years and don't care that you might not qualify, or qualify for premium rates, at the reentry period down the road. Of course, the reentry term is less expensive because it gives the insurance company a chance to eliminate you from its rolls when you are ill but have not yet died!

Convertible Term

This is a provision worth choosing in your term insurance. At some point down the line you may decide that instead of paying steadily increasing premiums for term, you'd like to switch to a cash value policy. You could start the search for a good cash value policy, but your health might not be as good as it was when you first purchased the term policy. If your term policy is convertible into whole life without another medical examination, you'll be glad you paid for this provision.

Waiver of Premium

This is an expensive provision that says you do not have to pay your annual premiums to keep the policy in force if you become disabled. *Waiver of premium* is just an expensive form of disability insurance. Read chapter 49, and purchase disability insurance. Do not pay for the waiver of premium on your insurance policy, just as you would not take the "choke and croak" policy on your automobile (see chapter 47).

Age of Expiration

Age of expiration is the statement on your policy that says it is renewable either annually or every five years until a certain age, generally 70. If you expect to keep it longer, you can ask for insurance that is renewable to age 80—but beware because the premium levels can be nearly as much as the death benefits!

You may think you won't need term insurance after the specific age limit in your policy, and in that case the limit has no importance. But many people are buying 15- or 20-year level term policies when they are in their fifties. It makes no sense to pay for a long-term level premium policy that cannot be renewed when you reach age 70. Look for a policy that can be renewed until age 90.

HOW TO BUY TERM INSURANCE

Term Insurance-Buying Strategy #1: Use a Quote Service

The services listed below will give you quotes on the least expensive term insurance, with no obligation to purchase a policy. Except where indicated, all of the application paperwork can be done by mail should you choose to purchase a policy. In cases where a medical exam is required, they will arrange to have a service take the appropriate tests at your convenience, either in your home or office. (In some instances medical tests requiring X-rays or treadmill tests must be done in licensed facilities.)

Before contacting any of these services be prepared to list your policy amounts and requirements. For example, decide first whether you want:

guaranteed annual renewable or reentry term;

level premiums of 5, 10, 15, or 20 years, or traditional annual premium increases;

guaranteed premiums, and if so for how many years.

They'll also need to know your name, address, age, sex, general health category (i.e., preferred, nonsmoker), and amount of insurance you are requesting.

I have tried each of these services, and each has knowledgeable people to answer your questions. But don't call without some idea of your requirements. It's a waste of time to get the least expensive quotes if they are all for reentry term, which you don't want. All of these services deal with top-rated insurance companies, but you should check ratings of individual companies. Many of these services cannot deal with some of the major insurance companies that restrict sales of their policies solely to their own and independent commission agents. So you may not have quotes from the largest and best-known companies that avoid dealing with agents who discount or rebate commissions. The quotes are given without charge, and this information can help you in evaluating prices and policies presented by your own insurance agent.

The following three companies will send you quotes on five of the least expensive term policies that meet your requirements. There is no obligation to purchase, but they will handle transactions in most states by mail:

InsuranceQuote Services, Inc., Chandler, AZ (800-972-1104);

SelectQuote, San Francisco, CA (800-343-1985);

TermQuote, Dayton, OH (800-444-TERM);

LifeRates, Newton, PA (800-45-RATES).

One insurance quotation service advertises rebates on commissions:

Direct Insurance Services (DIS), San Diego, CA (800-622-3699), is an insurance-buying service that rebates one half the commission on insurance policies it sells in Florida and California, the only two states that allow rebates on commissions. To give you proof of the commission rebate, they'll show you the insurance company's commission statement.

Since this company rebates commissions, it can only sell or mail quotation information to people with addresses in Florida and California. If, after receiving the information you decide to purchase a policy, you must fly to one of those locations and sign the policy personally. But on a large policy, the commission savings can be well worth the trip.

Terry's Tips:

$$$ If you are purchasing a policy in California or Florida from an agent or firm that promises to rebate your commission, be sure to ask whether rebates of commissions on subsequent year renewals are also included. Also compare several years' projected premiums to see if you are purchasing a policy that has given the agent large commissions in the second through fifth year to make up for the amounts rebated in the first year.

$$$ Determine whether any rebate of commission is taxable to you, and if the seller of the policy is going to send you a Form 1099 at income tax time as evidence of this taxable payment.

The following is the one service that does not sell any insurance but only gives information:

Insurance Information, Inc., Hyannis, MA (800-472-5800)
Gives you five illustrations on term life costs from top-rated companies. The cost is $50, charged to your bankcard, which is refunded if you are not satisfied. This service will give you the name and number of the insurance company, which in turn will refer you to a local agent.

Term Insurance-Buying Strategy #2: Buy Insurance Direct

Two companies sell both term and cash value insurance (more about that in the next chapter) direct to the public, without using agents. They sell what is called "no-load" insurance. These policies tend to be less expensive because they avoid paying agents' commissions. Instead, much like no-load mutual funds, they charge a slightly larger annual fee that is taken out of your premiums. You can use these quotes as a comparison to make sure you are getting the best deal from your agent. For more information, contact:

USAA Life, San Antonio, TX (800-531-8000)
Individual representatives—not commissioned salespeople—will answer your questions and send you policy quotations based on your individual needs. The only policies they offer are underwritten by USAA Life Insurance, which is rated A + + by A. M. Best, AAA by S&P, and AA-1 by Moody's.

Ameritas, Houston, TX (800-552-3553)
Individual representatives—not commissioned salespeople—offer policies underwritten by Ameritas Life Insurance, based in Lincoln, Nebraska. The company is highly rated: A+ by A. M. Best; AA by S&P; and A by Weiss Research.

Term Insurance-Buying Strategy #3: Get Independent Advice

When you read the policy illustrations sent to you by the quote services listed in Strategy #1, and the no-load price illustrations sent to you by the companies listed in Strategy #2, you may still have some questions.

If you are buying a large amount of term insurance, it may pay to check with the advisors listed in Smart Insurance-Buying Strategy #1 in chapter 54. These advisors can help you evaluate the price quotations you have received. If your term insurance needs are substantial, they may help you qualify for larger discounts or rebates. Also, be sure to read Strategy #5 in the same chapter for advice on checking the safety rating of any insurance company before you buy.

Chapter 52

Cash Value Life Insurance

Cash value insurance is sometimes referred to as permanent insurance because it is designed to cover longer-term needs such as providing money for estate taxes. If you need to keep your insurance coverage until you are much older, term insurance becomes too expensive. So now you'll have to consider insurance policies with names like whole life, universal life, interest-sensitive whole life, and blended policies with term life and cash value riders. I can see your eyes glaze over!

If you'll just stick with me long enough to understand some basic definitions, you can then skip to chapter 54, where I'll show you how to have any cash value insurance policy (one you already own or are thinking of buying) analyzed to see if it is a good, competitive investment in today's economic environment, and how to get prices on the most competitive policies being offered today. But first, a word of caution:

Understand this section before buying any cash value policy!

When an insurance agent explains a cash value policy, you'll be presented with rows of numbers that are called *policy illustrations*. These illustrations demonstrate how cash values will build up inside the policy and may be used in the future to pay premiums or to provide a fund against which you can borrow.

The most important thing for you to know is that these illustrations are just part of the sales pitch and are not guaranteed. In fact, if interest rates drop, the policy will not build up nearly as much cash as illustrated—leaving you, the policyholder, in a tough spot. If you were counting on the cash buildup to pay future premiums, you could be forced to pay additional money to keep the insurance in force—money you might not have available when you're older and retired.

It's easy to be misled about interest rates, not only when you purchase a cash value policy, but again over the years as the insurance company announces the new interest rate it will pay for the current year. In order to keep the policyholder happy, the insurance company may promise a high rate, but then increase its expenses and its charges for mortality (the death benefits). Those are subtracted from your cash value before the interest rate is paid. The result: yes, you get a higher interest rate, but it is paid on a smaller amount of cash value. Bottom line: You really earn less than the promised rate.

The biggest thing that can affect your cash value in the early years is the insurance agent's commission and total compensation package, which includes other agent perks such as bonuses and luxury vacation trips. Because it is built right into the premium you pay for the insurance, many people are unaware that as much as 90 percent of the first year's premium may be paid to the agent in commission! Start-up costs and expenses may eat up much or all of the remaining premiums in the first year. So at the end of year one, your cash value is ZERO! Those charges may also remain high in the next few years. The result is that money you thought was building up as cash value and earning interest is hardly earning interest at all. Only in the later years will the "true return" on your cash value equal the insurance company promises.

How can you tell what amount is going to the insurance company and agent—and what amount is going to the investment and savings portion of your insurance policy? Just take a look at the ledger shown to you by the agent. Look under the heading *surrender value*. If the amounts shown in the first few years are zero, the agent and company are getting all those premium dollars (see chart V-2 and note the arrows).

By the time many people figure this out, they get angry and decide to cancel their cash value policies. In fact, the insurance industry counts on the fact that a number of people will drop out early. That leaves more assets for remaining policyholders and boosts their return in later years—making it easier for the insurance company to deliver promised returns over the

CHART V-2

A G E	Y E A R	PLANNED PREMIUM OUTLAY FOR YEAR(a)	CURRENT COST OF INSURANCE AND CURRENT INTEREST OF 8.000/ 8.500%(b) -----END OF YEAR-----			GUARANTEED COST OF INSURANCE AND GUARANTEED INTEREST OF 4.000% -----END OF YEAR-----		
			POLICY VALUE	SURRENDER VALUE	NET DEATH BENEFIT	POLICY VALUE	SURRENDER VALUE	NET DEATH BENEFIT
43	1	2400	1848	0 ←	190000	1767	0	190000
44	2	2400	3791	0 ←	190000	3552	0	190000
45	3	2400	5835	94 ←	190000	5356	0	190000
46	4	2400	7985	2336	190000	7172	1523	190000
47	5	2400	10683	5129	190000	9001	3447	190000
		12,000		7559			4470	

long run. So it may make sense to hold on to that older policy. How will you know?

As you'll see in Smart Insurance-Buying Strategy #1 in chapter 54, there are two consulting services (not brokers or sales agents) that for a fixed fee will help you analyze both proposed and currently held policies—to see how the promises stack up given current interest rates. With this advice, you can decide whether to purchase a proposed policy, cancel or stick with an older policy, or contact your insurance company about increasing your variable premiums to make sure your current policy is building enough cash value.

The other thing you can do to avoid these big charges against your cash value in the early years is to purchase your life insurance from a *discount insurance broker* or a broker who specializes in *low-load life insurance*. Did you know that many insurance companies sell the exact same policies, with commission loads that are as much as 50 percent lower? Usually those policies are offered to buyers who are purchasing multi-million-dollar policies. But if you deal with the right companies, you can get that kind of discount on much smaller policies. We'll introduce you to those insurance brokers in Smart Insurance-Buying Strategy #2 in chapter 54.

The other way to get good cash value policy quotes is to deal with the few insurance companies that do not have agents, but sell directly to the public. They are identified in Smart Insurance-Buying Strategy #3 in chapter 54. They may not always have the lowest prices, but their reputations for pricing and promises are excellent—and you can use their quotations as a guideline against which to measure other policies.

I promised to make life insurance simple. But you really should have a few definitions before skipping to these Smart Insurance-Buying Strategies in chapter 54.

Whole life

Whole life is the simplest cash value life insurance policy. Your premium stays the same every year. The amount of the premium is much more than would be needed to pay the death benefits in the early years, so the extra money inside the policy earns interest that grows and compounds tax-deferred. There is a fixed death benefit, which does not drop unless you take a policy loan against your cash value. If you die with a policy loan in place, the amount of the loan is subtracted from the death benefits that are paid to your beneficiary.

When you own a whole life policy, you keep paying the same level premiums into your old age. At that point you may decide to use the cash value in the policy to continue paying premiums—or you may decide to borrow against the policy to get some extra cash in your retirement years.

Some whole life policies are structured so that you only pay premiums for a fixed number of years—and then the cash value inside the policy is used to pay for future premiums. This is called *vanishing premium*, but unless the cash value builds up enough to pay those future premiums, it could be the entire policy that vanishes!

You may have been told that traditional whole life policies do not earn "enough" interest. That's hard to figure out, since insurance companies do not reveal the amount of interest that is actually credited toward your cash buildup. There may be an illustration of an interest rate, but the insurance company does not reveal its expenses and mortality charges, which are subtracted from your annual premiums before interest is credited. The higher these expenses, the lower your cash value, and the less interest you earn.

To find out what your policy is really earning, see Smart Insurance-Buying Strategy #1 in chapter 54. You might be surprised by the numbers revealed in this computerized study of individual policies offered by the National Insurance Consumer Organization, or by the policy evaluation that graphs your projected return in the Beacon policy survey. These are invaluable services for any buyer of cash value policies.

Interest-sensitive Whole Life

Some insurance buyers prefer to know how much interest they're receiving on their whole life policy. Interest-sensitive whole life policies reveal the annual market rate that is being credited to the cash values. Most of these policies have a fixed premium, although a few promise a narrow range of premiums with a guaranteed top limit.

But you can't really beat the insurance company just by knowing the promised interest rate. If the company raises its expenses or mortality charges, you have less cash value against which the interest is being credited. So even though the published interest rate remains high, your return will drop. That's another reason to check on your current policy.

Universal Life Insurance

While both the death benefit and premiums are fixed on standard whole life policies, universal life gives you some flexibility. A universal life policy has all the features of the previously described whole life—but allows you the choice of varying (at any time)—the premium payments or the amount of the death benefit.

For example, you can design the policy to have constant level premiums—like a standard whole life policy—and guarantee the death benefit forever. Or you can design the policy so that you'll have to pay minimum premiums, much like term insurance. Of course, that means your premiums will have to increase each year to keep the death benefits fully in force. You can pay large premiums and design the policy to accumulate tax-free cash so that after seven or ten years it's unlikely you'll ever need to pay premiums again. (The cash buildup inside the policy should grow fast enough to pay future premiums in this case.)

And you can change your mind midstream. You can start today to pay premiums for life—and then later decide to increase your premium payments so the need for premiums will vanish. Or you can start with large payments now, designed to vanish the premium, and then later decide to make only smaller payments.

You can even change the amount of the death benefits, to make them smaller and alter premium payments to cover this change. You can choose how much death benefit you want your premium to purchase. With the same premium dollars you can opt for lower death benefits and a larger cash buildup, or smaller cash buildup and higher death benefits.

You may withdraw excess cash and lower the death benefit with no interest expense. That cash withdrawal will permanently lower the death benefits, even if you repay the cash. If, however, you take the withdrawal as an interest-bearing loan, when you repay the money, the death benefit will be increased by the amount you repay.

The real advantage of universal life is that you have this flexibility. You can design the policy just like a similar whole life policy—with fixed premiums and death benefits. But if you buy a straight whole life policy, you never have any flexibility to skip payments or increase them if circumstances in your life happen to change.

The potential disadvantage of a universal life policy is that you must check carefully and be very disciplined to insure that you make enough payments to keep the insurance in force. Yes, for a while you can depend on your growing cash value to make premium payments. But if you decide on that route, you could run out of cash value before you run out of the need for life insurance. You must ask your agent for an *in-force ledger* every year or two, as a sort of policy "checkup" to make sure it is growing adequately. The insurance company will tell you how much you must pay every year to keep the insurance in force until you reach age 100.

You see the catch here: If there isn't enough cash value in the policy, your insurance could lapse. That's why you should always make extra premium payments in the early years, so you'll have a cash cushion. There's another catch: If the interest rates illustrated when you buy the policy are higher than the rates the insurance company can earn, your cash value will not build up enough to pay premiums in later years.

So, while you want to rely on the insurance company "target" premiums, it's also worthwhile to check on the current status of your universal life policy by using Smart Insurance-Buying Strategy #1 in chapter 54. If your policy is underfunded, you'll want to know about it early enough to make additional premium payments before the gap gets too large. Otherwise your insurance could lapse in your old age—just when it is too expensive to replace with it with a new policy.

One other warning about universal life (and all cash value insurance policies): You might decide to invest extra money in the policy to benefit from the tax-deferred compounding feature. But Congress has placed limits on this tax benefit, and too much cash can turn your policy into a *modified endowment contract*, which would restrict your ability to take tax-free loans out of the policy in later years.

Variable Life Insurance

If you really want to gamble with your life insurance policy, you can choose a variable form of either whole life or universal life. With *variable whole life*, the annual premiums are fixed—but instead of getting a fixed interest return, the growth of the cash value in the policy depends on investment choices you make.

With *variable universal life*, you still have the flexibility in choosing your premiums and death benefits, but the variable portion is the amount by which your cash value will grow. That depends on your investment choices, not on a fixed rate promised by the insurance company.

Do you think you're a good enough investor to beat the rates promised by the insurance company? You'll have a choice of a number of mutual funds in which to invest the cash inside your policy. If you're planning to stick with this variable life policy over the years, you'll probably want to invest in a growth stock mutual fund that will outperform fixed interest rates. Otherwise it's not worth paying the extra charges and fees associated with variable life policies.

And that brings up the biggest problem with variable life policies. You may think your investments are doing well, but your cash value may not be growing quite as much. You see, the insurance company gets to take out its fees and mortality charges *before* the investment return is credited to the cash value. That can substantially lower your total investment return.

Terry's Tip:

$$$ If you want to speculate in the markets on a tax-deferred basis, do so through a variable annuity (see chapter 29) instead of with your life insurance policy. You're buying life insurance to eliminate risks, not enhance them. Don't speculate with your family's security blanket.

Single Premium Life

Single premium policies are designed for the older person who has a lump sum of money to invest and seeks tax-deferred growth of principal plus insurance benefits for beneficiaries. The buyer of this single premium policy has access to the cash buildup, as described below, but he or she should be over age $59\frac{1}{2}$. That's because any money withdrawn by a younger policyholder, even as a policy loan, will be subject to that 10 percent federal tax penalty, plus ordinary income taxes if the policy had enough cash to qualify as a modified endowment contract.

This single premium policy is really a form of modified endowment contract, as described above, where the purchaser invests far more money than is needed to buy life insurance—only because that extra money will grow tax-deferred. Before June 21, 1988, these policies were an especially great deal; you could borrow money out without paying any taxes. For single premium policies sold after June 21, 1988, all borrowings (up to the total amount of earnings inside the policy) are considered to be taxable income.

Single premium policies may be simple whole life policies or universal life policies that earn a fixed rate of interest. Or they may be variable policies, allowing you to choose your own investments. Either way, the same considerations apply as listed in the warning above when it comes to believing the interest rate projections. Be sure you understand just how much cash value is accumulating—*after* charges for mortality and expenses.

Blended Policies

Blended policies are the latest wrinkle in life insurance. Done properly, they can lower your initial commission costs and increase the cash value that is available to earn interest. Done incorrectly, they can present you with problems later in life when there may not be enough cash value to keep paying premiums on the blended policy—leaving you with a choice of paying additional premiums or letting the policy lapse.

Expert agents, like the discount specialists listed in chapter 54, use blending to lower the cost of cash value insurance in states where rebating of commissions is not allowed. These policies are also frequently recommended by fee-only advisors.

Simply stated, blended policies mix a combination of higher cost cash value insurance with smaller amounts of term insurance. Sometimes the agent packages a combination of policies to lower the overall commission on the same dollar amount of death benefits. Some blends offered by major insurance companies like Prudential and Guardian carry lower sales commissions, resulting in a larger amount of cash value available to earn interest. The overall cost of the policy is lower because the term portion of the package carries a lower premium.

Some of the cash value in the policy is used to pay for the term insurance portion. Also, over the years, the dividends on the whole life portion of a blended policy are used to buy something called *paid-up additions*. They are essentially little whole life policies on which all the premiums are prepaid in one lump sum. These paid-up additions gradually increase the death benefits of the whole life portion, just as the term insurance becomes too expensive to keep. But by that time the death benefits have increased enough to eliminate the term portion of the insurance.

The advantage of using paid-up additions to increase the death benefit is that they usually have a much lower commission rate than regular whole life, so more money goes into the cash value buildup. The disadvantage is that the death benefits build up more slowly than with a policy that is completely whole life and starts out with a larger, fixed death benefit.

Warning: If promised cash value illustrations are too optimistic, they may not be able to pay for the rising cost of the term portion or the paid-up additions. Then the annual premiums would have to rise sharply—or the insured would have to cancel the coverage. Most blended policies use about 25 percent term insurance, and some of the more aggressive policies may use 50 percent term. When using a higher percentage of term, it may be wise to pay in extra premium dollars in the first years to build a cash cushion.

One way to judge a blended policy is to ask how much cash value there will be at the end of the first year. If the cash value is equal to at least half of the first year's premium payment, you're probably off to a good start. Or use one of the insurance analysis services cited in chapter 54 for an unbiased appraisal of the blend.

Some Insurance "Buzzwords"

Dividends: These are simply a way of expressing the amount of money, over the guaranteed minimum, that is credited to your policy each year. Some companies use the term *excess earnings*. It is really just the additional money that comes from higher investment earnings, lower expenses, or return of excess premium that the insurance company credits to your whole life cash values. (There used to be a big difference between mutual and stock insurance companies and how dividends were treated for tax purposes. Those differences are no longer significant.)

Surrender charges: Another marketing term that consumers often hear. You've learned already that if you decide to cancel a policy in the first few years, you won't have much cash buildup because of all the money that goes to pay agents' commissions and sales expenses. So, if you decide to cancel a policy, these costs are considered surrender charges. If you borrow against your policy, you can only borrow against your cash surrender value. But if you die, there are no surrender charges!

Policy loans: These are simply a way of taking some of the excess cash out of your cash value policy. Frequently the interest rates on borrowings are lower than rates you could find elsewhere, but you should be aware of some of the drawbacks of borrowing against your insurance policy:

1. The amount you borrow reduces the death benefit to your heirs should you die with the loan outstanding.

2. While the interest rate may appear low, there is a hidden cost. Not only do you pay interest on the amount you borrow, but a portion of your cash value inside the policy is set aside as collateral for your loan. This portion of your cash value earns only the minimum guaranteed rate inside the policy, while your remaining cash value may be earning higher rates. This lower crediting rate on your collateral reduces your policy earnings.

3. In certain types of policies, the borrowings may be treated as taxable income, if the policy was an overfunded modified endowment contract (see p. 417). Check on this before you borrow.

4. If you have outstanding policy loans and decide to surrender your policy, or it lapses for some other reason, at the time the policy ends you will owe taxes on the total amount of the loans you have taken in previous years. You may have already spent the cash, and now owe tax dollars you do not have.

Paid-up policy: A paid-up policy means that the insurance company has *guaranteed* that you will not need to make one more penny in premium payments to keep this policy in force for the rest of your life. That's a lot different from illustrations of "vanishing premiums," which are simply predictions that no more premium payments will be required. You'll usually see the term *paid-up* used in connection with single premium policies or in connection with *paid-up additions* used in blended policies.

Preferred rates: Preferred rates are the premiums paid by the best insurance risks: those in good health, with no recent illnesses or congenital problems. Obviously, preferred rates are the lowest rates the insurance company charges. All too often an agent will quote you the preferred rate, and then after you've filled out the application and gone through the medical examination, you'll be told that you don't qualify for preferred rates. Instead, you're considered "standard." By this point, many people feel they've gone through so much hassle they might as well accept the higher standard rates.

In some situations, it's an obvious case of "bait and switch." The attractive preferred rates are used to get you into the process. Later you're switched to the higher standard rates. But standard rates can be as much as 20 percent higher.

So you should ask the agent to go back and ask the insurance company to review your file. In the meantime, the agent should check with other companies to see if you'll qualify as preferred. Not all companies rate individuals in the same way. It's worth taking a little more time and trouble to try to find preferred rates. But if you know before you apply that you have medical problems, then inform your agent and ask for price quotes on standard rates.

In-force ledger: This is simply an updated version of the illustration you were shown when you purchased your policy. Only this current version will show exactly how much cash you've been building up in the policy—and whether it will be enough to pay the future premiums as predicted at the time of purchase. To receive an in-force ledger, contact your company's policyholder service department. They will have the original illustration used when the policy was first sold and the current in-force ledger. They can also draw up ledgers to illustrate any changes that would occur if rates should drop farther or move higher. Always ask for an illustration of what you'll have to pay to keep this coverage until age 95. This service is free—and it should come to you directly, without an agent seeing it first.

Policy switching: Beware of insurance agents who tell you to switch from your old policy to a new one. That's how many agents do most of their commission business. In chapter 54 you'll learn how to get an independent and unbiased analysis of whether it pays you—not the agent—to switch out of an old policy and into a new one.

There is one aspect of policy switching that might come in useful. Suppose you decide that you want to continue your insurance policy and not cancel it, but you are a bit concerned about the insurance company itself. (See Smart Insurance-Buying Strategy #5 in chapter 54 for ways to check on insurance company safety.)

If you take the cash values out, to the extent you exceed the total amount of premium payments you have made, you'll have to pay ordinary income taxes. Plus you'll owe that 10 percent penalty if you're under age 59½ and the policy is a modified endowment contract. And you might want to keep the cost basis (total premiums already paid) on the old policy intact. You can transfer those cash values and cost basis to a new policy with a different company if you're careful to follow the rules.

It's called a *1035 Exchange*, named after the tax law that makes this type of transfer tax-free. First you'll have to apply for a new policy at a different company and be officially approved at rates you consider favorable. Then you must fill out the proper documents at each insurance company, agreeing to assign your old policy to the new company. You'll probably have to make the first premium payment on the new policy to put it in force. Then you'll assign the cash value of your old policy to the new policy—*without ever touching the money yourself.*

That part is critical. In order to avoid taxes on the cash value portion, the policy must be transferred directly from one insurance company to the other. Get top-notch professional advice to make sure a 1035 Exchange goes through without a hitch. And remember, the transfer to a new insurance company starts a new two-year contestability period.

Chapter 53

Life Insurance Strategies

When you purchase a life insurance policy, you're thinking about money that will be left to your survivors. But your concerns should not be limited to just the dollar amount and type of life insurance policy you're purchasing. You can own a huge amount of life insurance and still make a big mistake—if you don't understand the proper strategies to get the most money for your heirs with the least amount of taxes, while minimizing your premium outlays.

Life insurance can play a helpful role—in creating liquidity to pay estate taxes, in funding buy and sell agreements between partners, in equalizing inheritances among children, and in helping spouses increase their protection while cutting insurance costs.

The following tax-wise insurance strategies call attention to the importance of proper policy ownership and other techniques that can maximize your insurance dollars. Check out the benefits of these strategies before completing your insurance purchase.

Tax-Wise Insurance Strategy #1: Policy Ownership

There are four variables to consider before you actually sign the papers to purchase a policy.

1. Who is the insured?

2. Who is the beneficiary?

3. Who is the owner?

4. Who will pay the premiums?

The answers to these questions can make an important difference in tax consequences if the policy pays off.

The Insured

The insured is the person on whose life the policy is based. If the insured dies, the policy pays off. Some facts are obvious. The older the insured, the more expensive the policy. But as noted earlier, it makes little sense to buy life insurance on the life of a child, even though the premiums may appear very low.

The Beneficiary

The beneficiary is the person or persons who receive the money when the insured dies. But the beneficiary does not necessarily have to be an individual. In many cases it may be smarter to create a trust to be the beneficiary of an insurance policy, with a child or an otherwise less capable individual, such as a mentally disabled person, as the ultimate beneficiary of the trust. The trustees have a fiduciary duty to invest the proceeds of the policy for the ultimate beneficiary of the trust.

Sometimes a trust will be the beneficiary of a policy to avoid estate taxes. Sometimes a corporation will be the beneficiary of a life insurance policy on one of its key officers or owners. In this case, the money may be used to buy the owner's share of the company.

The Owner

The registered owner of an insurance policy is a critical concept that could have a big tax impact. First, the owner of the policy must have what is known as an *insurable interest* in the life of the insured when the policy is purchased. You cannot simply take out a life insurance policy on a stranger, or on your ex-husband—unless you have an insurable interest in seeing that his maintenance and child support obligations are covered.

Many women choose to actually own the insurance policy on the life of their spouse, even though the husband may provide money for making the premium payments. Then, if they divorce, the husband cannot cancel the policy on his life. His ex-wife is the owner, and the policy will remain in force as long as she keeps making premium payments.

Second, you should know that although death benefits of a life insurance policy are not taxed to the recipients, if the policy is owned by the deceased, it becomes part of his or her estate. As you'll see in chapter 55 on estate planning, a spouse can pass his or her entire estate, tax-free, to the surviving spouse. But when the surviving spouse dies, the heirs must pay hefty estate taxes on all amounts over $600,000.

Because of this situation, many people set up an *irrevocable insurance trust* to own the insurance policy. That means the proceeds at death are not included in the estate. The trust owns the policy and is also the beneficiary. The trustees can ultimately distribute the money received from death benefits in accordance with the instructions of the person who set up the trust. The death benefits can be used to purchase assets from the estate, providing liquidity, or can be loaned to the estate to pay taxes and legal fees.

It's very important that the trust be *irrevocable*. If the grantor of the trust can change his or her mind and reach into the trust to use its assets, then the proceeds of the life insurance policy will be considered part of the estate.

The Payer

The owner and the payer on a policy are generally the same person. But as noted above, one spouse may give cash to the other to pay premiums. Similarly, a trust may be the owner of a life insurance policy but may require cash to pay the premiums.

The person who created the trust makes an irrevocable gift to the trust every year—enough for the trustee to pay the insurance premiums. Since the assets of the trust cannot be touched, most people choose to put term insurance in the trust. The term policy does not build up cash value, and if the grantor ever changes his/her mind, he/she can simply stop gifting money to the trust to pay the premiums and the insurance will lapse. For more information on creating trusts, see chapter 57.

Tax-Wise Insurance Strategy #2: Life Insurance to Pay Estate Taxes

You may think you have built up a nice estate for your children and grandchildren, but how would you feel if Uncle Sam turned out to be the largest beneficiary of your life's work? That could happen. It's time to figure out just how much money could be subtracted from your legacy by federal estate taxes, state estate taxes (in some states), legal fees, and costs of processing or probating your estate plan.

Chart V-3 shows that estate tax rates start out at 37 percent and climb to 55 percent. The first $600,000 of an individual's estate is exempt from federal estate and gift taxes; using proper planning, a couple can shelter $1.2 million (see chapter 56). Above that amount, estate taxes are owed. And they must be paid, in cash, within nine months of death.

If a large portion of the estate is tied up in illiquid assets, such as ownership of a small business, the heirs could be forced to sell the

CHART V-3
Federal Estate Tax Rates
How They Diminish Your Estate and Deprive Your Family

Taxable Estate	Estate Tax*
$ 600,000	$ 0
750,000	55,500
850,000	153,000
1,250,000	255,500
1,500,000	363,000
1,750,000	475,000
2,000,000	588,000
2,250,000	710,000
2,500,000	833,000
2,750,000	965,500
3,000,000	1,098,000

ON EXCESS OVER $3 MILLION
THE ESTATE TAX IS 55%

* Assumes $600,000 deduction for Unified Tax Credit.
Example: $750,000 − $600,000 = $150,000 × 37% = $55,500

business at "fire-sale" prices to raise cash to pay estate taxes. Or they could be forced to get a bank loan to pay the taxes. That's not a good solution either, because they'd still have to sell the assets to repay the loan, plus they'd be paying large amounts of nondeductible interest on the loan.

If you think it can't happen, think again. The family of the late William Wrigley, heir to the chewing gum fortune, was forced to sell the Chicago Cubs baseball team to raise money for estate taxes. Even that wealthy family failed to make adequate provisions for estate taxes. When Sammy Davis Jr. died, his wife, Altovise, was forced to hold an auction of precious memorabilia in order to raise cash for the $7 million federal estate tax bill he left behind. And the IRS certainly believes Elvis is dead; it nicked his estate for a huge amount of taxes!

That's where life insurance strategies come in. Instead of paying a large fortune to the government in the form of federal estate taxes at death, it may be much smarter to spend less money now to buy life insurance which, properly owned, can be used to pay the estate taxes at death. Purchasing the right kind of policy now is like prepaying your death taxes at 25 cents—or less—on the dollar!

Here's an example: Nancy, a 55-year-old single woman, has built up an estate worth $2.6 million, which she wishes to leave to her heirs. The first $600,000 of her estate is not subject to federal estate taxes; but on the remaining $2 million, her estate would owe $588,000 before any money could be distributed to her heirs.

Now let's suppose that the majority of Nancy's wealth is tied up in her ownership of her business and in her home. Only a small amount is in cash and pension benefits. Her heirs could be forced to sell either the home or the business quickly to pay the taxes.

But Nancy is a smart businesswoman. She purchased $600,000 worth of life insurance that is owned by an irrevocable life insurance trust to keep the proceeds out of her estate. (Or she may have gifted the amount of the yearly premium to her children who own and pay for the policy. Remember, she is allowed to give $10,000 per year gift tax-free to each child.) At Nancy's death, the heirs will use the proceeds of the life insurance policy to pay the estate taxes, leaving them the $2.5 million she worked so hard to build up in assets.

What did the life insurance policy cost? Nancy chose a cash value policy that was designed to have the premium vanish in seven years. The premium outlay each year was $12,500 for a total of $87,500. (Nancy was a smart insurance buyer; before making the purchase she showed the illustrations to one of the analysis services listed in Smart Insurance-Buying Strategy #1 in chapter 54 to make sure the premium payments would be enough to make the premium vanish in the planned seven years.)

Nancy pays that $87,500 in premiums while she is alive, but she keeps the government from getting the $588,000 in estate taxes at her death— and her heirs get their full inheritance. That's the real benefit of life insurance properly used to pay estate taxes.

Tax-Wise Insurance Strategy #3: Joint and Survivor Life or Second-to-Die

In the case of a married couple, the real need for life insurance that will be used to pay estate taxes comes when the second spouse dies. A couple can save premium dollars by purchasing a *second-to-die* policy that covers their joint life expectancy, instead of purchasing two separate life insurance policies on each other.

A second-to-die insurance policy covers two lives—usually husband and wife—but pays off only on the death of the second person. Instead of paying for separate life insurance policies on each spouse, the insureds pay one lower premium on their joint lives. The premium is lower because the joint life expectancy is greater than a single life expectancy, resulting in a longer tax-free accumulation period before death benefits are to be paid.

The insurance cost savings can be dramatic, as you can see in chart V-4. (Note: Because women have longer life expectancies, the cost of the wife's insurance costs less than the husband's.)

It's very important to check and compare costs on second-to-die policies. As with other cash value policies, there are variables—including interest rate projections—that could affect the ability of the policy to continue providing cash value for future premiums. In fact, it's doubly important to check these illustrations because you're insuring two lives.

Terry's Tips:

$$$ Have the policy illustration on a second-to-die policy run with the assumption that the older insured dies within five or ten years. See what happens to the premium. If it increases, don't buy the policy.

CHART V-4
Last Survivor Plans Can Save You Money
Assumptions: Male, 65, nonsmoker / female, 65, nonsmoker
Need for estate liquidity: $1 million
Payment plan: 7-year quick pay

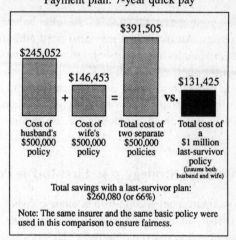

Total savings with a last-survivor plan:
$260,080 (or 66%)

Note: The same insurer and the same basic policy were
used in this comparison to ensure fairness.

SOURCE: David Phillips & Company.

$$$ Second-to-die policies are very useful because the current tax law
allows an unlimited marital deduction (for a complete explanation, see
chapter 56), which means there is no estate tax due on the death of the first
spouse. But that tax law could change, eliminating the marital deduction.
In that case, you would want two separate insurance policies to pay estate
taxes. Ask the insurance company if, in the case of divorce or tax law
change, the second-to-die policy can be split into two separate policies
without further evidence of insurability.

When a second-to-die policy is owned in an appropriate irrevocable
trust, the death benefits can provide ready cash to pay estate taxes.
Another alternative is to set up a family partnership involving the estate
owner's adult children. The partnership owns the second-to-die policy. See
your attorney regarding appropriate ownership of such a policy.

$$$ When purchasing a second-to-die policy be sure to use one of the
policy evaluation services in Smart Insurance-Buying Strategy #1, chap-
ter 54. Pricing of these policies is particularly important to make sure the
policy is not underfunded. These policies typically have very large pre-

miums that cover big commissions to agents, but some companies have restructured policies to minimize the distribution costs. You'll need guidance from an unbiased source to make sure you're buying a policy with a low commission built into it.

$$$ Consider your estate tax needs carefully before purchasing a second-to-die policy. An individual may also need additional individual life insurance to provide for some heirs who shouldn't have to wait for their inheritance until the spouse dies. A good example of such a situation is a second marriage in which the wife is much younger and there are older children from a first marriage. With only a second-to-die policy, the adult children must wait until their stepmother's death before receiving their inheritance.

Tax-Wise Insurance Strategy #4: First-to-Die Policies

Just when you've figured out second-to-die, along comes a way to reverse the order. But first-to-die insurance policies have very special applications for business partners and marriage partners. This is a relatively new but fast-growing type of cash value insurance policy.

First-to-die is designed so that one policy on two or more lives replaces two individual policies—saving as much as 25 percent over the cost of two separate policies. These policies are often aimed at small business partners who need to protect against a forced sale of the company when one partner dies. But there's an opportunity for spouses to use this type of policy.

Consider the case of a married couple with two incomes and several small children. Both incomes are required to pay the mortgage and other monthly expenses. So they each have a life insurance policy on the other, recognizing that the loss of one income would be devastating to the family's standard of living. If one spouse dies, then they won't really need the other policy—except, perhaps, to avoid estate taxes on the death of the second spouse.

In our hypothetical example, the separate $350,000 first-to-die universal life insurance policies on this 40-year-old couple are expensive: He pays $1,700 a year, and she pays slightly less, about $1,600. If they switch to a first-to-die policy, their annual premium will drop to $2,300.

In the case of two business owners, each may have a $5 million life insurance policy on the other, so that when one of the partners dies, the proceeds of the policy will be used to buy the deceased partner's share of stock from his or her estate. The surviving partner will then become the sole owner of the company.

Actually, the business partners didn't really need two insurance policies. They only needed one that pays off on the death of the first partner. But, of course, they had no idea who would die first, so they spent $60,000 a year on each policy for a total annual insurance cost of $120,000. And their insurance agent loved the business!

If they switched to this new policy, which pays $5 million on the death of the first to die, their annual premium would be $90,000. The real savings comes in when a small business wants to insure the first to die of three or four partners. Then the savings could be even greater.

There's one other benefit. When the first person dies, the survivor gets the money. But what if the survivor then decides to get an individual life insurance policy? With the best first-to-die policies, the insurance company will automatically make available life insurance in the same face amount for the survivor, with no evidence of insurability required. If spouses own the policy and decide to get divorced, they can continue the policy, or each will be allowed to convert to an individual policy for the same face amount. In the best of these policies, the survivor is automatically covered for a short period of time, and the policy should pay double death benefits in the event both insureds die simultaneously.

Tax-Wise Insurance Strategy #5: Living Benefits

Although not really a tax-oriented strategy, there are a few instances in which you may collect on your death benefits *before* you die. Several life insurance companies have established criteria that allow people to receive their death benefits if they are either terminally ill, facing catastrophic medical costs, or if they require extended long-term healthcare. This early access to death benefits is generally called *living benefits*.

Gaining early access to your death benefits is *not* the same thing as borrowing against the cash value of your policy. Living benefits are paid out based on the entire death benefit face amount of the insurance policy, not just the lower cash value. In fact, living benefits are often paid out against term insurance policies that have no cash value.

Using your death benefits while you are still alive is much like the old concept of "selling your inheritance" before receiving it. Only in the case of living death benefits on your life insurance, you—not your heirs—are selling the benefits in advance of receiving them.

There are two ways to realize living benefits if you find yourself in a situation where this is necessary. First, contact your insurance company to see if it will pay out the benefits directly to you. The insurance company will certainly require proof from your physician that your illness is terminal (as in the case of AIDS patients). Depending on your condition, a slightly discounted amount of insurance will be paid to you immediately. For instance, on a $100,000 policy you might receive a current cash payout of $90,000.

Other insurance companies now offer policies that have a living benefits rider that you pay for when you purchase the policy. Paying that advance fee might be worthwhile because it will reduce the discount when the benefits are ultimately paid out. Unless you are in a high-risk category for contracting a terminal illness such as AIDS, or you cannot get a good medical insurance policy, it is probably not worth purchasing this rider when you buy a policy.

The second way of realizing living benefits from your insurance is to contact one of several private companies that now offer to purchase policies of terminally ill or elderly persons at a discount. The amount of the discount depends on your current medical condition and life expectancy. In order for these companies to advance money to you, you have to accept less than the face value of the policy.

The IRS, as of this writing, has yet to determine whether the amount you receive in advance of death is taxable to the recipient. Some tax experts are saying that the cash advance should not be taxed because it is a collateralized loan. Also questionable is whether the buyer of the policy will be taxed on the difference between the amount paid to the owner of the policy and the amount ultimately received when the insured person dies. One way suggested to get around this problem is to make the buyer of the policy the irrevocably named beneficiary instead of actually transferring ownership.

You can get a list of life insurers that provide accelerated death benefits or living benefits by calling the National Insurance Consumer Helpline: 800-942-4242.

Some private companies that purchase your life insurance policy and advance the death benefits include:

Neuma, Inc. (312-786-5900)
Legacy Benefits Corporation (212-643-1190)
Accelerated Benefits of New York (800-666-1232)
Insurance Resources Group, Ltd. (301-652-9522)
Assured Lifetime Benefits (708-675-8856)

Some companies act as brokers, referring policy sellers to other companies with available capital. Others are direct buyers of life insurance policies. It is smart to get a price bid from more than one company.

Tax-Wise Insurance Strategy #7: A Private Pension

The one advantage of using life insurance to create a retirement program is that, if the policy is properly established, any money borrowed out of it is completely tax-free! In fact, you might consider this type of program superior to traditional retirement plans and even annuities. Money taken out of a retirement plan will be taxed as ordinary income. Money later taken out of a tax-deferred annuity will be at least partially taxable. But, if necessary, money can be borrowed out of a life insurance policy before age 59½ without the 10 percent federal tax penalty and without paying additional current income taxes. The one drawback to using life insurance as a retirement program is that you are paying mortality charges for the death benefits every year, and those amounts can rise significantly as you age.

The idea in using an insurance policy to build a pool of future retirement income is to find a policy that will build up the most cash value while you buy the least necessary amount of insurance. Most whole life or universal variable life policies offer tax-free policy loans and regular investment plans to create a "private pension" cash build-up program. When considering these plans, it's important to compare the annual cost of the life insurance mortality charges and the cost—if any—of the loans.

You must also get a reasonable projection of future cash values for the policy to make sure that once you start borrowing there will be enough money left inside the policy to pay for the ever-increasing mortality charges. It's very important to leave the excess cash growing inside the policy for the longest period possible, before borrowing money out.

Look for an insurer that credits your cash value at the same rate it charges you for the loan—effectively a no-cost loan. Inside the policy itself, the ratio of death benefits to premium (your original investment) is critical. If designed improperly the policy may be considered a *modified endowment contract,* and money taken out of the policy will be taxable. To obtain the maximum cash value, many companies structure premiums to be paid in over seven years, maximizing the ratio of cash value to death benefits. Finally, choose a strong, well-funded company that has a history of good earnings and of paying out competitive rates to policy holders.

Chapter 54

Strategies for Saving Money on Insurance

Now you understand how cash value life insurance policies work—and how difficult it is for the average consumer to judge whether he or she is getting a good deal. Since illustrations are not promises, you've seen how easy it is either to overpay for a policy (thereby giving the agent an excessive commission) or to buy a policy that looks less expensive (but creates the possibility of future underfunding).

You need help! Examining proposals from competing insurance agents is not the answer; they only confuse you more. Now you'll have at least two pages full of numbers swimming in front of your eyes, leaving you to wonder how prices on the same amount of insurance could be so dramatically different.

The following strategies will show you how to find unbiased help in evaluating current and proposed life insurance policies. You'll also learn where to find help in purchasing lower-cost policies, and how to design a buying strategy if you decide to go it alone.

Smart Insurance-Buying Strategy #1: Consult a Life Insurance Advisory Service

National Insurance Consumer Organization (NICO) has for several years offered an insurance policy evaluation service provided by consumer insurance advocate and expert James Hunt. You send a copy of illustrations on a proposed policy, or an *in-force ledger*, which your current insurance company will provide free of charge for any policy you already own. Armed with this information NICO will calculate your true rate of return on the cash value portion of your policy.

To get this figure, the computer subtracts what the death benefits *should* cost for term insurance on a person your age. The computer calculates whether you're earning enough on the policy to beat the investment returns you could earn elsewhere. This is where excessive charges for death benefits and insurance company expenses such as commissions are exposed. They lower the true rate of return.

In policies with higher initial costs, there is a lower cash value in the early years to receive the credited interest. It takes years before the true returns match those that are promised. And if, as is the case with nearly half of the cash value policies purchased, the policy lapses or is surrendered in the first seven years, this lack of return in the early years means consumers lose money on their insurance policies.

When you request a policy evaluation from NICO, you'll get a rate-of-return study for your policy (based on current interest rates and promises), and you'll get back a personal note from James Hunt, explaining why or how your policy is overpriced, along with his recommendations.

The cost for this service is $35 for each single life policy evaluated, and $25 for each additional single life policy submitted for analysis at the same time. Second-to-die policy analyses cost $75. Send a copy of the sales illustration on a new policy, or in-force ledger on an existing policy, to: National Insurance Consumer Organization, 121 N. Payne Street, Alexandria, VA 22314.

Beacon Company Policy Evaluation Service provides a way to sort out competing proposals or to evaluate your old policy based on current interest rate conditions. Its reports are designed to test for unrealistic pricing by using benchmark interest rates and cash value growth ranges.

When you submit either a policy illustration or an in-force ledger for a current policy, Beacon will send you a computer printout showing the illustrated cash value. The report also includes a chart that will show you the difference between the benchmark and the proposed policy illustration's cash value projections (see chart V-5).

The written analysis suggests some reasons for discrepancies, such as overly optimistic interest rate assumptions, and advises you either to

CHART V-5
Beacon Company Evaluation

Name: John Client
Description: XYZ Life Insurance Company Illustration
Issue Age: 45

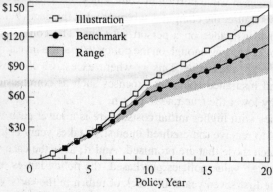

SOURCE: Beacon Company.

contact the company for more information about its policy assumptions, or simply to choose a more reasonable policy. Not all policies are projecting too much cash value growth; some promises underperform the benchmark. That suggests you are paying too much for a policy and should seek other alternatives.

The cost for each report is $108. An informative booklet explaining details of the Beacon reports is available for $9, which is credited against your first report. For reports sent within 72 hours by overnight express, add $25. Reports sent within 24 hours by fax cost an additional $50. To order or to obtain more information, call 800-824-1274.

Smart Insurance-Buying Strategy #2: Use a Discount Insurance-Buying Service or Fee Advisor

R.K. Nelson Associates (800-879-LIFE)

Rick Nelson uses low-load life policies, or creates blended policies to save consumers 40 to 70 percent on commissions. In Florida and California, where rebates are allowed, he will rebate similar percentages of commissions. Products offered include all types of cash value life insurance policies.

Assured Enterprises, Ltd. (312-993-0355)

Ted Bernstein is an insurance consultant who either charges an hourly fee averaging $150 an hour for straight advice, or $100 per policy for policy reviews. He will also research and sell either low-load or no-load life insurance policies for a fee. The fee for low-load is $1,500 per million of insurance, and for no-load the fee is $3,000 per million. These fees are substantially less than traditional commission costs.

Direct Insurance Services (DIS) (800-622-3699)

This company rebates at least 50 percent of the premium (including agent's commission, agency fee, and bonus) that you pay on policies sold in Florida and California (the only two states where rebating is legal). They will not sell by mail in any other state, but will mail information and price quotes to a California or Florida address. It may be worth a trip to their offices to sign for a policy and get the commission rebate.

Fee for Service (800-874-5662)

This service will direct you to financial planners who sell low-load cash value insurance. The fees for consultation or analysis of current policies run about $100–$150 an hour. The policies they offer typically charge less than 20 percent of usual agents' commission on similar policies.

Life Insurance Advisors Association (LIAA) (800-521-4578)

This group of fee-only advisors serves people considering $1 million or more in insurance purchases. Fees range from $3,000 to $10,000, and recommended policies are all low-cost, no-commission policies. Alternatively, they will work with buyers who want to get better value from agent-sold policies.

Smart Insurance-Buying Strategy #3: Buy No-Load Insurance Direct

Some companies sell their cash value insurance policies direct to consumers, bypassing agents, and thereby offering competitive premium prices with greater cash value buildup. You can call their toll-free numbers to request information on the specific policies offered:

USAA Life, San Antonio, TX (800-531-8000)

Individual representatives—not commissioned salespeople—will answer your questions and send you policy quotations based on your individual needs. The only policies they offer are underwritten by USAA Life Insurance, which is the rated A++ by A. M. Best; AAA by S&P; and AA-1 by Moody's.

Ameritas, Houston, TX (800-552-3553)

Individual representatives—not commissioned salespeople—of Ameritas Life Insurance respond to your questions. The company is highly rated: A+ by A. M. Best; AA by S&P; and A by Weiss Research. Note: Ameritas offers other policies that are sold by agents, but to get the direct sales office you must use the toll-free number listed above to reach the Houston marketing office.

Smart Insurance-Buying Strategy #4: Create Your Own Life Insurance Bid Checklist

Whether you're going to make a decision about life insurance on your own or use a policy evaluation service or consultant, you have to be able to compare the quotations and illustrations you'll be receiving. Unfortunately, the industry makes it almost impossible to do these comparisons.

When asking for insurance quotes, prepare your own checklist. First, make sure you are getting quotations on the same insurance:

1. Insured's name, sex, date of birth, and whether or not a smoker (include information for both insureds if seeking a joint and survivor policy).

2. Amount of insurance.

3. Type of insurance (term or cash value, single, joint life, etc.).

Second, list the agent's responses to the following issues:

1. When receiving an illustration, ask for all policy values (including cash values) to be shown for the first 20 years *and* to age 95 or 100. (This

makes sure there is enough cash in the policy to pay the premiums in years beyond the 20th.)

Don't settle for a policy illustration that covers values for only 20 years; tell the agent to illustrate the values at age 100 for you. The reason most policies only show the first 20 years of values is because that's the only legal requirement.

Another way of making sure your policy will give you coverage in your older years is to ask for an illustration of a policy that endows at age 95 to 100. *Endowing* means the cash value equals the death benefit. You want to make sure that even if the interest assumptions do not work out, the coverage will continue until age 100.

2. Ask each company to disclose the interest rate being used to calculate the premiums and policy values. Compare this rate with the rate the insurance company has actually averaged over the past ten years—although this is no guarantee of future performance in a lower interest rate environment. Ask if the company is projecting an interest rate bonus at any time in the future in order to meet its projections. If there is a projected bonus, ask if it's guaranteed.

3. Ask the insurance company to recalculate a second set of quotations and illustrations on the basis of a credited interest rate that is 2 percent lower than its current estimate. This will extend the number of years you will have to pay premiums. However, if it also increases the amount of premium that must be paid each year, do not purchase the policy. It is a sign that the assumptions are too optimistic.

4. Premiums should be sufficient to "vanish" in 15 years or sooner, based on each insurance company's current projections for credited interest rates, mortality rates, and expenses. (Note: "Vanish" does not mean paid-up insurance; it just means that based on current projections no more premium payments would be due after a specific number of years.)

5. Ask whether policy loans will be used to pay premiums when considering promises of vanishing premium. It's okay to use cash value buildup to pay future premiums, but you don't want to authorize policy loans.

6. When buying joint-and-survivor insurance, get a quote that shows what happens to policy values after the death of one of the insureds.

7. Always keep the policy illustration, but remember: The illustrated numbers are not guaranteed. When you receive the actual insurance policy, read it over for accuracy and remember to get all promises *in writing* on the policy itself. Then leave your policy in a safe place where your heirs can find it. Promise yourself to review your old policy—and request an in-force ledger to check on its current status—every two years on your birthday.

Smart Insurance-Buying Strategy #5: Check the Insurance Company's Safety Rating

This strategy is last, but most important. As Americans have learned to their misfortune in recent years, there is no federal government bailout fund or safety net for insurance companies that fail. There are only state guarantee funds in all 50 states (except Washington, D.C.) that come into existence when an insurance company doing business in that state fails.

These state funds usually have no assets; their job is to collect from other insurers doing business in the state to cover the policyholders of the failed company. This can be a time-consuming and confusing operation. In the most recent cases, other major insurers have stepped in to purchase the assets of the failed companies. But policyholders have had to cope with delays in getting both money and information; lower interest rates credited to their policies than they have been promised; limited, if any, ability to withdraw cash value from insurance or annuity policies; and, in a few cases, delays in paying death benefits.

Even when state funds step in to "rescue" policyholders of failed insurance companies, there are limits to the coverage. In most states, the maximum coverage is $100,000 for cash value in an individual life or annuity policy and $300,000 in death benefits, or $300,000 for all claims combined for an individual or family. Obviously this "insurance on your insurance" may not be enough to cover the amount you have invested in your policies, or the amount you expect to receive in death benefits.

Recent insurance company failures, combined with the decline in asset values of real estate and other assets owned by many insurance companies, make it most important for anyone purchasing an insurance policy to check the company's rating very carefully.

Here are the ratings services and their top ratings levels, below which you should not buy a policy, along with instructions for contacting the rating service. In most cases it will be easier to go to your nearest public library, which should have the current ratings books from these companies:

A. M. Best
To get a rating on any life or health insurer, call A. M. Best at 908-439-2200 to find out the company's AMB identification number; then call 900-420-0400 to get that company's rating. Cost of the 900 call is $2.50 per minute (you must have the AMB I.D. number to get a rating).

Highest ratings: A++ and A+.

Standard & Poor's (212-208-1527)
Ratings available at no charge during business hours;

Highest ratings: AAA, AA+, AA, AA-.

Moody's (212-553-0377)
Ratings available at no charge during business hours;

Highest ratings: AAA, AA-1, AA-2, AA-3.

Duff & Phelps (312-368-3157)
There is no charge for insurance company ratings; 100 companies are rated; .

Highest ratings: AAA, AA+, AA, AA-.

Weiss Research (800-289-9222)
This is the newest of the insurance rating services, and perhaps the most conservative. A. M. Best was still rating Executive Life (the large California insurer that failed in 1991) an A+, while Weiss Research was downgrading its rating to D.

Weiss's quarterly ratings service for life and health insurers is not available in libraries, but for an immediate, current rating, you can call the toll-free number and get the Weiss rating on any company for $15 charged to your bankcard. A one-page report is available for $25 by mail or fax.

Highest ratings: A+, A, A-, B+ (the last is the minimum rating to qualify for Weiss's recommended list).

PART VI

Strategies for Seniors . . . and Those Who One Day Will Be!

THIS SECTION of the book is intended for those who are senior citizens, those who expect they'll be seniors one day, or those who have parents who are seniors. In other words, there's something in this section for everyone.

Whether you're close to collecting Social Security or are suddenly aware that you'd better start doing some financial planning for that part of your future, you need to know the smart strategies that will assure you of a comfortable retirement and the ability to pass on stability and wealth to your children.

It's not only seniors who need estate plans, including a will or living trust; the young family with children may not have as many assets to pass along, but certainly needs to make sure there is a plan in place to take care of those children.

Middle-aged parents with children in college may not have thought about nursing home costs for themselves, but they may face that problem with their own parents at any moment. Long-term care insurance is a multi-generational issue.

An accident could leave any of us incapable of managing our assets; how much better you'll feel if you know you've arranged for a power of attorney to spare your family the need to go to court for the right to make decisions about finances or healthcare.

As interest rates have plummeted in the 1990s, many seniors have found their incomes cut in half as savings yields dropped. Strategies to extract equity without selling the family home (the reverse mortgage) or to use annuity plans to increase income allow seniors to receive more money each month without changing their lifestyles.

So, even if you're not a senior yet, you skip this section at your own peril. You or someone you love will need your planning efforts for the future.

Chapter 55

Planning Your Estate/Passing It On

It's never too early to start thinking about estate planning—even if your "estate" is just a few personal possessions. If you die without leaving any legal instructions for distribution of your property, the state in which you live will make the decisions in your place. Which government bureaucrat would you trust to assess the value of your property and decide when and how it should be distributed—or who will get custody of your children?

Many people put off making a will or estate plan because just thinking about the subject makes them uncomfortably aware of their own mortality. It may be difficult to push yourself—or a reluctant spouse—into a meeting with a qualified attorney to get your affairs in order. But until you do, there will always be a nagging feeling that you've left something undone. Every time you deposit a paycheck in your bank account, make a mortgage payment, or drive your child to school, you'll know that you've left a vital portion of financial planning in disarray.

Here's the mental argument that motivates me, and seems to work well on others, when it comes to making this type of financial arrangement. I'm superstitious. I figure that the unexpected disaster is less likely to happen if I've planned and prepared for it. On the other hand, if there is no will or estate plan, it's like tempting fate!

Whether you're motivated by fear, superstition, or just common sense and self-discipline, if you haven't made or reviewed your estate plan in the last two years, now is the time to do it.

By this time you know I'm a big believer in taking charge of your own financial assets, and in some instances, such as no-load funds and discount brokerage, I'm sure you can be successful taking a do-it-yourself approach. But estate planning is one arena in which I advise you to get competent professional help, and pay for the best. After all, if there's a mistake in your documents, you won't be around to correct it; it's your intended heirs who may suffer—and the government that may collect. Trying to avoid probate and estate taxes through self-written estate plans could be your most expensive financial mistake.

WHAT'S AN ESTATE PLAN?

An estate plan is simply a legal, written document or set of documents that provides for distribution of all your assets upon your death, and gives instructions for the care and protection of your children. In a broader sense, a good estate plan can have many uses. It can save on estate taxes, it can keep the details of your estate private, it can smooth transitions if you're incapacitated before you die, it can provide for succession in a family business, and it can help you keep your assets intact and growing.

Even if you're young and single, you should consider having a *simple will*. While you may have named a beneficiary for your IRA account, or for your benefits plan at work, you might want to distribute some personal items. Will your brothers fight over your car? Will your sisters know who should get the pearls you inherited from your grandmother, or the new watch you just purchased?

Some people think they have an estate plan if they simply put title to all their assets in *joint tenancy with rights of survivorship,* knowing that if one of the owners dies, the survivor will own the property. That plan has its drawbacks. If one of the joint owners is sued, the property could be tied up in legal battles. And joint ownership of property doesn't provide for distributions in the event of simultaneous death in an accident.

Or consider this scenario: You have no will because all your property and checking accounts are in joint name. You have no children. You and your spouse are driving home from a party and are involved in a terrible accident. You are pronounced dead at the scene of the accident, but your spouse survives for a few days before dying in the hospital. You died first; your assets go to your spouse. When your spouse dies—*all* of your assets go to your in-laws. Your spouse's parents are his or her legal heirs if there is no will to the contrary!

Yes, you need a will. Whether you're married or single, whether you have children or not, in all likelihood you have some assets you want to distribute and protect. And if you have enough assets, you'll want to protect them from estate taxes too.

For many people, a simple will that can be drawn by most attorneys will solve basic estate issues. But an even better solution for many people is a combination of a *living trust* with a simple *pour-over will*. As you'll see in the next chapter, the strategy of using a living trust can save you legal fees and probate costs, keep your estate planning documents private, and can simplify matters if you have a stroke or are incapacitated before your death.

Another important part of your estate plan may involve more than one *trust*—including trusts created and funded while you are alive (*intervivos trusts* or *living trusts*) or trusts that come into effect upon your death (*testamentary trusts*). These trusts may be used to reduce estate taxes, to hold insurance policies outside your taxable estate, to provide for distributions to minor children or others who may be incapable of making financial decisions, or to distribute assets to charities.

One other key element of your estate plan is the correct use of *powers of attorney*. Properly drawn, these documents give others the authority to make decisions in your place—as you would have wanted them to be made—if you are incapacitated. These powers may be limited to business and financial decisions, or may be separately drawn to give authority regarding healthcare decisions and your instructions regarding the use of extraordinary life-prolonging medical techniques. All of these strategies will be explained in the next chapter, but once again you must start with an understanding of the basics.

WHAT IF YOU DIE WITHOUT A WILL OR ESTATE PLAN?

The answer is simple: The laws of your state and the bureaucrats of your state government take over. The rules for distribution of assets are different in each state, but if you die without a will—*intestate*—the state will distribute the largest portion of your estate to your surviving legal spouse. Next in line are your children, your parents, and other relatives starting with those who are closest blood relations.

While each state may determine the proportions of your assets to be divided among your heirs if you die without a will, generally speaking a surviving spouse will inherit the entire estate, if there are no children—even if there are surviving parents.

If there is a surviving spouse and one child, the state may order your assets distributed equally. If there are several children, the spouse may get only one-third of the assets, and the children will divide the remaining amount. Other states require that a surviving spouse receive one-half of the estate. Some states provide that the spouse gets a small fixed sum of money from the estate before the division of the remaining assets.

Many people simply presume that because they have been living apart from a spouse, their children will inherit. In the absence of a formal divorce decree, a separated spouse will inherit his or her share. Other people assume that with no near living relatives, the person with whom they have been living will inherit. But the state may go to extreme lengths to find a distant relative to claim an estate. Living with a person does not create rights to an estate.

In the absence of a will that designates a guardian for minor children, the state will make the decision—and may even place children in temporary foster care. Then the state will designate the amount and timing of monetary distributions from the estate to the children's caretakers.

By now you get the picture. Unless you live alone and have no personal possessions, you should do some form of estate planning.

WHAT ARE ESTATE TAXES?

Federal estate taxes are the taxes owed to the federal government—in cash—nine months after the date of death. The amount of the taxes is based on the size of the estate (see chart VI-1—it's worth another look!), with certain exemptions listed below. Many states also have state death taxes, and 19 states not only tax your estate at death, but place an inheritance tax on your heirs. There are only 22 states in which you do not pay additional death taxes to state government.

Since 1981, the rules for federal taxation of estates have operated under the *Unified Tax Credit*, which currently exempts the first $600,000 of an estate from federal estate taxes. There is also an *unlimited marital deduction* which allows an unlimited transfer of wealth between spouses (either while both are living or at the death of the first spouse) without any taxes. Only at the death of the second spouse does the estate tax fall due.

CHART VI-1
Federal Estate Tax Rates
How They Diminish Your Estate and Deprive Your Family

Taxable Estate	Estate Tax*
$ 600,000	$ 0
750,000	55,500
850,000	153,000
1,250,000	255,500
1,500,000	363,000
1,750,000	475,000
2,000,000	588,000
2,250,000	710,000
2,500,000	833,000
2,750,000	965,500
3,000,000	1,098,000

ON EXCESS OVER $3 MILLION
THE ESTATE TAX IS 55%

* Assumes $600,000 deduction for Unified Tax Credit.
Example: $750,000 − $600,000 = $150,000 × 37% = $55,500

The law is called the "unified credit" because it combines the value of gifts transferred out of the estate while an individual is living with the value of the estate at death. In other words, you can give away $600,000 worth of assets free from gift taxes while you are alive, or you can give the same $600,000 away free from estate taxes when you die. Give away more than that amount—except to a recognized charity, or to the donor's spouse—and the donor will owe a gift tax.

However, there is an annual exemption from this portion of the unified tax: Each individual may give up to $10,000 per year to any number of people, free from the unified estate and gift tax. That means a married couple could jointly give away $20,000 a year to each of their children (or anyone else), thereby lowering the value of their estate for tax purposes.

The whole concept of estate planning is to use these basic federal tax laws to best advantage. For example, parents who wanted to give a child the $40,000 down payment on a home could take advantage of the annual exemptions. The parents could give $20,000 ($10,000 each) to the child in December, and another $20,000 in January of the following year—

avoiding any gift tax filings and getting the money out of their estate without a tax obligation.

That's just the easy stuff. An attorney who specializes in estate planning can help you set up trusts and organize your assets to take advantage of the laws as they currently exist.

But, as Mark Twain said: "No one's property is safe while Congress is in session!" These federal estate tax laws are subject to change, and that could require changes in your planning techniques.

Chapter 56

Estate Planning Strategies

Now that you're motivated and you know the basic tax considerations, it's time to examine some of the strategies that you might use in making an estate plan.

Estate Planning Strategy #1: A Will

Your will is the basic legal document around which all of your other estate planning tools are built. Your will serves three purposes: It carries your instructions for distributing your assets to the people or institutions you name as *beneficiaries*; it names people (*executors or trustees*) to handle the distribution of those assets; and it arranges the manner of those distributions to limit your estate tax liability.

A will is always full of legal jargon, including clauses that revoke prior wills, that relate to the state of mind of the person making the will, and that relate to the need to pay taxes and debts. That's why you need a qualified lawyer. In most states, handwritten wills are illegal unless they follow proper procedures, including witnessing of the signatures. Videotaped wills have been similarly outlawed (although a videotape might provide evidence of state of mind in a controversial case). Again, making a will is not a do-it-yourself project. Use an attorney who specializes in estate planning.

Who Gets What?

Let's start with the first part of the will: the beneficiaries and your gifts (*bequests*) to them. In general, you can make your own decisions about what amounts and to which people you decide to distribute your assets. There is one important exception: In most states, you must provide for your spouse if you are still married. *You cannot disinherit your spouse.* In most states, a spouse is legally entitled to at least one-third of your probate estate.

You can arrange to put the majority of this spouse's share into a restricted trust, but income from the trust must go to the spouse. The only way to eliminate a spouse from sharing in an estate is through a legal prenuptial agreement (or a postnuptial agreement) in which both parties agree, based on legal counsel, to the waiver of inheritance rights. (See chapter 35.)

Other beneficiaries, and the amounts of the bequests they receive, are designated by you. Your lawyer will advise you to designate and name as clearly as possible the recipients of your largesse. For instance, you will designate: "my brother, William Smith," instead of just saying: "I leave to my brother . . ."

In the case of children, all children whether natural or legally adopted are presumed to be your legal heirs. You may exclude them or provide separately for them, by name. If you have any illegitimate children, you must provide for them by name or specifically prohibit a claim by them to avoid a long and costly lawsuit in the future. Your attorney will also direct you to think about how distributions should be made among grand-children.

If you're making a will at a relatively young age, you might not know exactly how much money you'll want to leave each person. So you might designate a percentage of your assets or shares in a business or residence. A will may also include specific bequests of property, jewelry, or artwork, regardless of its share in the total value of the estate.

You'll also want to clearly describe the item being distributed, as in "the double strand of oriental pearls once owned by my mother." Beware, however, of specifically naming financial assets such as stocks. You may have sold them before your death, and the estate could be obligated to go out and buy the stock in order to distribute it if you designate someone to receive 100 shares of IBM.

Naming Executors, Trustees, and Guardians

You'll need to give careful thought to the people you name to carry out the wishes expressed in your will. Obviously these will be people you trust and whom you feel are competent to carry out the moral and legal duties you are asking them to perform.

In the case of children, you may designate a guardian if both you and your spouse should perish. But the state will presume that a surviving parent is custodian of a minor child, and that presumption will only be set aside by a custody battle to prove the surviving parent is unfit. Even a divorced spouse may have rights to custody, in spite of provisions otherwise that are written into your will.

The executor of the will has a double responsibility—to carry out the intent of your wishes, and to comply with the laws and tax rules that apply. In some cases, you may choose a co-executor, naming a bank or attorney to handle much of the paperwork. You may want to state which of the co-executors has the final word on questions other than clearly legal issues, such as those revolving around investment policy of estate assets.

Trustees may be either individuals, investment professionals, or banking institutions that will be responsible for investment and distribution of assets in trusts named in or created by your will. Again, you may choose a combination of trustees, but you should state who has the final word on decisions that must be made. You should also give the beneficiary the right to change trustees under certain circumstances so that your trust is not locked into an inept bank trust department.

Giving the trust beneficiary the ability to hire and fire trustees might have adverse estate tax results. One way to avoid that problem is to have the trust documents specify that an independent third party has the authority to fire any trustee. Then the trust beneficiary, usually the surviving spouse, can be empowered to designate a new trustee.

Executors and trustees may spend a lot of time handling your estate. For this service, they are paid out of the estate assets. These people are ordinarily required to post a bond to serve in the capacity of executor, but your will may eliminate that requirement.

Tax Strategies

The third aspect of the will are trusts and other arrangements made through your will to minimize the expenses of estate taxes and probate expenses. Those will be explained in the strategies below.

Making It Legal

When your will is finally prepared, you will be called in to sign it in your attorney's office in the presence of witnesses. Then you'll receive a copy and your attorney will offer to keep a copy in his or her "vaults." That's the one service an attorney offers free of charge—vault storage for your will. Of course, your will doesn't take up much space, and it's a nice courtesy to extend, but there's another reason.

Not only does your attorney send you a bill for the legal expenses of drawing up your will. When you die, your heirs will need an attorney to take your will through the court process of *probate*—changing the names on all your assets as directed by your will.

The legal fees for shepherding an estate through probate can be many times the fees charged for writing the will. In fact, in many states probate fees are based on a percentage of the gross value of the estate. If you have a young attorney, he or she will hope to outlive you and earn the probate fees. An older attorney will have shelves of wills in the "vault," just waiting to be probated by a younger partner. That's what makes an estate planning legal practice so valuable! In the next strategy, you'll learn how to avoid the costs of probate.

Estate Planning Strategy #2: The Living Trust

The living trust is not the answer to all estate planning issues, but it certainly does create flexibility in managing estate issues. The living trust, by itself, *does not* save federal or state death taxes. But it *does* save all the costs of probating your will, while giving your estate a high degree of privacy both in death and during your lifetime should you become incapacitated and require a conservator to look after your financial affairs. Let's look at the issue of probate first.

What Is Probate?

Probate is simply the process of legally changing the title on assets owned by the deceased person into the names of his or her heirs. *Probate has nothing to do with taxes.* The probate court is the only institution that is authorized to change the title of assets owned by a dead person. This court is also responsible for resolving disputes, paying off creditors, taking an inventory of the assets of the estate, and then distributing those assets to the named beneficiaries with good legal title. If there is no will, the probate court distributes the assets according to state law.

With all this legal responsibility, you might have already guessed that the process of probate can be very expensive—and very time-consuming. While a simple probate process may be finished in less than a year, many estates take two years or more to pass through the process of probate.

Probate is also a very public process. Every detail of your finances will be available to anyone who searches these public papers at the local courthouse. And probate takes place not only in your state of residence, but in every state where you own real estate, adding to the expense.

As noted above, legal fees for taking your estate through the probate process can cost your estate plenty—perhaps as much as 10 percent of the total value of your gross estate. In states where gross valuation of assets is the basis for setting legal fees, the court will consider the value of your assets without deducting the amount of any loans such as mortgages. Probate courts in other states allow attorneys to charge any "reasonable fee." Probate costs are in addition to any federal or state death taxes.

When you have a living trust, almost the entire process of probate, and all its costs, are avoided. You have already transferred title to your property to the living trust; at your death it is simply a matter of having a successor trustee step into your place.

What Is a Conservatorship?

There is a distinct possibility that as you age you could acquire some disease such as Alzheimer's, or spend an extended period of time in the hospital for a physical illness, which makes it impossible for you to handle your own financial affairs. You'll need someone to pay your bills, write your checks, and perhaps make decisions about your assets. If you don't plan ahead, your family will have to go to court and petition to have one of them named your *conservator* or *guardian*. The guardian must then report to the court regularly on all aspects of your finances.

While a will protects you in death, it has absolutely no effect on management of your assets while you are alive but incapacitated. That's another area where a living trust has an advantage.

What Is a Revocable Living Trust?

A revocable living trust is simply a different way of holding title to your assets. You don't give up any control over your property when you establish a living trust, and you don't pay any additional taxes. You simply change the title to your assets while you are alive, into the name of the living trust. You still retain control over your assets and may dispose of them or replace them at any time because you are both the trustee and the beneficiary of the living trust. If you like, you and your spouse can be co-trustees. Your trust documents also name a successor trustee if you should die or become incapacitated.

There are some big advantages to creating a revocable living trust. First, when you die the assets titled in the name of your living trust do not pass through the probate process. Assets pass directly to your beneficiaries without any legal or probate fees because title is already held by the living trust (not by a dead person). Second, if you become disabled there will be no need to petition the court for a conservatorship. The successor trustee whom you named will automatically take over management of your assets.

This same living trust document also provides instructions for the distribution of trust assets upon your death. You can have your successor trustee manage the assets until your children reach an age you have specified. You can even include a "no-contest" clause that prohibits beneficiaries from attacking your estate plan.

Placing Your Assets Inside the Trust

When you do create a revocable living trust, it's important that you immediately retitle all your assets in the name of the trust so that those assets can avoid probate at your death. For instance, the title of your house must be transferred and your attorney will provide the necessary papers. If there is a mortgage, you'll have to notify the lender and get an approval, which should not be a problem. Your state may require that a new deed be issued when you put real estate into a trust, and that could cost about $25 for a filing fee.

You will also rename your mutual fund accounts, bank CDs, and any other major financial assets. You can do this yourself by writing to the bank or mutual fund company and enclosing a certified copy of only the first and last pages of your revocable living trust documents, and the page that grants the trustee's power.

Your account will now be named the "Susan Smith revocable living trust dated ____ / ____ / ____ , Susan Smith trustee." And when you write a check on this account or sell stocks, you'll simply add the word "trustee" after your name. Or the trust can be a joint one, such as the "Susan and John Smith revocable living trust," or the "Smith family revocable living trust dated ____ / ____ / ____ ."

There are some assets that will simply be too inconvenient to transfer into your living trust. For example, while you'll change the name on your bank CDs and money market account, you'll probably keep your ordinary checking account in your own name. (Imagine explaining to the grocery store checkout clerk why you signed your check "Susan Smith, trustee"!) Unless your car is a very expensive one, it will probably be more convenient to register it in your own name.

For the very few items left out of your living trust, you'll need a *pour-over will* to distribute those items after your death. This is the only part of your estate that will go through probate, and it should be of minimal cost because your valuable assets are already owned by your living trust.

Tax Consequences of a Living Trust

Remember, there is *no tax consequence* when you change title to these assets. Even if you have held the assets a long time, you don't have to worry about incurring a capital gains tax. Your tax basis remains the same when you transfer assets into the living trust. You'll include any trust income (such as interest from your CDs) or capital gains (on the sale of stocks and bonds held in the trust) as part of your own personal income tax return. There is no additional tax return to file for this trust. The taxpayer I.D. number for the living trust is the donor's Social Security number.

You'll note that simply establishing a revocable living trust does not save on estate (death) taxes. That type of tax savings is accomplished through the trusts established in the strategies described in the following chapter.

Advice on a Living Trust

Your estate planning attorney knows the advantages of a living trust. But most people simply ask their attorneys to "write a will," so the subject of a living trust may not come up. You may need to state specifically that you want your attorney to create a living trust estate plan, and follow through by transferring your assets into the living trust.

If you don't know a local attorney who specializes in these matters, you might want to contact Estate Planning Specialists, Inc. (800-223-9610). For a fee of $69 they'll give you a complete personalized estate analysis with recommendations for living trusts, insurance trusts, and other estate tax-saving strategies. All you have to do is fill out a simple form. They'll either send you the analysis (at least 50 pages of easily understood directions) or have a qualified estate specialist in your area explain it to you personally.

Then for a flat fee of $1,295, less your $69 estate analysis fee, they'll have all the legal forms for a living trust drawn up for your signature. And they'll assist you in transferring your assets into the trust. For an additional $500 fee they'll create your own insurance trust (see Tax-Wise Insurance Strategy #2 in chapter 53). Or you can use their recommendations as a checklist for your own personal lawyer. Either way, you've taken the first step to getting your estate problems solved.

Chapter 57

Estate Tax-Saving Strategies

There are two aspects to estate planning. The first we've already covered: getting your assets to the people you want to have them, with as little time and expense as possible.

The second aspect revolves around saving the maximum dollar amount possible on estate taxes by using the existing laws. I cannot emphasize enough that the strategies in this section require the expertise of your qualified estate planning attorney and accountant who specialize in these issues and can keep up with changes in the laws. Some of these strategies will be used in conjunction with the life insurance strategies shown in chapter 53.

Estate Tax-Saving Strategy #1: The A-B Trust

The *A-B trust* technique (also known as a *credit shelter trust*) is the simple basis for your largest estate tax savings. If you do only one estate tax planning strategy, this is the one that will save married couples and their families estate taxes on up to $1.2 million in assets.

To understand how this A-B concept works, you have to remember the basic rules of estate taxation. Every person gets a $600,000 exemption from estate taxes. Married people have a special deal called the *unlimited marital deduction*. There is no taxation on the estate of the first spouse to

461

die; on the death of the second spouse, everything over $600,000 is subject to estate taxes.

It sounds like a great deal, but think again. When the first spouse dies, you lose the $600,000 exemption on his or her estate if all assets pass to the surviving spouse. That means as much as $235,000 in tax savings would be lost forever.

But using an A-B trust correctly will preserve the $600,000 exemption and its tax savings when the first spouse dies. Here's how it should be set up in your will or living trust to come into existence at your death.

The "A" trust—including as many assets as desired—goes to the surviving spouse at death, to be managed, used, or spent by the surviving spouse in any way the survivor desires. The "A" trust, sometimes called the *marital trust*, is simply a convenient way of passing the assets along; it does not save on taxes, as there would have been no taxes on an estate passed to a surviving spouse by virtue of the unlimited marital deduction. However, on the death of the surviving spouse, all assets above $600,000—even if part of this trust—will be subject to federal estate taxes.

It's important to stress that these marital assets really do not have to be held in trust at all for tax purposes. Many female spouses are told that putting the marital estate in trust is a protection against estate taxes. Putting limitation on use of marital assets is really only a control device that is sometimes designed by male spouses and their lawyers to demonstrate a lack of trust in a woman's money management capabilities, or to "save" some assets for children at the death of the surviving spouse. Any assets that are meant to be passed to children or other beneficiaries should be placed in the restricted "B" trust.

The "B" trust is designed to hold assets that will go to the children or grandchildren at the death of the surviving spouse. But during the lifetime of the surviving spouse, income from the assets in the "B" trust (and in some instances the assets themselves) can be used for the surviving spouse's needs for health, education, or support. The trustee is generally someone other than the surviving spouse.

Where's the tax advantage of the "B" trust? The first $600,000 of assets placed in the "B" trust are exempt from federal estate taxes. Those assets can continue to grow above $600,000 within the trust, and even the growth of the assets will not be subject to estate tax. That's why it's a good idea to place assets that may appreciate rapidly inside this trust. At the death of the surviving spouse, the entire "B" trust will pass tax-free to the children for whom it was intended.

You'll need an attorney to draw up this plan to comply with your individual estate needs and your state's tax law. But when things get complicated, just remember the "A" trust stands for "alive"—money that goes directly to the surviving spouse. The "B" trust stands for "buried"— money buried in a trust at the death of the first spouse, held in the trust until the second spouse dies, whereupon it is disbursed to the children and grandchildren.

If you already have a living trust and don't have the A-B trust provision incorporated into your living trust documents, you can simply create a separate trust to function as the "B" trust. It should be funded with at least $600,000 worth of assets, and your children should be named as beneficiaries upon the death of your spouse. Income and assets from the trust can be used to support the surviving spouse. But you have taken $600,000 out of your unlimited marital transfer and out of your spouse's subsequent estate, saving on estate taxes when your spouse dies.

Remember, assets held in joint name cannot be put into separate trusts, so title your assets in the name of a living trust, or in separate names.

The Uniform Simultaneous Death Act provides that if two persons die together—for example, in an automobile or airplane accident—each is presumed to have survived the other. For instance, the husband's will is read as if the wife died first, and the wife's will is read as if her husband died before her. In that case, the marital deduction would be lost to each spouse and the estate taxes would be substantially higher. When creating an A-B trust, the possibility of simultaneous death should be addressed in the basic will or living trust documents.

Estate Tax-Saving Strategy #2: Gifts to an Irrevocable Trust

This strategy relies on the basic estate and gift tax rules that allow anyone to give away up to $10,000 per year per recipient with no tax consequences. And it assumes that you have enough assets in your estate that you'd like to start giving some of it away each year to your children or grandchildren so it won't be included in your taxable estate. This strategy also makes the assumption that you're not sure those children and grandchildren will use (spend) the money wisely if you give it to them directly.

So instead of giving money directly to children or grandchildren, you establish one or more *irrevocable trusts* and name the children or grand-children as beneficiaries of the trust. The trustee must be someone other than the donors.

Each year you make your $10,000 gift to each irrevocable trust you have set up in the name of your children or grandchildren. The trust documents will specify when the beneficiaries can receive income or assets from the trust. The donor cannot use the assets of the trust for personal benefit, but the donor may generally direct the investment of trust assets unless the assets consist of stock in the family business.

When a grandparent makes a gift to an irrevocable trust for a grandchild in order to take advantage of the annual $10,000 gift tax exclusion, there is a possibility that the gift will trigger the generation-skipping tax (see Estate Tax-Saving Strategy #4) unless the trust meets specific require-ments of the Internal Revenue Code.

The assets inside the trust grow free from estate taxes (although the trust will have to file an income tax return of its own). You have accom-plished the goal of reducing your taxable estate while allowing those assets to grow free from estate taxes.

NOTE: There's one important consideration in making gifts to an irrevoca-ble trust. In order to qualify for the gift tax exclusion, the beneficiaries of the trust must legally have an interest, or a right to get at those assets for even a brief period of time. So when you make the gift, the trustee must notify the beneficiary of his or her right to withdraw the amount of that year's gift. This is called the "Crummey provision" of the trust, after the case that tested it in court.

Estate Tax-Saving Strategy #3: The Irrevocable Life Insurance Trust

The real leverage of making an annual $10,000 gift to an irrevocable trust is to use the gift money to pay the premiums on an insurance policy every year. The death benefits are not included in the estate because the policy is owned by an irrevocable trust.

You learned in the section on life insurance that death benefits from a policy owned by the deceased are part of the estate for federal estate tax purposes, no matter who is the beneficiary. A policy owned by an insur-ance trust is *outside* the estate of the deceased.

The money that you gift to the trust each year can be used to purchase the maximum amount of term or cash value life insurance on the life of a single person, with the trust as both the owner and beneficiary of the policy. Using term life insurance inside an irrevocable life insurance trust has the advantage of allowing a younger person to buy more insurance coverage without placing a large amount of cash value buildup out of reach inside the trust. But remember that term insurance becomes very expensive at more advanced ages.

The best compromise would be to purchase a convertible term insurance policy that can later be switched into a cash value policy. In the case of a married couple, the trust can maximize its life insurance premium dollars by purchasing a second-to-die life insurance policy (see Tax-Wise Insurance Strategy #3 in chapter 53).

An independent trustee must be appointed to handle the assets of the trust. The creator of the trust cannot be the trustee. The trust has its own checking account, and the trustee uses this account to write the checks that pay the insurance premiums. Only the trustee has the power to sign the checks.

NOTE: The irrevocable life insurance trust must be set up *before* the life insurance policy is applied for, in order to avoid the inclusion of the trust assets inside the taxable estate if death occurs within three years after the purchase of the policy.

Estate Tax-saving Strategy #4: Educational Gifts to Grandchildren

If you're a grandparent who would like to leave something to your grandchildren, you really need professional advice to help you avoid something called the Generation Skipping Transfer Tax. This is basically a form of taxation designed to prevent you from saving on estate taxes by skipping over your children (who would then have estate taxes due on their death) and leaving money directly to your grandchildren.

So, if you leave money to your grandchildren, it may be taxed at 55 percent—per generation! That leaves after-tax bequests of only 20 percent of what you originally intended your grandchildren to receive. One solution is to use a special provision of the tax rules that applies only to grandparents.

In addition to the $10,000 per person per year exemption and the lifetime $600,000 exemption, grandparents may make unlimited gifts of money for the education of their grandchildren—from kindergarten through college—without incurring any gift taxes. That means the grandparent can pay the full tuition for private school or college without cutting into those other exemptions. No forms need to be filed at any time if a grandparent chooses to make this type of gift. In order to qualify, the tuition payment must go directly to the institution.

Caution: When the grandparent makes a gift of tuition, it could have income tax consequences for the grandchild's parents. When the parent has an obligation under the law to support the children, the IRS has at times construed that the amount of the tuition payment is taxable to the parents, because it relieved the parent of the legal obligation for support and education.

Terry's Tip

$$$ Grandparents who want to leave a fortune to their grandchildren can also utilize the irrevocable life insurance trust to own a second-to-die policy on the grandparents' lives, with the grandchildren as beneficiaries of the trust that receives the death proceeds.

$$$ Twentieth Century Giftrust Investors (800-345-2021) is a no-load mutual fund that allows you to set up an irrevocable trust account for a child or grandchild. Gifts to children must stay in the fund for at least 10 years or until the child reaches the age of majority, whichever is longer. The giver can designate the date, at least 10 years in the future, when the beneficiary can receive the funds. The fund invests for long-term growth and has an outstanding record. The minimum investment is $250.

Contributions must be reported on IRS Form #709 and taken against your lifetime $600,000 unified credit. (Contributions do not count against your annual $10,000 exclusion, since they are a gift of a future interest.) Annual taxes are paid directly by the fund, which sells shares to cover the tax liability, so there is no income tax reporting requirement on the part of the giver or beneficiary.

When the child reaches the age of majority, he or she can redeem the account (paying any capital gains tax on the sale of the shares), convert the account into another Twentieth Century fund, or allow the money to remain in the Giftrust fund. The advantages of this strategy are that the giver can designate the specific time in the future when the child or grandchild may receive the funds, and there is no expense to set up this irrevocable trust account.

Estate Tax-Saving Strategy #5: Use the $600,000 Exemption Now

It's entirely possible that Congress could lower the lifetime $600,000 exemption from estate and gift taxes. After all, in 1976 the exemption was only $60,000, and it was as low as $175,000 in 1981 before the current law was passed. In an era of tax attacks on the "rich," Congress might well consider lowering the estate tax exemption amount.

Some people have chosen to lock in that exemption now. Remember, the $600,000 is a *unified* credit, which means it exempts a combination of taxable gifts made during your lifetime and on your death. So wealthy people who worry about the potential reduction in the amount of the exemption being reduced have decided to make a current gift of $600,000 to an irrevocable trust.

The gift assets continue to grow and compound inside the trust, removed from any future estate tax. But the assets are now under the control of an independent trustee. As with all irrevocable trusts, the trust itself must file an income tax return.

Estate Tax-Saving Strategy #6: The Family Limited Partnership

This is a strategy that is still making its way through the legal system and may yet be challenged by the government. Simply put, the idea is to create a legal family limited partnership (or several of them) to hold assets outside the taxable estate.

One of the spouses, acting as *general partner*, holds 10 percent of the assets of the partnership. The general partner also has the voting interest. The remaining 90 percent of the assets are divided among the *limited partners*, who initially are the husband and wife.

After the partnership is established, each year the parents gift a small partnership interest to their children, subject to the $10,000 per year per person gift tax exclusion. Over a period of years, the children will own the 90 percent limited partner shares in the family limited partnership.

The general partner retains voting control over the assets, controls their investments, and can block payouts to limited partners. The general partner can even charge the family limited partnership a reasonable fee each year for managing its assets. Thus, substantial assets such as real estate can be transferred outside the parents' taxable estate over the years. In fact, the parents can even choose to make their $600,000 gift out of their limited partnership shares—transferring assets all at one time, but still maintaining control over the growth and distribution of the partnership wealth.

In addition to estate tax benefits, the real advantage of the family limited partnership may be the provision that shelters these assets from almost every type of lawsuit and from bankruptcy proceedings as well, once the assets are transferred to the limited partners. Be sure to consult your attorney before embarking on this strategy.

Estate Tax Saving Strategy #7: Dynasty & Generation Skipping Trusts

If you've accumulated wealth in your lifetime, you'd like to pass it on to the next generations free from estate taxes. Unfortunately, our estate tax laws make that almost impossible. However, in addition to the $600,000 lifetime exemption and $10,000 annual gifts exemption, each individual is allowed to give (by gift or bequest) up to $1 million to be placed in an irrevocable trust for future generations. (If you don't have $1 million, you might have the trust own an insurance policy on your life for that amount.) The trustee is instructed not to distribute the assets of the trust to beneficiaries on your death so that those assets are not subject to estate taxes when your beneficiary ultimately dies.

Indeed, the object is just the reverse: to include investments and growing assets in the trust so they can build in value as they pass to succeeding generations without being subject to estate taxes. Limited payouts can be made to your descendents, however, at the discretion of the trustees.

Eventually, however, the proceeds must be paid out in full to avoid the *rule against perpetuities* which requires that the trust terminate no later than 21 years after the death of the last possible person named under the terms of the original trust. Some states such as Idaho, South Dakota and Wisconsin do not limit the number of years that the dynasty trust can exist. Consult your professional advisor for specific advice.

Chapter 58

Charitable Trusts and Estate Planning

You don't have to be altruistic to help a favorite charity. There are several estate planning strategies that can reduce estate taxes, increase current income, benefit your favorite charity—and deal with a particular problem such as leaving money in trust for a handicapped child or grandchild.

Charitable Giving Strategy #1: An Outright Gift

The tax laws say you may make a gift to a charity in any amount without incurring any estate or gift tax consequences. In fact, a gift to a charity is an outright deduction on your income tax return—within certain limitations.

Under current tax law, individuals are entitled to itemized deductions for cash (nontangible property) contributions to a public charity in an amount up to 50 percent of adjusted gross income each year. Deductions for contributions of appreciated property such as artwork or securities are generally limited to 30 percent of AGI. Any excess amount may be carried forward and deducted in the five-year period after the year of contribution.

There are additional limitations on deductions for gifts of tangible personal property made to a recognized charity. If the gift is not used for the charity's tax-exempt purpose, you may deduct only your cost basis, not the appreciated value. That is, if you give a piece of art to a museum, you may deduct the current, appreciated value. If you give the artwork to a hospital which sells your gift to raise money for research, then you may only deduct its cost basis. Consult your tax advisor before making such a gift.

Until the Tax Act of 1993, the appreciation over cost of all gifts of tangible personal property such as artwork and securities was considered a tax preference item for the alternative minimum tax. The 1993 act provides that if the property was owned for at least one year before being gifted, the gain is exempt from the alternative minimum tax. Also, starting in 1994, charitable deductions in excess of $250 are not allowed without a written substantiation of receipt from the charitable organization.

Charitable Giving Strategy #2: Fidelity Charitable Gift Fund

As of this writing, only Fidelity Investments offers this unique concept in charitable giving. It allows you to have the benefits of your own private charitable foundation—without any of the legal expenses or paperwork.

The Fidelity Charitable Gift Fund (800-682-4438) allows donors to contribute to one of three Fidelity-managed asset pools: a growth pool, an equity-income pool, and an interest income pool—all of which are managed by Fidelity mutual fund managers. The donor may contribute cash or securities, including securities that have already appreciated in value. The donor then takes an immediate tax deduction for the contribution.

The money remains in the funds (it can be switched between pools once a year) until the donor issues instructions to have a contribution made to an IRS-recognized charity. While the money is in the investment pools, it grows tax-free, just as in a charitable foundation, so the ultimate gifts to selected charities can be larger. The donor has no tax liability for the increase in value of the shares in the fund. If the donor makes a gift of appreciated stock to the fund, there is no capital gains tax.

Fidelity handles all the paperwork, including making the donations, which can be sent in the donor's name, in any other name, or even anonymously. The donor receives quarterly and year-end account statements. At the death of the donor, the proceeds can be automatically distributed to the charities of choice, or the donor can name a successor to continue to oversee the account and its distributions.

The minimum amount required to open an account in the Fidelity Charitable Gift Fund is $10,000, with a minimum of $2,500 in any one pool. Additional investments in the fund can be made for a minimum of $2,500. The minimum gift designation amount is $250—and for accounts under $50,000, the donor may designate five distributions per calendar year. Larger accounts may distribute funds more frequently.

The cost of this service is intended to be minimal, and the fund is charging no fees through December 31, 1993.

Those who might benefit from using this fund are people who want to make regular contributions to charity over the years, but take an immediate tax deduction to offset a year of high current income. People who have appreciated securities can donate them via the fund without paying capital gains tax—and spread their contributions over future years. And younger givers might use the fund as the start of a long-term program of gifting, allowing assets to grow over the years.

Charitable Giving Strategy #3: The Charitable Remainder Trust

Here's a strategy that allows you to give assets to your favorite charity at a future date, get tax benefits, and still continue to receive a stream of income from the gifted assets during your lifetime. No wonder charitable remainder trusts are receiving more and more attention from estate planners. Here's the concept.

Your attorney sets up a charitable remainder trust. You make a gift of money or assets to the trust—preferably assets that have appreciated, such as stocks you have held over the years. By gifting, you remove the asset from your estate and therefore eliminate the estate tax on its value. The trust will then sell the asset and use the proceeds to purchase an income-producing asset in its place.

Then the assets remain in trust, but you—or whomever you designate—receive a stream of income from the trust for the rest of your life, or the lives of your beneficiaries. That stream of income can start immediately, or you can wait until later, perhaps after retirement.

The charitable remainder trust pays no capital gains tax when it sells the appreciated asset. As a result, there is more money to be invested in income-producing assets such as bonds or money market funds, which will produce a stream of income for the beneficiary of the trust—probably you.

You, as the grantor of the trust, are allowed a sizeable immediate income tax deduction on your gift of assets to the fund. You can't deduct the entire amount of your contribution because this is a gift of a *future interest* to the charity. You will still be receiving income from the gift on a current basis. The amount of your immediate deduction depends on your age, the value of your property transferred, and the amount of the payout you retain.

Here's an example: You paid $100,000 for a piece of property that has now appreciated to $500,000. You want to sell it, but you know that the capital gains tax will take a huge bite out of the proceeds. Instead, you donate the property to your charitable remainder trust, which sells it and invests the entire proceeds of $500,000 in bonds that pay all income to you, the beneficiary of the trust.

You've increased your income and taken a portion of the gift as an immediate tax deduction. At your death (or the death of you and your spouse), the assets of the trust will go to the charity of your choice. This is only a good deal if you know you won't have to dip into those assets in the future. You certainly don't want to place all your assets in a charitable remainder trust.

There's one other element of this strategy. You might have already noticed that in order to get your current tax deduction and higher income, you've sacrificed some of the assets you hoped to leave for your children. So, along with the charitable remainder trust you'll want to set up an irrevocable insurance trust, following the guidelines in Estate Tax-Saving Strategy #3 in chapter 57. Use a portion of the higher income you're now earning to gift an annual amount and buy a life insurance policy in that trust—with your children as the beneficiaries of the trust. The death benefits will replace the assets given to the charity.

Now you've avoided capital gains taxes, taken a current tax deduction, increased your income, reduced the size of your taxable estate, given a gift to your favorite charity, and maintained a sizable tax-free estate for your children.

This strategy can work particularly well when the income beneficiary is a person who is disabled or incapable of handling money. The charitable remainder trust will manage the assets and distribute income to the beneficiary for life. When the beneficiary dies, the charity gets the remainder.

Your attorney, financial planner, or even attorneys for your favorite charity will be able to advise you of the latest legal and tax consequences of this maneuver.

Charitable Giving Strategy #4: The Charitable Lead Trust

The charitable lead trust is really just the reverse of a charitable remainder trust. Under this grantor trust, you give your money to the charity now— and take a deduction for the present value of the charity's interest in the gift. The charity earns income from the assets for at least ten years, but no longer than 20 years. Then, at your death, the assets revert to your heirs— with a substantial savings on estate taxes.

Charitable Giving Strategy #5: Charitable Gift Annuity

This is another strategy designed to give appreciated assets to a charity, which can sell them without worrying about capital gains taxes and use the principal to provide an income for the donor.

The charitable gift annuity allows an individual to transfer cash, stock, or other property to a qualified charity in exchange for a guaranteed fixed amount of income for the remainder of his or her (or both spouses') life. The charity gets the value of the liquidated property over the amount that it costs to purchase the annuity. The donor receives a current deduction, which is based on the amount ultimately given to the charity.

There are some disadvantages to this type of strategy. The income from the annuity is fixed and not adjustable for inflation. Also, the arrangement must be structured correctly with the donor and donor's designated survivor as the only annuitants, or else any gain must be reported on the sale of the original donated securities.

Again, your attorney and the attorney for the charity you designate will be able to guide you in this strategy.

Chapter 59

Estate Planning Strategies: Giving Away Power

When you think about estate planning, it's usually in conjunction with giving away money or other assets. But an equally important aspect of estate planning is judiciously giving away *power*—authorizing someone else to make decisions in your place.

Before giving someone else the power to make decisions, commit your money, or sign your name, you must carefully think over the potential consequences and consider how that power might be used. The following strategies show how some of these powers might be granted.

Power Transfer Strategy #1: The Nondurable Power of Attorney

The nondurable power of attorney, sometimes called a *limited-term power of attorney*, is a strategy you might use when you want to grant someone the authority to act in a specific case. Perhaps you will be out of town and you want your attorney to close a real estate transaction, or you will be in the hospital for a week and need someone to sign a business contract on your behalf. This type of power can be used only if you—the principal—could have acted on your own behalf in a specific instance.

Power Transfer Strategy #2: The Durable Power of Attorney

The durable power of attorney goes into effect immediately after you sign it, authorizing your agent to make all types of decisions on your behalf, and specifically stating that it remains in effect if the grantor of the power becomes incompetent.

This is the type of power that needs to be granted by someone who is in the early stages of Alzheimer's disease, for example, to allow a relative or an attorney to act on his or her behalf. Generally there are two types of durable power of attorney—one for *property* and one for *healthcare*.

The *property durable power of attorney* will authorize someone to make business or financial decisions on your behalf. It can allow your agent to renew your certificate of deposit at the bank, or instruct your broker to sell stocks, or even allow your agent to sell your home or business, based on the agent's determination of what is best for you. Clearly, this is not a power you want to designate lightly.

The *healthcare durable power of attorney* authorizes your agent to make decisions relating to choice of hospital, doctors, or medication. If an elderly person requires special medical care or if surgery is required, the healthcare power of attorney will allow someone else to sign the required consent forms.

In some cases, two or more people may be named to serve simultaneously to make decisions under the durable power of attorney—to act as a sort of balance against bad decisions. A successor should also be named, in case the originally named person cannot serve.

Power Transfer Strategy #3: The "Springing" Power of Attorney

While each of the durable powers of attorney described above goes into effect immediately after the papers are signed, there is another way to put these powers into effect at a delayed date. The *springing power of attorney* becomes effective only once a specific test for incompetency or incapacity is met. Then the power "springs" to life. This type of power can be challenged in court—even by the person who originally granted it—and the court will ascertain whether the person is really incompetent.

Power Transfer Strategy #4: The Living Will

Generally the healthcare power of attorney has a separate paragraph that allows you to initial your choice of options in case of a terminal condition. On most forms, these options range from taking a conservative attitude about treatment to aggressively terminating life support. But the health-care power of attorney is not a substitute for a separate *living will*, which specifically directs those in charge of your care to "pull the plug" under hopeless and terminal circumstances, and if you are being kept alive only by artificial means. In most states, the living will is a separate form created by statute.

If you do not have this type of document, the presumption is that you want treatment to continue. In the absence of a living will, medical treatment will be prolonged unless a lawsuit is brought by family members to stop such treatment. It is far less expensive and emotionally taxing to make your wishes known while you still have the capacity to do so.

Chapter 60

Social Security

It's only appropriate to start this coverage of issues that concern seniors and their families with a discussion of Social Security. Social Security has an impact on everyone's life right from birth. Today, parents can apply for a Social Security number for a newborn at the same time they fill in the information for the birth certificate. The IRS requires a Social Security number on parents' income tax returns in order to claim all dependents age one and older.

There are three major Social Security trust funds: the Old Age and Survivors (OASI) fund; the Medicare fund; and the Disability fund. Earlier in this book we noted the debate about the solvency of these funds into the 21st century. For those retiring now, that's not likely to become a problem. If you're turning 65 this year and spent your lifetime working for a nongovernmental agency, you've probably paid into Social Security for your entire working history. Now, it's time to collect.

Just to make sure you collect all the benefits to which you (and your family) are entitled, and to help you make smart decisions about when to start collecting your Social Security benefits, you should carefully consider the rules and strategies in this chapter.

Your first step should be to contact Social Security to make sure your earnings record is correct and to ask for their estimate of your potential benefits. It's a smart strategy to check your Social Security earnings record every three years to make sure it is correct.

477

To get this information, call 800-772-1213 and ask for a Request for Earnings and Benefit Estimate Statement. You'll receive a simple form in the mail. Complete it and return it to the address listed on the form. Within about three weeks you'll receive a complete statement of your earnings history, along with estimates for your benefits if you retire at 65, at 70, or at any age below 65.

Social Security Strategy #1: Understand Your Basic Benefits

Before you can make good decisions about when to collect on Social Security, you must understand how your benefits are calculated. This information may affect your decision to keep working or to retire earlier.

How You Qualify for Benefits

When you work and pay Social Security (FICA) taxes, you earn Social Security *credits* or *quarters of coverage*. In 1995, you earn one credit (or quarter) for each $630 of earnings. That dollar amount is indexed upward every year.

You need a certain number of credits to qualify for retirement benefits. If you were born in 1929 or later, you need 40 credits, representing ten years of work. People born before 1929 need slightly fewer credits to qualify (39 credits if you were born in 1928, for example).

Many people stop working at some point in their life and stop paying into Social Security. But those credits you have already earned remain on your Social Security records, and if you later return to work you can add more credits so that you can qualify for benefits.

You must have the required number of credits to qualify for benefits— but the number of credits on your record does not determine the size of the monthly benefit you will receive.

How Monthly Benefit Amounts Are Determined

The size of your monthly retirement check from Social Security is based on your earnings averaged over most of your working life. If you earned higher wages—and paid more money into Social Security—you will receive a higher monthly check at retirement. If you had lower earnings, or did not work in some years, your monthly check will be lower.

For everybody born after 1928, and retiring in 1991 or later, your highest 35 years of wages are used to compute Social Security benefits. For people born before 1929, fewer years of wages are averaged. The total of covered wages, divided by the number of years, determines your average adjusted earnings. That average number is then multiplied using a formula weighted to favor low-income workers. Still, higher-income workers receive higher monthly checks.

Once you start receiving monthly benefits from Social Security, you can expect the size of your check to increase annually in line with inflation. This is called a COLA, or cost-of-living adjustment.

The size of your monthly check is also determined by the age at which you retire. Currently, 65 is the earliest age at which you can get full retirement. However, the retirement age is scheduled to increase gradually to age 67. As you can see from chart VI-2, this change in full retirement age will affect people born in 1938 and later.

How Early Retirement Affects Your Benefits

If you start taking your benefits at the earliest possible retirement age, 62, your benefits will be permanently reduced by 20 percent of what you

CHART VI-2
Age to Receive Full Social Security Benefits

Year of Birth	Full Retirement Age
1937 or earlier	65
1938	65 and 2 months
1939	65 and 4 months
1940	65 and 6 months
1941	65 and 8 months
1942	65 and 10 months
1943–1954	66
1955	66 and 2 months
1956	66 and 4 months
1957	66 and 6 months
1958	66 and 8 months
1959	66 and 10 months
1960 and later	67

would have received. If you retire at age 63, the reduction is 13.33 percent; and if you retire at age 64, your benefits are permanently reduced by 6.66 percent.

But early retirement can affect your level of benefits in another important way. As noted above, the size of your check depends on averaging your years of earnings. In 1995, up to $61,200 of earnings can be credited to your account. But 20 years ago, the maximum was $7,800 a year. Of course, those differences are indexed to today's dollars, so the discrepancy is not as large as it appears. Still, adding those higher earnings years can result in a higher monthly benefit. If you retire early, you will get 80 percent of a smaller basic benefit. (See Social Security Strategy #5 in this chapter for help in deciding whether to retire early.)

Terry's Tip:

$$$ Always work at least 35 years, if possible, before retiring. Because the calculations require the use of 35 years of wages, if you retire with fewer years, a "zero" year or two will be added into your average, substantially reducing your benefits.

How Delayed Retirement Affects Your Benefits

If you wait until after age 65 to retire, your Social Security benefits may be increased because of two factors:

1. You are probably adding high-earning years to your record, and that will increase your basic monthly benefits.

2. Your benefit will be increased by a specific percentage amount for every extra year you work. The percentage by which your monthly benefit will increase for every year you delay retirement is dependent on the year in which you were born (see chart VI-3).

Terry's Tip:

$$$ Even if you delay your retirement past age 65, be sure to sign up for Medicare insurance at your Social Security office.

CHART VI-3

Effects of Delayed Retirement on Social Security Benefits

Year of Birth	Yearly Percentage Increase
1916 or earlier	1 %
1917–1924	3
1925–1926	3.5
1927–1928	4
1929–1930	4.5
1931–1932	5
1933–1934	5.5
1935–1936	6
1937–1938	6.5
1939–1940	7
1941–1942	7.5
1943 or later	8

Social Security Strategy #2: Understand Family Benefits

Once you have started receiving Social Security benefits, other members of your family may also be entitled to a monthly check.

Family members who may collect benefits include:

Your spouse if he/she is age 62 or older;

Your spouse if he/she is taking care of your child who is under age 16 or disabled;

Children up to age 18;

Children age 18–19, if they are full-time secondary school students;

Children age 18 or older, if they are disabled before age 22.

Benefits for Ex-Spouses

A divorced spouse who is age 62 or older and unmarried can claim benefits on the account of an ex-spouse if the worker is at least age 62, and if the marriage lasted at least ten years. That rule applies even if there is no support order. Even if the worker has not retired but is eligible for benefits, the divorced spouse can get benefits if he or she has been divorced at least two years. (The benefits granted to an ex-spouse do not affect benefits paid to a current spouse.)

A divorced spouse is entitled to reduced survivor's benefits after the death of the former spouse, if the survivor is at least 60 years old (50, if disabled) and was married at least ten years before the divorce. The surviving divorced spouse is entitled to full benefits at age 65, or at any age if caring for a child who is either under 16, or disabled, or receiving benefits on the same record.

A divorced spouse can get benefits on the basis of childcare only if the former spouse dies, and only if the child is the deceased spouse's natural or legally adopted child. A separation short of divorce has no effect on a spouse's right to benefits.

Benefits for Widows or Widowers

A widow or widower receives a lump sum burial payment of $255. The survivor also is entitled to a monthly benefit if he or she is at least 60 years old (50, if disabled) or is caring for a child who is under 16, disabled, or who was receiving benefits on the same account.

A widowed person who remarries at age 60 or older may continue to receive either a full survivor's benefit or a spouse's benefit on the new spouse's account, whichever is larger. If a widowed person remarries under the age of 60, survivor's benefits are terminated. If that subsequent marriage ends, survivor's benefits will be reinstated upon application.

Amount of Family Benefits

A spouse who retires at age 65 receives one half of the retired worker's full benefit. If the spouse takes benefits before age 65, the benefit will be reduced. For instance, if a spouse retires at age 62, the benefit will be 37.5 percent of the worker's full retirement benefit. If the worker is getting reduced benefits from early retirement, it does not reduce the spouse's benefits.

At the worker's death, the surviving spouse age 65 or older will get 100 percent of what the worker was receiving. However, a surviving spouse may retire as early as age 60 and receive a reduced benefit on the deceased worker's account. The survivor's benefit would also be reduced if the worker had been receiving lower early retirement benefits.

If both spouses, or previous spouses, have earned credits, Social Security will automatically calculate benefits on both a spousal basis and an individual basis and pay the higher of the two amounts. The form you fill out to apply for benefits will alert Social Security to accounts of spouses, or former spouses, on which you might be eligible to collect benefits.

Eligible children each receive up to one-half of the full benefit. But there is an annual limitation on total benefits that can be paid to spouses and children in one year. It's called the *family maximum*. If the eligible benefits exceed the limit, spousal and children's benefits are reduced proportionately, but the worker's benefit remains the same.

Social Security Strategy #3: Understand How Postretirement Work Reduces Benefits

You may decide to continue to work after you start receiving your Social Security benefits. If you earn wages above a specific limit, your Social Security benefits will be reduced. However, people who are age 70 or older can earn an unlimited amount of extra wages with no reduction in benefits.

Earnings Limits

The earnings limits for 1995 are as follows:

   Age 65–69: $11,280;

   Under age 65: $8,160.

If you are age 65 through 69, $1 is deducted from your benefits for every $3 you earn above the limit. If you are under age 65, $1 is deducted from your benefits for every $2 you earn above the limit. If a worker earns income well above the limit, family member benefits may be similarly reduced. Also, if family members who are collecting benefits on the account of a worker earn more than the limits, their benefits will be reduced.

What Income Is—and Is NOT—Included

For purposes of reducing your Social Security benefits, only gross wages and income from self-employment are considered. But "wages" include bonuses, commissions, fees, vacation pay, tips, severance pay, and non-cash compensation such as meals or living quarters. In determining income from self-employment, you may have to prove that you have substantially reduced your time at work from the amount you worked before retirement, so keep records of the time you spend in business activities. Any income earned outside the United States is subject to the same earnings test—even if those earnings are not covered by Social Security.

You are allowed unlimited amounts of the following types of income: investment income, interest, capital gains, rental income, pensions from work that was covered by Social Security, other government benefits such as veterans benefits, annuities, gifts, or inheritances, moving or travel expenses, jury duty pay.

If you receive a pension from work that was not covered under Social Security, such as federal civil service (before 1984) or some state or local government pensions, then your Social Security benefits may be reduced or offset by the other pension.

The Monthly Rule

In your first year of retirement, your earnings may get special treatment. Under the monthly rule you can receive a full Social Security check for any month you are retired, no matter what your yearly earnings. However, to be eligible for a Social Security check that month, your earnings must be under a monthly limit. (Earnings are counted in the month they were earned, not the month they were paid.) For 1995, the monthly earnings limit for ages 65 to 69 is $940. The monthly earnings limit under age 65 is $680.

Terry's Tip:

$$$ It may make sense to retire at the beginning of the year. If you retire in September of the previous year, you can use the monthly earnings test for only four months—September, October, November, and December. But if you wait until January to retire, you can use the monthly earnings test for the entire year—and only lose benefits for any month in which you exceed the $880 gross earnings limit.

Filing Requirements

If you earn above the limits, you must report those earnings to Social Security by April 15 of the year following the calendar year in which the income is earned. This Annual Report of Earnings is a separate report from your federal income tax return, and there is a penalty for failure to file a timely report.

If you know in advance that you will earn wages above the limit, you must file an estimate with Social Security. If your estimate is incorrect, an adjustment will be made. Either you will receive a refund of benefits withheld, or you will have to repay some of the benefits you were given during that year.

In the year you turn 70, you must report excess earnings for the months before your birthday month. Earnings in your birthday month or later in the year will not affect your Social Security benefits. In subsequent years you do not have to file a report at all.

When Social Security Benefits Are Taxed

The examples above concern instances where the amount of your Social Security benefits may be *reduced* because of wage income above specific limits. But there is also a situation where the actual Social Security benefits may be *taxed* based on a combination of your wages and investment income, your Social Security benefits, plus other income that would normally be considered nontaxable.

There are two elements to determining how much you might be required to pay in taxes on your Social Security benefits. First, you must determine the threshold at which Social Security benefits *begin* to be taxable for you. Second, you must determine *how much* of your benefits will be taxed.

You start by calculating a figure called Modified Adjusted Gross Income (MAGI)—which is used only for the purpose of calculating taxes on Social Security benefits. MAGI includes your Adjusted Gross Income (the last line on page one of your tax return) plus two other items: a) all tax-exempt income you received during the year (such as municipal bond income), and b) one-half of the Social Security benefits you received during the year. Add them all together and you have your MAGI.

MAGI is the critical number for determining the threshold at which Social Security benefits *begin* to be taxed. If you're filing a joint return and

MAGI is larger than $32,000, then some portion of your Social Security benefits will have to be added back to page one of your tax return as taxable income ($25,000 MAGI on a single return). If MAGI is more than $44,000 on a joint return ($34,000 on a single return), then an even greater portion of your Social Security benefits will be taxed as income.

Social Security Strategy #4: Deciding Whether to Keep Working

Should you continue to work? You'll need a pencil and paper to answer this question. The earnings test is based on gross wages. But to balance the issue, you'll need to figure out what you might earn—and then subtract any income taxes you might owe, plus the Social Security (FICA) taxes that you would owe on this income. Then you have to subtract the expenses of going back to work: transportation, lunch, work clothes, etc. Then you have to subtract the $1 reduction in Social Security benefits for every $3 you earn above the $11,280 limit in 1995.

You might factor in one other calculation. The penalties on earning income continue only until age 70. After that, you can earn an unlimited amount of wages or self-employment income without being penalized. If you delay the start of Social Security benefits until age 70, you will receive a higher monthly check. If you do not need the income now, and plan to continue working—and if you plan to live a very long time—you might postpone collecting Social Security (but not Medicare) until age 70. Or, as in the case of most people, you can decide to limit your earnings just to the amount that will not reduce your Social Security benefits.

There is no one "right" answer. If the financial and psychological benefits of working exceed the financial penalties and costs, you can join the millions of Americans who continue to work after starting to collect their Social Security benefits.

Social Security Strategy #5: Deciding Whether to Retire Early

You know that if you retire at age 62, the monthly benefit you collect from Social Security will be permanently reduced by 20 percent (see Strategy #1 above). Is it worth taking the reduced benefits now, at age 62?

In 1995, the maximum annual benefit you can collect if you retire at age

62 is $973 per month. You'll also collect the same amount in 1996 and 1997. By the time you reach age 65, you'll have collected a total of $35,028—money you would not have received if you'd waited to collect at age 65.

Now, figure that the maximum benefit at age 65 (based on current maximums) is $1,199 per month in 1995. (Your maximum might have been slightly higher because it will rise in the course of three years.) That's an extra $2,712 a year, over the benefits you get by retiring at age 62.

Divide the extra $35,028 you received for ages 62–64 by the extra $2,712 you would be receiving from age 65 on. The result shows you'd have to live 12.9 years longer just to break even.

There's a real advantage to having the money in the early years as opposed to spread out over the later years. There's that time-value-of-money concept again. And, of course, I've ignored cost-of-living increases, which you'd receive under either situation.

At first, it may not seem worthwhile to take the early retirement cut of 20 percent in your benefits forever. But you'll have to decide how long you're likely to live and whether it pays to start taking those lower benefits sooner. It's a decision only you can make for yourself—but at least now you have the facts. To make your own decision in future years, check with the Social Security administration for the current benefit levels.

Keep in mind that those who will be eligible for retirement at age 67 in the future will still have the opportunity to retire early at age 62. But they will suffer an even greater reduction in benefits, and it will take more years to break even.

Social Security Strategy #6: Electing Disability Benefits

Social Security may cover disabilities at any age. However, for purposes of retirement, it is important to note that disability benefits are higher than most reduced retirement benefits. So if you become seriously disabled *after* taking early retirement, but *before* age 65, you should switch to disability benefits if you qualify. Disability benefits end at age 65; but if you were disabled for several months, your post-65 retirement benefit will be slightly higher because those months do not count as early retirement.

Social Security: A Final Note

The discussion of Social Security in this chapter has been based on retirement issues and strategies to deal with Social Security rules and regulations. But only about 60 percent of people who receive Social Security are retirees. The remaining hundreds of millions of dollars each year are paid out in benefits to survivors, to dependents of retirees and disabled workers, and to Medicare recipients. Social Security also administers the SSI (supplemental income) program, which is paid out of general revenue funds.

For more information on your Social Security entitlements, call the Social Security Administration toll-free at 800-772-1213. Remember: You *must apply* for Social Security benefits in order to receive them.

Use that same toll-free number to make an appointment at your local Social Security office, where you will apply for benefits, and to find out what documentation you'll need to prove your eligibility claim. You should sign up at least three months before you become eligible.

And one more strategy: Consider having your benefits check deposited directly into your bank account. It doesn't cost any more, but it is safer and more convenient—and it saves money for the government!

Chapter 61

Medicare and Medicare Supplement Insurance

When you reach your 65th birthday, if you have met the work requirements to be eligible for Social Security, you are automatically eligible for Medicare—a national health insurance program for seniors. You are also eligible if you are qualified to claim benefits on the account of someone else, such as a spouse, or an ex-spouse if you were married at least ten years. You can even qualify for Medicare before age 65 if you have received Social Security disability payments for at least two years, or if you have severe kidney disease. But Medicare is a voluntary program, and you must apply for your benefits through your local Social Security office.

As you'll see in the health insurance strategies described below, Medicare will not provide enough coverage to protect you completely, so you'll need some additional insurance as well. This is usually called a *Medicare supplement policy* or a *Medigap policy*. Or you may be covered through your employer's health insurance if you continue to work. Strategies to maximize your healthcare coverage are detailed below. But first you need to understand just what Medicare covers, what it doesn't cover, and what expenses you may be obligated to pay.

MEDICARE COVERAGE

There are two parts to Medicare: Part A is the hospitalization portion, which also covers *skilled* nursing care, hospice care, and some home healthcare. You automatically qualify for this free hospitalization portion of Medicare if you have enough Social Security credits from working in covered jobs. If you do not have enough credits to qualify for premium-free Medicare hospital insurance, you may be able to buy it. The premium for Medicare hospital insurance is $261 per month in 1995.

Medicare Part B is the medical insurance part of the plan, which covers physicians' services, certain lab testing, outpatient treatment and surgery, plus certain medical supplies, and some prescription drugs. Part B of Medicare is optional, and anyone who receives Medicare medical insurance must pay a monthly premium $46.10 in 1995, which is automatically deducted from your monthly Social Security check.

People who buy the hospital insurance (Part A) must also buy the medical insurance (Part B), but they can cancel the hospital coverage and continue to buy the medical insurance.

Terry's Tip:

$$$ Plan to sign up for both parts of Medicare at least three months before your 65th birthday to get prompt coverage and the lowest premiums.

Always sign up for Part A because it doesn't cost you anything if you are eligible. Even if you are covered by a company health plan, Part A will pick up the deductibles that are not covered by your company plan.

Also sign up for Part B—unless you continue to be covered by your own or your spouse's healthcare plan at work. Even then, Part B would pick up the expenses the company plan does not cover. Check the rules of your company plan, because many require employees or spouses over age 65 to use Medicare as their primary health insurance, although the company plan may cover some of the expenses left uncovered by Medicare.

How to Enroll in Medicare

Several months before your 65th birthday, you should start checking on your eligibility for both Social Security and Medicare. Contact your nearest Social Security office to get started.

The initial enrollment period for Medicare begins three months before you turn 65. If you wait, it could delay start of your coverage by several months. If you don't apply for Part B during the initial period, which lasts for three months after the date of your 65th birthday, your coverage could be further delayed, and you will be required to pay premiums that are 10 percent higher for each year you delayed applying. You can sign up for Part A of Medicare at any time after you reach age 65 with no penalty.

The exception to this premium increase for delayed signup for Part B is for people who can demonstrate that they were covered by an employer health plan when they were first eligible to enroll in Medicare.

If you don't sign up for Medicare medical insurance during the initial enrollment period, there is a general enrollment period held every year from January 1 through March 31. For those who sign up during this general enrollment period, coverage begins on July 1 that year. The one exception is for people who were previously covered by an employer plan: In that case, you may sign up at any time in the seven months following the end of your employer's coverage, and coverage will start the first day of the following month.

What Medicare Doesn't Cover

When you sign up for Medicare, you'll get a list of everything the program covers—and it may seem very complete. But a little study will show you that there are a number of medical costs that Medicare doesn't begin to pay for, and a number of costs that Medicare requires you to share. Understanding these gaps in coverage will be important when you look around for Medicare supplement policies in the strategies listed below.

Here's what you still must pay, even if you have Medicare.

Medicare Part A:

1. You must pay a deductible of $716, in 1995, which you must pay when you enter the hospital for each benefit period. Depending on the number of hospitalizations and their frequency, you could be required to pay more than one deductible amount in a calendar year.

2. You must pay a portion of hospital costs only if your stay lasts longer than 60 days. (You must, however, pay hospital costs such as private nurses, and the extra cost of a private room, unless they are determined by Medicare to be medically necessary.)

For your 61st to 90th day in the hospital you must pay a co-payment of $179 a day in 1995. If your hospital stay lasts longer, Medicare will not pay—unless you choose to dip into your lifetime reserve of 60 additional days, in which case you must pay $358 a day for coverage.

If you need skilled nursing care, Medicare will pay nothing toward the first 20 days, and you must pay $89.50 per day in 1995 for the 21st to 100th day of skilled nursing care. Medicare pays nothing after the 100th day.

Medicare Part B:

3. You must pay a $100 annual deductible, and 20 percent of doctors' services and other outpatient services—plus, any amount the doctor charges above what is considered "reasonable and ordinary" fees.

To make sure that Medicare will pick up at least 80 percent of your doctors' bills, make sure your physicians will accept *Medicare assignment*. That means the doctor will waive any charges above Medicare's reasonable standard fee for the service he or she provides.

4. You must pay for routine physical examinations, glasses, hearing aids, dentures, ordinary dental and podiatric care, and most prescription drugs, except those administered while you are in a hospital.

5. You must pay for medical and hospital bills you incur while traveling abroad (with a few exceptions for Canadian or Mexican hospitals if they are the closest facility to your home).

As you can see from this list, you need some extra insurance to plug all those "gaps." That's where Medicare supplement or Medigap policies step in.

MEDICARE SUPPLEMENT POLICIES

In July 1992, a new law went into effect that made it much easier to pick a Medicare supplement policy. Recognizing that many seniors were confused and often pushed into buying multiple supplement policies, the new law established ten standard Medigap policies and prohibited insurance companies from selling duplicate coverage to people who already have policies. Now companies must compete on service and price instead of different product design or salesmanship. Here's how the new policies work.

Medigap Strategy #1: Understand the Ten Standard Supplement Policies

The ten new policies are named by letter, from A to J. All companies must offer the basic policy A but can choose among the others the ones they want to offer. Each state also has the right to decide which policies can be offered within its borders. As a consumer, you know that any policy with the same letter will cover the same services—no matter which company is offering that policy.

Only in three states (Massachusetts, Minnesota, and Wisconsin) are there slight differences in the core policies that are allowed. But even in those states, insurers must follow the rules against selling duplicate policies.

What do the policies cover? Policy A, the most basic policy, and all other policies cover the following:

Part A: 20 percent co-insurance for days 61 through 90 and lifetime reserve days;

365 additional days of hospitalization, above 60 lifetime reserve days;

Part B: co-insurance (the 20 percent of Medicare-approved expenses);

First 3 pints of blood each year.

Medicare supplement policies B through J offer increased coverage (see chart VI-4). They pick up the annual hospital deductible and then add co-insurance for skilled nursing, benefits for foreign travel emergency care, and at-home recovery care. The policies with the maximum coverage will pay for the portion of doctors' bills that are above the "reasonable" Medicare limit. Some also pay for preventive care, and for prescription drugs up to limits of either $1,250 or $3,000 per year.

As the coverage goes up, so does the cost!

Medigap Strategy #2: Compare Costs

Although each policy is standardized, the costs certainly vary from company to company—and within the same company from state to state. Those differences occur because large national plans recognize there are

Chart VI-4

Ten Standard Medicare Supplement Insurance Plans

Medicare supplement insurance can be sold in only ten standard plans. This chart shows the benefits included in each plan. Every company must make available Plan A. Some plans may not be available in your state. The newly standardized policies make it easy for you to compare the costs of identical policies issued by different companies.

A	B	C	D	E	F	G	H	I	J
Basic Benefits	Basic Benefits	Basic Benefits	Basic Benefits	Basic Benefits	Basic Benefits	Basic Benefits	Basic Benefits	Basic Benefits	Basic Benefits
		Skilled Nursing Co-Insurance	Skilled Nursing Co-Insurance	Skilled Nursing Co-Insurance	Skilled Nursing Co-Insurance	Skilled Nursing Co-Insurance	Skilled Nursing Co-Insurance	Skilled Nursing Co-Insurance	Skilled Nursing Co-insurance
	Part A Deductible	Part A Deductible	Part A Deductible	Part A Deductible	Part A Deductible	Part A Deductible	Part A Deductible	Part A Deductible	Part A Deductible
		Part B Deductible			Part B Deductible				Part B Deductible

CHART VI-4 (continued)

				Part B Excess (100%)	Part B Excess (80%)		Part B Excess (100%)	Part B Excess (100%)
		Foreign Travel Emergency	Foreign Travel Emergency	Foreign Travel Emergency	Foreign Travel Emergency	Foreign Travel Emergency	Foreign Travel Emergency	Foreign Travel Emergency
		At-Home Recovery			At-Home Recovery		At-Home Recovery	At-Home Recovery
						Basic-Drugs ($1,250 Limit)	Basic-Drugs ($1,250 Limit)	Basic-Drugs ($3,000 Limit)
			Preventive Care					Preventive Care

Basic Benefits: Included in all plans.
Hospitalization: Part A co-insurance plus coverage for 365 additional days after Medicare benefits end.
Medical Expenses: Part B co-insurance (20 percent of Medicare-approved expenses).
Blood: First 3 pints of blood each year.
SOURCE: Health Insurance Association of America.

different costs for medical services in different localities. So you must be sure you are comparing the same coverages for the same state of residence.

One way to compare coverage is to start with one of the largest offerers of Medicare supplement policies—the American Association of Retired Persons (AARP). Its Medicare supplement policies are underwritten and administered by Prudential Insurance. You can call the AARP Group Health Insurance Program at 800-523-5800 to get an information package.

By way of example, in Illinois you'd pay $33 a month for the Plan A basic benefits. But Plan J—which covers preventive care, prescription drugs to $3,000, excess medical charges in full, and all other possible options—costs $125.50 a month in Illinois.

Of course, other insurance companies may charge less, or more, for similar packages. Check prices of policies for your age, but ask also if there are price increases for older people. The best companies do not increase premiums as you age or if you enter at an older age. Beware of policies that have an "attained age" premium, which increases your premiums when you reach a specific age.

Some companies offer a discount when couples buy two policies. Under the new regulations, all policies now must be guaranteed renewable without regard to health, as long as you keep paying the premiums.

Before buying a policy that charges lower prices, you'll want to check the safety rating of the insurance company (see Smart Insurance-Buying Strategy #5 in chapter 54).

Medigap Strategy #3: Take Advantage of Initial Six-Month Entry Period

For six months after you turn 65, you cannot be denied Medigap coverage at regular prices—even if you are already sick. The insurer may impose a six-month waiting period on coverage for preexisting conditions, but you must be accepted into the plan.

If you know you already have a health problem or require expensive prescription drugs, purchase the maximum coverage supplement plan that you can afford. Once they start covering your existing conditions, the expensive plan will be worth the additional monthly cost.

If you're using the AARP supplement plans, you should know it's their policy to accept all applicants into the first seven of their plans at any time. But after the initial six-month application period, if you are already in poor health you will not be accepted into the top three levels of the plan, which offer prescription medicine coverage.

If you delay purchasing Medicare Part B because you are still working and covered by a company plan, your six-month window starts on the day you apply for Part B.

One other note: If you already satisfied a waiting period for a preexisting condition in your current supplement plan, you do not have to do so again if you decide to switch plans. But if you have a preexisting condition it may be difficult to get coverage after the initial six-month window, which starts when you turn 65.

Medigap Strategy #4: Don't Buy Duplicate Coverage

It is now against the law for a company to sell you duplicate coverage. Before selling you a policy, the agent must ask if you already have Medigap insurance. If you have a current policy, the agent is obligated to give you a written comparison between the two policies.

Don't ever buy a Medicare supplement policy for someone who is already on Medicaid because Medicaid already covers all bills not paid for by Medicare.

You may already have a policy that pays daily hospital benefits (an indemnity plan) while you are hospitalized, or a special policy that covers specific illnesses such as cancer. The combination of Medicare and a good supplement policy already covers almost all of these costs, so these policies may provide mostly duplicate coverage. They're also expensive ways to insure your health.

Medigap Strategy #5: Consider an HMO

Many health maintenance organizations (HMOs) have contracted with Medicare to provide services to Medicare patients. In fact, most HMOs are required to provide additional benefits at little or no additional cost—including preventive care, dental care, hearing aids, and eyeglasses. They may also provide extended hospital and skilled nursing facility stays and coverage for certain drugs.

To receive Medicare coverage through an HMO, you must be enrolled in Medicare Part B and pay the premiums. An HMO is usually not a substitute for a Medigap policy, but you might consider combining it with a basic Medicare supplement Plan A policy. There are a few HMOs with programs designed specifically for Medicare patients.

Medigap Strategy #6: Be Informed

Collect all the information you need about the current rules and payment levels for Medicare Parts A and B from your local Social Security Office. The government also offers a free booklet called *The Medicare Handbook*, which can be obtained by calling 800-772-1213.

Write to AARP, 601 E. Street N.W., Washington, D.C. 20049 for their free booklet entitled *Medigap: A Consumer's Guide*.

Contact the office of your state insurance commissioner for any special state rules regarding Medicare supplement policies. Many states also have an "office on aging," which will help seniors and their families evaluate Medicare supplement policies.

Remember, the deductibles, co-insurance, and premium costs of Medicare are increased every year, so get the current numbers from Social Security. Also remember that the premiums for Medicare supplement policies vary by state, so when you request prices, be sure to give your state of residence. Finally, make sure you have not chosen a policy that has a low cost in the first year, but whose annual charges will rise rapidly in later years.

Chapter 62

Catastrophic Illness and Nursing Home Care

Living too long may be the biggest financial problem facing the baby boom generation—and their parents. According to the U.S. Census Bureau's latest projections, Americans over age 65 will make up 20 percent of the U.S. population in 2020—compared with 13 percent now. Within the next 30 years, the number of dependent elders may be greater than the number of dependent children in the United States.

The American Association of Retired Persons points out that nearly one third of all people who reached age 65 in 1990 will spend at least three months in a nursing home. In fact, nearly 25 percent of today's seniors will spend at least one year in a nursing home. And, according to the same report, nearly two-thirds of the people using nursing homes will be women.

Every healthy senior will, at this point, turn to an adult child and extract a promise not to put him or her into a nursing home. But as Americans live longer naturally, and submit to medical treatments that can prolong life, that promise may not be a fair situation in which to place your adult children. Anyone who has ever been through the emotional and physical demands of caring for a loved parent with Alzheimer's knows the value of trying to plan in advance for a debilitating long-term illness.

Here's what you may not know: Although Medicare and Medicare supplemental insurance policies may cover almost every medical cost,

Medicare provides no coverage for long-term custodial nursing care.

Medicare only provides extremely limited coverage for treatment at "skilled nursing facilities" that must be entered only after at least three consecutive days in a hospital and on the specific instructions of a doctor who certifies that you need skilled, daily nursing care. That eliminates coverage for most elderly patients who need help dressing, feeding, and otherwise caring for themselves. And even for skilled nursing situations, Medicare pays only for the first 20 days in full, another 80 days in which the patient is responsible for a good portion of the bill, and nothing at all after 100 days.

A good nursing home costs anywhere from $30,000 to $60,000 a year today—depending on where you live. But costs of nursing home care have been escalating far beyond the general rates of inflation. If you assume a 7 percent annual cost increase, and if you are 60 today and enter a nursing home at age 80, today's $45,000-a-year home would cost $175,000 a year when you enter! Who will pay for this expensive care? And what money will remain for a surviving spouse, or in an estate to pass on to children?

How does a family deal with that kind of cost burden? Without some advance planning, an elderly person or couple paying $30,000 a year for nursing home care would become completely impoverished within a few months or years. And only then would Medicaid—the federal/state health-care program designed for the destitute—take over and cover nursing home bills. As you'll see in a moment, both the nursing home patient and his or her spouse, who may not need nursing home care, would be left with only minimal assets and income.

PLANNING AHEAD FOR LONG-TERM CARE

By the time nursing home care is required, it's too late to do much planning. The first instinct is to transfer any assets of the patient into other family members' names. But there are laws against that. Any assets transferred within 36 months of entering a nursing home must be used to pay for care, before Medicaid will step in. Applicants for Medicaid are even required to submit back tax returns, and budget-squeezed states that administer the Medicaid programs are checking carefully before offering this aid program.

There are two ways to approach the problem of expensive long-term care—and you'll need to understand, and perhaps combine, both methods to deal with the problem. The first method revolves around structuring the assets of older people so that if the need for long-term care arises, Medicaid can step in sooner.

Many people find an ethical dilemma in arranging their estates to pass money on to their children while accepting federal and state aid for nursing care costs. Yet those same people employ tax consultants to search for every break in the income tax laws. It's a dilemma to consider, but you should at least know the facts and the strategies.

The second approach is to purchase long-term care insurance, sometimes known as nursing home insurance. This is a relatively new form of insurance, but today there are more than 140 companies selling these policies. Some can provide excellent long-term benefits; others are questionable. A recent congressional hearing into long-term care policies found that many of these policies were "filled with loopholes and limitations that limit insurers' liability when a claim is incurred." This chapter will show you how to identify the best policies and the coverage they should give.

The best strategy of all may be a combination of the two approaches: purchasing a long-term care policy to cover at least three or four years of nursing home care, which will give you time to activate some of the asset-preserving strategies outlined below. It's a sad but true fact that almost half of those who enter a nursing home either die or leave within a year. But one patient in five will stay five years or more. It makes sense to plan ahead.

LONG-TERM CARE INSURANCE

Here's how long-term care insurance policies work: You purchase a policy while you're still relatively young and healthy—55 is not too young to consider a long-term care policy purchase. Premiums stay level over the life of the policy (with exceptions noted below), so the younger you are when you take out a long-term care policy, the easier and less expensive it is to get this coverage.

Unlike life insurance, there's no certainty that you'll ever need the coverage. You may be one of the fortunate ones who never needs nursing home care. On the other hand, also unlike life insurance, if you do need to collect, this policy is for *your* benefit, as well as for your heirs. If you purchase a well-constructed policy, you should have coverage to pay for even the increasing cost of nursing home care.

There is also the possibility that a future national health insurance reform program could include some type of coverage for nursing home care. Under that scenario, it is possible that premiums already paid for private long-term care insurance would have been wasted.

Deciding whether you really need a long-term care policy comes first. Then you need to know what your policy should cover and how to buy the most coverage for the best price.

Long-Term Care Insurance Strategy #1: Decide If You Need It

Do you—or your parents—need a long-term care policy? The answer is no—*if* you're very wealthy and could easily cover the cost of care in a nursing home. In that case, you'd be better off investing the money in a good mutual fund, because you might never need the insurance you're paying for.

The answer is also no if you're single and do not plan to leave money to your children or other heirs. As long as your assets are large enough to pay for the first few months of private nursing home care, and get you into a home that accepts both private and public aid patients, you can use your own assets and Social Security benefits to get started. When your assets are exhausted, the state will take over. You have no need to protect your estate for the ultimate care of your spouse or your children, so you do not need a long-term care policy.

But the answer is yes if you are concerned that a long-term stay in a nursing home would exhaust assets that your spouse needs to live on, or would drain the assets from an estate that you want to leave to your children. Then, a combination of a long-term care policy and smart planning can keep your assets from being swallowed in a healthcare catastrophe.

Long-Term Care Insurance Strategy #2: Get Proper Coverage

The following are the key ingredients to look for when purchasing a long-term care policy:

1. A policy that covers *all levels of care*—from skilled to custodial.

2. A policy that has reasonable "gatekeepers"—the actual require-ments you need to meet for coverage. For example, choose a policy that *does not require a prior hospital stay* before receiving benefits. Many seniors have no acute care problems before entering a nursing home.

3. A policy that specifically says it covers Alzheimer's disease, senility, Parkinson's disease, and stroke.

4. A policy that *guarantees the rates* for the first few years. (While the policy may quote a flat rate for the rest of your life, the insurance company does retain the right to increase premiums for an entire class of policyholders—such as everyone in your age bracket, or everyone living in a certain state.) A few policies (including the AARP policy listed below) will guarantee rates for five years.

5. A policy that has *level premiums*, as opposed to rates that increase at specified periods.

6. A policy that is *guaranteed renewable*, meaning the insurer cannot cancel unless you fail to pay the premium.

7. A policy that has *inflation protection*, specifically at least 5 percent compound annual increase in benefits.

8. A policy with a *premium waiver* that says you do not have to continue to pay the premiums once you enter a nursing home.

9. A policy that offers *home care* as well as care received in a nursing home.

10. A policy that is offered only after the company has thoroughly checked your medical records.

11. A policy that is offered by a safe, highly rated insurance company with experience insuring against long-term care risk.

All of the above ingredients are essential in purchasing a long-term care policy, and particularly the last point about purchasing a policy from a safe, reliable, and experienced company. See Smart Insurance-Buying Strategy #5 in chapter 54 for a listing of the services that rate insurance companies for safety, and check the company's rating before purchasing a policy. If you buy a policy at age 60 but do not use it for 20 or more years, you want to be sure the insurance company will be around to pay off!

Terry's Tip:

$$$ There's one more reason to use a large, reliable insurance company for nursing home care policies: This type of policy is so new that the basic coverages are regularly being enlarged. For instance, Travelers and John Hancock, two larger insurers offering this type of policy, recently rewrote all their previously issued policies, at no cost to the policyholders, to increase various portions of the coverage.

Long-Term Care Insurance Strategy #3: Get a Good Price/ Use Money-Saving Techniques

There are some smart ways to save money on a long-term care policy, but you may have to point these out to your insurance agent.

Buy a Policy to Cover Only Three or Four Years

Lifetime benefits are expensive. You have 30 months after entering a nursing home to transfer assets to a trust or to a relative so that your level of income and assets will be low enough to qualify for Medicaid. Therefore, three or four years of nursing home care coverage is the most you'll need; after that, with proper planning, the state will take over.

Choose a Longer Deductible Period

Like other types of insurance, your long-term care policy will have a deductible, commonly called an *elimination period*. Some plans offer coverage from the first day you enter a nursing home; others use a 20-day deductible as standard. But if you have enough assets to cover the first three or six months of nursing home care before your insurance policy kicks in, you can save on your premiums.

For example, a 60-year-old woman seeking a four-year plan with $100-a-day benefits would pay $470 in annual premiums for a 20-day deductible plan—and only $350 in premiums if she chose the same plan with a 100-day deductible.

Get Adequate Daily Benefits

This is an aspect of nursing home care that will cost you *more* money, but it is worth paying for. Check the level of benefits offered by your plan. You'll probably want at least $100 a day in coverage, although some plans may offer as little as $60 a day. To learn what costs are in your area, call some of the nicer nursing homes and ask for the average daily cost.

Get Inflation Protection

The second, expensive, but important aspect of a good long-term care plan is inflation protection, sometimes called the *benefit increase option*. Each policy will define this differently, but at least it should offer a 5 percent increase of your original daily benefit each year on the anniversary of your policy.

Avoid Premium "Step-ups"

Avoid policies that step up the premium to a higher level each year. The costs could be prohibitive by the time you really need the insurance. Remember, you're at risk for rising premiums if the insurance company raises its prices to an entire class of policyholders, unless you have a guaranteed premium for a set number of years.

Ask for Spousal Discounts

Many companies will offer a discount of from 10 to 15 percent if both spouses purchase a policy. And some companies waive further premiums after the first spouse dies if the policies have been in effect for at least ten years.

Long-term Care Insurance Strategy #4: Comparison Shop for Policies

AARP (the American Association of Retired Persons) offers a choice of long-term care policies to all its members. The basic coverage is called AARP Plan FF, and you can get an information package by calling 800-523-5800.

Plan FF is AARP's basic comprehensive coverage for long-term care. It lasts for four years and pays up to $100 a day in coverage, after a 90-day deductible. This plan pays for home healthcare or adult daycare visits after a 45-visit deductible. The plan will then pay up to $70 a visit for home healthcare or $60 a visit to an adult daycare center. This 45-day deductible can be combined for both home healthcare and adult daycare.

The AARP plan meets all of the requirements listed above in Strategy #2 above except one: There is no annual inflation protection from the year of purchase, although this policy offers you the option to purchase additional insurance (at new, higher prices) at least once every four years without evidence of insurability. And one year *after you begin to receive benefits*, the daily benefit amounts increase 8 percent during each benefit year, starting from your original base coverage. As you can see, with the AARP long-term care plan, it is your responsibility to increase coverage to keep up with inflation.

Other than that gap, the AARP plan has some coverage above what you might consider the minimum requirements, such as four years of coverage instead of three. Plus, its rates are guaranteed for five years. In fact, if you're willing to pay more each month, you can have the rates guaranteed for ten years. That coverage comes under AARP plan FN, which also will extend benefits for a short grace period even after you might decide to cancel the policy in the future after paying premiums for at least ten years. The additional monthly cost for ten-year guaranteed rates depends on your age when you purchase the policy.

AARP has given me permission to reprint their rate schedule as of 1992 (see chart VI-5). Once you purchase a policy, the rate is guaranteed for five years—but the rate schedule might rise before you sign up, so check their current literature carefully.

Also, I used David T. Phillips & Co. (800-223-9610), an independent broker offering a variety of long-term care plans, to research a comparable plan, with $100 a day in benefits, a 100-day deductible, inflation protection of 5 percent in addition to the original daily benefit each year from the date of purchase (not, as above, the date of usage), and coverage to last four years.

Here is the proposal from AMEX Life, a company rated A+ by A. M. Best and one of Phillips & Co.'s top-recommended policies (see chart VI-6).

You'll note that these prices are quoted on an annual basis. The company does allow you to pay monthly, but the price is 8 percent higher. If

CHART VI-5

AARP Nursing Home Insurance Rates

Plan FF

(Rates are for each person applying for coverage)

If your application is not accepted, your payment will be completely refunded or credited to your account.

Age as of Effective Date	Monthly Rate*	Age as of Effective Date	Monthly Rate*
50	$29	65	$102
51	31	66	113
52	35	67	123
53	37	68	135
54	40	69	149
55	43	70	164
56	46	71	180
57	50	72	197
58	54	73	217
59	59	74	238
60	64	75	261
61	70	76	284
62	77	77	307
63	85	78	332
64	93	79	358

* Your monthly rate will be based upon your age when your insurance takes effect.

SOURCE: American Association of Retired Persons.

you do a little math, you'll see that at age 65 the AMEX policy would cost $990 per year, while the AARP policy is $1,224. Part of that difference is explained by the 10-day shorter deductible under the AARP policy. The AARP rates are guaranteed for five years. There is no rate guarantee with the AMEX policy, but AMEX Life has not raised rates in the 18 years it has offered this coverage. Also, the AMEX policy pays your actual benefit amount up front, while the AARP program requires you to submit invoices and be reimbursed.

You can contact either of these organizations for current prices, or use these numbers as a basis for judging proposals presented by your own insurance agent.

CHART VI-6

AMEX Life Nursing Home Insurance Rates
(Annual Premiums)

1460 Day Plan (Four Years)
$100 Daily Benefit
100 Day Deductible

Age	Basic Plan*	With Inflation Protection†	Age	Basic Plan*	With Inflation Protection†
40–45	$ 130	$ 230	65	$ 650	$ 990
46	140	240	66	690	1050
47	140	240	67	770	1140
48	140	250	68	860	1270
49	150	260	69	940	1380
50	150	260	70	1040	1510
51	160	280	71	1140	1630
52	160	280	72	1260	1790
53	170	290	73	1410	1980
54	180	300	74	1560	2170
55	200	330	75	1710	2360
56	230	370	76	1900	2580
57	250	410	77	2140	2890
58	280	440	78	2360	3140
59	300	480	79	2600	3430
60	350	560	80	2830	3680
61	410	640	81	3070	3960
62	440	690	82	3350	4250
63	510	800	83	3650	4600
64	560	870	84	3950	4900

* No inflation protection rider.

† Benefit increases by 5% of original amount each year. (Prices quoted are for annual payments; paying monthly increases cost 8%.)

Chapter 63

Strategies to Save Your Estate from Nursing Home Costs

If you don't have long-term care insurance, you'll have to pay for nursing care yourself—and pay, and pay, and pay. Only when almost all of your assets are spent will the state step in and start paying your nursing home care costs. There are some strategies for getting your assets out of your estate for Medicaid purposes, but first you should understand just how little you must have in the way of assets in order to qualify for Medicaid.

NOTE: Each state may have slightly different requirements, so check on the current rules in your state. But in these days of state budget crunches, most states are limiting income and assets more strictly before they'll pay for custodial care.

Maximum Assets to Qualify for Medicaid:

Life insurance with a face value up to $1,500;
Cash up to $2,000;
Some "reasonable" amount of personal property (jewelry including one wedding and one engagement ring), approx. total value $2,000;
Term life insurance with no cash value;
Burial fund up to $2,500 and a burial plot;

Car (usually only if less than $4,500 value);
Home, if it is the principal residence.

Maximum Income to Qualify for Medicaid:

All states: All income of institutionalized person must be applied against cost of care;

21 states: Income over a set amount (about $1,266 a month) for person receiving care automatically results in denial of Medicaid assistance. These income limitations are called *caps*. More and more states are enacting caps, which result in the denial of Medicaid benefits even if the patient's income is just slightly over the cap. There are restrictions on transferring income to a healthy spouse or other relative. Before changing state of residence, check on whether that state caps income for Medicaid recipients. Florida and Arizona, two states that are favorite retirement destinations, cap income to qualify for Medicaid.

Spousal assets that may be retained:

The spouse of a Medicaid recipient may also keep one-half of the family's total assets—up to a maximum of $66,480 in 1994—and some additional income (depending on the state). Some states have far lower maximums.

Assets that must be "spent down" to qualify for Medicaid:

Cash, IRAs, Keoghs, CDs, savings bonds, Treasury bills, stocks, bonds, mutual funds, life insurance policies that have cash value, vacation homes, jewelry other than wedding and engagement ring, must all be "spent down."

Assets "not counted" for Medicaid determination:

• Assets that you've given away or spent at least 36 months prior to entering the nursing home;
• Assets held in certain irrevocable trusts where potential Medicaid recipient has no control over distribution of assets or income.

Determination date for Medicaid qualification:

Your assets are counted as of the date you entered the nursing home or hospital, *not* on the date you applied for Medicaid.

Special issues regarding income:

Note also that if you receive a company pension, rental income, or
annuity income and Social Security which, combined, put you over
the monthly income limits, you may not qualify for Medicaid in 20
states (Alabama, Alaska, Arkansas, Colorado, Delaware, Florida,
Georgia, Idaho, Iowa, Kansas, Louisiana, Nevada, New Jersey, New
Mexico, Oklahoma, South Carolina, South Dakota, Tennessee,
Texas, and Wyoming).

If married, only the income of the spouse entering the nursing
home is considered. But for jointly received income, the at-home
spouse can keep only between $1,149 and $1,717 a month, depending on the state of residence.

In other words, they really mean it when they say Medicaid is meant to
cover costs for the truly impoverished. There are some ways to put
yourself in that class—before spending all your money. Again, you must
think clearly about the ethical as well as financial issues of taking these
steps.

Medicaid Strategy #1: Understand the 36-Month Rule

The 30-month rule is the critical ingredient in transferring assets. The rule
says that any assets transferred to anyone else in the period of 36 months
before entering a nursing home must still be counted toward your nursing
home care before Medicaid steps in.

So, if you transfer your savings account to your daughter six months
before entering a nursing home, the money in the account must be used to
pay bills for 24 months. If the assets that were transferred, plus the assets
remaining that are over the allowed limit, run out before 24 months, then
Medicaid will start paying the nursing home bills.

There is one other exception to the 36-month rule. If you divide the
amount of assets transferred by the average cost of a nursing home in your
community, the resulting number is the amount of months before you are
eligible for Medicaid. Transfers to spouses and to disabled children are
exempt from this rule.

For example, let's suppose a mother had $50,000 in cash and transferred

$25,000 to her daughter. In that city, nursing home costs are $2,500 a month. Then it would take ten months ($25,000 divided by $2,500) before the mother became eligible for Medicaid. In the meantime, she would have to pay for ten months of nursing home care out of her own assets—the remaining $25,000 she had kept. Then Medicare would take over. But her daughter would still have the $25,000.

Warning: In a worst-case scenario, the mother might have been incapacitated by a stroke and unable to transfer any assets at all. That's one more reason for executing a power of attorney as described in chapter 59.

Medicaid Strategy #2: Special Rules for Residences

You've probably already noticed that the one potentially valuable item that can be retained is the personal residence. As explained in this strategy, there are special rules for transfer of title to a primary residence. However, if the Medicaid recipient is single and deemed unlikely to return to that residence, the state can order it sold and the money used to pay for nursing home care. Or Medicaid can place a lien on the home to recapture money when it is ultimately sold.

If the home is owned jointly by a married couple, the person entering the nursing home can transfer it entirely to the name of the well spouse, who can then transfer a portion to a child or another relative—making the residence fully protected from Medicaid spend-down requirements.

Whether single or married, a house or apartment can also be transferred to either a child who is blind, disabled, or under the age of 21; a child of any age who lived in the home for at least two years before the parents go into a nursing home (and cared for the parents at home); or a sibling who owns a share of the home and lived there for at least one year before the co-owner goes into a nursing home.

Of course, there is no restriction on selling the home for fair market value, as long as the proceeds are included in the asset valuation for Medicaid purposes.

Selling the home and then giving away the money shortly before entering a nursing home would violate the 36-month rule (see below) but may be a useful strategy if there is a large capital gain involved and the person entering the nursing home can use his or her once-in-a-lifetime, over-55 capital gain exclusion. But a portion of the proceeds would still be required to be used to pay for the first 36 months of nursing home care.

Placing title to the home in a revocable living trust may be one of the few ways to shelter a residence from Medicaid liens. In most states, liens are not placed on a Medicaid recipient's home until he or she dies, and then a lien is placed only if the property is in the deceased's name only. A home placed in a revocable living trust is owned by the trust, not the Medicaid recipient. Check with your attorney for the latest rulings on this issue of whether a revocable living trust can shelter assets from Medicaid. One other option to discuss with your attorney is the creation of a *life estate interest* in the home, even though you no longer own the property.

Medicaid Strategy #3: Transfer of Assets to Spouse

The first strategy most married couples think of is to transfer all the assets into the name of the spouse who is not entering the nursing home. But, as noted above, there are limitations on the amount of assets, besides the residence, that the well spouse can keep. The maximum is $70,740 in 1993, and the amount is indexed upward every year. But many states have lower maximums.

Well, then, you might suggest, why not transfer the well spouse's assets to the children? Foiled again. Since November 1989, the law has stated that any assets transferred by the well spouse within 36 months of the ill spouse entering the nursing home are also considered countable assets if transferred within 36 months of the spouse entering the nursing home!

The well spouse must use excess assets above that level to pay for nursing home care, even if the ill spouse is impoverished. The well spouse is also allowed a higher income level, depending on the state. In 1993, the maximum amount of joint income that can be kept by the well spouse is $1,769 per month.

There have been instances when the well spouse simply refused to contribute money toward nursing home care. In that case Medicaid may bring a lawsuit, and the amount the well spouse must contribute may be decided by a judge.

Since asset transfers, with the exception of the primary residence and income allowances, are limited, many elderly married couples reluctantly conclude that the only way out of the Medicaid impoverishment trap is to divorce after years of marriage.

There is another potential alternative.

Medicaid Strategy #4: Establish an Irrevocable Trust

It is possible to use irrevocable trusts to transfer assets out of the reach of Medicaid. But if the trustee has any right to distribute income from the trust to the Medicaid patient, all the assets are considered to be yours—even if the trustee refuses to give you some of the money. The state can go to court to collect.

To really protect assets from Medicaid using an irrevocable trust you need specialized legal assistance. The trust may have a provision to divide the income between husband and wife. Then if one spouse enters a nursing home, only half the income would be countable toward nursing home costs (unless the income lifted the remaining spouse above maximum income levels). Some trusts have provisions that income payments to an ill spouse are to be discontinued automatically, with all payments going to the well spouse.

Congress has changed the laws on the use of irrevocable Medicaid trusts several times. And there is always the possibility that the laws will change again, making it harder to shelter assets in this manner. That's another reason for having a continuing relationship with an attorney who specializes in this type of practice.

Medicaid Strategy #5: Hold Assets in Joint Name

This is a strategy that won't work. Many elderly people hold assets, especially bank accounts, in joint name with an adult child on an either/or basis. But Medicaid considers this type of account to be completely owned by the nursing home patient, unless it can be proved otherwise.

Many elderly couples have joint accounts. In this case, half of the assets are presumed to be available to pay for the nursing home care. An exception would be if the account required the signatures of both parties; then the remaining signer could simply refuse to co-sign a check and release the money.

Medicaid Strategy #6: Give Most of Your Assets Away

One unpleasant strategy may be to give away most of your assets well before you think you'll need to enter a nursing home—and trust the child or friend to whom you give the assets to use the money to take care of you. You would keep only enough assets to pay for the first few months of nursing home care—to get yourself situated in a private nursing home that will one day accept Medicaid assignment.

That's one advantage of having a long-term care insurance policy. It will give you time to distribute your assets before the 30-month rule takes effect. That way you can retain control of your assets until you're absolutely sure you must enter a nursing home permanently.

Of course, you must really trust the person to whom you give the assets. But if you hadn't wanted to leave that person some assets in the first place, you would have just let Medicaid take everything.

There is one other reason to put some assets in the hands of a person you trust. Medicaid pays for room and board and basic care in a nursing home. But patient loads are heavy, and even in the best homes the nurses' aides are spread thin. A person you trust, and have left in a position to spend money on your behalf, may be able to provide additional caregivers to "baby-sit" an aging patient.

Terry's Tip:

$$$ It is impossible to cover every aspect of Medicaid transfers, and states are changing their rules frequently. If you are contemplating such a transfer of assets, you should consult an attorney who specializes in geriatric law. And if you are currently facing this situation for yourself, your spouse, or your parents, I strongly recommend you purchase an excellent, comprehensive paperback, *How to Protect Your Life Savings from Catastrophic Illness and Nursing Homes*, by attorney Harley Gordon (available by mail for $19.95 from Financial Planning Institute, P.O. Box 135, Boston, MA 02258). The FPI also offers a referral service for attorneys in your area specializing in elder law (call: 617-965-8120).

Chapter 64

Lifecare Communities

In planning for the later stages of life, don't automatically assume that an immediate transition will be made from your present home into custodial care. As the population ages, more and more senior citizens in good health are moving into transitional communities designed to accommodate their needs.

These communities come in several different forms—with different financial requirements and commitments. You should have an idea of choices and costs in these senior living strategies.

Senior Living Strategy #1: Senior Rental Community

The least complicated move for a senior citizen to make is to a senior rental community. Many seniors sell their homes and simply rent an apartment in a development specifically designed for senior citizens. There may be grab-bars in the bathrooms to assist the unsteady, and the instructions in the elevators will be in large print. Typically these apartments have their own kitchens and complete living facilities, but the complex may also offer extra service in the monthly rental that includes one or two meals a day in a group dining room. There is usually a recreation center and planned group activities for seniors. There may be trips away from the complex as well as activities on the premises.

Many of these senior living communities also offer some form of physical therapy on the premises and keep a nurse or doctor on call. But these communities are not designed for continuing care, and a senior who needs that type of assistance may be asked to move out.

Senior Living Strategy #2: Lifecare "Buy-In" Community

In a lifecare "buy-in," an individual or couple buys into the community, much like purchasing a condo. The entry cost depends on market conditions and could be as much as $75,000 for a one-bedroom apartment. Plus there will be a monthly charge, typically ranging from $850 to $1,250 for complete services—including all utilities, laundry, housekeeping, and one or two meals a day.

The community may offer the conveniences listed above, along with some form of nursing home insurance for its residents. For instance, they may pay a fixed amount toward nursing home confinement or offer a certain number of days per year in nursing care as part of the monthly package.

One of the things to consider before getting involved in this type of community is whether you will get any of your money back if you (or your parents) move out, or die. In the best communities there is a strong resale market. And some communities even guarantee that a large percentage of your initial investment will be returned, along with a portion of any appreciation in the value of your unit.

The ability of a buy-in community to make this kind of commitment depends on its overall financial stability. It's your responsibility to check on the finances before you buy into the community. The best way to check is to ask to see the current financial statements and show them to your accountant. Another good idea is to ask for a bank reference. Does the community have a mortgage? Ask them to write a letter to the bank, authorizing the bank officials to speak freely to you about the financial condition of the community. Ask for a credit report on the owner of the community.

Many senior citizens are selling their homes and moving into this type of senior center. It offers security, medical care, and the companionship of other active seniors. It should also offer a chance that your unit will appreciate in value.

Senior Living Strategy #3: Endowment Communities

Many religious organizations sponsor endowment communities that require an up-front, nonrefundable payment in return for a promise of lifetime care. There will be an additional monthly fee, as well. These communities are generally tied to a hospital and nursing care center run by the same organizations.

In choosing this type of plan, you are making several commitments. The longer you live, the better bet this type of living center will turn out to be. But if you die shortly after entering the community, there will be no refund of your endowment to give to your heirs. You cannot be removed, except to their own nursing center or hospital. On the other hand, you may be restricted to the doctors and specialists at the affiliated hospital.

Read the documents carefully before entering an endowment community because this is truly a lifetime decision, unless you want to move out and forfeit your up-front payment.

Terry's Tip:

$$$ The American Association of Homes for the Aging (AAHA) has a commission that accredits continuing care retirement communities (CCRCs). For a list of more than 100 of these communities, send a self-addressed, stamped envelope to: Continuing Care Accreditation Commission, 901 E Street N.W., Washington, D.C. 20004.

Chapter 65

Pension and IRA Distributions

After you've spent a lifetime building up your retirement accounts, you will be faced with some decisions about when and how to take the money *out*. Some of those decisions will be dictated by tax laws or corporate policy, but other issues revolve around your retirement budget and the amount of money you need to have to live on.

KEY RULES TO RETIREMENT DISTRIBUTIONS

1. You want your money to continue to grow and compound tax-deferred as long as you possibly can.

2. You want to leave a small portion of your retirement assets in growth investments. The amount of risk you're willing to take depends on your age and total amount of retirement funds.

3. You want to maintain flexibility of your retirement funds so that you can react to changing levels of inflation and changing market conditions.

4. You want to take maximum advantage of the tax laws that cover distributions from qualified retirement plans.

Important New Tax Rule Regarding Distributions

In January 1, 1993, a new tax rule went into effect that will have an impact on rollovers between qualified retirement plans. Under the old rule, you could take possession of your IRA or pension funds for a period of 60 days before placing the money into another qualified account. That meant that if you left your old job or decided to switch investments, you could simply ask the trustee of your plan to write you a check. Then you had 60 days to deposit it (or an equivalent amount of money) into a new, qualified plan.

Under the new rules, if you take possession of the money for any length of time you will be subject to 20 percent federal income tax withholding. To avoid this withholding, the transfers must be made directly from the trustee of your old plan to the trustee of your new plan.

There's another important tax aspect to this rule. Unless you replace the 20 percent that was withheld with other funds that you contribute to your rollover account, the amount that was withheld will be treated as a withdrawal. You'll owe ordinary income taxes on it. If you contribute enough money from your own pocket to make up the difference, you'll have to file for a refund of the amount withheld. And, if you are under age 59½ and do not replace the amount withheld, you could face a 10 percent federal tax penalty, as well as income taxes, on the amount withheld.

Remember, you may not touch any distribution from a qualified plan before it is rolled over into a new plan—or you will walk into this trap of tax withholding.

The new law does allow more flexibility in taking a portion of the distribution and rolling over the balance. Under the old law, you had to roll over at least 50 percent of your distribution in order to continue tax deferral. Under the new law, you can take any portion yourself (and pay the withholding tax), and then transfer the remaining amount into your IRA or your new employer's plan.

NOTE: When transferring money, do not add this rollover to a previously existing IRA account. Establish a new and completely separate account for your rollover every time you leave a company. That preserves your right to roll that account subsequently into a new employer's plan, if allowed. And it greatly simplifies your tax records.

The following strategies are designed to help you make the most of retirement distributions.

Retirement Distribution Strategy #1: Lump Sum Rollovers

Ask your employer if you have the option of taking your retirement benefits in a lump sum rather than fixed monthly benefits. If you do have access to the lump sum and can live on other income, you will probably want to use the new rules listed above and roll over the lump sum into an IRA rollover account with a bank or no-load mutual fund.

If you take the lump sum but do not roll it over into a qualified plan, you will owe substantial taxes. That's a good reason for consulting with your accountant before taking any distributions—and for considering the strategies listed below.

Retirement Distribution Strategy #2: Forward Averaging

If you reached age 50 before January 2, 1986, you have some interesting choices. You can elect to use five-year tax averaging (under the current rates) or ten-year forward averaging (under the 1986 tax rates).

You'll need to calculate the tax both ways before you decide, but generally the ten-year option is better for amounts under $475,000. Still, you also need to weigh the benefits of simply rolling over the entire amount. If you do not think you'll have to use this retirement money for a number of years, it might be better to roll over the entire lump sum. Since you won't be paying taxes, you'll have more money working for you.

Withdrawals from IRAs and SEPs are not eligible for income averaging. You can only use lump sum averaging once in your lifetime, so if you are going to receive several different retirement amounts, consider carefully which one should receive the averaging treatment.

Terry's Tip:

$$$ There's a 15 percent excise tax on distributions in excess of $150,000 annually, or on lump sums over $750,000. You'll definitely need a tax professional to guide you through these issues.

Retirement Distribution Strategy #3: Avoiding Penalties on Early Distributions

If you take money out of a qualified plan or IRA before you reach age 59½, you are subject to a 10 percent penalty on the taxable amount of the distribution. There is one exception to this penalty, which you should try to take advantage of if you are withdrawing money early from your retirement account.

The penalty may be avoided if you take "substantially equal periodic payments" for the life of the recipient. There are three methods for calculating the amount of those payments:

The *life expectancy method* is the simplest calculation, but it results in the smallest payments. It simply uses a mortality table to determine how much must be distributed. Since your life expectancy changes every year, the amount of the withdrawal must be recalculated each year.

The *amortization method* calculates the withdrawal amount based on the earnings your fund can be expected to develop over your life expectancy. You can get much larger annual withdrawals using this method.

The *annuity method* is similar, but it requires far more calculations and must be determined by an actuary.

If you're trying to get the *largest* amount, choose the amortization method. If you're trying to make your funds last the longest, use the life expectancy method. Your custodian for the funds will easily make the dollar calculations for you.

Terry's Tip:

$$$ Once you start an early withdrawal plan, you must continue it for at least five years and until you reach age 59½ or you will owe the 10 percent tax penalty on all previous withdrawals. However, once you've met these criteria, you can subsequently change your withdrawal method.

Retirement Distribution Strategy #4: When You *Must* Take Distributions

You must start taking distributions from your IRA by April 1 of the year *after* you reach age 70½. That is, if you turn 70½ during this year, you must start taking money out of your IRA before April 1 of next year.

If you withdraw funds from your IRA before 70½ there are no limitations on how much or how little you can take out—except if your bank or mutual fund custodian sets its own rules for minimum distributions. And, of course, if you withdraw money before age 59½, you'll have to pay that 10 percent federal penalty.

Once you reach age 70½, however, you run into a whole new set of regulations. The rules state that you must take out enough each year to deplete your IRA account over your life expectancy. Your IRA custodian will help you calculate that amount, and it can be done in several different ways.

If you have IRAs at different institutions, you must base your withdrawals on the total of all your IRAs. But you can remove the funds from just one account, or divide withdrawals from several accounts.

You might want to take out the most money you can, while still making the account last over your lifetime. Or, if you have other money to pay your living expenses, you might want to take out as little as possible—leaving the balance to continue growing tax-deferred.

If you elect to take regular payments, your custodian will divide your account (or the total of your IRA accounts) balance by your life expectancy based on IRS mortality tables. The tables are unisex: at 70½ the life expectancy for men and women is 16 years. If you wait to take the money out until the year in which you will turn 71, then your life expectancy is only 15.3 years. (Remember, these are IRS tables. You could live a lot longer and you'd want to have other money set aside in that case.)

There are several methods of calculating the required withdrawals:

The recalculation method: Each year the amount distributed from your account is recalculated based on the current balance in your account and your new life expectancy.

The joint life expectancy method: Use this method if you want to make your money last longer. The annual distributions are based on the joint life expectancy of both you and your spouse. If your spouse is much younger, that would stretch the payments over a greater number of years, and each annual payment would be smaller. Or you are allowed to have the figures calculated on the life expectancy of you and your beneficiary—with ten years as the maximum age difference.

Terry's Tips:

$$$ Once you reach age 70½, you want to make sure you have your IRA money invested in places that do not charge a penalty when you make withdrawals, as would be the case with some bank CDs. Or a mutual fund may have minimum withdrawal limits. Ask about these minimums and see if they apply to monthly required IRA distributions.

$$$ You can actually be penalized for earning too much in retirement benefits. If you withdraw more than $150,000 in retirement benefits in one year you will have to pay a 15 percent excise tax on the portion above $150,000 in addition to regular income taxes.

The excise tax does not apply to lump-sum distributions from a retirement plan that are taken using either five- or ten-year averaging, unless the distribution exceeds $750,000. But that $750,000 exemption can only be taken once in a lifetime and is not applicable for IRA payouts, or for payouts taken before age 59½. Ask your tax advisor about these provisions if you have a very large pension or IRA account.

Retirement Distribution Strategy #5: Tax Consequences of an IRA at Death

The tax consequences of an IRA at death depend on who is the beneficiary—an individual such as a surviving spouse, an unrelated person, or a trust.

If the beneficiary is a surviving spouse, the survivor may roll the deceased's IRA into his or her own IRA and, in effect, treat it as if it were his or her own. That is, the survivor may name a new beneficiary for this combined account, and will calculate the combined benefits for required minimum distributions at age 70½. Only a surviving spouse is entitled to this privilege of combining accounts.

Or, if the deceased spouse was already receiving minimum required distributions because he or she was over age 70½, the surviving spouse can continue to receive minimum distributions at the same rate. If distributions had not begun, the surviving spouse has the option of taking distributions based on the survivor's life expectancy, or taking a full distribution of all assets by December 31 of the fifth year following the IRA owner's death.

If the beneficiary of an IRA is a child, or anyone other than the surviving spouse, the tax rules depend on whether the deceased was already receiving minimum required distributions. If that is the case, the distributions must continue for the beneficiary at the same rate they were being issued for the decedent. If the deceased was not already taking distributions, the beneficiary can receive distributions based on his or her life expectancy—or make full distribution by December 31 of the fifth year following the owner's death. But the choice must be made in the year following the IRA owner's death—and if lifetime distributions are chosen, they must begin in that year.

$$$ If your estate, including your own revocable living trust, is the beneficiary of your IRA or other retirement plan, you could face costly taxes. Adding the value of your retirement account to your estate could push you into a higher estate tax bracket. Excess retirement plan assets also trigger an excise tax. And your ultimate beneficiary could be forced to pay income taxes on the distribution as well. So if you have a large retirement fund you should consult your estate planning professional. Sometimes the solution to avoiding taxes on retirement fund assets is to set up a private charitable foundation as the beneficiary of your retirement fund.

Chapter 66

Senior Income Strategies

The 1990s have been an era of lower interest rates. Senior citizens who were used to earning double-digit rates and living off their interest checks had a rude awakening. Interest income has dropped by $150 billion in the first two years of the decade. That's left many seniors struggling—and considering risky investments to boost their yields.

In chapter 23, we discussed strategies to earn higher interest rates, and how to measure the extra risk involved. This chapter presents some unique strategies designed especially for seniors, to boost monthly income without incurring additional risk. Not everyone may qualify to use these techniques, but they're certainly worth exploring.

Senior Income-Boosting Strategy #1: The Reverse Mortgage

Many senior citizens prefer to stay in their own homes. They feel perfectly able to care for themselves and their property, but because of rising property taxes, maintenance costs, and the general increases in the cost of living, their limited incomes seem to dictate that they must move. Not necessarily so. In recent years a new concept has been gaining popularity and availability. It's the *reverse mortgage plan*.

A reverse mortgage is simply a way of turning your paid-up home into a pension fund—withdrawing monthly checks that you cannot outlive, while still living in your home and holding title to it. Only since 1989 has the Federal Housing Administration (FHA) been insuring these mortgages, which are made through private companies and many banks and S&Ls.

Before reverse mortgages became available, the only way to take money out of a home was to sell the home and move, or to take out a home equity loan or line of credit. But many seniors have incomes too low to qualify for this type of loan. Now there are three types of reverse mortgages that allow seniors (over age 62) to withdraw money that does not have to be repaid until the homeowner either moves and sells the house or dies. To qualify, the home must be owned without a mortgage, or with only a small mortgage balance.

The most comforting factor in the reverse mortgage is that you cannot be forced to move and repay the loan, nor can your heirs wind up owing any more than the total value of the home. The FHA insurance protects lenders against the risk that the loan balance could be greater than the value of the home itself. If you outlive the actuarial tables and die owing more than the home is worth, the lender cannot go after your other assets to pay off the loan.

Remember, the FHA insurance protects the lender from risk, not you. So it doesn't matter to you whether your reverse mortgage is FHA-insured or not. You'll just find more FHA-insured reverse mortgages because the insurance encourages lenders to go out and offer the loans.

How Much Money You Can Receive

The amount of money you can take out of the home depends on your current age, the current market value of the home, and current interest rates. Generally speaking, the older the person and the greater the value of the house, the more money will be available for a reverse mortgage loan. Also, as interest rates are lower, the greater the value of the loan that can be taken.

Every reverse mortgage lender can calculate the monthly payments slightly differently, and so it might be worthwhile to check the offers from several lenders. An FHA-insured reverse mortgage generally will give you a lower monthly payment than a reverse mortgage that is insured by the lender itself.

You can use the money from your reverse mortgage for any purpose you choose. You might decide to use it for monthly living expenses, to pay some big bills, or simply to go on a vacation. It's your money, and nobody can tell you what to do with it.

The income you receive does not affect your Social Security benefits.

How Reverse Mortgages Are Structured

Here's how the three FHA-insured plans work.

The tenure plan: Under this plan, you will get a fixed monthly loan amount for as long as you live in the home as your principal residence or until you die. (If your reverse mortgage is being insured by the lender instead of the FHA, this is the only type of plan you will be offered.)

The term plan: Under this type of reverse mortgage, you decide how many years of payments you want to receive. The shorter the term, the higher the monthly payments. But when the term ends, the payments stop. At the end of the term you still do not have to repay the loan until you sell the home or until your heirs repay it out of the home equity when you die.

The line-of-credit plan: This is the most flexible plan because you sign up for a line of credit (which automatically increases as you age). You can take out money at any time, to use for home improvements or to pay a major bill.

Terry's Tip:

$$$ You should reserve some of your home equity if you are taking either a term or line-of-credit plan. On the other hand, if you are just opting for the highest monthly income you can receive, you'll need to use all of the equity available in your home.

The Costs

As with any mortgage, there are up-front costs associated with a reverse mortgage, but most of those costs can be financed as part of the loan balance. Each lender sets its own fees and costs, but you can expect to pay normal closing costs, plus a fee of from 1 to 2 percent of the home's value. Then there is the insurance premium of about 2 percent of the home's value. This fee is charged at the closing, plus an additional ½ of 1 percent is added to the interest rate on your loan. All of these amounts can be financed as part of the loan—except for the portion of the origination fee that exceeds 1 percent of the home value.

For example, on a $100,000 home you'd pay two percentage points or $2,000 in FHA insurance fees, another two percentage points ($2,000) to the lender as an origination fee, and perhaps as much as $1,000 or $1,500 in fees for appraisals, title insurance, and other closing costs. Altogether, you'd be talking about paying $5,500 to close this loan, and all except $1,000 (part of the origination fee) can be financed.

The Loan Interest Rate

Each lender may set its own interest rate on the loan. Some will charge a fixed interest rate, but a more popular way to do it is to use an adjustable rate. The adjustable rate will have a cap limiting overall interest increases. Of course, the lower the rate at closing, the higher the monthly payment you'll receive. But on a variable-rate reverse mortgage, your monthly check never changes. Instead, what changes is your outstanding loan balance. If rates move higher, you'll be building up a larger outstanding loan. But don't worry, because you still can't outlive your regular monthly payments.

The Limits

For FHA-insured reverse mortgages there are limits on the amount of home equity that can be used to determine loan payments. This limit varies by state and county; the current maximum is $124,875 in expensive urban areas.

NOTE: Not all reverse mortgages are made by FHA-approved lenders. Other private lenders also make these mortgages and may offer a greater use of home equity, although usually at a slightly higher rate.

Where to Get a Reverse Mortgage Loan

You can call the FHA at 800-732-6643 to find the names and numbers of lenders in your area that make reverse mortgage loans. Other lenders that privately insure their loans will advertise through local publications.

The Negatives

There are a few drawbacks to reverse mortgages, and you should understand them. In fact, many states require that potential reverse mortgage borrowers undergo independent counseling before they sign an agreement with a mortgage firm.

First, these mortgages can be expensive in terms of up-front costs, so only those planning to remain in their homes for several years should consider reverse mortgages.

Second, unless your plan has a formula for sharing the increase in property values, you could forfeit appreciation of the value of your home. If the home's value is locked in at the time the reverse mortgage is made, you can live there and receive monthly checks until you die. But unless specifically stated in the loan document, your heirs would not benefit from the sale of the house at a higher price.

Also, check the terms of your loan carefully. Many reverse mortgages have language stating that in the event of a lengthy nursing home stay you could be forced to sell your home and repay the loan.

Terry's Tip:

$$$ For more information on reverse mortgage loans, AARP offers an excellent free booklet: *Consumer's Guide to Home Equity Conversion*, available by writing to AARP, 601 E Street N.W., Washington, D.C. 20049.

There is a nonprofit organization that will give you a list of lenders that make reverse mortgages. To get this list send $1 and a self-addressed, stamped, business-size envelope to NCHEC Locator, 1210 E. College—#300, Marshall, MN 56258.

Senior Income-Boosting Strategy #2: Residential Sale-Leaseback

There is another strategy that may allow elderly owners of fully paid residences to liberate some of their cash while remaining in their residence. It's called a sale-leaseback.

The parents sell the home to one or more of their children, who then lease the home back to them at a fair market rental rate. The parents are required to pay taxes on the gain realized from the sale of the house, but if at least one of the parental homeowners is age 55 and has lived in the home as a principal residence for three of the past five years, up to $125,000 of the gain can be excluded from income. (See Everyday Tax Strategy #8 in chapter 45.)

The child (or a partnership of several children) can either pay cash for the sale, secure a mortgage on the house, or ask the parents to provide mortgage financing at current rates. The latter arrangement keeps the entire transaction more private and also reduces costs involved with obtaining a mortgage. If the parents become the lenders, they no longer have the problem of what to do with the proceeds of the sale; instead, they'll be collecting monthly mortgage payments.

Obviously, the idea is to have the parents earning more mortgage (or investment) income than they will be paying in rent. This will increase the parents' cash flow, while allowing them to remain in the home. Expenses associated with the upkeep of the home become the responsibility of the new owners—the children—who may use the expenses as described below, to offset the rental income.

The newly purchased house qualifies as rental property for the children who buy it. The rental income they receive from the parents is taxable, and expenses related to upkeep of the property are deductible, subject to the income tax limitations on passive losses. At some point in the future, the children may sell the house and realize a gain—which would offset any current negative cash flow.

Because of the tax implications of a sale-leaseback, you should definitely consult your own tax advisor about the benefits of entering into this type of arrangement. You should also carefully consider the personalities of family members involved in this plan, because it will be a difficult transaction to unravel emotionally, as well as financially, if one family member has a change of heart.

Senior Income-Boosting Strategy #3: Split-Funded Annuities

This is a strategy designed to increase your monthly income while preserving your principal. To fully understand the advantages of this strategy, you'll need to reread chapter 28 on annuities.

Right up front, I'm going to tell you the "catch" to this program. Once you've started on this investment program, you have to stick with it. You lose some liquidity—the ability to get at your cash—but the monthly returns can be substantially higher than the interest checks you're receiving now. So you might want to consider this plan for part of your savings.

Remember that there are two kinds of annuities. An *immediate annuity* lets you start receiving a monthly check for life, based on the amount of money you put into the annuity plan, your current age, and the current level of interest rates. A *deferred annuity* lets your cash grow and compound tax-deferred until you choose a way to take the money out.

If you receive a check from a monthly annuity, it will be for a greater amount than if you simply invested the money in a bank certificate of deposit. That's because a portion of the check is a return of your own principal. The portion of the monthly check that is a return of your own principal is not subject to income tax. The exact amount of your monthly check, as noted above, depends on certain variables such as age, sex, interest rates, and the amount contributed to the annuity.

Here's the plan. Let's assume you have $40,000 to work with. We're going to divide it into separate "pots" of money and set each pot to "cooking" a slightly different way!

First you take half of your money ($20,000) and purchase an immediate annuity. This annuity is designed to pay out all of your original investment and interest earnings in a period of ten years. Then take the second half of your investment and divide it into two more "pots"—each with $10,000. Those will be invested in two separate deferred annuities, which will build up income over the years but will not start paying your cash out until later.

Here's how our example works. For ten years you are receiving monthly checks from the first $20,000 annuity. A portion of each monthly check is tax-free because it is a return of your original investment. The check will be larger than a simple interest check on a bank CD because of this return-of-capital feature. At the end of ten years you've used up all your cash in the first annuity, plus the interest it earned along the way.

But at the same time, the money you've invested in the second and third annuities has been growing tax-sheltered at exactly the same rate at which you were taking money out of the first annuity. Each of these $10,000 annuities was earning interest at a rate of at least 7 percent a year. Remember the Rule of 72 in chapter 13? At a rate of 7.2 percent, your money will double in ten years.

So, at the end of ten years, each of those original $10,000 annuities is worth $20,000. You wind up with the same principal amount of money you started with, although the buying power has been reduced somewhat by inflation.

In the 11th year, you take one of the remaining annuities and ask the insurance company to start sending you ten years of monthly payments—of which a substantial portion (about 40 to 45 percent) will be tax-free. At the end of this second ten-year period, you'll still have the remaining annuity which could be worth as much as $40,000 or more, depending on the rate at which it is earning interest!

There is no other drawback, beyond the general restrictions on annuities that you learned about in chapter 28. If inflation were to return, you might be locked into fixed rates that seem relatively low, but you could always switch your remaining deferred annuities into higher-yielding ones, if rates move high enough to offset the surrender charges.

This is the kind of strategy that requires some help from a financial planner or annuity expert, so you can pick high-yielding annuities from safe insurance companies.

This strategy can be modified to ensure that the payments you receive after the 11th year are completely tax-free. Instead of purchasing two additional annuities with the second half of your investment, you purchase a life insurance policy designed to create the largest amount of cash build-up with the least amount paid for life insurance.

This type of policy is completely explained in Tax-Wise Insurance Strategy #6 on page 433. If the correctly designed policy is purchased at the same time you purchase your immediate annuity, your borrowings from the insurance policy starting in the 11th year will be completely tax-free. Care must be taken not to borrow too much money out of the life policy. Only the interest earnings should be taken out each year, leaving the balance to pay the mortality charges and generate cash earnings for the future. But this stream of tax-free borrowings can continue indefinitely—over your life, your spouse's life, and even your child's life as described on page 433.

Conclusion

It's all in your hands now. You have learned financial planning strategies for every stage of your life, while gaining some perspective about the need to apply these strategies. But none of it will work until you take action. The first two letters of the word GOAL are GO!

No matter what your age, it's never too late—or too early—to get started. The knowledge you now have will help you adjust your plan to changing economic circumstances, while you move steadily toward your financial objectives. The road to success is always under construction!

Every person has special dreams. Don't rest until you turn those dreams into realities—by creating and following a plan. While you're setting goals, don't limit yourself to financial targets; include all the dreams that have whispered to your heart.

Sit down right now and take a few minutes to make a list of the desires you have for the next ten years. Then pick out two goals for this year. Make a list of reasons why you want to reach these goals. With enough reasons you can accomplish anything. Write a step-by-step plan of how you will approach your mission. Then start working your plan!

Remember, the best way to predict the future is to create it. We live in a country that gives us the opportunity to set unlimited goals—and to reach those goals through our own efforts. When it comes to finances, it's simply a matter of mind over money!

Appendix A

No-load Mutual Fund Management Companies

FUND FAMILY	ADDRESS	PHONE #
AARP Funds	P.O. Box 2540 Boston, MA 02208	800-253-2277
Jones & Babson	3 Crown Center 2440 Pershing Rd. Kansas City, MO 64108	800-422-2766
Benham Capital Management	1665 Charleston Rd. Mountain View, CA 94043	800-472-3389
Berger Funds	210 University Blvd. Suite 900 Denver, CO 80206	800-333-1001
Blanchard Group Funds	41 Madison Avenue, 24th Fl. New York, NY 10010	800-458-8621
Boston Company	53 State St. Boston, MA 02109	800-225-5267
Bull & Bear Advisors	11 Hanover Square New York, NY 10005	800-847-4200

FUND FAMILY	ADDRESS	PHONE #
Columbia Funds	1301 S.W. 5th Ave. Portland, OR 97201	800-547-1707
Dimensional Fund Advisers	1299 Ocean Ave., Suite 650 Santa Monica, CA 90401	310-395-8005
Dodge & Cox	One Sansome St. San Francisco, CA 94104	415-434-0311
Dreyfus Funds	200 Park Ave. New York, NY 10166	800-829-3733
Eclipse Financial Services	144 East 30th St. New York, NY 10016	800-782-6620
Evergreen Funds	2500 Westchester Ave. Purchase, NY 10577	800-235-0064
Fidelity Investments	82 Devonshire St. Boston, MA 02109	800-544-8888
INVESCO Funds	INVESCO Funds Group P.O. Box 2040 Denver, CO 80201	800-525-8085
Flex-Funds	R. Meeder & Associates 6000 Memorial Dr. Box 7177 Dublin, OH 43017	800-325-3539
Founders Funds	2930 East Third Ave. Denver, CO 80206	800-525-2440
GIT Investment Funds	1655 Fort Meyer Dr. Arlington, VA 22209	800-336-3063
Gabelli & Company	Corporate Center at Rye Rye, NY 10580	800-422-3554
The Galaxy Funds	P.O. Box 0007 Worcester, MA 01653	800-628-0414
The Gateway Trust	400 Techneccenter Dr. Suite 220 Milford, OH 45150	800-354-6339
Gintel Equity Management, Inc.	Greenwich Office Park #6 Greenwich, CT 06831	800-243-5808

FUND FAMILY	ADDRESS	PHONE #
Gradison McDonald	580 Walnut St. Cincinnati, OH 45202	800-869-5999
Harbor Fund	One Seagate Toledo, OH 43666	800-422-1050
IAI Mutual Funds	3700 First Bank Plz. 601 2nd Ave., South Minneapolis, MN 55402	800-945-3863
Janus Funds	100 Fillmore St. Suite 300 Denver, CO 80206-4923	800-525-8983
Legg Mason Mutual Funds	111 South Calvert St. Baltimore, MD 21203	800-822-5544
Lexington Management Corp.	Park 80 West, Plaza 2 P.O. Box 1515 Saddlebrook, NJ 07662	800-526-0056
Lindner Group	P.O. Box 11208 St. Louis, MO 63105	314-727-5305
Merriman Investment Management	1200 Westlake Ave., North Suite 700 Seattle, WA 98109	800-423-4893
Monetta Financial Services	1776-A South Naperville Rd., #207 Wheaton, IL	800-666-3882
Mutual Series Fund, Inc.	Mutual Series Service Center 440 Financial Group P.O. Box 74 Worcester, MA 01653-0074	800-553-3014
Neuberger & Berman Management	605 Third Ave. 2nd Fl. New York, NY 10158	800-877-9700
Nicholas Family of Funds	700 North Water St. Suite 1010 Milwaukee, WI 53202	800-227-5987
Portico Funds	615 East Michigan Milwaukee, WI 53202	800-982-8909

FUND FAMILY	ADDRESS	PHONE #
T. Rowe Price Investor Services	100 East Pratt St. Baltimore, MD 21202	800-638-5660
Rushmore Funds	4922 Fairmont Ave. Bethesda, MD 20814	800-621-7874
SAFECO Mutual Funds	4333 Brooklyn Ave., N.E. Seattle, WA 98185	800-426-6730
Sit Investment Associates	4600 Norwest Center 90 South 7th St. Minneapolis, MN 55402	800-332-5580
Scudder Funds	175 Federal St. 12th Fl. Boston, MA 02110	800-225-2470
Selected Funds	P.O. Box 419782 Kansas City, MO 64141-6782	800-553-5533
Stein Roe & Farnham	300 West Adams 12th Fl. Chicago, IL 60606	800-338-2550
Strong Funds	100 Heritage Reserve Menomonee Falls, WI 53051	800-368-3863
Twentieth Century Investors	4500 Main St. P.O. Box 419200 Kansas City, MO 64111	800-345-2021
USAA Investment Management	USAA Building San Antonio, TX 78288	800-531-8181
United Services Advisors	P.O. Box 659 San Antonio, TX 78293-0659	800-873-8637
Value Line	711 Third Ave. New York, NY 10017	800-223-0818

FUND FAMILY	ADDRESS	PHONE #
Vanguard Group	Vanguard Financial Center Valley Forge, PA 19482	800-662-7447
Warburg, Pincus Counsellors	466 Lexington Ave. New York, NY 10017-3147	800-257-5614
Weiss, Peck & Greer	One New York Plaza 31st Fl. New York, NY 10043	800-223-3332

Appendix B

Federal Reserve Banks

For In-Person Visits:	For Written Correspondence:
FRB Atlanta	
104 Marietta Street, N.W.	Securities Service Dept.
Atlanta, Georgia	104 Marietta Street, N.W.
404-521-8657 (recording)	Atlanta, GA 30303
404-521-8653	
FRB Baltimore	
502 South Sharp Street	P.O. Box 1378
Baltimore, Maryland	Baltimore, MD 21203
301-576-3500 (recording)	
301-576-3300	
FRB Birmingham	
1801 Fifth Avenue, North	P.O. Box 10447
Birmingham, Alabama	Birmingham, AL 35283
205-731-8702 (recording)	
205-731-8708	
FRB Boston	
600 Atlantic Avenue	P.O. Box 2076
Boston, Massachusetts	Boston, MA 02106
617-973-3805 (recording)	
617-973-3810	

FRB Buffalo
160 Delaware Avenue
Buffalo, New York
716-849-5158 (recording)
716-849-5000

P.O. Box 961
Buffalo, NY 14240-0961

FRB Charlotte
530 East Trade Street
Charlotte, North Carolina
704-358-2424 (recording)
704-358-2100

P.O. Box 30248
Charlotte, NC 28230

FRB Chicago
230 South LaSalle Street
Chicago, Illinois
312-786-1110 (recording)
312-322-5369

P.O. Box 834
Chicago, IL 60690

FRB Cincinnati
150 East Fourth Street
Cincinnati, Ohio
513-721-4787 Ext. 334

P.O. Box 999
Cincinnati, OH 45201

FRB Cleveland
1455 East Sixth Street
Cleveland, Ohio
216-579-2490

P.O. Box 6387
Cleveland, OH 44101

FRB Dallas
400 South Akard Street
Dallas, Texas
214-651-6362

Security Dept. Station K
400 South Akard Street
Dallas, TX 75222

FRB Denver
1020 16th Street
Denver, Colorado
303-572-2475 (recording)
303-572-2470 or 2473

P.O. Box 5228
Denver, CO 80217-5228

FRB Detroit
160 West Fort Street
Detroit, Michigan
313-963-4936 (recording)
313-964-6157

P.O. Box 1059
Detroit, MI 48231

FRB El Paso
301 East Main
El Paso, Texas
915-544-4730

P.O. Box 100
El Paso, TX 79901

FRB Houston
1701 San Jacinto Street
Houston, Texas
713-649-4433

P.O. Box 2578
Houston, TX 77252

FRB Jacksonville
800 West Water Street
Jacksonville, Florida
904-632-1178 (recording)
904-632-1179 or 1190

P.O. Box 2499
Jacksonville, FL 32231-2499

FRB Kansas City
925 Grand Avenue
Kansas City, Missouri
816-881-2767 (recording)
816-881-2409

P.O. Box 440
Kansas City, MO 64198

FRB Little Rock
325 West Capitol Avenue
Little Rock, Arkansas
501-324-8272

P.O. Box 1261
Little Rock, AR 72203

FRB Los Angeles
950 South Grand Avenue
Los Angeles, California
213-624-7398

P.O. Box 2077
Terminal Annex
Los Angeles, CA 90051

FRB Louisville
410 South Fifth Street
Louisville, Kentucky
502-568-9240 (recording)
502-568-9236 or 9238

P.O. Box 32710
Louisville, KY 40232

FRB Memphis
200 North Main Street
Memphis, Tennessee
901-523-7171 Ext. 622 or
Ext. 641 (recording)

P.O. Box 407
Memphis, TN 38101

FRB Miami
9100 N.W. Thirty-Six Street
Miami, Florida
305-471-6257 (recording)
305-471-6497

P.O. Box 520847
Miami, FL 33152

FRB Minneapolis
250 Marquette Avenue
Minneapolis, Minnesota
612-340-2051 (recording)
612-340-2075

250 Marquette Ave.
Minneapolis, MN 55480

FRB Nashville
301 Eighth Avenue, North
Nashville, Tennessee
615-251-7236 (recording)
615-251-7100

301 Eighth Ave., N.
Nashville, TN 37203-4407

FRB New Orleans
525 St. Charles Avenue
New Orleans, Louisiana
504-593-3290 (recording)
504-593-3200

P.O. Box 61630
New Orleans, LA 70161

FRB New York
33 Liberty Street
New York, New York
212-720-5823 (recording)
212-720-6619

Federal Reserve
P.O. Station
New York, NY 10045

FRB Oklahoma City
226 Dean A McGee Avenue
Oklahoma City, Oklahoma
405-270-8660 (recording)
405-270-8652

P.O. Box 25129
Oklahoma City, OK 73125

FRB Omaha
2201 Farnam Street
Omaha, Nebraska
402-221-5638 (recording)
402-221-5636

2201 Farnam Street
Omaha, NE 68102

FRB Philadelphia

Ten Independence Mall
Philadelphia, Pennsylvania
215-574-6580 (recording)
215-574-6680

P.O. Box 90
Philadelphia, PA 19105

FRB Pittsburgh

717 Grant Street
Pittsburgh, Pennsylvania
412-261-7988 (recording)
412-261-7863

P.O. Box 867
Pittsburgh, PA 15230-0867

FRB Portland

915 S.W. Stark Street
Portland, Oregon
503-221-5931 (recording)
503-221-5932

P.O. Box 3436
Portland, OR 97208-3436

FRB Richmond

701 East Byrd Street
Richmond, Virginia
804-697-8355 (recording)
804-697-8372

P.O. Box 27622
Richmond, VA 23261

FRB Salt Lake City

120 South State Street
Salt Lake City, Utah
801-322-7844 (recording)
801-322-7900

P.O. Box 30780
Salt Lake City, UT 84130

FRB San Antonio

126 East Nueva Street
San Antonio, Texas
512-978-1330 (recording)
512-978-1303
512-978-1305

P.O. Box 1471
San Antonio, TX 78295

FRB San Francisco

101 Market Street
San Francisco, California
415-974-3491 (recording)
415-974-2330

P.O. Box 7702
San Francisco, CA 94120

FRB Seattle

1015 Second Avenue
Seattle, Washington
206-343-3615 (recording)
206-343-3605

Securities Services Dept.
P.O. Box 3567
Terminal Annex
Seattle, WA 98124

FRB St. Louis

411 Locust Street
St. Louis, Missouri
314-444-8602 (recording)
314-444-8665

P.O. Box 14915
St. Louis, MO 63178

United States Treasury
Washington, D.C.

Bureau of the Public Debt
Securities Transactions Branch
1300 C Street, S.W.
Washington, DC 202-874-4000

Mail Inquiries to:
Bureau of the Public Debt
Division of Customer Services
Washington, DC 20239-0001

Device for hearing impaired
202-874-4026

Mail Tenders to:
Bureau of the Public Debt
Department N.
Washington, DC 20239-1500

Commonly Used Public Debt Forms:

5174-1	Tender for 2–3-Year Treasury Note
5174-3	Tender for 5–10-Year Treasury Note
5174-4	Tender for Treasury Bond
5176-1	Tender for 13-Week Treasury Bill
5176-2	Tender for 26-Week Treasury Bill
5176-3	Tender for 52-Week Treasury Bill
5178	Transaction Request
5179	Security Transfer Request
5180	Reinvestment Request (for Treasury Bills)
5262	Reinvestment Request for Treasury Notes or Bonds

Index

AAA Auto Pricing Service, 323
AAII Guide to No-Load Mutual Funds, 140
AAII Journal, 140
A-B trust, 461–63
Account maintenance fee, 130
Adam Network, 113
Adjustable-rate mortgage (ARM), 316–19
Adjustable-rate mortgage funds, 159–60
ADRs (American Depository Receipts), 187, 196
Age groups. *See* Generations
A. M. Best insurance rating service, 441
American Association of Homes for the Aging
    (AAHA), 518
American Association of Individual Investors,
    140
American Association of Retired Persons
    (AARP), 499
  Insured Tax-Free General Bond Fund, 171
  long-term care insurance of, 505–7
  Medicare supplement policies of, 494
American College, 47–48
American Depository Receipts (ADRs), 187, 196
American Express Express Cash program,
    250–51
American Numismatic Association, 195
American Pacific Bank, 244–45
American Stock Exchange, 146
Ameritas, 410, 438
AMEX Life, 506–9
Amica Mutual Insurance Company, 377
Annuities, 203–19
  charitable gift, 473
  definition of, 204
  guaranteed-rate, 204–5, 208, 216–19
    choosing, 217–19

    definition of, 216–17
    rules on, 217
  insurance company safety and, 208–9
  lump sum distribution from, 206
  rules and costs of, 205
  split-funded, 531–33
  surrender charges for, 205
  switching, 207
  taking money out of, 205–6
  tax-deferred, 203–9. *See also* Annuities,
    variable-rate
    definition of, 204
    retirement plan using, 344–45
  taxes and, 206–7
  variable-rate, 210–15
    choosing a plan, 212–15
    costs associated with, 212
    definition of, 204–5, 210–11
    guaranteed death benefit, 211
    mutual funds in, 211–14
    surrender charges, 211
    tax-deferred compounding feature, 211
Annuitizing, 205–6
Annuity shopping service, 213–14, 219
Arbitration of disputes with stockbrokers, 129
Argus Research Utility Spotlight and Rankings
    (monthly), 165
Asset allocation, 62–68
  changing your, 66–67
  market timing and, 67–68
  risk and, 62–65
  your own, 65–66
Assets in balance sheet, 39–41
Assured Enterprises, 437
Audits, 353–54

Auto Advisor, 323
Automatic deductions from paychecks, 226
Automobile insurance, 370–79
  additional coverages, 377
  bodily injury liability coverage, 373
  chargeable claims and pricing of, 372
  choosing a policy, 372–73
  collision coverage, 376
  comprehensive coverage, 376–77
  denial of coverage, 380
  medical payments coverage, 375
  no-fault, 370–71
  pricing of, 371–72
  property damage liability coverage, 374
  saving money on, 377–80
    annual premiums, 379–80
    applicable discounts, 378–79
    car-buying decision, 379
    comparison price shopping, 377
    raising your deductible, 378
    track record of insurance company, 378
  underinsured motorist coverage, 375
  uninsured motorist coverage, 374–75
Averaging down, 88

Babson Group, 20
Baby boom generation, 11, 17–20, 22
Back-end charges, 59
Back-end load, 106
Bad money habits, 32–34
Balance sheet, 39–42
Bank accounts, foreign currency, 190–91
Bankcard Holders of America, 242
Bankruptcy, 232–33, 238–39
  tax aspects of, 355
Banks
  establishing a relationship with, 226–27
  safety rating for, 97
Beacon Company Policy Evaluation Service,
    435–36
Benchmarks, 93
Benham
  European Government Bond Fund, 186
  GNMA Income, 158
  Gold Equities Index, 196
  Treasury Note Fund, 157
Best of America IV, 214
Beta, 59
Better Investing (magazine), 140
"Bigger is better" habit, 33–34
Bill-paying system, establishing a, 228–29
Blanchard Short-Term Global Income, 185
Bodily injury insurance in automobile policy, 373
Bond Buyer Municipal Bond Index, 153
Bond equivalent yield of Treasury bills, 100
Bond ladder, 154–55
Bond mutual funds, 155–57
  closed-end, 165–66
  of longer-term bonds issued by foreign govern-
    ments and corporations, 185–86

Bonds, 148–75
  benchmarks for measuring yields of, 153, 169
  call provision in, 150
  convertible, 162–63
  increasing yield of, 154–66
    adjustable-rate mortgage funds, 159–60
    bond, 155–57
    bond mutual funds, 155–57
    building a bond ladder, 154–55
    closed-end bond funds, 165–66
    Ginnie Mae funds and CMOs, 158–59
    LYONs (Liquid Yield Option Notes), 163–64
    strategic income funds, 166
    U.S. savings bonds, 160
    zero coupon bonds, 160–62
  interest rate-risk relationship, 150–51
  risk-price relationship, 151
  terms used in discussing, 149–50
  total return, 150
  zero coupon, 160–62
    convertible, 163–64
Brinson Associates, 67
Broker loan rate, 143–44
Brokerage firms, 49
  discount, 130–31
    no-load mutual funds purchased through,
      111–12
    short sales of mutual funds, 125
  800 numbers for, 131
  stock, 128–30
    account maintenance fee charged by, 130
    arbitration of disputes with brokers, 129
    commissions, 130–31
    discount, 130–31
    wrap accounts at, 130
Budget, 42
Budget deficit, federal, 28, 30, 69
Budget Kit, The, 42
Budget notebook, 42
Bull & Bear Gold Investors, 196
Bullion, 195
Bullion coins, 195
Business expenses
  deducting legitimate unreimbursed, 301–2
  home office, 306–7
Buying power, taxes and, 70–71
Buyout offers, 296–98

C corporations, 306–7
Call options, 145–46
Call provision, 150
Capital gains taxes, 74–75
  "first in, first out" (FIFO) method,
    125
Capital Preservation money market fund, 161
Car/Puter International, 323, 326–27
Cars, 322–29. *See also* Automobile insurance
  buying vs. leasing, 327–29
  cash purchase vs. financing, 327
  getting the best price on, 322–24

new vs. used, 325–27
unnecessary extras and buying, 324–25
Cash. *See also* Currencies
on hand, 95
Cash flow statement, 42–43
Cash management accounts, 229–30
Cash value life insurance, 411–22. *See also* Life
insurance
blended policies, 418–19
dividends, 419
illustrations for, 411–12
in-force ledger, 421
loans on, 420
paid-up policies, 420
preferred rates, 420–21
single premium, 417–18
start-up costs and expenses, 412
surrender charges, 419–20
surrender value of, 412
switching policies, 421–22
universal, 415–16
variable, 416–17
whole life, 414–15
Casualty losses, 354
Catastrophic health insurance, 384
Catastrophic illness, 499
Cato Institute, 70–71
Certificates of deposit (CDs)
foreign, 190–91
interest rates on, 97
jumbo (above $100,000 insured limit), 97
rate of return on, 53–54
risk and, 54
as safe investment, 96–97
Certified Financial Planners (CFPs), 47
Chapter 7 bankruptcy, 238
Chapter 11 bankruptcy, 238–39
Chapter 13 bankruptcy, 238
Charitable giving, estate planning and
charitable gift annuity, 473
charitable lead trusts, 473
charitable remainder trusts, 471–73
Fidelity Charitable Gift Fund, 470–71
outright gifts, 469–70
Charitable lead trusts, 473
Charitable remainder trusts, 471–73
Charting, 137–38
Check registers, 228
Checkbook
balancing your, 228
desk-style, 227
Checking accounts, 226–27
automatic deductions from, 226
with overdraft line of credit, 227, 249
style of, 227–28
Chicago Board Options Exchange, 146
Chicago Mercantile Exchange International Monetary Market, 192
"Chicken money," 94–96. *See also* Safe money
strategies

Child support, 263
Children, 290–92. *See also* College saving strategies
economic education of, 291–92
educational gifts to grandchildren, 465–67
employing, in your own business, 309–10
financial hobbies for, 291
investments and, 290–91
savings accounts for, 290
taxes and, 292
Citibank (South Dakota), 244
Civil Service Retirement System (CSRS), 344
Closed-end bond funds, 165–66
Closed-End Fund Digest, 109
Closed-end municipal bond mutual funds,
172–73
Closed-end mutual funds, 108–9
foreign, 188–89
COBRA period, 297–98
COBRA provisions, 388
Coins, gold and silver, 194–95
Co-insurance provision, 382
Collateralized mortgage obligations (CMOs),
158–59
College aid, 283–89
adjusting your finances to increase, 284–85
applying for, 286–89
choosing college based on offer, 286
need assessment for, 283–84
College Cost Explorer Fund Finder (software pro-
gram), 289
College costs, 8, 267–70, 272, 277, 279
College saving strategies, 275–82
CollegeSure CDs, 277–80
forecast of costs and, 270–71
life insurance, 281–82
prepaid tuition plans, 281
Series EE U.S. savings bonds, 276–77
state, 280–81
stock market mutual fund, 275–76
tax-exempt college bonds, 280–81
tax rules that could affect, 271–75
College Savings Bank, 271, 277, 280
College scholarships, 288
CollegeSure CDs, 277–80
College tuition, U.S. savings bonds for, 276–77
Collision coverage in automobile policy, 376
Colonial Strategic Income Fund, 166
Commodity funds, 147
Commodity futures, 146–47
Common-law property, 263
Common stocks. *See also* Investment strategies;
Stocks
risk in owning, 54, 57–59, 65
Community property, 263
Community property states, 259
Compounding, Rule of 72 and, 88–89
Computer programs, 231
Conference Board, 19
Conglomerates, 25

Congress, regulations and, 75–76, 78
Conservatorship, 457–58
Continental Bank (Chicago), 193
Continuing Care Accreditation Commission, 518
Convertible bond funds, 163
Convertible bonds, 162–63
Convertible preferred stock, 164
Corporate bond mutual funds, 157
Corporations, Subchapter S, 305–6
Coupon rate, 149
Credit, 232–39
    divorce and, 263–64
    getting help with problems, 236–38
    in your own name, 235–36
Credit bureaus, 233–34
Credit cards, 224, 240–47
    cash advances from, 249–51
    choosing, 242–43
    cost of charging on, 3
    costly billing practices of, 243–44
    debt owed on, 41–42
    disputes involving, 246–47
    fraud involving, 247
    gold and platinum, 33–34
    interest rates paid on, 242
    keeping a list of your, 245
    rights of holders of, 246
    secured, 244–45, 264
    transferring your balance to a lower-rate card,
        243
Credit life insurance, 325
Credit reports, 224, 233–36
Credit shelter trust, 461
Credit unions, 254
Currencies, 176
    buying, 189–90
    mutual funds, 191
    price quoted for, 181–82
    stocks and, 180–81
    strong vs. weak, 179–80
    trade and, 180
Currency exchange rates, 176
Currency futures and options, 192
Currency risk, 178
    hedging, 181
Current yield of bonds, 149

Daily Graphs, 138
Debit cards, 247
Debt, 3. *See also* Credit; Liabilities; Loans
    getting out of, 224
    in the 1980s, 4–5, 27–28
    in the 1990s, 28–29
Defensive investment strategies, 193–202
    gold and silver, 194–97
    natural resources, 201–2
    real estate, 197–201
Defined benefit plans, 342–43
Defined contribution plans, 344
De Gaulle, Charles, 178

Depression of the 1930s. *See* Great Depression of
    the 1930s
Direct Insurance Services (DIS), 408–9, 437
Disability insurance, 324, 391–97
    amount of coverage needed, 392
    company disability benefits and, 397
    definitions of disability and, 393–94
    with guaranteed premium, 395
    inflation and income increases and, 395–96
    noncancellable, 395
    price comparisons before buying, 396–97
    pricing of, 392–93
    residual benefit disability payments and,
        393–94
    term of benefits from, 394
    waiver of premiums clause in, 395
Discount brokerage firms, 130–31
    no-load mutual funds purchased through,
        111–12
    short sales of mutual funds, 125
Discover cards, cash withdrawal on, 250
Dividend reinvestment plans (DRPs), 132–33
Divorce, 262–66
    credit and, 263–64
    division of property and, 263
    financial fairness and, 266
    spousal maintenance and child support and,
        263
    taxes and, 264–65
Dohmen, Bert, 139
Dollar. *See also* Currencies
    strong vs. weak, 179
Dollar cost averaging, 84–87
Dollar discipline, 83–84
Donahue's Money Letter, 122
Dow Jones Bond Average, 153
Dow Jones Industrial Average (DJIA), 65, 93
Dreyfus
    asset-allocation program, 124–25
    Convertible Securities, 163
    GNMA, 158
    Insured Municipal Bond Fund, 171
    short sales of mutual funds, 125
Duff & Phelps, 441

Earned income credit (EIC), 353
Earthquake insurance, 363
Educational gifts to grandchildren, 465–67
Eighties, the, 27–28
Elimination period, 504
Emotion, risk of, 61
Employee Stock Ownership Plans (ESOPs), 299
Employer identification number (EIN), 304
Empty-nesters, 20
Endowment communities, 518
Enrolled agents, 352
Equifax, 233
Equitable distribution, 263
Estate planning, 447–76
    charitable giving and

charitable gift annuity, 473
charitable lead trusts, 472–73
charitable remainder trusts, 471–72
Fidelity Charitable Gift Fund, 470–71
outright gifts, 469–70
definition of, 448–49
dying without a will or estate plan, 449–50
giving away power and, 474–76
wills and, 453–56
dying without a, 449–50
living, 475
pour-over, 449, 459
Estate taxes, 8, 450–52
life insurance to pay, 426–28
saving on, 461–68
A-B trust, 461–63
educational gifts to grandchildren, 465–67
family limited partnership, 468
gifts to an irrevocable trust, 463–64
irrevocable life insurance trust, 464–65
$600,000 exemption, 467–68
Estimated taxes, filing, 351–52
Everyday money strategies
balancing your checkbook, 228
cash management accounts, 229–30
computerizing your records, 231
direct deposit of paychecks, 225–26
establishing a banking relationship, 226–27
establishing a bill-paying system, 228–29
paying yourself first with automatic deductions, 226
Excess major medical health insurance, 384
Executors, 455
Extended warranties, 328–29
for cars, 323

Fabian's Investment Resource, 123–24
Face value of bonds, 149
FAF (Financial Aid Form), 284
FAFSA (Free Application for Federal Student Aid), 283–84
Family income, median pretax, 8
Family limited partnership, 468
Family members, employing your own, 309–10
Family Service America, 237
Fashion. *See* Styles of handling money
Fear, 7
Federal Deposit Insurance Corporation (FDIC), 96
Federal Deposit Insurance Corporation Improvement Act (FDICIA), 76
Federal Employees Retirement System (FERS), 345
Federal Housing Administration (FHA), reverse mortgages and, 527–30
Federal Reserve Banks, 99
Federal Reserve System, 27, 74–78
creation of credit by, 76
lowering of interest rates by, 76
recession of 1992 and, 76–78

Fee for Service, 437
FICA (Social Security or payroll tax), 70, 71, 478
Fidelity Asset Manager, 118
Fidelity Insight (newsletter), 122
Fidelity Investment
Aggressive Tax-Free Bond Fund, 171
Brokerage Services, 137
Charitable Gift Fund, 470–71
Convertible Securities Fund, 163
direct annuity sales, 215
European Fund, 188
fund match program, 124
Ginnie Mae, 158
Global Bond Fund, 186
Government Securities Fund, 156
Insured Tax Free, 171
natural resource specialty funds, 202
Portfolio Advisory Services, 124
Real Estate, 199
short sales of mutual funds, 125
Short-Term World Income Fund, 185
Ultra Service Account, 229–30
Utilities Income Fund, 165
Worldwide Fund, 187
Fifties, the, 25
Financial aid for college. *See* College aid
Financial Institutions Reform, Recovery, and Enforcement Act (FIRREA), 75
Financial planners, 46–52
education of, 47–48
fees of, 48–49
questions to ask, 49–51
questions that should be asked by, 51–52
Financial planning, 12–15. *See also* Investment plan
age and generational issues and, 16–22
goals of, 14, 44–45
professional help in, 14–15
Financial Strategic
Energy, 202
European, 188
Gold, 196
Pacific Basin, 188
Utilities, 165
First-to-die policies, 430–31
Fixed rate, 149
Flood insurance, 363
Forward averaging, 521
401(k) company savings plans, 339–41
401(k) plans, 298–99
403(b) plans, 342
Franklin U.S. Government, 158
Franklin Value Mark II, 214
Fundamental analysis, 137
Futures contracts
on currency, 192
on gold and silver, 195–96

Galaxy of Funds, 113
Generation gap, 22

Generations
  baby boom, 11, 17–20, 22
  financial planning and, 16–22
  55- to 64-year-old, 20–21
Gift tax, college saving plan and, 273
Gifts
  charitable, estate planning and, 469
  to an irrevocable trust, 463–64
Ginnie Mae mutual funds, 158–59
Global income funds, 185
Goals, 44–45
Gold bullion, 195
Gold coins, 194–95
Gold futures contracts, 195–96
Gold mining stocks, 196
Gold mutual funds, 196–97
Gold standard, 25, 178
Gordon, Harley, 515
Government bond funds, 156–57
Government bonds. *See also* Municipal bonds
  foreign, longer-term bond funds, 185–86
Government employees, retirement planning for,
  344
Government regulation, 75
Government spending, federal, 28, 30
Grandchildren, educational gifts to, 465–67
Great Depression of the 1930s, lessons of, 24
Great Income Reshuffle, The (Conference Board),
  19
Greed, 7, 27
Guardians, 455

Habits of the past, 32–34
Hardy, Dorcas, 21–22
Health insurance, 381–90
  basic healthcare policies (hospital/surgery),
    383
  COBRA provisions and, 388
  co-insurance provision, 382
  comprehensive policies, 382–83
  cutting costs of, 389–90
  disease-specific policies, 384
  excess major medical policies, 384
  group plans, 385–87
  guaranteed renewable, 389–90
  health maintenance organizations (HMOs), 383
  hospital indemnity policies, 384–85
  individual policies, 387
  leaving a job and, 298
  long-term care policies, 385
  loss of job and, 388
  owning a business and, 308–9
  preexisting conditions and, 388
  preferred provider organizations (PPOs), 384
  self-insured plans, 386
  short-term coverage, 389
Health maintenance organizations (HMOs), 383,
  497–98
Hedging currency risk, 181
Hewitt Associates, 296, 334

Home-based businesses, 307–8
Home equity loans and lines of credit, 242–54,
  252–54, 321
Home office, 306–7
Home ownership. *See also* Mortgages
  baby boomers and, 17–19
Homeowners insurance, 361–69
  additional coverages and exceptions, 367
  claims, 368–69
  contents coverage and scheduled items,
    365–66
  credit card losses coverage, 367
  cutting the cost of, 368
  forms of coverage, 361–63
  getting enough coverage, 364–65
  liability insurance and umbrella policies,
    366–67
  medical payments section of, 367
  for renters, condo owners, and co-op owners,
    363–64
  replacement cost coverage, 366
Hospital indemnity policies, 384–85
Households, 19
*How to Protect Your Life Savings from
  Catastrophic Illness and Nursing Homes*
  (Gordon), 515
Hulbert, Mark, 67
Hulbert Financial Digest, The, 67, 123, 138–39
Huntington
  Global Currency Portfolio, 191
  Hard Currency Portfolio, 192
  High-Income Currency Portfolio, 191
  International Currency Portfolios, 191

Ibbotson & Associates, 54
Income
  family, 8
  of senior citizens, 21
  taxes' effect on, 69–70
Income tax. *See also* Tax-free investments
  children and, 292
  deferring, 167
Independent Advantage Financial Services,
  213–14, 219
Index funds, 114–16
Indexes
  bond, 153
  stock market, 92–93, 127
    international, 183
Individual Retirement Account (IRA), 4, 9, 203,
  305, 335–38. *See also* Retirement
  distributions
  at death, 524–25
  rollovers, 346–47
  Simplified Employee Pension Plans (SEPs)
    and, 307
Inflation
  asset allocation and, 65
  buying power and, 9
  of the 1970s, 26

return on investment and, 9
Rule of 72 and, 88–89
Initial public offerings (IPOs), 140–42
Installment loans, 41
Institute of Certified Financial Planners, 47
Insurance, 13, 52
  automobile. *See* Automobile insurance
  credit life, 324
  disability, 324, 391–97
    amount of coverage needed, 392
    company disability benefits and, 397
    definitions of disability and, 393–94
    with guaranteed premium, 395
    inflation and income increases and, 395–96
    noncancellable, 395
    price comparisons before buying, 396–97
    pricing of, 392–93
    residual benefit disability payments and,
      393–94
    term of benefits from, 394
    waiver of premiums clause in, 395
  earthquake, 363
  flood, 363
  health. *See* Health insurance
  homeowners, 361–69
    additional coverages and exceptions, 367
    claims, 368–69
    contents coverage and scheduled items,
      365–66
    credit card losses coverage, 367
    cutting the cost of, 368
    forms of coverage, 361–63
    getting enough coverage, 364–65
    liability insurance and umbrella policies,
      366–67
    medical payments section of, 367
    for renters, condo owners, and co-op
      owners, 363–64
    replacement cost coverage, 366
  life. *See* Life insurance
  long-term care. *See* Long-term care insurance
  umbrella, 60
Insurance brokers, discount, 413
Insurance companies
  annuities and ratings of, 208
  safety rating of, 440–41
Insurance Information, Inc., 409
InsuranceQuote Services, 408
Interest rate investments, 148–53
Interest rates
  Federal Reserve's lowering of, 76
  margin, 144
  for mortgages, 314–19
  in the 1970s, 26–27
  overall trend of, 148
  risk and, 150–51
  on Treasury bills, 99–100
Internal Revenue Service (IRS), help when
    dealing with, 355–56
International Association for Financial Planning, 48

International Board of Standards and Practices for
    Certified Financial Planners, 47
International bond funds, 157
International investing, 176–92
  currencies and stocks and, 180–81
  currencies and trade and, 180
  currency quotes and, 181–82
  currency risk and, 178
  hedging currency risk and, 181
  strategies for, 183–92
    bank accounts, 190–91
    closed-end country funds, 188
    currencies, 189–90
    currency futures and options, 192
    currency mutual funds, 191
    global income funds, 185
    longer-term bond funds, 185–86
    stock market funds, 187–88
  strong vs. weak currencies and, 179–80
International Monetary Market, 192
INVESCO Funds Group, 271
Investech Mutual Fund Advisor (newsletter),
    122
Investment, 37
  need for, 43
Investment clubs, 139–40
Investment newsletters, 138–39
Investment plan, 38
Investment strategies, 81. *See also* Safe money
    strategies
  averaging down, 88
  dollar cost averaging, 84–87
  dollar discipline, 83–84
  leverage, 90–91
  rating investment performance, 92–93
  Rule of 72, 88–89
  selling short, 91–92
  time value of money, 89–90
Irrevocable trusts, 463–64
  Medicaid and, 514

Japan Fund, 188
Job
  financial considerations in leaving a, 298–300
  finding the best, 295–96
Job-related business expenses, deducting,
    301–302
John Hancock Strategic Income Fund, 166
Joint tenancy
  in common, 259
  with rights of survivorship, 259, 448
Junior Achievement program, 291

Keogh plan, 305, 338–39
  defined benefit, 339
  money purchase, 339
  profit-sharing, 339
Key Federal Savings Bank, 244
Kiddie Tax, 271, 292
Kleinwort Benson International, 187

LEAPS (Long-term Equity Anticipation Securities), 146
Lehman Brothers Long Treasury Bond Index, 153
Leverage, 90–91
  investing using, 143–47
    commodity futures and funds, 146–47
    margin accounts, 143–44
    options and LEAPS, 144–46
Lewis, Michael, 18
Liabilities in balance sheet, 41–42
Liability insurance homeowners policy and, 367–68
Life insurance, 60, 398–441
  amount needed, 401–2
  borrowing on, 254–55
  cash value. *See* Cash value life insurance
  for college savings, 281–82
  first-to-die policies, 430–31
  joint and survivor vs. second-to-die policies, 428–30
  living benefits, 431–32
  low-load, 413
  modified endowment contract, 433
  need for, 400–401
  ownership of, 423–25
  to pay estate taxes, 426–28
  premiums, 398–99
  private pension, 433
  reasons to buy, 398
  strategies for buying
    advisory services, 434–35
    creating your own bid checklist, 438–40
    direct purchase of no-load insurance, 437–38
    discount services or fee advisors, 436–37
    safety rating of insurance company, 440–41
  term. *See* Term life insurance
Life Insurance Advisors Association (LIAA), 437
Life insurance trust, irrevocable, 464–65
Lifecare communities, 516–18
Limited partnership, family, 468
Lincoln National American Legacy II, 214
Lindner Dividend Fund, 165
Liquid Yield Option Notes (LYONs), 163–64
Liquidity, 95
Liquidity Fund, 200
Liquidity risk, 60
Living benefits, 431–32
Living trusts, 449, 456–60
  advice on, 460
  placing your assets inside, 458–59
  revocable, 458
  tax consequences of, 459
Living wills, 475
Loans
  home equity, 242–54
  life insurance, 254–55
  on life insurance, 420
  personal, 254
Long-term care, 500–501

Long-term care insurance, 501–9
  comparison shopping for, 505–7
  key ingredients of, 502–4
  money-saving techniques for, 504
  need for, 502
Low-income housing tax credits, 200–201
LYONs (Liquid Yield Option Notes), 163–64

Managed Account Reports (newsletter), 147
Margin accounts, 143–44
Marital property, 263
Marital trust, 462
Mark Twain Bank, 190
Market Facts, 105
Market timing, timing techniques for mutual funds, 123–24
Market value of bonds, 149
Marriage (married couples), 256–61
  discussing money before, 257
  prenuptial agreements and, 260–61
  titling assets and, 258–60
MasterCard, cash advances from, 249–51
Maturity, 149
Medicaid, 500
  assets "not counted" for qualification, 510
  assets "spent down" to qualify for, 510
  determination date for qualification for, 510
  establishing an irrevocable trust, 514
  giving most of your assets away and, 514–15
  joint accounts and, 514
  maximum assets to qualify for, 509–10
  maximum income to qualify for, 510
  residences and, 512–13
  spousal assets that may be retained, 510
  30-month rule and, 511–12
  transfer of assets to spouse and, 513
Medical expenses, owning a business and, 308–9
Medical insurance. *See* Health insurance
Medical payments coverage in automobile policy, 375
Medicare, 488–91
  long-term custodial nursing care and, 499
  Part A, 489–91
  Part B, 489, 491
Medicare supplement policy (Medigap policy), 489, 492–98
  cost comparisons, 493–94
  duplicate coverage and, 496
  health maintenance organizations (HMOs) as alternative to, 497–98
  information on, 498
  initial six-month entry period, 494, 497
  ten standard policies, 493
Merrill Lynch CMA Account, 230
MetLife State Street Government Fund, 156
Money market deposit accounts, 96, 225–26
Money market mutual funds, 26, 58, 97–98
  tax-free, 99
Money purchase plans, 344
Moody's, 441

Morningstar, 115
Morningstar Closed-End Fund Survey, 109, 173
Morningstar 5-Star Investor (newsletter), 122
Morningstar Mutual Funds Service, 121
Morningstar Mutual Fund Survey, 171
Mortality rate, 403
Mortgages, 41, 311–21
  adjustable-rate vs. fixed-rate, 316–19
  biweekly payments on, 320–21
  making additional principal payments on,
    319–20
  refinancing, 313–14
  reverse, 321, 526–30
  30-year vs. 15-year, 314–16
  where to get, 311–12
Motivation, 7
Municipal bond mutual funds, 170–72
  closed-end, 172–73
  for short-term, tax-free income, 174–75
Municipal bonds, 71, 167–73
  best price for, 170
  call provision, 170
  college bonds, 280–81
  commissions and, 170
  general obligation, 169–70
  insured, 170
  of Puerto Rico, Guam, the Virgin Islands,
    172
  rating of, 169
  revenue, 169–70
  for short-term, tax-free income, 174–75
Mutual Fund Encyclopedia, The (Perritt), 121
Mutual Fund Forecaster (newsletter), 122
Mutual Fund Letter, The, 122
Mutual funds, 20, 104–25. *See also* Money market mutual funds
  adjustable-rate mortgage funds, 159–60
  with back-end load, 106
  bond, closed-end, 165–66
  buying, 110–13
    automatic investments, 112–13
    discount brokerage firms, 111–12
    through financial planners, 113
  choosing, 120–25
    asking the fund family, 124
    managers, 120–21
    newsletters, 121–22
    past performance as basis for, 120
    surveys of mutual fund performance, 121
  closed-end, 108–9
    foreign, 188–89
  convertible bond, 163
  currency, 191
  direct purchase of no-load funds, 110–11
  dollar cost averaging and, 85–87
  families of, 106–8
  of foreign securities, 183–84
  Ginnie Mae, 158–59
  global income, 185
  load vs. no-load, 105–6

municipal bond, 170–72
  closed-end, 172–73
  for short-term, tax-free income, 174–75
  for mutual funds, 123–24
  natural resource, 201–2
  net asset value of, 104
  objectives of, 107
  popularity of, 104
  precious metals, 196–97
  prospectus for, 106
  short sales of, 125
  simple strategies for investing in, 114–19
    growth vs. income, 116–17
    index funds, 114–16
    one-fund approach, 118
  stock market, foreign, 187–88
  strategic income, 166
  and taxes, 125
  in variable annuities, 211–14
  zero coupon bond, 161

NASDAQ (National Association of Securities
    Dealers Automated Quotation System),
    127
National Association of Auto Dealers' (NADA)
    Official Used Car Guide, 326
National Association for the Cottage Industry, 307
National Association of Investment Clubs, 139
National Association of Personal Financial Advi-
    sors, 48
National Association of REITs, 198
National College Services, 289
National Debt, 30
National Foundation for Consumer Credit, 237
National Insurance Consumer Helpline, 432
National Insurance Consumer Organization
    (NICO), 434–35
National Partnership Exchange, 200
National Scholarship Research Service, 289
Nationwide Auto Brokers, 323
Natural resource funds, 201–2
Needs, 43
New York Stock Exchange, 127
Newsletters
  investment, 138–39
  mutual fund investment, 121–22
Nineties, the, 28–30
Nixon, Richard, 25
No-fault automobile insurance, 370–71
No-load bond funds, 155
No-Load Fund Investor (newsletter), 122
No-load mutual funds, 105–6
Nomura Pacific Basin, 188
Numismatic coins, 194–95
Nursing home care, 500. *See also* Long-term care
    insurance; Medicaid
Nursing homes, 9

Official Used Car Guide (National Association of
    Auto Dealers), 326

Olympia & York, 77
100 Highest Yields (publication), 97
Opportunity cost, 89
Optimism, reasons for, 11
Options, 144–46
    on cash currency contracts, 192
Organization of Petroleum Exporting Countries
    (OPEC), 25–26
Outplacement counseling, 300
Overdraft line of credit, 227, 249

Partnership Profiles (newsletter), 200
Partnerships, real estate, 199–200
Paychecks
    automatic deductions from, 226
    direct deposit of, 225–26
Paying yourself first, 224
    with automatic deductions, 226
    strategy of, 37–38
Payroll tax. *See* FICA
Pell Grant, 286
Pension Benefit Guaranty Corporation (PBGC),
    343–44
Pension plans, 294–95. *See also* Retirement plan-
    ning
    distributions. *See* Retirement distributions
    leaving a job and, 299
Perkins Loan Program, 288
Perritt, Gerald, 121
Personal injury protection (PIP) in automobile
    policy, 375–76
Personal loans, 254
Peterson's College Money Handbook, 286
Philadelphia Stock Exchange, 192
Planning, 10–11
PLUS Loan Program, 288
Pour-over wills, 449, 459
Power of attorney, 449
    durable, 475
    nondurable, 474
    springing, 475
Precious metals mutual funds, 196–97
Preferred provider organizations (PPOs), 384
Preferred stock, 164–65
    convertible, 164
Prenuptial agreements, 260–61
Prepaid tuition plans, 281
Price/earnings ratio (P/E), 136
Probate, 456–57
Profit-sharing plans, 344
Property damage liability insurance in auto-
    mobile policy, 374
Prospectus for mutual funds, 106
Put options, 146
Putnam Diversified Income, 166

Qualified plans, 167

Rate of return, 45
    traditional, 58–59

Rating investment performance, 92–93
Real estate
    defensive investment in, 197–201
    distressed, 199
    low-income housing credit, 200
    Tax Reform Act of 1986 and, 74–75
    vacation time shares, 200–201
Real estate investment trusts (REITs), 198–99
Real estate partnerships, 199–200
Recession
    of 1980-82, 27
    of 1990-92, 18–19
Recordkeeping, tax-related, 352–53
Rental property, 197–98
Renters, homeowners insurance coverage for,
    363–64
Residential sale-leaseback, 530–31
Retirement. *See also* Social Security
    buyout offers and, 296–98
Retirement distributions, 519–25
    avoiding penalties on early, 522
    forward averaging, 521
    lump sum rollovers, 521
    new tax rule regarding, 520
    tax consequences of an IRA at death, 524–25
    when you *must* take, 523–24
Retirement Equity Act, 265
Retirement planning, 331–48. *See also* Pension
    plans
    company plans, 342–44
    deciding when, Social Security and, 486–87
    early start in, 331–34
    401(k) company savings plans, 339–40
    403(b) plans, 342
    for government employees, 345
    Individual Retirement Account (IRA), 335–38
    investing your retirement funds for the long
        run, 334–35
    Keogh plan, 338–39
    rollovers, 346–47
    sheltering your retirement funds from current
        income taxes, 334
    taking money out of retirement funds, 347–48
Reverse mortgage plans, 526–30
Reverse mortgages, 320
RHM Convertible Survey (newsletter), 162
Risk, 53–65
    asset allocation and, 62–65
    assumptions and, 56–57
    in avoiding risk, 53–54
    bond prices and, 151–52
    of emotion, 61
    getting out of an investment, 59–60
    hidden, 59–60
    historical, 57–58
    insurance and, 60
    interest rates and, 150–51
    liquidity, 60
    in the long run, 54
    measuring, 59

time horizon and, 56–57
Risk premium, 59
R.K. Nelson Associates, 436–37
Rollovers, lump sum, 521
Rule of 72, 88–89

Safe money strategies, 53, 94–103
  bank accounts, 96–97
  "chicken money" concept and, 94–96
  higher-yielding, 103
  as one-decision investments, 95–96
  Series EE U.S. savings bonds, 101–3
  Treasury bills, 99–101
Sale-leaseback, 530–31
Salomon Brothers Mortgage-Backed Index, 153
Saving bonds, U.S. *See* U.S. savings bonds
Savings, 9
Savings accounts for children, 290
Savings and loans (S&Ls), 26–27
  bailout bill for, 76
Schedule C, 304
Scholarships, private, 288
Scudder
  direct annuity sales, 215
  GNMA, 159
  International Bond Fund, 186
  International Fund, 187
  Managed Municipal Bonds, 171
  Medium Term Tax-Free, 175
  Short-Term Global Income Fund, 185
Second-to-die life insurance policies, 428
Secondary offerings, 141
Section 1035 exchange, 207
"See it, spend it" habit, 32–33
Select Information Exchange, 139
SelectQuote, 408
Selling short, 91–92
Senior citizens, 21–22. *See also* Estate planning;
    Medicare; Social Security
  home sale exclusion for, 354
  income strategies for, 526–33
    residential sale-leaseback, 530–31
    reverse mortgage plans, 526–30
    split-funded annuities, 531–33
  taxes and, 354–55
Senior rental community, 516–17
SEOG (Supplemental Educational Opportunity
    Grant), 287
Series EE U.S. savings bonds, 101–3. *See also*
    U.S. savings bonds
  for college saving plan, 276–77
  as a higher-yielding strategy, 160
Series HH U.S. savings bonds, 102
Seventies, the, 25–26
Severance pay, 298–300
Shopping, 224
Short sales, 91–92
  of mutual funds, 125
Silver, futures contracts, 195–96
Silver bullion, 195

Silver coins, 194–95
Silver mining stocks, 196
Silver mutual funds, 196–97
Simplified Employee Pension Plan (SEP), 307
Sixties, the, 25
Social Insecurity (Hardy), 21
Social Security, 8, 331, 477–88
  basic benefits, 478–81
  deciding whether to keep working and, 486
  deciding whether to retire early and, 486–87
  delayed retirement and benefits, 480–81
  determination of monthly benefit amounts,
    478–79
  disability claims through, 391
  early retirement and benefits, 479–80
  electing disability benefits under, 487
  family benefits, 481–83
  filing requirements, 485
  information on, 488
  postretirement work and benefits, 483–86
  qualifications for benefits, 478
  Request for Earnings and Benefit Estimate
    Statement, 478
  taxation of benefits, 485–86
    Modified Adjusted Gross Income (MAGI),
     485–86
Social Security tax. *See* FICA
Sole proprietorships, 303–5
Spain Fund, 188
Specialists, 127
Spectrum
  Growth Fund, 116–17
  Income Fund, 116
Speculation, 37
Split-funded annuities, 531–33
Spousal support, divorce and, 263
Stafford Nonsubsidized Student Loan Program,
    287
Stafford Student Loan Program, 287
Standard & Poor's, 441
Standard & Poor's 500 Stock Index, 4, 54, 57
  index funds and, 114–16
Standard & Poor's/Lipper Mutual Fund Profiles,
    121
Standard & Poor's Stock Reports, 136–37
Starting your own business, 303–10
  employing and, 309–10
  home-based businesses, 307–8
  regular C corporations, 306–7
  sole proprietorships, 303–5
  Subchapter S corporations, 305–6
State grants for college, 287
State income tax, Treasury bills not subject to,
    100
"Status is significant" attitude, 33–34
Stein Roe
  High-Yield Municipals, 171
  Intermediate Municipals, 175
Stock brokerage firms, 128–30
Stock market averages or indexes, 92–93, 127

Stock market averages or indexes (*cont'd*)
  international, 183
Stock market mutual funds
  for college saving plan, 275–76
  foreign, 187–88
Stock markets, 126–27
  in the 1960s, 25
  in the 1970s, 25–26
Stock options, 144–46
  leaving a job and, 300
Stock report services, 136–37
Stockbrokers, 129
Stocks. *See also* Common stocks
  borrowing against, 251–52
  children and, 291
  currencies and, 180–81
  gold and silver, 196
  investing in, 126–33
    direct purchase/dividend reinvestment plans,
      132–33
    discount brokerage firms, 130–31
    with margin accounts, 143–44
    options and LEAPS, 144–46
    stock brokerage firms, 128–30
  preferred, 164–65
    convertible, 164
  strategies for choosing, 134–42
    American Association of Individual Inves-
      tors, 140
    brokerage firm reports, 135–36
    initial public offerings (IPOs), 140–42
    investment clubs, 139–40
    investment newsletters, 138–39
    looking around you, 134–35
    stock report services, 136–37
    technical analysis, 137–38
  utility, 164
Stop-loss orders, 84
Strategic income funds, 166
Strategic minerals and resources, 202
Styles of handling money, 23–30
  in the 1920s, 24
  in the 1930s and 1940s, 24
  in the 1950s and 1960s, 25
  in the 1970s, 25–26
Subchapter S corporations, 75, 305–6

Takeovers, 27–28
Target Maturity Funds, 161
Tax Act of 1993, 69, 70, 72, 74, 75, 200, 319
Tax anticipation notes, 175
Tax preparers, 352
Tax Reform Act of 1986, 75
Tax returns, filing, 349–50
Tax shelters, 27, 45, 71–72
Tax-deferred annuities, 203–9. *See also* Annu-
    ities, variable-rate
  definition of, 204
  retirement plan using, 344–45
Tax-deferred investments, 72–73

Taxes
  buying power and, 70–71
  children and, 292
  divorce and, 264–65
  everyday tax strategies, 349–56
    audits, 353–54
    estimated taxes, 351–52
    extensions, 353
    filing tax returns, 349–50
    recordkeeping, 352–53
    special tax rules, 354–55
    tax preparation assistance, 352
    withholding taxes, 350–51
  income as affected by, 69–70
  investing power and, 71
  as 2 percent of income (1948–1990), 7–8
Tax-free investments, 72, 167–75
  money market funds, 99
  municipal bonds. *See* Municipal bonds
  short-term, tax-free income, 174–75
  unit investment trusts, 173–74
Teachers Insurance and Annuity Association-
    College Retirement Equities Fund (TIAA-
    CREF), 342
Technical analysis, 137–38
Tenancy in entirety, 259
1035 Exchange, 207, 422
Term insurance, 403–10
  age of expiration, 407
  convertible, 406–7
  direct purchase of, 409–10
  independent advice on, 410
  level premium vs. annually increasing pre-
    mium, 404–5
  quote services for, 407–9
  reentry term vs. annual renewable, 405–6
  waiver of premium, 407
TermQuote, 408
TIAA-CREF (Teachers Insurance and Annuity
    Association-College Retirement Equities
    Fund), 342
Time value of money, 89–90
Timing techniques for mutual funds, 123–24
Titling your property, 258–60
Total return, 153
  on bond investments, 150
  on bond mutual funds, 156
Tranches, 159
Trans Union Credit, 233
Travel and entertainment expenses, deducting,
    301–302
Traveler's checks, in a foreign currency, 189–90
Treasury bills, 57–58
  auctions for, 99–101
  interest rates on, 99–100
  money market funds that purchase only, 98
  purchasing, 99–101
  rollover option, 100
  as safe investment, 99–101
  when interest is taxable, 101

Treasury bonds, 57
  bond ladder and, 154–55
Treasury direct system, 100
Treasury securities, money market funds that invest only in, 98
T. Rowe Price
  asset mix worksheet, 124
  college planning package, 271
  European Stock, 188
  GNMA, 159
  International Bond Fund, 186
  International Stock Fund, 187
  New Asia, 188
  New Era, 202
  retirement planning work-book, 333
  Spectrum Income Fund and Spectrum Growth Fund, 116–17
  Tax-Free High-Yield Fund, 171
  Tax-Free Income, 171
  Tax-Free Short-Intermediate Fund, 175
Trustees, 455
Trusts
  charitable lead, 472–73
  charitable remainder, 471–72
  living. *See* Living trusts
  for minors, college saving plan and, 274
TRW Credit Services, 233
Tuition. *See also* College costs
Twenties, the, 24
Twentieth Century International Equity, 187
Twentieth Century U.S. Government Fund, 157

Umbrella liability policy, 366–67
Underinsured motorist coverage, 375
Understanding Options (pamphlet), 146
Unified Tax Credit, 450
Uniform Gifts to Minors Act, college saving plan and, 273–74
Uniform Simultaneous Death Act, 463
Uniform Transfer to Minors Act, 274
Uninsured motorist coverage, 374–75
Unit investment trusts, 173–74
United Services
  All American Equity Fund, 115, 275
  Automobile Association (USAA), 377
  Global Resources, 202
  Gold Shares, 196
  Intermediate Treasury Fund, 157
  Near Term Tax Free Fund, 175
  Real Estate Fund, 199
  U.S. Government Securities Savings Fund, 275
  World Gold, 196
Universal life insurance, 415–16
  variable, 417
Unlimited marital deduction, 461–62
U.S. savings bonds, 160
  for college tuition, 102
  information on, 103
  maximum amount that can be purchased, 103

purchasing, 103
retirement and, 103
Series EE, 101–3
  for college saving plan, 276–77
  as a higher-yielding strategy, 160
Series HH, 102
USAA Life, 410, 438
Utility Forecaster (monthly), 165
Utility stocks, 164–65

Vacation time shares, 201
Value Line Composite Index, 93
Value Line Convertible Strategist (newsletter), 162
Value Line Investment Survey, 133, 136–37
Value Line U.S. Government Securities Fund, 157
Values, changes in, 23
Vanguard
  Convertible Securities, 163
  direct annuity sales, 215
  Fixed-Income GNMA, 159
  International Equity Index European, 188
  International Equity Index Pacific, 188
  Long-Term U.S. Treasury, 157
  Short-Term Federal Bond Portfolio, 157
  Specialized Energy, 202
  World International Growth, 187
Vanguard Advisor, The (newsletter), 122
Vanguard Star Fund, 118–19
Veribanc, 97
Veterans disability benefits, 391
Visa, cash advances from, 249–51

Wall Street Journal, 153
Warranties, extended, 329–30
  for cars, 324
Weiss Research, 209, 217
  insurance rating service, 441
Wellington Letter, The, 139
Whole life insurance, 414–15
  variable, 416–17
Wills, 453–56
  dying without a, 449–50
  living, 475
  pour-over, 449, 459
Withholding taxes, 350–51
World Currency Certificates of Deposit, 190
Wrap accounts, 49, 130

Yankelovich Partners, Inc., 23
Yield to call, 150
Yield curve, 58, 151
Yield to maturity, 150

Zero coupon bond mutual funds, Benham Capital Management, 161
Zero coupon bonds, 160–62
  convertible, 163–64

About the Author

TERRY SAVAGE is a nationally recognized financial authority and television money advisor. She writes a weekly syndicated column on personal finance for the Chicago *Sun Times*, and her regular column in *Bloomberg Personal Finance* magazine answers readers' money questions. She is also the author of the bestselling *Terry Savage Talks Money*.

Savage appears regularly on PBS's "Nightly Business Report" and is the money expert on Lifetime Cable's "Our Home" show. You see her frequently on CNN and CNBC commenting on the markets and investments. She's often a guest on "Oprah," "Donahue," and "The 700 Club," and her advice is quoted in *Bottom Line Personal, Boardroom Reports*, and other national magazines.

For 12 years Savage appeared daily on the evening news for CBS in Chicago, reporting on business and market news and offering financial advice. She's a registered investment advisor for both stocks and futures. After starting her career as a stockbroker, Savage became a founding member—and the first woman trader—on the Chicago Board Options Exchange. And she traded currencies on the Chicago Mercantile Exchange's International Monetary Market.

Among numerous honors, Savage has received the Outstanding Consumer Journalism Award from the National Press Club and an Emmy for her hour-long special on money, "It Doesn't Grow on Trees!" In 1993 she was given the Directors Choice Award by the National Women's Economic Alliance honoring outstanding women corporate directors.

Terry Savage serves on the board of directors of McDonald's Corporation and The Broadway Stores, Inc. She is in demand nationally as a speaker at corporate and association meetings on the subject of the economic outlook and personal financial planning.